Antitrust and Monopoly

Antitrust and Monopoly

Anatomy of a Policy Failure

Dominick T. Armentano
University of Hartford

1807 1982

A Wiley-Interscience Publication

JOHN WILEY & SONS

New York   Chichester   Brisbane   Toronto   Singapore

Library of Congress Cataloging in Publication Data:

Armentano, Dominick T.
  Antitrust and monopoly.

  "A Wiley-Interscience publication."
  Includes index.
  1. Industry and state—United States. 2. Trusts,
Industrial—United States. 3. Competition—United States.
4. Monopolies—United States. I. Title.

HD3616.U47A77   343.73'072   81-16440
ISBN 0-471-09931-7   347.30372   AACR2
ISBN 0-471-09930-9 (Pbk)

Printed in the United States of America

10 9 8 7 6 5 4 3 2 1

To my wife, Rose,
and to my son, Paul

Preface

This book is a revised and expanded version of *The Myths of Antitrust: Economic Theory and Legal Cases*, which was published in 1972.

My trenchant opposition to orthodox competition theory and antitrust policy has not mellowed over the years. Indeed, if anything, I have become even more convinced that the theory and practice of antitrust is fundamentally flawed, and that all of the antitrust laws ought to be promptly repealed. When I first made this recommendation in 1972, I was warned that repeal of the antitrust laws was both intellectually unwarranted and politically unthinkable. Few observers of the antitrust scene would be as certain of such conclusions today. I would hope that even fewer still will be as certain after reading this book.

There are some special individuals who have been very supportive of this volume and I would like to thank each of them.

I would like to thank Edward H. Crane and Robert L. Formaini of the Cato Institute, Washington, D.C., for their early interest in the publication of this manuscript. I would especially like to thank Robert Hessen of the Hoover Institution at Stanford University and Walter Grinder of the Institute for Humane Studies, Menlo Park, California, for their unfailing encouragement on my behalf. Special thanks are also due William Hammett, President, the International Center for Economic Policy Studies (ICEPS) in New York City, for his friendship and interest in my work.

I have benefited from informal discussions with Yale Brozen, Harold Demsetz, Donald Dewey, Armen Alchian, M. Bruce Johnson, Israel Kirzner, Murray N. Rothbard, Wesley J. Liebeler, and other professors and economists who have blazed the trail toward needed antitrust reform and, I hope, repeal. Although I have learned much from them, they cannot be held responsible for any of my errors or omissions.

I would also like to thank Pamela Joerg and Marilyn Baleshiski for typing various drafts of the manuscript.

Finally, I would like to thank John B. Mahaney, my editor at Wiley, for his entrepreneurial alertness and courage. The free competitive market in publishing is sustained by businessmen like John who rush in where angels may fear to tread.

DOMINICK T. ARMENTANO

West Hartford, Connecticut
November 1981

Contents

Introduction

It is now admitted that contrary to the conventional wisdom, the enforcement of the antitrust laws may have made the economy less efficient, and may have been an important contributing factor in the steady decline of business productivity in America.[1]

Horizontal business mergers that would have generated important economies of scale have been thoroughly discouraged by a rigid and lockstep enforcement of Section 7 of the Clayton Act. Price discrimination, clearly an important element of rivalrous competition, has been routinely attacked by the Federal Trade Commission since the late 1930s for fear that it might eliminate some competitors. Aggressive business growth to gain and hold market share has often been found illegal by the courts even though such practices may, in the courts' own words, have been productive of economies and efficiencies. And tying agreements have been judged almost entirely illegal on the faulty assumption that the very existence of such agreements was itself evidence of unreasonable monopoly power.

In short, it can be argued that extremely competitive and efficient business behavior has been legally restricted or prohibited on the misguided assumption that such actions endanger the competitive process and result, or may result, in monopolistic abuse. Clearly the time has come for a thorough reevaluation of the antitrust policies of the United States.

Such a reevaluation has been in process within the legal and academic community for some time. As an example of the current antitrust revisionism, attorney Ira M. Millstein has acknowledged that there has been a very significant shift in theoretical antitrust thinking over the last decade.[2] According to Millstein, most antitrust enthusiasts now have recognized the severe limitations of the "competitive" or "atomistic" model, and its handmaiden, structuralist economics, and have adopted, accordingly, a substantially more realistic vision of competition and monopoly under the antitrust laws.

This enlightened change in thinking—if it has occurred—must surely be applauded, but the point to be focused on in this study is Millstein's admission elsewhere in his article that this atomistic model of competition had

1

"formed the basis for antitrust thinking" for the last ninety years. But what now becomes of the hundreds of legal decisions under the antitrust laws during this ninety-year period of nonenlightenment? If the simple economic theory that had formed the very foundation of antitrust law is now to be rejected as impractical, isn't it reasonable to assume that previous court decisions based upon that simple theory were just as impractical, even nonsensical? For example, were the business organizations indicted in some of the classic monopoly cases really raising prices and restricting outputs—was the competitive process actually endangered—or is the conventional historical wisdom just as confused on this issue as is the atomistic model? And finally, if the simple models of economic theory are now to be rejected as inappropriate, what is the appropriate theoretical approach to competition and monopoly power under the antitrust laws? Even more fundamentally, are the laws themselves appropriate in a competitive economy?

This book is an attempt to analyze critically the theory and practice of an American sacred cow—the antitrust laws of the United States. Like all sacred cows, antitrust laws appear shrouded with an aura of authenticity and legitimacy. By and large, Americans still accept the view that antitrust has served to make the market economy more competitive and efficient, and that business monopoly would triumph in the absence of such legal prohibition.

Academic economists, for the most part, have created and sustained the public's impression concerning monopoly and the antitrust laws. Two generations of economists, both liberal and conservative, have generally accepted antitrust as an important social force in maintaining competition and in limiting the difficulties commonly associated with monopoly power. Although some economists have disapproved of particular sections of the laws and particular enforcement procedures, and although a very few have called for repeal of specific antitrust statutes, the bulk of the academic economists have historically supported—and continue to support—antitrust and a vigorous enforcement policy.[3] Indeed, some influential economists are committed to a substantial beefing up of antitrust enforcement, particularly in the price-fixing area, or alternatively, to additional legislation aimed at radically restructuring concentrated American industries. Despite the recent criticism, the antitrust philosophy is still a firmly entrenched part of the conventional wisdom of a mixed-enterprise system.

Yet importantly, this public and professional acceptance of the efficacy of antitrust depends upon important assumptions that are rarely made explicit or challenged. One assumption, for instance, is the belief that the standard theories of competition and monopoly developed by the economists are a correct perspective and can be applied meaningfully in the antitrust area. Another crucial assumption is the belief that antitrust history contains impressive empirical verification of the resource misallocations and monopolistic abuses suggested by the standard theoretical approach.

This study will maintain that neither of these important assumptions are valid. It will argue that orthodox competition and monopoly theory is inherently flawed and misleading and cannot rationally support antitrust policy. Further, it will demonstrate that the business organizations under indictment in the classic antitrust cases were expanding outputs, reducing prices, improving technology, and engaging generally in an intensely competitive process. It will conclude that both antitrust theory and history are an elaborate mythology with no solid foundation in either logic or fact.

This is not to say that the notion of monopoly power itself is a myth, or that there is an absence of abusive monopoly in the American business system; far from it. It is to say only that our formal antimonopoly policies have been a fraud, and that public attentions concerning the monopoly problem in America have been totally misdirected. Government, and not the market, is the source of monopoly power. Government licensing, certificates of public convenience, franchises, patents, tariffs, and other legally restrictive devices can and do create monopoly, and monopoly power, for specific business organizations protected from open competition. Abusive monopoly is always to be associated with governmental interference of production or exchange, and such situations do injure consumers, exclude sellers, and result in an inefficient misallocation of resources. But importantly, for this discussion, such monopoly situations are legal, created and sanctioned by the political authority for its own purposes. Thus, ironically or intentionally, the bulk of the abusive monopoly in the business system has always been beyond the scope of antitrust law and antitrust policy. Antitrust, as we will demonstrate, is both a myth and a hoax.

This work differs in two fundamental ways from many others that have discussed competition, monopoly, and antitrust problems. First, most of the previous volumes have accepted the essential correctness of the neoclassical theories of competition and monopoly; serious criticism of this perspective has been marginal at best and frequently reduced to a footnote. The overwhelming impression received from these works is that the criticism does not subtract substantially from the logic and policy implications of neoclassical theory. Second, almost all volumes on the subject have presented a welter of antitrust cases, void of relevant conduct and performance information. Consequently, any serious consideration of the indicted firms' actual behavior has been conspicuously absent. Apparently, these volumes expect readers to assume that the firms indicted under the antitrust statutes were actually raising prices, reducing outputs, producing shoddy products, colluding successfully with competitors, driving competitors from the market with predatory practices, and generally abusing consumers in the marketplace.

This book will reverse explicitly the two positions outlined above. The neoclassical theories will be shown to be static equilibrium models that tell us almost nothing meaningful concerning efficiency and the competitive process. Moreover, the antitrust cases to be examined—the classic cases only—will be presented in a context that attempts to make the conduct and performance of the firms involved comprehensible. Wherever possible, readers will be provided with information enabling them to make independent judgments as to the economic guilt or innocence of the defendant.

Finally, the overall purpose of this book is to provide teachers, lawyers, students, businessmen, and other interested citizens with a convenient guide to a comprehensive body of dissenting thought concerning competition theory and antitrust policy. In the light of this intention, this volume does not necessarily present a balanced set of contrasting opinions. Instead, it advances an extreme position, buttressed with specific arguments and facts that, hopefully, will encourage serious readers to rethink critically the antitrust policies of the United States.

NOTES

1. "Antitrust Grows Unpopular," *Business Week*, January 12, 1981, p. 90–91. See also "Antitrust: Big Business Breathes Easier," *The New York Times*, February 15, 1981, pp. 1f, 22f and Lester Thurow, *The Zero Sum Society* (New York: Basic Books, 1980), pp. 146–150.

2. *Harvard Law Review*, Vol. 93 (1980), pp. 618–632.

3. In a recent study of public policy attitudes, 85 percent of the economists sampled agreed with the proposition that "the antitrust laws should be used vigorously to reduce monopoly power from its current level." See J. R. Kearl, Clayne L. Pope, Gordon C. Whiting, Larry T. Wimmer, "A Confusion of Economists?" *American Economic Review, Papers and Proceedings*, Vol. 69, No. 2 (May 1979), p. 30.

CHAPTER ONE

The Legitimacy of Antitrust Policy

The competitive business process is central to an appreciation of the market economy. If competition exists in the market, business organizations tend to allocate resources efficiently, engage in innovation and technological development, and generally respond effectively to consumer demand. If competition is weak or nonexistent, however, it is not at all evident that the interplay of free market forces will automatically generate beneficial economic behavior and performance. Indeed, it is often alleged that if business organizations could extinguish the market process through monopoly or collusion, they could presumably misallocate resources and create a utilitarian justification for extensive governmental regulation.

THE RATIONALE FOR ANTITRUST

While the American economy may still primarily employ the institutions of private ownership and voluntary exchange, it certainly has never adhered to strict laissez-faire principles.[1] The decline of the free-market system accelerated with the rise of large-scale business enterprise in the post-Civil War period. At that time, spokesmen for business interests, labor, government, and even a few economists asserted that some regulatory control of the economy was required in order to protect consumers from the "trusts" and their attendant unfair practices.[2] Presumably, the Sherman Antitrust Act (1890) and the rest of the antitrust laws* were passed in order to halt the spread of business monopoly and to restore effective competition to the market economy.

The conventional perspective on the origins of antitrust regulation is that the laws were enacted to stem the rising tide of "monopoly power."[3] Yet revisionist analysis of the Clayton Act, the Federal Trade Commission Act, and

---

* See the Appendix for the relevant sections of the antitrust laws.

the Robinson-Patman Act has severely shaken this conventional view; various scholars have demonstrated that these particular "antitrust" statutes were often supported and employed by established business interests in an attempt to restrain and restrict the competitive process. Unable to compete effectively with more efficient business organizations, certain special interests sought political and legislative restrictions in an attempt to secure or enhance existing market positions. According to this view, therefore, much of the antitrust movement should more accurately be seen as conservative rather than as "progressive," and as an important part of the "triumph" of conservatism in American politics.[4]

Interestingly, and perhaps ironically, the Sherman Antitrust Act has managed to escape the revisionist assault almost entirely. It is still widely accepted as a statute whose sole purpose was to protect consumers from monopoly power, and to prevent "an artificial enhancement of prices" in the market.[5] And while some economists can now admit that the Sherman Act has not always been employed to that end, they presumably have little doubt that its intention was to advance the general consumer welfare.

But there has always been some reason to doubt the orthodox interpretation of the origins of the Sherman Act. It is true that it was Senator Sherman's expressed intent to make illegal those business arrangements that tended to "advance the cost to the consumer," and this precise language appeared in the original draft of his bill.[6] However, this wording was stripped from the legislation as approved by the U.S. Senate; the Sherman Act as enacted into law does not mention the alleged "sole" purpose, that is, the "enhancement of prices by combination." Moreover, at least through 1911, the legal enforcement of the Sherman Act had absolutely nothing to do with the substantive conduct and performance of the indicted corporations or, in other words, with whether there *had* been any "enhancement of prices" to the consumer. The courts were totally immune to defense arguments that the indicted trusts had not increased prices and had not resticted outputs—indeed, that they had lowered prices and expanded outputs—and had not restrained trade in violation of the law. Nor is there the slightest shred of evidence that the U.S. Congress, on observing that its alleged "intent" was being misconstrued by the courts, ever sought to revise the wording in the law (or the enforcement of the law) to conform to Senator Sherman's original vision. In short, reasonable doubts can be raised about the purity of the intentions of the men in government and in business at the very birth of the antitrust movement.

More to the point, as this volume will demonstrate, the Sherman Act—like its sister antitrust legislation—has been continuously employed to restrain competition and the free-market process, whatever its alleged intent. It will be shown that the antitrust laws have been fundamentally protective of the existing economic structure of business organizations. This protectionism may or may not have been the specific intent of the laws, but it is the way the laws have operated in practice.

THE LEGALITY OF ANTITRUST

While the precise intent of the antitrust laws must always remain somewhat obscure, the legality of legislation regulating interstate commerce has never really been in doubt. In the first place, the Constitution of the United States states explicitly in Article One, Section 8, that Congress has the authority and the legislative power "to regulate commerce among the several states . . ." Even more importantly, repeated court decisions made it perfectly clear that the government could legally regulate the use of private property whenever it was devoted "to a use in which the public has an interest." For example, in the famous *Munn v. Illinois* case decided in 1877, Munn and his partner, Scott, had argued that their private grain-storage business was of no concern to the State of Illinois legislature, and that the government had no right to require them to make their rates public, to get a license to operate from the state, or to comply with maximum-price limits. A majority of the U.S. Supreme Court did not agree. Instead, the high court declared, with plenty of English common law as precedent, that the use of private property which involved the public "must submit to be controlled by the public for the common good." In explicitly utilitarian rhetoric, Chief Justice Waite argued that this interest could justify extensive public regulation.

> Property does become clothed with the public interest when used in a manner to make it of public consequence, and affect the community at large. When therefore, one devotes his property to a use in which the public has an interest, he, in effect, grants to the public an interest in that use, and must submit to be controlled by the public for the common good. . . . He may withdraw his grant by discontinuing the use; but, so long as he maintains the use, he must submit to the control.[7]

Since all private property in an exchange economy involves the public, this decision and many subsequent ones established clear legal precedent that legislatures had the authority to regulate practically any private business activity. As Justice Roberts so clearly puts the matter in *Nebbia v. New York* in 1934: ". . . a State is free to adopt whatever economic policy may reasonably be deemed to promote the public welfare, and to enforce that policy by legislation adapted to its purpose."[8]

Actually, the ending of a strict private-property rights approach in law and its replacement with utilitarian public-welfare analysis had begun well before

Munn v. Illinois. Morton J. Horwitz has demonstrated conclusively that there were dozens of important court decisions at the state level in the early nineteenth century that clearly embody the triumph of utilitarian public interest over common law property right.[9] In the name of technological progress, for instance, the courts in some of the early water pollution cases were more than willing to sacrifice the traditional common law principle of strict tort liability in favor of a more instrumentalist concern for promoting the general economic welfare. In many instances, upstream property owners were allowed to victimize downstream owners when the public benefits associated with industrial progress exceeded the social costs, in the courts' view. Thus *Munn v. Illinois* and *Nebbia v. New York* represent the logical culmination of a philosophical change in the law that justified extensive governmental regulation of property in the so-called public interest.

THE LEGITIMACY OF ANTITRUST

While regulation such as antitrust laws have admittedly been judged legal, is such legislation proper in a free society? From a strict natural rights perspective, such regulation and legislation would not be proper.[10] This theory holds that individuals have inalienable rights to life, liberty, and property. These rights imply the liberty of any person or persons to enter into any noncoercive trading agreement on any terms mutually acceptable, to produce and trade any factor or good that they own, and to keep any property realized by such free exchange. This perspective would hold that it is right to own and use property; it is right to employ that property in any manner that does not infringe on anyone else's property rights; it is right to trade any or all of that property to anyone else on any terms mutually acceptable; and that it is right to keep and enjoy the fruits of that effort. These activities are right because they can logically be derived from man's natural right to life and life-sustaining action. Consequently, it would be wrong to initiate force against someone else's private property; wrong to forcibly interfere with someone else's voluntary property transaction; and wrong to outlaw or regulate certain types of business contracts, organizational structures, or business cooperation. These activities would be wrong since they would infringe upon the natural rights of individuals to do with their own property what they see fit.

So interpreted, government's function in such a social system would be to define and protect rights to life and property, and to adjudicate disputes over alleged violations of rights. Government could not legitimately regulate the manufacture and price of agricultural commodities, limit the production of petroleum, prohibit the sale of labor services below certain fixed terms of exchange, or restrain the voluntary merger of private properties. Such state activities would be invasive of property rights and thus would violate the principle of free and voluntary exchange. Antitrust laws, therefore, to the extent that they restrict voluntary agreement or the exchange of private property, would not be consistent with a social system based on natural rights. Thus, part of the case against antitrust can be couched in strictly normative terms.

ECONOMISTS AND GOVERNMENT REGULATION

The philosophical position on property rights outlined above is clearly still a minority position. Many intellectuals, and certainly most economists assume that private-property rights are not inalienable or natural. They hold that such relationships are useful social conventions that governments sanction because they tend, under special conditions, to promote the public welfare. For example, if sufficient degrees of competition exist, free trade is desirable because it is said to maximize the value of social output or minimize social cost. If business monopoly or collusion exist, however, economic activity might be regulated, through legislation, in society's own interest. Because this view makes voluntary-exchange relationships conditional or dependent upon their alleged effect upon social efficiency and the public "welfare," it can be designated as the instrumentalist–utilitarian position.[11]

Historically, almost all economists have rationalized their belief in a capitalistic market system and justified sporadic government regulation of that system by arguing in essentially instrumentalist–utilitarian terms. For example, in the first systematic economic treatise, *The Wealth of Nations*, Adam Smith indicted all the old regulatory economic systems, especially Mercantilism, for their economic inefficiency.[12] Smith opposed government restrictions on production and trade because, in his view, they held down the accumulation of capital and the creation of national wealth and welfare. Removal of the restrictions and regulations would allow self-interest, regulated by competition, to produce the greatest economic good for the greatest number.

Smith did not extend his argument for free trade to all economic areas. *The Wealth of Nations* contains numerous examples which demonstate that Smith did not believe that private wills or interest always synthesized into the public good. And where they did not, government involvement and even regulation were clearly necessary. National defense was an obvious example, but other exceptions to the general rule of noninterference in the areas of schools, bridges, canals, roads, and the post office were even more revealing.[13] Smith, it appeared, often qualified his general laissez-faire whenever he felt that private pecuniary interests could not, or would not, operate in the general public interest as he conceived it.[14]

Jeremy Bentham and the Philosophic Radicals made the semiutilitarian economic philosophy of Adam Smith even more explicit.[15] Bentham believed that the interests reflected in the private, selfish economic activities of individuals were harmonious, and created a stable economic system; that is, that a universal order was "surely and instinctively established by the spontaneous division of tasks and by the automatic mechanism of exchanges." The Philosophic Radicals supported free-market capitalism because that view of political economy extended the "greatest good to the greatest number." Government intervention, not condemned *a priori*, was rejected, for the most part, simply because the "hedonistic calculus" and experience had shown that its benefits rarely exceeded its costs. Thus, as with Smith, the Radicals made the question of legitimate state intervention in economic affairs a utilitarian issue: They supported economic arrangements that appeared to function in the general public interest as they conceived it.

This approach seems to have been the essential methodological and ideological position of most of the classical economists, and certainly is the position of almost all neoclassical economists. Neither Smith, Ricardo, Mill, McCulloch, Senior, Marshall, or certainly Keynes[16] ever admitted to a belief in an undiluted laissez-faire, nor did they imply it in any clear and consistent theory of public policy.[17] For the most part, their only guide to the important questions of legitimate governmental regulation was utilitarian: though free-market activity might be generally acceptable, the state could and should intervene whenever its duly elected, well intentioned representatives thought the intervention to be, on balance, in the public's interest.

ANTITRUST POLICY AND THE PUBLIC INTEREST

There may, however, be inherent difficulties associated with this approach to public policy. The most central observation, aside from the normative considerations already examined, is that this instrumentalist perspective may not be able to be as pragmatic or scientific as it pretends. Utilitarians and instrumentalists implicitly assume that there is some generally acceptable method to determine the precise economic costs and benefits of public action, so that the public interest might be intelligently pursued.[18] Yet, individual costs and benefits are inherently subjective and personal; it is not possible to sum up subjective evaluations of cost and benefit for different individuals in society and arrive at any meaningful aggregate.[19] In short, there may be no unambiguous way to calculate precisely the greatest good for the greatest number, or to determine the aggregate social costs associated with achieving any collective objective. Accordingly, there may be no scientific way to demonstrate that antitrust policy promotes efficiency in some collective utilitarian sense.[20]

Most policy analysts would assert that this conclusion is emphatically not the case. They would argue, presumably, that there is persuasive economic theory and historical data to support the belief that antitrust policy does, on balance, promote the public welfare. And while they might admit that the empirical evidence does not lend itself to exact measurement, they would hold that the general weight of economic theory and historical fact would strongly suggest that antitrust policy—at least antimonopoly policy—is appropriate in a competitive market system.

The material to follow in this volume will challenge this widely held presumption among economists and the general public. It will argue, instead, that the weight of the general evidence is that the firms indicted under the antitrust laws were not abusing consumers, and that the laws have tended, instead, to protect competitors and reduce efficiency throughout the market. Further, it will hold that this misguided social policy is not an accident, but flows logically from an irrelevant and deeply flawed theory of competition. Finally, it will suggest that the antitrust laws should be more accurately understood as consistent with a wider spectrum of legal interventions (tariffs, price controls, licensing), that are openly acknowledged to restrain competition and promote monopoly throughout the economy. That antitrust tends to make the economy less competitive and less productive is the ultimate irony and myth inherent in antitrust policy. The rest of this volume is devoted to making this perspective comprehensible and believable.

NOTES

1. Jonathan Hughes, *The Governmental Habit: Economic Controls from Colonial Times to the Present* (New York: Basic Books, Inc., Publishers, 1977).

2. Jerrold G. Van Cise, "Religion and Antitrust," *The Antitrust Bulletin*, Vol. 23, No. 3 (Fall 1978), p. 462. The platform of the American Economic Association founded in 1885 declared that "the doctrine of *laissez-faire* is unsafe in politics and unsound in morals." Among those who subscribed to this view were such rising young economists as John R. Commons, Richard T. Ely, and Simon N. Patten, who wielded considerable influence in the following century. See "Report of the Organizations of the American Economic Association," Merle Curti et al., eds., *American Issues: The Social Record*, 4th ed. rev., Vol. 2 (Philadelphia: J. B. Lippincott Company, 1971), pp. 158–62. See also Joseph Dorfman, *The Economic Mind in American Civilization: 1865–1918* (New York: Viking Press, 1949), pp. 206–208.

3. Robert H. Bork, "The Legislative Intent and the Policy of the Sherman Act," *Journal of Law and Economics*, Vol. 9 (October 1966), pp. 7–48. See also, Hans Thorelli, *The Federal Antitrust Policy* (Baltimore: Johns Hopkins Press, 1955), esp. Chapter 4, and William Letwin, *Law and Economic Policy in America* (New York: Random House, 1965), esp. pp. 88–99.

4. Gabriel Kolko, *The Triumph of Conservatism: A Reinterpretation of American History 1900–1916* (New York: Free Press of Glencoe, 1963).

5. Alan Stone, *Economic Regulation and the Public Interest: The Federal Trade Commission in Theory and Practice* (Ithaca, N.Y.: Cornell University Press, 1977), p. 24.

6. Thorelli, *op. cit.*, p. 169. Sherman's motives for sponsoring such legislation may have been ambiguous. See Thorelli, *op. cit.*, p. 168.

7. *Munn v. Illinois*, 94 U.S. 113 (1877).

8. *Nebbia v. New York*, 291 U.S. 502 (1934).

9. Morton J. Horwitz, *The Transformation of American Law: 1780–1860* (Cambridge, Mass.: Harvard University Press, 1977).

10. Roger Pilon, "Corporations and Rights: On Treating Corporate People Justly," *Georgia Law Review*, Vol. 13 No. 4 (Summer 1979), pp. 1245–1370. See also Robert Hessen, *In Defense of the Corporation* (Stanford, Cal.: Hoover Institution Press, 1979).

11. Gordon C. Bjork, *Private Enterprise and Public Interest: The Development of American Capitalism* (Englewood Cliffs, N.J.: Prentice-Hall, 1969), esp. chapters 1, 3, and 5 for a discussion of this position.

12. Adam Smith, *The Wealth of Nations* (New York: Modern Library, 1937).

13. *Ibid.*, pp. 682–90 and 737. Also see Mark Blaug, *Economic Theory in Retrospect* rev. ed. (Homewood, Ill.: Richard D. Irwin, 1968), p. 63.

14. Yet Smith did not favor laws prohibiting business collusion, since such laws could not be executed in a manner "consistent with liberty and justice." Smith, *op. cit.*, p. 128.

15. Elie Halévy, *The Growth of Philosophic Radicalism* (Boston: The Beacon Press, 1955). See Chapters 3 (part 1) and 4 (part 3).

16. John Maynard Keynes, *Essays in Persuasion* (New York: W. W. Norton and Company, Inc., 1963), esp. pp. 312–322.

17. William D. Gramp, *Economic Liberalism: The Classical View*, Vol. 11 (New York: Random House, 1965), p. 75. Also, see Edmund Whittaker, *Schools and Streams of Economic Thought* (Chicago: Rand McNally Co., 1960), pp. 168–175.

18. H. H. Liebhafsky, *American Government and Business* (New York: John Wiley & Sons, 1971), pp. 23–26.

19. Murray N. Rothbard, *Toward a Reconstruction of Utility and Welfare Economics* (New York: The Center For Libertarian Studies, 1978). See also S. C. Littlechild, "The Problem of Social Cost," in Louis M. Spadaro, ed., *New Directions in Austrian Economics* (Kansas City: Sheed Andrews and McMeel, Inc., 1978), pp. 77–93.

CHAPTER TWO

Competition Theory
and the Market Economy

It might be appropriate to begin a theoretical discussion of the foundations of antitrust law with the familiar historical observation that business competition was declining in the post-Civil War period. Joseph W. McGuire, in his classic *Business and Society,* provides a typical expression of the conventional wisdom regarding the state of competition in the marketplace:

> There have always existed many forces which tend to reduce competition. In the thirty years following the Civil War, these forces began to predominate in the United States. . . . Competition, so effective as a regulating force on business operations in the decades prior to the war, was steadily decreasing as a few firms began to dominate our important industries and as these and other concerns turned more and more to collusion.[1]

Now this seems entirely straightforward. Competition was an effective process prior to the Civil War, but in the post-war period it steadily declined. Major industries came to be dominated by large combinations that either monopolized the market or conspired to restrain trade and competition. The impression here and elsewhere is that these combinations were effective, and that the Sherman Act was a logical response to a deteriorating economic situation. In short, the free market was amended to save it.

And yet there is something curious about this perspective, particularly in the McGuire text. For only a paragraph earlier it had informed the reader that:

> From 1865 to 1897, declining prices year after year made it difficult for businessmen to plan for the future. In many areas new railroad links had resulted in a nationalization of the market east of the Mississippi, and even small concerns in small towns were forced to compete with other, often larger firms located at a distance. At the same time there were remarkable advances in technology

13

and productivity. In short it was a wonderful era for the consumer and a frightful age for the producers especially as competition became more and more severe.[2]

Something appears amiss here. It is not immediately obvious how competition could be "steadily decreasing" on the one hand while it was becoming "more and more severe" on the other. In addition, if competition was declining as large firms came to dominate certain industries, how could the period have been a "wonderful era for the consumer"? If the growth of large-scale enterprise reduced competition in the market, why did overproduction occur, and why were there "remarkable advances in technology and productivity"? Further, how are we to reconcile increasing monopoly and collusion with the general price deflation that occurred in this period, and with McGuire's conclusion that this era was a "frightful" age for the producer? And finally, if the second perspective quoted above is in fact the correct one, what becomes of the standard explanation for regulatory antitrust?

It should be apparent that a theory of competition—and monopoly—is required before we can proceed further. We must have a theory of competition before we can judge whether it is increasing or decreasing. And we must have a theory of "resource allocation" before we can assert, or understand the assertion that monopoly power can arise in a free market and can misallocate economic resources and reduce consumer and social welfare. As the quotations from McGuire have illustrated, the facts in any historical situation can provide an ambiguous picture of what is occurring. What is required is a theory that can integrate the relevant facts and make business history intelligible.

NEOCLASSICAL COMPETITION THEORY

Competition can be defined as "the effort of two or more parties acting independently to secure the business of a third party by offering the most favorable terms."[3] This definition is entirely consistent with the everyday usage of the term. In business, for instance, competition is seen as a continuous process of rivalry between sellers for the patronage of potential customers. The emphasis is upon strategies involving price, product differentiation, advertising, service, research and development, technological change, and a whole host of activities that are designed to secure sales and ultimately profits for the business organization. Competition is not simply a mechanical optimization within known constraints, but is seen as an exploratory process whereby opportunities for profit are discovered and exploited over time under uncertain circumstances. Resources are allocated efficiently if rival producers (entrepreneurs) are in the process of discovering and responding correctly to the uncertainties of changing market conditions.

Economists, by and large, have held sharply differing views of competition and resource allocation, and it is their views which have tended to legitimize antitrust regulation. This is not to say that the views of the economists have been correct and that antitrust policy is appropriate in a market economy. Indeed, it will be argued below that such views are fundamentally misguided. Yet it is vitally important to understand the orthodox theories of competition and monopoly, and to understand how to criticize them, since they still serve as the intellectual foundation of antitrust policy. Indeed, it is difficult to comprehend the classic antitrust cases to be discussed in this volume, and the decisions reached in those cases, without a clear understanding of conventional competition and monopoly theory.

Perfect Competition and Resource Allocation

For more than 100 years, economists have been building economic models describing an ideal or optimal competitive situation, that is, a situation that would produce the greatest benefit to consumers and to society at the lowest possible economic cost. If this optimal condition could be achieved, scarce resources would be employed in their highest valued use, and their efficient employment would imply that no alternative allocation could make anyone better off without making someone else worse off. This situation is referred to as a *Pareto optimal* condition and it can occur in a perfectly competitive equilibrium.[4]

In its simplest expression, pure and atomistic competition is said to exist in any market if all suppliers of commodities in the market are small relative to total market supply; the commodity produced and sold by the various suppliers is homogeneous in the minds of the consumers; and resources are mobile and no artificial restrictions exist with respect to entry, demand, supply, or price. In addition, a condition of perfect competition is said to exist if all relevant market information is correct and fully known to market participants.[5]

To understand why many economists hold this conception of competition as optimal, it is necessary to review briefly the mechanics of the competitive model. The model begins by assuming that a substantial number of small firms already exist in some relevant market, and that they are already producing homogeneous products, that is, products that are identical in the mind of the consumer. If the firms are small, such that their individual outputs cannot noticeably affect the total market output of the product under discussion, then all sales by these sellers are made at some given market price that is determined by market demand and market supply (see Figure 1).

In a purely competitive market, atomistic firms are said to have no control over their own prices. No firm could sell its output at a price higher than the market price since the same homogeneous product is available from all other suppliers at the (lower) market price. And no firm would charge a price lower

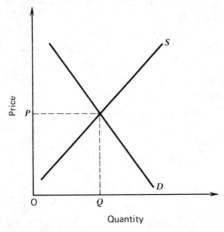

Figure 1   Supply and demand determine market price and output.

than the market price, since all of its output can be sold at the market rate. Hence, the market price becomes a horizontal demand schedule facing each and every firm in the market, and indicates, at any relevant price, how many units of the commodity consumers would be willing and able to purchase.

Firms under short-run competitive conditions are assumed to be powerless to adjust the price of their commodity or of any other relevant product variable (e.g., quality). Consequently, sellers are induced to maximize their profits by adjusting their outputs such that their marginal costs of production and sale just equal the market price of the commodity. At such output levels, the extra costs (marginal cost) of producing and selling the commodity would just equal the extra revenue (marginal revenue) received from the sale of the commodity. And if average costs including "normal" profits are below average revenues at such outputs, total net income (economic profit) would then be maximized for some representative firm (see Figure 2).

Economic profits would only be temporary under pure competition. Eventually, it would pay entrepreneurs to mobilize additional resources and supply additional homogeneous products (entry is easy) in an effort to earn the economic profits available in this industry. But the entrepreneurial adjustments in output will soon lower the market price of the commodity and narrow the economic profits of any representative supplier. In fact, pushed to its logical conclusion, it is possible to argue that outputs will be increased until market prices fall and eliminate all economic profits (normal profits included as a "cost" still being earned). With appropriately drawn average-cost functions, price will settle at the very minimum point of the average cost function where there is a triple identity between price, marginal cost, and minimum average cost (see Figure 3). And since economic profits and losses are entirely absent, and demand and supply are assumed to be known and stable, an *equilibrium* condition is now established in this industry. Resource allocation is as efficient as possible and social welfare, given the distribution of income, is said to be maximized.

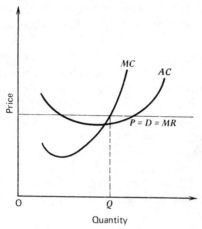

Figure 2 A firm's marginal costs are equated with market price (marginal revenue) to determine firm output.

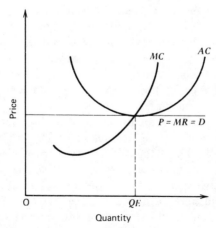

Figure 3 Equilibrium for the individual firm in pure competition.

Perfect Competition and Regulatory Policy

It should be apparent that there may be important policy implications associated with this equilibrium condition and with this theory of atomistic competition. For instance, if this is a correct theory of competition, and if this is the sort of competition that actually exists in the marketplace, antitrust policy would be unnecessary. Since a perfectly competitive market would automatically generate socially beneficial conduct and performance on the part of the suppliers, little if any additional social benefit could be accomplished by antitrust intervention.

On the other hand, if economic markets are not perfectly competitive, then there can be no corresponding guarantee that resources would be allocated efficiently. Indeed, from a perfectly competitive perspective, economic resources would be misallocated and some waste and inefficiency would exist under imperfectly competitive conditions.[6] Markets that contain large firms, locational advantages, price discrimination, differentiated products, tie-in sales, promotional advertising, collusion, and interdependent rivalry are not perfectly competitive markets, and firms in such markets are said to possess some *monopoly power*. Consistent with this perspective, such markets might require government antitrust regulation to make them more competitive and more socially efficient.[7]

This is not to say that regulatory enthusiasts believe that the actual business world can (or even should) be transformed by law, into pure or perfect competition. That would be the ultimate "straw man" position and it is not being maintained here or elsewhere in this volume. It is to say, however, that the atomistic model described above is still the standard welfare benchmark, the guidepost, the optimal referent that most proponents of regulation employ when they argue that concentrated industries can misallocate resources, or that waste and inefficiency can occur under imperfectly competitive market conditions.[8] It is the implicit acceptance of perfect competition as some sort of optimal standard of economic performance that allows a condemnation of activities such as large mergers, or product differentiation and advertising. Consumers that prefer product variety are said to be willing to sacrifice "efficiency" in order to obtain it.[9]

Reference to the perfectly competitive model also allows proponents of business regulation to talk of "more competition" as an industrial situation that structurally approaches atomistic competition; alternatively, resource misallocation is any allocation that does not coincide with the pattern of resource use under perfect competition. From a neoclassical perspective, competition declines, and some economic waste occurs, as we move away from perfect competition, and competition increases, and markets become more efficient, as we move towards perfect competition. The explicit relationship between this perspective and government antitrust regulation should now be clear. As a leading microtheorist puts it:

> ... in the theory of a market economy pure competition tends to lead toward the set of conditions defining maximum economic welfare or well-being, given the distribution of income. The actual performance of the economy can then be appraised against its potential 'best' performance. Imperfectly competitive or monopolistic forces are important in preventing the attainment of the 'best' allocation and use of economic resources. Thus, the purely competitive model frequently is used as the basis for public regulation of imperfectly competitive situations. Presumably it underlies the philosophy and enforcement of the Sherman Antitrust Act of 1890 ...[10]

Imperfect Competition and Resource Misallocation

It is important to understand why business organizations are judged to be misallocating resources under monopoly or imperfect competition. The explanation begins with the observation that under imperfectly competitive conditions, firms have some control over the prices of their products. This control may stem from the fact that the commodities being produced by suppliers are differentiated, or that market knowledge is not perfect, or that firms are colluding to restrict production. Differentiation of product, imperfect knowledge, and collusion are the primary ingredients of imperfectly competitive situations.

For instance, if products are differentiated, individual sellers discover that the demand curve for their own product is downward sloping and not horizontal, and that they will not lose all of their customers with a price slightly higher than a competitor's. Such sellers are said to have price control or *monopoly power* relative to competitive sellers of homogeneous products. And it is this price and product control, and the subsequent business rivalry, that so typify monopolistically competitive or imperfectly competitive market situations.

Similarly, if firms collude to restrict production, prices can be higher than under perfectly competitive conditions. Consumers may buy less and pay more, and are said to be injured by the restriction of production. Moreover, there is said to be a social welfare-loss due to the misallocation of resources associated with the collusive output restriction.

Firms under monopolistic or imperfect competition still attempt to maximize their profit by selling an output where marginal revenue equals marginal cost. But if products are not perfect substitutes, the demand function each firm faces is downward sloping, and the price that each firm charges will

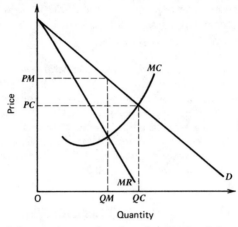

Figure 4 A firm with "monopoly power" produces less (*QM*) and charges more (*PM*) than a "competitive" firm.

tend to be greater than both marginal revenue and marginal cost (see Figure 4). Thus, when profits are maximized, the prices that consumers pay will exceed the extra costs associated with bringing those products to the consumers. Even if economic profits are zero, prices will still exceed marginal costs, production will not occur at minimum average costs, and resources are said to be misallocated due to monopoly power.

Most economists would hold that this particular economic situation compares unfavorably with price, output, and cost under perfect competition. Under atomistically competitive conditions, price is always identical to marginal cost, and within a competitive equilibrium, market price is always driven to the minimum point of the average-cost function such that production tends to occur at its most efficient point. Thus neoclassical analysis appears able to demonstrate scientifically what has always been assumed concerning monopoly, namely, that the prices tend to be higher, the outputs less, and the equilibrium costs greater than under comparably competitive conditions.[11]

The Cost-Benefit Welfare Model

Since a classic journal article by Arnold Harberger in 1954, it has been convenient to portray the economic difference between monopoly and competition, and the consequent welfare loss and resource misallocation, as a so-called welfare-loss triangle[12] (see Figure 5). In this basic diagram, OX is the

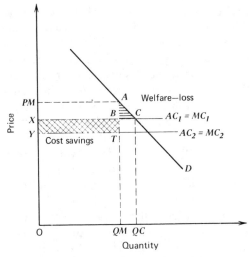

Figure 5   The cost-benefit model.

competitive price and is equal to long-run average and marginal cost. OPM is the monopoly price and is higher than the competitive price for reasons explained previously. It should be clear that if governmental antitrust regulation could prevent or reduce this monopoly power, it could, consistent with this perspective, improve economic performance and allocative efficiency by lowering prices and increasing output. Presumably it is this fundamental economic principle that underlies any rational antitrust policy in this country.[13]

The basic economic model outlined above can be broadened to highlight the economic effects, and regulatory implications, of business collusion, merger, deconcentration, and increased business efficiency. If, for example, monopoly power established through collusion or horizontal merger threatens to reduce output and increase prices, resources would be misallocated and social welfare would be reduced (as explained above). The triangle area ABC in Figure 5 is said to represent the deadweight welfare-loss associated with a restriction of output from QC to QM. Or, alternatively if antitrust policy could prevent or end such output restrictions, it could increase social welfare by improving the allocation of scarce economic resources. This analysis would also apply, similarly, to proposals aimed at the governmental decentralization of highly concentrated industries. Presumably, a reduction in economic concentration would lessen monopoly power and lead to increased outputs at lower prices.

Whether society would gain on balance from such governmental regulation would depend upon whether costs were affected adversely by such policies.[14] With respect to so-called naked price-fixing and market division agreements, the standard economic literature is practically unanimous: to prevent or end such agreements by law would not raise business costs and thus, would clearly serve the public interest in terms of increased social efficiency.[15] Indeed, costs might even be reduced since it has been maintained by some commentators that firms expend resources to attain monopoly power, and then expend monopoly profits in socially wasteful non-price competition. Thus, the social costs of monopoly are alleged to be greater than just the deadweight welfare-loss triangle.[16]

The matter becomes still more complicated with antimerger and business deconcentration policies. As can be observed from Figure 5, even the slightest gains in actual economic efficiency associated with a merger or increased business concentration (the decrease in costs from AC_1 to AC_2), could easily overwhelm the strict allocative welfare losses associated with pure monopoly power (output restriction). In general, if area XYBT exceeds area ABC, regulatory action to prevent the merger or reduce the industrial concentration is said to harm society's welfare, and could not be justified even from a utilitarian perspective. If output restriction is difficult or impossible, and if there are more than negligible economies and effiences associated with large-scale business organization, antimonopoly policy—even on its own terms—would not tend to improve social welfare.

A CRITICISM OF NEOCLASSICAL COMPETITION THEORY

The orthodox theories of competition and monopoly just reviewed have hardly gone unchallenged by economists over the last thirty years. Baumol, for instance, has admitted that if monopoly were to exist in every industry in the economy, it would be difficult to conclude that resources were misallocated.[17] Lipsey and Lancaster have acknowledged that it is uncertain whether a public policy that leads to a reduction in some but not all monopoly would necessarily result in a more efficient allocation of resources.[18] Further, it has long been admitted that the entire long-run cost function might be lower under monopoly than under competition. And finally, the traditional analysis and its welfare implications does not take account of market externalities, factor indivisibilities and noneconomic elements of social welfare.

Horizontal Demand and Resource Misallocation

Although these critical observations are interesting, the orthodox approach to competition and monopoly theory is open to more serious and fundamental difficulties. The first difficulty concerns the internal logic of the competitive model itself, and specifically the logic of the horizontal demand function that is the hallmark of competition and its welfare implications. Atomistic competition assumes that the demand curve that faces each firm is horizontal and that the coefficient of elasticity is infinite. But is such a circumstance logically possible?

There are several objections that can be raised to the notion of a perfectly horizontal demand function. The first is that market price is determined by total market demand and total market supply. At the equilibrium price consumers are purchasing (or are willing to purchase) some *precise* amount of market product—and no more. It would seem logical, therefore, to conclude that any increase in supply—if it is to be sold—must have some perceptible effect on market supply and market price. The effect may be "small" but there must be some effect in order to sell the additional output.

It will not suffice to assert that an atomistic firm is so tiny that its output has no "appreciable" effect on the market. What *is* an appreciable effect? If the additional output is to be sold there must be an appreciable effect as far as *consumers* are concerned. The economic world, unlike the pure mathematical model in which price can be parametric, does not contain the "infinitely small steps" of the calculus or limit. Output adjustments, even small ones, are nonetheless *discrete* changes, and must have some noticable effect on prices. Although individual demand functions may appear to be *nearly* horizontal, and may indeed be extremely elastic under certain circumstances, a perfectly elastic demand function confronting each seller would not appear to be logically possible.[19]

Prices in openly competitive markets may tend to remain stable even though there are "small" increases in supply. But this observation does not demonstrate that individual demand functions are perfectly horizontal or that sellers have no influence on market price. It simply demonstrates that market demand has shifted (slightly) to purchase the (slightly) larger supply that is in the market. If the demand curve is held constant, however, the slightly larger output must be sold at a slightly lower market price.

An additional objection to the horizontal demand curve is that in strict mathematical terms, the curve is not a "function." In the mathematics methodology, a functional relationship between two variables always implies that for every value of the *independent* variable there exists one, and only one, value for the *dependent* variable. In economic models, although the familiar axes have been reversed, "price" is clearly the independent variable and "quantity demanded" is the dependent variable. Yet a perfectly elastic demand curve implies that there are an infinite number of values for the dependent variable ("quantity demanded") associated with any one independent variable ("price"). Clearly, then, the perfectly elastic line in competition (assuming for the moment that it could exist) is not a demand *function*.

We must conclude, therefore, that the notion of a perfectly elastic demand function is not legitimate and must be rejected even on its own terms, aside and apart from any criticism of the realism or optimality of the atomistic model.

This criticism has important welfare and policy implications. If actual demand curves cannot even in theory be perfectly horizontal, the entire orthodox theory of resource misallocation under imperfect competition simply collapses. The fact remains that if all demand curves are downward sloping, price diverges from marginal revenue under *all* selling conditions. All sellers now must restrict their output to a point where marginal cost is just equal to marginal revenue and not price. It should be obvious, however, that such behavior can no longer be uniquely associated with market power, but is, instead, the natural conduct and performance of all business organizations.

Orthodox theory is able to conclude that resources are misallocated under such circumstances only by comparing these selling situations with the perfectly competitive equilibrium. Since price is greater than marginal cost and since output is restricted, the result is termed socially inefficient. But if such an equilibrium situation with a horizontal demand function is logically impossible, then this particular notion of resource misallocation is incorrect. "Misallocation" is relative to what possible standard? "Restricted" output is relative to what possible standard of output? "Inefficient" is relative to what possible standard of efficiency? Without perfect competition as a standard, monopoly power and monopolistic competition are indistinguishable from any selling situations where firms face a downward sloping demand curve, and where they attempt to maximize their profits by equating marginal revenue with marginal costs.

Indeed, why continue to refer to such situations as "monopolistic"? All firms in a free market tend to produce an output where marginal revenue and marginal cost are equal. This allocation of resources is the allocation that one would expect under free-market competition with legally open entry; monopoly power has nothing to do with this at all. Such openly competitive markets would *tend* towards an equilibrium condition where marginal revenue and marginal costs were equal, and where firms were earning returns comparable to returns earned elsewhere in the market (see Figure 6).

This general theory of entry, pricing, and output determination can easily be broadened to incorporate the competitive process in which several large firms sell the bulk of the market output. The primary behavioral characteristic of oligopoly and, indeed, of all business competition, is that there is extreme interdependence (rivalry) between the sellers in the marketplace. Business organizations realize that their competitors will respond and react to their actions. The demand function facing each seller, therefore, would incor-

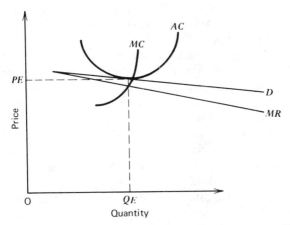

Figure 6 Equilibrium for a firm in an openly competitive market.

porate the most likely reactions of rivals to price and non-price changes. The equilibrium solution towards which such markets theoretically tend, would be precisely the same as depicted in Figure 6.

Competition as a Dynamic Discovery Process

There are still more fundamental difficulties with the perfect competition perspective. Certainly one of the most important is that perfect competition theory is not really concerned with the process of competition. Perfect competition theory is fundamentally static, and not a theory of market process.[20] Standard competition theory assumes conditions to exist that automatically result in an equilibrium. But such assumptions avoid the tough questions concerning the nature of the competitive process and can easily lead to inappropriate policy conclusions.

Neoclassical competition theory begins with given conditions—with information that is already known, and correctly known, to all market participants. The economic activity that occurs under such conditions is purely routine, that is, maximization of profit, with no room for discovery, error, or learning. Correctly understood, the perfectly competitive model does not actually move toward equilibrium but is, itself, an equilibrium condition.

Since perfect competition theory starts with equilibrium assumptions, it must assume away the significant aspects of a genuinely competitive process. For instance, the question of how businessmen come to understand what consumer demand *is* becomes, in the standard analysis, the assumption that such information is already known, and correctly known, to all businessmen. How businessmen discover which factor combinations are the most efficient becomes, in the orthodox model, the assumption that such combinations are already known and have already been adopted by suppliers. How businessmen determine which products to produce with what degree of differentiation, becomes the assumption that all the products are already homogeneous. In short, the model assumes the existence of information that a competitive process aims to discover.

Moreover, the competitive equilibrium condition is optimal in an entirely trivial sense. Perfect competition is optimal if all relevant information is given, and then only if that information never changes. The optimality of the perfectly competitive solution depends upon a static world of unchanging data and preferences. But it should be apparent that the passage of time in any real market situation must change knowledge and preferences and, thus, must weaken seriously the relevance of the neoclassical model. A perfectly competitive equilibrium in a changing world could not be efficient, since a changing world would allow for new products, new factor combinations, and new insights into what consumers prefer and at what prices. A changing world would allow for rivalry, for error and error corrections, and for continuous entrepreneurial activity. But such a perpetual disequilibrium process is incompatible with the assumptions of the perfectly competitive model and with its static perspective.

Entrepreneurial Competition.   Business competition is always a dynamic process, not a given static state of affairs, in which suppliers continually strive to offer improved alternatives to market participants. Unlike the perfectly competitive world, competition is a process of discovering opportunities for profit, and then adjusting market conditions so that these opportunities tend to be exploited. If there is any movement toward equilibrium, this process of discovery and market adjustment is that movement, and this is why it occurs. Competition is the equilibrating process, not the equilibrium condition, in which businessmen attempt, in the absence of perfect knowledge and homogeneous products, to more closely coordinate their supply plans with the anticipated plans of other market participants.

As an illustration of the process, imagine that we are concerned with the buying and selling of ballpoint pens. If we assume at the start that market knowledge is perfect, then we have assumed away the entire competitive process. If, instead, we assume that the knowledge concerning consumer preferences, technology, factor prices, advertising, location, and dozens of other variables is only understood vaguely, then the competitive process is the social vehicle through which a closer economic coordination is achieved. During the process some firms may differentiate their products; others may not. Some firms may stress durability and choose to sell their pens in retail stores; others may stress only price and choose to mail order. Some pens may be produced by large business organizations that formerly offered only fountain pens to consumers. Other pens may be sold by new organizations equipped with radically different manufacturing technologies. Since market knowledge is imperfect, some firms may choose to spend substantial amounts of resources on advertising and on alerting and persuading potential consumers to purchase; others may decide on minimal amounts of advertising, or even, perhaps, on none at all. The point to be emphasized here is that all of these entrepreneurial activities are competitive, and it is only through this discovery process that firms are able to determine how to allocate resources efficiently. These entrepreneurial activities do not spoil competition or efficiency, as they would in the atomistic model, but are the very essence of market competition.

Neoclassical Competition and Social Welfare.   The real perversity inherent in the traditional competitive perspective is that it can treat as resource-misallocating the very business practices that are, in fact, essential to any competitive process. Business organizations compete by differentiating products, innovating new products, discounting list prices, locating in areas convenient to consumers, advertising prices and services, and purchasing resources cheaper than rivals. Yet because these activities are not discovered in the competitive maximization process or in the equilibrium condition, they have often been classified as monopolistic and inefficient. What some have labeled monopolistic may simply be a competitive market process in a necessary state of disequilibrium.

This mislabeling is most pernicious in the case of product differentiation. Since the atomistic model starts with the given assumption of homogeneous product, it is forced by its own logic to treat product differentiation as inefficient. But why begin an analysis of competition by assuming that products are already homogeneous? If, instead, a competitive model is begun with revealed consumer preferences, homogeneous products become one, but only one, possible competitive outcome. Other competitive outcomes include various degrees of product differentiation that are supported by the voluntary demonstrated preferences of consumers. Once it is acknowledged that differentiated goods have subjective value that buyers are willing to pay for, perfect competition with homogeneous products can no longer be considered universally optimal or efficient.

It is a serious analytical error to mistake a competitive market process for resource-misallocating monopoly. It is also a serious error to continue to associate the simple price-and-profit behavior of atomistic firms (in equilibrium), with competitive business conduct and performance. For example, it is now arbitrary to associate zero economic profits with efficient resource allocation or alternatively, to associate the total absence of a pricing policy with competitive behavior; price takers are now no more competitive than price makers. Indeed, radically different price-and-profit strategies are compatible and desirable if competition is defined in dynamic terms. Nor ought anyone to expect any actual industrial situation to settle down into some impossible, long-run equilibrium (if we could only wait long enough); long-run equilibria are not of this world. In short, every aspect of the perfectly competitive model must be rejected for policy purposes. Far from being useful or predictive, as has often been maintained, the atomistic model leads to incorrect expectations concerning socially desirable structure, conduct, and performance. To attempt to apply the model as a standard in antitrust for determining competition or monopoly power would be nothing short of disastrous.

The Welfare Models Revisited

The welfare model analysis reviewed earlier in this chapter can now be confronted directly. It will be recalled that resource misallocation in that model occurred relative to some objectively determined "competitive" price and output. But if perfect competition is both illogical and non-optimal, the standard of optimality and efficiency for measuring welfare-loss evaporates. If all firms in open markets face downward sloping demand functions, then price diverges from marginal cost in all economic markets, and outputs are always restricted. Further, even if this "restriction" was meaningful, why do the higher prices and profits *not* attract entry, increase production and lower prices? In the absence of a governmental restriction on production, why is the welfare triangle not competed away?

But even more fundamentally, the standard welfare models assume that both costs and benefits are measurably objective phenomena, knowable to outside observers. From a strictly theoretical perspective, however, the notion of objective and aggregate costs and benefits for society as a whole is seriously misleading. Not only are costs imprecise and difficult to measure in an accounting sense, but a strictly theoretical understanding of costs and benefits is that they are ultimately and fundamentally personal and subjective.[21] The costs of an action are the subjective values attached to the foregone opportunities by the decision maker at the moment of the decision. Such subjective values can never be known to any outside observer and thus, cannot be objectively aggregated for society as a whole.

If social costs and social benefits cannot be known or aggregated, the alleged usefulness of the neoclassical welfare models in support of a rational antitrust policy is now open to the most serious question. In short, how is it to be demonstrated that, say, "restrictive" agreements between business organizations are socially inefficient when the gains and losses associated with such arrangements are incapable in principle of discovery, measurement, or comparison? How are we now to know that cartel prices injure consumers or "society"? How are we now to compare social utility before and after some cartelization or monopolization? How are we now to conclude that certain forms of non-price competition are socially wasteful? It would appear that even the best and most reasonable neoclassical analysis is mired in a serious *methodological* difficulty.

An Alternative Theory of Efficiency

A very different perspective on economic efficiency and resource allocation can be developed directly from a strict subjectivist approach to cost and utility. This approach would hold that individual human action is purposeful and aims at accomplishing selected ends by adopting patterns of resource use (plans) consistent with those ends. If the means employed in the pursuit of selected ends are consistent with those ends, then the means or plans are said to be efficiently employed.

The efficient accomplishment of ends in a social context requires that particular planned activity dovetail or coordinate with the planned activity of other market participants. Yet given the complex division of labor and the difficulty of obtaining accurate information, such a dovetailing is not automatic; indeed, mutually inconsistent plans must be anticipated. If market participants had perfect information, all plans would be fully coordinated and markets would be efficient, by definition. But to assume perfect information is to assume away the problem of explaining social efficiency. The question of social efficiency is not how resources would be allocated if everyone had perfect information. The issue, instead, is an understanding of the process by which more accurate information is produced, transmitted, and utilized such that a more consistent pattern of social plan coordination can be achieved.

An unhampered market economy automatically generates price information that can be utilized by decision makers in an effort to coordinate divergent plans. Decision makers are able to monitor behavior with strong incentives to pursue patterns of resource use that are more fully coordinated with the plans of others. Since information is not perfect and is constantly changing, this process of plan adjustment can never achieve any final equilibrium. What must be emphasized, however, is that the competitive market process creates powerful incentives to discover and utilize information and to correct plans that fall short of objectives. In short, an unhampered market provides the context within which individuals and institutions can engage in efficient action. It is both a necessary and a sufficient condition for an efficient market process.[22]

Seen in this light, voluntary market agreements—even agreements that intend to "restrict" production in some neoclassical sense—can be efficient, since they aim to more fully coordinate the plans of the respective parties. Such arrangements are judged appropriate *ex ante* to bring about some desired end or goal. To prohibit or restrict (by law) such agreements, from this perspective, would result in an unambiguous reduction in efficiency and social coordination.

There are some distinct advantages associated with this theory of efficiency. The first is that the entire professional tirade against highly advertised differentiated products simply collapses as an irrelevant discussion of ends; social efficiency relates only to means. Second, nothing said or implied in this discussion of efficiency requires the aggregation of individual costs and benefits; individual decision makers perform all of their own cost/benefit calculations, and social welfare can be enhanced by free trade since individuals can coordinate their plans more fully and engage in any arrangements that they judge to be efficient. Finally, all government restrictions or prohibitions of trade and contractual agreement are now revealed to be socially inefficient in a scientific sense that is independent of the natural rights argument for open markets sketched briefly in Chapter 1.

Economists and Competition Theory

Some of the preceding criticism of the atomistically competitive paradigm and its regulatory implications has been noted in the orthodox literature, although it has yet to dislodge that perspective from its foremost position in matters of public policy. Some economists have argued eloquently that perfect competition is a misleading notion, and that simple welfare comparisons between the real world and the model are fraught with danger. This criticism first became important in the 1930s when Joan Robinson and Edward Chamberlin developed their respective theories of imperfect and monopolistic competition. Joan Robinson, for instance, stated that:

> In order to make a valid theoretical comparison between competitive output and monopoly output in a particular industry it is necessary to make very severe assumptions. First, we must have a definite idea of what we mean by the commodity that we are considering. Secondly, if we wish to discuss what will happen to output and prices if a certain commodity, heretofore produced by competing firms, is monopolized, we must assume that neither the demand curve for the commodity nor the costs of production of any given output are altered

by the change. These assumptions are unlikely to be fulfilled in any actual situation.[23]

In addition, there were whole classes of industrial activity (she specifically mentioned railways and the distribution of gas and electricity) where, because of vast cost differentials, any general comparisons were meaningless.[24]

Professor Chamberlin was even more explicit in his criticism of neoclassical competition theory. He put the matter bluntly:

> The explicit recognition that product is differentiated brings into the open the problem of variety and makes it clear that *pure competition may no longer be regarded as in any sense an ideal for purposes of welfare economics*. . . . Differences in tastes, desires, incomes, and locations of buyers, and differences in the uses which they wish to make of commodities all indicated the need for a variety and the necessity of substituting for the concept of a 'competitive ideal' an ideal involving both monopoly and competition. How much and what kinds of monopoly and with what measure of social control become the questions.[25]

In addition, economists such as J. M. Clark, J. K. Galbraith, and Sumner H. Slichter all rejected pefect competition as a welfare ideal as far as public policy is concerned.[26] Finally, two intellectual giants, Joseph Schumpeter and F. A. Hayek, while holding quite different views of the competitive process, were unanimous in their condemnation of the purely competitive model as a benchmark for policy analysis.

The Schumpeter Criticism.   Schumpeter constantly chided his fellow economists for thinking of competition, and hence, of capitalism, in static terminology. Instead, competition was always a continuous process of "creative destruction" that came from the "new commodity, the new technology, the new source of supply, the new type of organization—which commands a decisive cost or quality advantage and which strikes not at the margins of the profits and the outputs of the existing firms, but at their foundations and their very lives."[27] This sort of innovative competition was incompatible with perfect competition, and incompatible with the sort of ideal business organization envisioned under competitive conditions. Instead, the large capital-intensive firm was "the most powerful engine" of dynamic competition. Schumpeter concluded that

> perfect competition is not only impossible but inferior, and has no title to being set up as a model of ideal efficiency. It is hence a mistake to base the theory of government regulation of industry on the principle that big business should be made to work as the respective industry would work in perfect competition.[28]

The Hayek Criticism.   Austrian economist F. A. Hayek delivered a severe attack on the neoclassical theory of competition in a talk at Princeton University in 1946.[29] Hayek argued that most economists assumed away the competitive process, or simply took it for granted, when they postulated that firms already knew the tastes of consumers, the least-cost combination of resources, and all other relevant market information. If these bits of information were already known, Hayek reasoned, then the markets must already be in equilibrium. As Hayek put it so cogently, the "modern theory of competitive equilibrium *assumes* the situation to exist which a true explanation ought to account for as the effect of the competitive process."[30]

For Hayek, and for all modern neo-Austrians, competition is the discovery process itself, and not the final and static equilibrium condition. Equilibrium theory, which assumed away the entrepreneurial process, was simply no help in an understanding of market competition.

Summary

Perfect competition theory is both illogical and irrelevant. Moreover, it simply assumes conditions to exist which necessarily result in an equilibrium. Business competition, on the other hand, is always a process in which entrepreneurs, with imperfect information, attempt to make adjustments in market conditions such that a closer coordination between supply and demand plans is achieved. Importantly, these adjustments are not limited to price and output, as in the standard model, but may encompass any aspect of exchange that consumers believe to be relevant. Finally, even collusive agreements can be efficient if one adopts a coordinating theory of efficiency and market process.

These theoretical arguments concerning competition have important practical implications. Antitrust policy in the United States has often been associated with that vision of competition inherent in the perfectly competitive equilibrium. Consequently, many of the elements of the entrepreneurial adjustment process, such as product differentiation, price cutting, and advertising have been consistently misidentified by business critics as inefficient, and as resource-misallocating activities. In addition, horizontal price agreements have almost always been seen as inherently inefficient and antisocial.[31] Yet if this standard theory of competition and resource allocation is incorrect or irrelevant, then the legitimacy of all antitrust policy must be open to the most serious question.

MARKET STRUCTURE AND INDUSTRIAL ORGANIZATION

One might think that this criticism of the standard competitive perspective would have settled the policy issues decisively. It would seem that no serious student of antitrust could hold perfect competition as an optimal benchmark, or attempt to employ the perfectly competitive structure as an ideal one for real-world competition. And yet this position, far from being abandoned, is the essence of the still popular "structural" approach to competition, and forms the core of industrial organization theory. This is not to say that all economists—even those who support antitrust—support the structuralist approach, or that there are not vigorous disagreements over the significance of certain structural factors. It is to say, however, that much of the academic and nonacademic support for antitrust regulation is based primarily on structural considerations.[32]

The tie-in between a structuralist approach to competition and a perfectly competitive perspective ought to be made explicit. The market-structure approach to competition assumes that structure "determines the behavior of firms in the industry, and that behavior determines the quality of the industry's performance."[33] But this is precisely the perspective of the perfectly competitive benchmark school. Perfect competition theory assumes the same sort of one-way determinism between structure, conduct, and performance. And as will be shown, what is in fact proper behavior and performance for the structuralists is identical to what is proper behavior and performance from a perfectly competitive perspective.[34]

An attack on the perfectly competitive perspective, therefore, is an attack on the entire structuralist methodology. If perfect competition is illogical and irrelevant, then market structures, or market structure changes, reveal nothing *a priori* concerning competition or welfare. And without reference to some acceptable welfare ideal, structuralist discussions of concentration, barriers to entry, high-profit rates, product differentiation, wasteful advertising, and mergers are indeterminate discussions at best, and totally misleading discussions at worst. It will be useful to review, critically, some of the more common tools of analysis in industrial organization theory to further substantiate this position.

Lerner Index

The so-called Lerner Index is one of the oldest devices for measuring monopoly power and estimating social welfare loss.[35] Assume that some commodity is produced and sold under imperfectly competitive conditions. For reasons already explained, the price of the product and the marginal costs associated with producing it will not be the same: the price will always exceed the marginal costs. The Lerner coefficient of monopoly is determined by dividing the price of the product into the difference between the price of the product and its marginal costs. The index number will be greater if there is a wider divergence of price from marginal costs. If perfect competition exists, on the other hand, the index number is zero.

But what is all of this supposed to mean? If perfect competition is a welfare ideal—and Lerner accepted it as such—it is apparent that the index number is intended to be a handy, short-cut method for measuring monopoly power and the subsequent resource misallocation associated with such power. With little encouragement, many economists have proceeded to determine the degree of monopoly power and the subsequent welfare losses due to monopoly in the economy as a whole, under the Lerner-like assumption that a simple divergence of price from marginal cost is indicative of wasteful economic performance.[36]

It should be apparent that if costs and benefits are subjective, and if perfect competition is not a welfare ideal, then all of this so-called measurement of monopoly and welfare-loss is illegitimate. Once it is recognized that heterogenous firms, products, and tastes are desirable facts of economic life, and that equilibria with perfect information and product homogeneity cannot actually exist in a dynamic market, a divergence of selling price from marginal cost cannot prove inefficiency or resource misallocation in any meaningful sense. Prices diverge from marginal costs in all market situations since demand curves are never perfectly elastic. The alleged comparison of the real world with the perfectly competitive wonderland is simply not legitimate.

Profit-Concentration Studies

The same sort of methodological error is made in the ever-popular profit-concentration study, where economists seek to discover the relationship between profit rates (rates of return on investment or equity) in various industries, and the degree of concentration in those industries.[37] The idea for such a relationship is derived directly from neoclassical competition theory where, under perfect competition, economic profits are eliminated and accounting profits among industries are brought into equality, neglecting risk, in equilibrium.

A handy way to determine which industries might require antitrust attention, therefore, would be to correlate industrial concentration with rates of return. If industries really behave competitively, it is argued, such correlations should be weak or nonexistent. If correlations are high and persist over time, however, serious resource misallocation may be occurring, and the U. S. Justice Department might do well to correct such market failure.[38]

But as with the welfare-loss studies already criticized, all this measurement of monopoly and misallocation is meaningless. If zero economic profits or equalized accounting returns are not a competitive or a welfare ideal in a dynamic and changing world, profit differences need not demonstrate monopoly power or resource misallocation and consumer injury. The fundamental error here is to assume that long-run equilibria actually exist, or that the movement toward equilibrium is smooth and continuous after some initial exogenous shock to the system. Long-run equilibria cannot actually exist, and changes in tastes, costs, risk, information, and uncertainty are not short-run phenomena whose effects on profitability somehow disappear in the static long-run. Change and entrepreneurial adjustment to change are continuous in the market process and are as much in evidence in the long view as in the short. There is, to be sure, an ever present process of equilibration and coordination occurring, but it would be sheer fantasy to assume or expect such a process ever to be completed. Thus profit rate differentials, should they exist between industries, would be explainable within the context of a fully competitive market process that has not achieved, and could never achieve, any final long-run equilibrium.

Even if the differentials in profit rates were to statistically correlate with particular market structures, the results need not be interpreted negatively, that is, that monopoly power in concentrated markets produce the high rates of return and the social inefficiency. As Harold Demsetz has suggested, it may make more sense to reason that efficient business organizations expand their market share faster than less efficient rivals and that, therefore, efficiency and profits tend to produce specific levels of concentration (rather than vice-versa).[39] Far from concluding that resources are misallocated, one should conclude that such resource allocations are entirely consistent with social efficiency and consumer preferences.

Cross-Elasticity and Competition

Cross-elasticity tests have been another popular method of attempting to measure competition and monopoly in markets. The cross-elasticity coefficient records the responsiveness of buyers of one commodity to a change in the price of some other commodity. Assume that pencils are made and sold by a group of small manufacturers in some market area. A change in the price of pencils made by manufacturer X might well affect the sales of pencils by manufacturer Y. For example, higher X prices, other things being equal, might mean higher Y sales; lower X prices might mean lower Y sales. If changes in the price of one commodity affect sales of another commodity in the manner just described (termed high cross-elasticity), then one might infer that the products are relatively good substitutes for each other, that is, that the goods are competitive with each other in the market. On the other hand, if a change in the price of X has little or no effect on the sales of Y (termed low cross-elasticity) then one might infer that the goods are not close substitutes, and do not really compete with each other in the market. Indeed, the relevant market itself might be defined in terms of cross-elasticity coefficients.

There are serious methodological difficulties in attempting to measure competition in this manner, or to infer anything meaningful concerning an efficient allocation of resources. The most serious difficulty is that any cross-elasticity test over time would inevitably confuse a change in sales due to a price change, and a change in sales due to any and all other factors. Since other things are never constant in an actual situation, there is never any guarantee that one is, in fact, testing cross-elasticity at all. Economic principles such as elasticity are unlikely to be verified by empirical experiments that are, of necessity, a mosaic of complex and nonrepeatable historical events.

Further, all close substitutes in markets differ on the basis of appearance, reliability, quality, service, technical assistance, ease of shipment, warranty, and many other factors that buyers may consider important. If final selling price were the only relevant variable then, in principle, cross-elasticity might indicate which products compete in the market at some point in time. But if price were not the only relevant selling factor, and if everything else were not constant, then such measurements might only indicate the relative insignificance of price differentials as a competitive factor in the market. Cross-elasticity tests implicitly assume that competition is one-dimensional; they neglect non-price-competitive factors employed by firms in rivalrous market situations.[40]

Finally, even if cross-elasticity could measure competition, it would have nothing unambiguous to say concerning social welfare. If consumers decide a product is special and don't abandon it because of a price reduction in a supposed substitute, so what? Does low cross-elasticity imply injury to buyers or society when it is presumably the very same buyers that decide to ignore the price change? Once it is recognized that disequilibrium and differentiation are inherent in all competitive situations, cross-elasticity tests cannot reveal anything meaningful concerning resource allocation and welfare.

Barriers to Entry

The subject matter of so-called barriers to entry occupies a crucial position in the structuralist orthodoxy. For it is these supposed barriers, erected by leading firms in an industry, that limit competition and misallocate resources away from their highest valued use. The three most important barriers for the critics are: product differentiation, scale economies, and advertising.

Product Differentiation.   Product differentiation allegedly limits competition and injures consumers since it makes competitive market entry more costly. Relative to the ease of entry into homogeneous product markets, firms must expend extra resources to differentiate their products. To use a favorite example of the critics, the fact that the major automobile companies change styles each year increases the entry costs of competing in this industry.[41] Would-be-entrants must be willing and able to undergo similar style-change procedures (e.g., retooling) or they cannot compete in the industry. Hence the high costs of differentiation (a "phony" product differentiation for most critics) block entry into the business and tend to perpetuate the market positions of the leading companies. Even worse, once competition is limited, the auto companies routinely pass along the higher costs in the form of higher prices which contribute to a further reduction in consumer and social welfare.

It can be argued that the critics have gotten the matter completely and precisely backwards. It is only because consumers find resources satisfactorily allocated that potential competitors find entry difficult or impossible. Product differentiation, especially a differentiation that increases prices, can act as a barrier to entry *only if* consumers prefer that differentiation, and are willing to pay the presumably higher prices associated with, say, new annual auto style changes. If consumers do not prefer such changes and instead reward the firms that change styles less often, or not at all, then product differentiation could hardly act as a barrier to entry. Indeed, in the case just suggested, differentiation would be an open invitation to entry and to a more rivalrous competition.

To condemn commercially successful product differentiation as a misallocation of resources, therefore, is to condemn the very allocations that consumers apparently prefer and support. It is the faulty vision of an allegedly optimal allocation under purely competitive conditions that product differentiation upsets, and not any allocation that can be associated with free buyer choice in open markets.[42]

Scale Economies.   The barriers-to-entry argument become particularly irrational when applied to cost savings associated with large-scale production. The fact that certain firms realize lower average costs because of larger volumes may, indeed, make it difficult for smaller, higher-cost firms to enter or compete in the market.[43] Thus we are supposed to regret the reduced competition and the consequent resource misallocation, since relatively inefficient firms cannot compete successfully with relatively more efficient firms! But consumers do not regret the economies nor the consequent reduction in competition; why should critics? Consumers could increase competition any time they choose by indicating their willingness to pay higher prices to cover the higher costs of the smaller less efficient firms. That consumers do not usually do this indicates that resources are correctly allocated as far as they are concerned. Again, it is the vision of the purely competitive wonderland that is threatened by large, efficient firms, and not efficiency from a free-market perspective.

Advertising.   The same sort of errors in analysis are evident in much of the orthodox criticism of advertising. Certainly it can be admitted readily that advertising might be wasteful in the perfectly competitive equilibrium. But advertising is wasteful there only because that model already assumes perfect information.[44] To simply *assume* perfect information, however, is not to explain how information comes to exist, or how information comes to be noticed by market participants. In the competitive world, noticed information cannot be assumed; it must be accounted for within a theory of market process.

Product advertising is a legitimate way of accounting for noticed information, and information transfer, within a theory of market process. Indeed, it is difficult to imagine how any products could be sold without some advertising, since they could not even be known without it.

A popular criticism of advertising holds that it attempts to persuade rather than to inform. But once it is recognized that advertising occurs in disequilibrium, where selling is not automatic, it is difficult to appreciate the relevance of this criticism. All advertising, even the so-called informational advertising, is intended to sell products. Why advertisements that are loaded with "pure" information ought to be preferred to advertisements that are highly emotional and persuasive is not immediately obvious from this perspective.[45]

It is also difficult to appreciate the traditional distinction that some economists have made between production costs and selling costs. All expenditures, including advertising, are selling costs in the sense that they are made only in order to sell products to consumers. Products only sell themselves in the perfectly competitive equilibrium. Since products are intended to be sold, advertising expenditures are as legitimate as any other resource expenditure for the firm, and are a crucially important activity in a competitive market. To separate out such expenditures for special treatment and special criticism thus appears arbitrary and indefensible.[46]

It is also indefensible to assert that advertising is socially efficient only if it shifts market demand and allows scale economies to be realized. It is still common in some elementary textbooks to see a comparison of the costs and prices of a product before advertising with the costs and prices of the same product after advertising.[47] But such comparisons cannot be legitimate, since the alleged products being compared are *not* the same product. The price and cost of apples after advertising cannot be meaningfully compared to the price and cost of apples before advertising; in the mind of the consumers, they are now different products. Whether higher expenditures are socially efficient or legitimate is to be determined ultimately by competition and not by outside observers.

Advertising may, of course, lower the average total costs of a product and act as a barrier-to-entry to competition. This could occur if media advertising expanded the market for a product or if it substituted for more expensive and less effective marketing techniques. But as with the achievement of any economy in the use of resources, such circumstances are never to be regretted, and certainly not from any consumer perspective. If consumers want more competition between products they are always free to increase their patronage of the higher-cost, higher-priced sellers; indeed, consumers in legally open markets should have all the competitors they are willing to pay for.

On the other hand, if advertising tends to raise costs and prices, then it could hardly act as a barrier to entry or to competition. To raise costs and prices in markets where there are no legal restrictions on entry is to encourage entry and competition. Therefore inefficient advertising would always act as an invitation to entry and to competition, and requires no remedial antitrust activity.

Concentration

Concentration has been the most popular and important tool of analysis in industrial organization. *Market concentration* (concentration ratio) refers to the percentage of assets or sales held by the largest firms in a particular industry or market. *Average market concentration* measures the degree of concentration in all markets sampled, by averaging the market concentration data for those markets. *Aggregate concentration* refers to the percentage of assets (sales) held by the largest manufacturing firms in the economy, without reference to specific industries or markets. All three concentration indicators have been used by structuralists to imply that certain degrees of market control, or changes in these percentages over time, infer something significant concerning monopoly power, competition, and social welfare. The implication is that a high level of concentration, or increasing concentration in an industry, or in the economy, is bad for competition and is socially inefficient.[48]

Once the arbitrary optimality of the atomistic model is admitted, however, concentration or changes in concentration reveal little concerning business competition or consumer welfare. An industry or industrial sector with a high level of concentration, or one with increasing concentration, is quite compatible with competition defined in dynamic terms. If competition is a process of rivalry between firms in open markets, then that process could increase in intensity and could be more efficient because of increasing concentration. Concentration could increase as smaller firms grow larger due to increased efficiency, relative to other firms. Concentration could also increase as firms innovate new products that are popular with consumers, relative to other firms. Companies could merge to enjoy economies of scale in production, distribution, research and development, or capital financing, and the resultant economies could also result in growth and concentration, relative to other firms. In all of these cases, concentration could increase, but it is not at all clear that business competition would necessarily decline, or that social welfare would automatically be lowered (even if we could measure welfare) and resources wasted. Concentration may upset the perfectly competitive wonderland, but it is not clear that it upsets the efficiency of the competitive process.

This perspective is even more apparent when consumers themselves concentrate an industry or market by concentrating their expenditures on the products of one firm or group of firms, to the consistent neglect of others. Are we to equate this concentration with monopoly power, with a misallocation of resources, and with a reduction in consumer satisfaction? Here as elsewhere, structuralists have gotten the matter backwards. Starting with given levels of concentration they proceed, using neoclassical price theory, to pessimistic conclusions about conduct and market performance. Yet if they started with revealed consumer preferences in an open market, they would see that concentrated market structures may only reflect buyer choice and entrepreneurial efficiency: that is, that structure is determined by performance and not vice versa. If concentration reflects tastes, technology, and increased coordination, then it clearly would be absurd to condemn such situations as wasteful or inefficient.

But even on its own structural terms, the concept of market concentration is subject to much criticism.[49] What are "high" levels of concentration, how much of an increase in concentration is dangerous, and are the benchmarks the same for all markets? If concentration in a market stays the same over time, and yet the leading firms change position and shares of the market or are replaced by new firms, what conclusions are to be drawn from the structural information? How are the markets under discussion to be defined in the first place: are imports and used goods to be included in the concentration data, and are foreign and nonindustrial assets to be excluded from the calculations? How are these questions to be answered objectively and unambiguously?

As an example of the ambiguity, an influential government study of concentration was released in 1969, titled *Studies by the Staff of the Cabinet Committee on Price Stability*. The study employed data for 213 industries, even though the Census of Manufacturers classifies over 400 different industries in manufacturing. Nearly half of all industries in the economy were excluded from the study, since their product in 1963 had become too differentiated from their product in 1947, making it infeasible to draw any valid comparisons. The trends in concentration, therefore, were developed for the older, more conservative industries, whose product lines had not changed markedly. Further, the study employed unweighted averages of concentration ratios for the different markets, did not exclude foreign assets and nonindustrial assets held by the domestic manufacturing firms included in the study, and made no allowances for imports or second-hand goods in the concentration ratios.[50] And even though it concluded that "average market concentration of manufacturing industries has shown *no* marked tendency to increase or decrease between 1947 and 1966,"[51] no unambiguous conclusions concerning competition or consumer welfare could ever be drawn from such a methodological nightmare.,

Even if market concentration were a completely reliable measure of competition, there is surprisingly little empirical evidence that there has been any marked tendency for average market concentration to increase sharply over time (with a resultant decline in competition in the economy). Studies of industrial concentration in the period 1901–47, and some through 1976, reveal a modest upward trend, at best. The early work of Adelman,[52] Nutter,[53] and Nelson[54] all tend to support the idea that general levels of industrial concentration reached at the turn of the present century have remained relatively stable since.

If average market concentration is a methodological nightmare, aggregate or overall concentration is still more ambiguous in terms of competition and consumer welfare.[55] Market concentration is at least concerned with competition between business organizations in the same market; aggregate concentration, on the other hand, is not derived from microeconomic market data, but is determined by computing the percentage of the total manufacturing industry's sales or assets held by the largest corporations in manufacturing. But what a given level of concentration, or rising or falling aggregate concentration would mean in terms of prices, costs, innovation, competition or resource allocation in any given industry is unknowable. In short, aggregate concentration even on its own terms cannot measure competition or social inefficiency.

Conclusions

It has been argued here that atomistic theory and the structuralist approach to competition are inherently flawed notions that cannot serve as the foundation for any rational antitrust policy. What these theories identify as manifestations of monopoly power are simply economic advantages and efficiencies that specific business organizations have earned—absolute and scale economies, for instance—or they are consumer preferences for one brand of product over another. Moreover, what these theories describe as a misallocation of resources is only inefficient when compared with the irrelevant perfectly competitive equilibrium. Clearly, this theory of monopoly power must be rejected for antitrust purposes.

MONOPOLY AND THE MARKET PROCESS

To reject the standard theory of monopoly power and resource misallocation is not to reject all such theories. If competition is a process in which entrepreneurs are free to offer more "attractive opportunities to other market participants,"[56] then the power to arbitrarily restrict such offers and market adjustments can be defined as monopoly power. And since the adjustment process is inherent in the very working of the free market itself, the power to restrict entry and market adjustment must arise from outside the market.

Government can impede the competitive process with certain legal restrictions as barriers to exchange and entry. Such legal restrictions harm consumers (and excluded suppliers) by restricting or preventing mutually advantageous exchanges and plan coordinations from occurring.[57] Consequently consumers can be injured and resources can be misallocated since production and resource use is not fully determined by the voluntary preferences of market participants. Government franchises, certificates of public convenience, licenses, tariffs, price-support programs, patents, and any other governmental interference with voluntary trade and production are all instances of monopoly, and all can prevent plan coordination and generate monopoly power for the firms protected from open competition.[58] With this perspective, government, and not the free market, would be the actual source of resource-misallocating monopoly.

One of the implications to be drawn from this perspective is that monopoly power could not exist without direct governmental support. Yet it has been widely believed that competitive markets could deteriorate into monopoly without antitrust protection. Certain business organizations could presumably attempt to eliminate rivals through predatory practices and eventually monopolize the market. Moreover, once in control of a market, such firms could exploit their power by restricting output and raising prices to consumers.

But there have always been serious problems with this argument. Even if such a scenario were likely (it is unlikely, since predatory practices to eliminate rivals are expensive in open markets[59]), the process of attempting to eliminate rivals is inherently competitive. Large firms bent on eliminating competitors would presumably seek to reduce final prices, increase their own efficiency and productivity, and offer additional services to potential buyers, all in order to secure business from rivals. But such competitive activity is delightful from a consumer perspective, and ought not to be discouraged in any way.

In addition firms are driven ultimately from open markets by consumer choice. It is buyers that decide to end supplier rivalry (temporarily, perhaps) by abandoning some producers in favor of what they perceive to be more desirable alternatives. They could ignore the lower prices and better services and stay with the existing market structure. Instead, they reduce the number of firms in the market by concentrating the bulk of their purchases on outputs that promise to maximize their subjective utility. Are consumers to be prevented from exercising free choice in order to protect these very same consumers from the consequent monopoly? Resources are not misallocated when they are allocated in accordance with revealed consumer preferences in open markets.

Finally a free-market monopolist does not "control the market" (a misleading phrase of the industrial-organization theorists) and cannot misallocate resources, as traditional theory assumes. The market, far from being "monopolized" or controlled, is still perfectly open to competition; that is, open to any entrepreneur who correctly sees a way to more efficiently service consumers than the existing firm. The existing firm is correctly seen as monopolizing existing preferences, and not the market for the product or service.[60] Should such preferences change, the open market monopoly can dissolve into a more familiar supply pattern.

Actually, extended discussions of monopoly in a completely free-market context strain credibility since such situations, though not regrettable—as already argued—would be extremely rare in fact. To establish monopoly in a free market would require perfect entrepreneurial foresight, both in the short run and the long run, with respect to consumer demand, technology, location, material supplies and prices, and thousands of other uncertain variables; it would also require an unambiguous definition of the relevant market. Few, if any, firms in business history, before or since antitrust, have ever approached such unerring perfection, let alone realized it for extended periods of time. The so-called quiet life that is reputed to be enjoyed by the free-market monopolist is, as we shall discover below, part of the folklore of antitrust history.

Business interests, however, have employed the state in an attempt to achieve legal monopoly positions of influence and power within the capitalistic system. Indeed it may have been their inability to achieve free-market monopoly that prompted such interests to seek government regulatory control over entry and restricted competition in many industries. In the chapters that follow, we will attempt to document both the fact that free-market monopoly is an illusion, and the fact that pernicious monopoly power can be associated with government regulation of the economy.

NOTES

1. Joseph W. McGuire, *Business and Society* (New York: McGraw-Hill Book Co., 1963), pp. 39–40.

2. *Ibid.*, pp. 38–39.

3. By permission. From Webster's New Collegiate Dictionary © 1981 by G. & C. Merriam Co., Publishers of the Merriam-Webster Dictionaries.

4. On the development of this model of competition between 1880 and 1933, see Donald Dewey, *The Theory of Imperfect Competition: A Radical Reconstruction* (New York: Columbia University Press, 1969), pp. 5–10.

5. For a review of the assumptions and operations of the perfectly competitive model, see any modern microeconomics text, or specifically, Richard H. Leftwich, *The Price System and Resource Allocation*, 7th ed. (Hinsdale, Ill.: Dryden Press, 1979).

6. F. M. Scherer, *Industrial Market Structure and Economic Performance*, 2nd ed. (Chicago: Rand McNally College Publishing Company, 1980), p. 18. For a contrasting view, see Harold Demsetz, "The Nature of Equilibrium in Monopolistic Competition," *Journal of Political Economy*, Vol. 67 (February 1959), pp. 21–30, and "The Welfare and Empirical Implications of Monopolistic Competition," *Economic Journal*, Vol. 74 (September 1967), p. 623.

7. This is a widely held view among academic economists. See Robert L. Bishop, "Monopolistic Competition and Welfare Economics," in Robert E. Keunne, ed., *Monopolistic Competition Theory: Studies in Impact* (New York: John Wiley & Sons, 1967), pp. 251–63; Edwin Mansfield, *Microeconomics* (New York: W. W. Norton and Company, 1975), pp. 282, 315; Willard Mueller, *A Primer on Monopoly and Competition* (New York: Random House, 1970), p. 8; Richard E. Low, "Introduction," in R. E. Low, ed., *The Economics of Antitrust: Competition and Monopoly* (Englewood Cliffs, N.J.: Prentice-Hall, Inc., 1968), pp. 1–42. See also Lee Preston and Benjamin King, "Proving Competition," *The Antitrust Bulletin*, Vol. 24, No. 4 (Winter 1979), p. 787.

8. See the discussion by Roger Sherman in *Antitrust Bulletin* (January 1976), p. 947. See also Milton H. Spencer, *Contemporary Microeconomics* (New York: Worth Publishers, Inc., 1975), pp. 240–243 and Peter Asch, "Industrial Concentration, Efficiency and Antitrust Reform," *The Antitrust Bulletin*, Vol. 22, No. 1 (Spring 1977), pp. 129–143, esp. p. 130.

9. Douglas F. Greer, *Industrial Organization and Public Policy* (New York: Macmillan Publishing Co., 1980), p. 44.

10. Leftwich, *op. cit.*, p. 32 [Copyright 1979 by Dryden Press, Inc., Reprinted by permission of Dryden Press, Inc.].

11. Antoine Cournot made this determination as early as 1838. See Joseph A. Schumpeter, *History of Economic Analysis* (New York: Oxford University Press, 1954), pp. 972–977. And despite some qualifications this is still the determination today. See Roger A. McCain, *Markets, Decisions, and Organizations* (Englewood Cliffs, N.J.: Prentice Hall, Inc., 1981), pp. 257–259.

12. "Monopoly and Resource Allocation", *American Economic Review, Papers and Proceedings*, Vol. 44 (May 1954), p. 77.

13. William Long, Richard Schramm, and Robert Tollison, "The Economic Determinants of Antitrust Activity," *Journal of Law and Economics*, Vol. 16, No. 2 (October 1973), pp. 351–364. See also Philip Areeda, *Antitrust Analysis: Problems, Text, Cases*, 2nd ed. (Little, Brown & Company, 1974), pp. 12–23, and esp. p. 195.

14. Oliver Williamson, "Economics as an Antitrust Defense: The Welfare Trade-offs," *American Economic Review*, Vol. 68, No. 18 (March 1968), and a correction in *American Economic Review*, Vol. 69 (December 1969), pp. 954–959. For an excellent discussion of the cost-benefit trade off model, see Wesley J. Liebeler, "Market Power and Competitive Superiority in Concentrated Industries," *UCLA Law Review*, Vol. 25 (1979), pp. 1232–1297.

15. This position has recently been stated most emphatically in Robert Bork, *The Antitrust Paradox* (New York: Basic Books, 1978).

16. Richard A. Posner, *Antitrust Law: An Economic Perspective* (Chicago: University of Chicago Press, 1976), pp. 10–15.

17. William Baumol, *Economic Theory and Operations Analysis* (Englewood Cliffs, N.J.: Prentice-Hall, 1961), p. 257.

18. R. G. Lipsey and K. Lancaster, "The General Theory of Second Best," Review of Economic Studies, Vol. 24 (1956–57), p. 11.

19. This is admitted in some of the older and more careful microeconomic texts. See Albert Levenson and Babette Solon, *Outline of Price Theory* (New York: Holt, Rinehart and Winston, Inc., 1964), p. 111.

20. The discussion that follows draws heavily on the following works: Murray N. Rothbard, *Man, Economy and State*, Vol. 2 (Princeton: D. VanNostrand & Co., 1962); Israel M. Kirzner, *Competition and Entrepreneurship* (Chicago: University of Chicago Press, 1973); Friedrich Hayek, "The Meaning of Competition," *Individualism and Economic Order* (Chicago: Henry Regnery Company, 1972), pp. 92–106; Paul McNulty, "Economic Theory and the Meaning of Competition," *Quarterly Journal of Economics*, Vol. 82 (1968), reprinted in Yale Brozen, *The Competitive Economy: Selected Readings* (General Learning, 1975), pp. 64–75. Also, see a recent treatment by Arthur A. Thompson, Jr., "Competition as a Strategic Process," *The Antitrust Bulletin*, Vol. 25, No. 4 (Winter 1980), pp. 777–803.

21. James M. Buchanan, *Cost and Choice* (Markham Publishing, 1969). Also see an excellent discussion by Thomas Sowell, *Knowledge and Decisions* (New York: Basic Books, Inc., 1980), pp. 50–52, and Bork, *op. cit.*, pp. 110–113.

22. Israel Kirzner, *Market Theory and the Price System* (Princeton: D. Van Nostrand, Inc., 1963), pp. 34–45. See also Roy E. Cordato, "Austrian Theory of Efficiency and the Role of Goverment," *Journal of Libertarian Studies*, Vol. 4, No. 4 (Fall 1980), pp. 393–403.

23. Joan Robinson, *The Economics of Imperfect Competition*, 2nd ed. (New York: St. Martin's Press, 1961), pp. 143–144.

24. *Ibid.*, p. 166.
25. Edward H. Chamberlin, *The Theory of Monopolistic Competition* (Cambridge, Mass.: Harvard University Press, 1948), p. 214.
26. J. M. Clark, "Toward a Concept of Workable Competition," *American Economic Review*, Vol. 30 (June 1940), pp. 241–56, and *Competition as a Dynamic Process* (Washington: Brookings Institution, 1961). See Sumner H. Slichter, "In Defense of Bigness in Business," and John Kenneth Galbraith, "The Economics of Technical Development," in Edwin Mansfield, ed., *Monopoly Power and Economic Performance: The Problem of Industrial Concentration*, 3rd ed. (New York: W. W. Norton and Company, 1974), pp. 13–18 and pp. 36–44.
27. Joseph Schumpeter, *Capitalism, Socialism and Democracy* (New York: Harper and Row, 1962), p. 84.
28. *Ibid.*, p. 106.
29. Hayek's talk is reprinted as "The Meaning of Competition," in his *Individualism and Economic Order* (Chicago: Henry Regnery Company, 1972), pp. 92–106.
30. *Ibid.*, p. 94.
31. An interesting exception to this general position is taken by Donald Dewey, "Information, Entry, and Welfare: The Case for Collusion," *American Economic Review*, Vol. 69, No. 4 (September 1979), pp. 588–593.
32. See, for example, Stanley E. Boyle, *Industrial Organization: An Empirical Approach* (New York: Holt, Rinehart and Winston, 1972). See also, Joe S. Bain, *Industrial Organization*, 2nd ed. (New York: John Wiley & Sons, 1968); F. M. Scherer, *Industrial Market Structure and Economic Performance*, 2nd ed. (Chicago: Rand McNally & Company, 1980).
33. Richard Caves, *American Industry: Structure, Conduct Performance*, 2nd ed. (Englewood Cliffs, N.J.: Prentice-Hall, 1967), p. 17 [emphasis added].
34. Boyle, *op. cit.*, p. 8.
35. A. P. Lerner, "The Concept of Monopoly and the Measurement of Monopoly Power," *Review of Economics and Statistics*, Vol. 1 (June 1934), pp. 157–175. For a review of the other "monopoly indexes," see Eugene M. Singer, *Antitrust, Economics and Legal Analysis* (Columbus, Ohio: Grid Publishing, Inc., 1981), pp. 181–186.
36. Arnold Harberger, "Monopoly and Resource Allocation," *American Economic Review*, Vol. 44 (May 1954), pp. 77–87; David Schwartzman, "The Burden of Monopoly," *Journal of Political Economy*, Vol. 68 (December 1960), pp. 627–630; Dave R. Kamershen, "An Estimation of the 'Welfare Losses' from Monopoly in the American Economy," *Western Economic Journal*, Vol. 4 (Summer 1966), pp. 221–36; Keith Cowling and Dennis Mueller, "The Social Costs of Monopoly," *Economic Journal*, Vol. 88 (December 1978), pp. 727–748.
37. There have been dozens of such studies and we cannot review them here. For a good review and criticism of the more important profit/industrial organization studies, see John M. Vernon, *Market Structure and Industrial Performance: A*

Review of the Statistical Findings (Boston: Allyn & Bacon, 1972). The first and perhaps most influential concentration/profit study was Joe S. Bain, "Relation of Profit Rates to Industry Concentration," *Quarterly Journal of Economics* (August 1951). For an important criticism of the Bain study, see Yale Brozen, "Concentration and Profits: Does Concentration Matter?", *The Antitrust Bulletin*, Vol. 19, 1974. For an important methodological criticism of all such studies, see Almarin Phillips, "A Critique of Empirical Studies of Relations Between Market Structure and Profitability," *Journal of Industrial Economics*, Vol. 24 (June 1976), pp. 241–249.

38. H. M. Mann, "Seller Concentration, Barriers to Entry, and Rates of Return in Thirty Industries: 1950–1960," *Review of Economics and Statistics*, Vol. 48 (August 1966), pp. 296–307, esp. p. 300.

39. Harold Demsetz, "Industry Structure, Market Rivalry and Public Policy", *Journal of Law and Economics*, Vol. 16 (April 1973), pp. 1–70, and "Economics as a Guide to Antitrust Regulation," *Journal of Law and Economics*, Vol. 19 (August 1976), pp. 371, 384. For an independent confirmation of the Demsetz hypothesis, see John R. Carter, "Collusion, Efficiency, and Antitrust," *Journal of Law and Economics*, Vol. 21, No. 2 (October 1978), pp. 434–444.

40. Edward H. Chamberlin, *Towards a More General Theory of Value* (New York: Oxford University Press, 1977), pp. 78–83. See also, Ken D. Boyer, "Degrees of Differentiation and Industry Boundaries," in Terry Calvani and John Siegfried, eds., *Economic Analysis of Antitrust Law* (Boston: Little, Brown, 1979), pp. 88–106.

41. Mark J. Green, *The Closed Enterprise System* (New York: Bantam Books, 1972), p. 396. See also Franklin Fisher, Zvi Griliches, and Carl Kaysen, "The Costs of Automobile Model Changes Since 1949," *Journal of Political Economy*, Vol. 70 (October 1962), pp. 433–451.

42. Some structuralists attempt to meet this criticism by simply asserting that consumers, in the absence of perfect knowledge, really don't know what they are doing! See Boyle, *op. cit.*, p. 73.

43. Caves, *op. cit.*, pp. 24–25.

44. Yale Brozen, "Entry Barriers: Advertising and Product Differentiation," in Goldschmid, Mann & Weston, eds., *Industrial Concentration: The New Learning* (Boston: Little, Brown and Company, 1974), pp. 115–37. Also see Dean A. Worcester, Jr., *Welfare Gains from Advertising: The Problem of Regulation* (Washington, D.C.,: American Enterprise Institute, 1978).

45. Kirzner, *Competition and Entrepreneurship, op. cit.* pp. 159–163.

46. *Ibid.*, pp. 146–151.

47. See, for instance, Milton Spencer, *Contemporary Economics*, 2nd ed. (New York: Worth Publishers, Inc., 1974), p. 433.

48. For example, the influential *Studies by the Cabinet Committee on Price Stability* (Washington, D.C.: U.S. Government Printing Office, 1969) boldly asserted that "market concentration is directly related to the intensity of competition in

an industry" (p. 54). For an excellent criticism of the notion that high concentration endangers competition or consumer welfare, see John S. McGee, *In Defense of Industrial Concentration* (New York: Praeger Publishers, 1971).

49. Sanford Rose, "Bigness is a Numbers Game," *Fortune*, Vol. 80 (November 1969), pp. 113, 115, 226, 228, 230, 232, 234, 237–38.

50. *Ibid.*, pp. 230–32.

51. *Studies by the Cabinet Committee on Price Stability*, p. 58.

52. Morris A. Adelman, "The Measurement of Industrial Concentration," in Mansfield, *op. cit.*, pp. 83–88.

53. G. Warren Nutter, *The Extent of Enterprise Monopoly in the United States, 1899–1939* (Chicago: University of Chicago Press, 1951).

54. R. L. Nelson, *Concentration in the Manufacturing Industries of the United States* (New Haven: Yale University Press, 1963).

55. Morris A. Adelman, "Monopoly and Concentration: Comparisons in Time and Space" in Richard E. Low, ed., *The Economics of Antitrust: Competition and Monopoly* (Englewood Cliffs, N.J.: Prentice-Hall, 1968), p. 52. See also Willard F. Mueller and Larry G. Hamm, "Trends in Industrial Concentration, 1947 to 1970," *Review of Economics and Statistics*, Vol. 56 (November 1974), pp. 511–513.

56. Kirzner, *op. cit.*, p. 20.

57. Legal barriers are to be distinguished sharply from the nonlegal barriers discussed earlier in this chapter. As we have already argued, nonlegal barriers are created or perpetuated by free consumer choice and cannot be said, therefore, to harm consumer welfare.

58. Yale Brozen, "Is Government the Source of Monopoly?" *Intercollegiate Review* (Winter 1968–69), reprinted in Tibor R. Machan, ed., *The Libertarian Alternative: Essays in Social and Political Philosophy* (Chicago: Nelson-Hall Company, 1974), pp. 147–169.

59. Wayne A. Leeman, "The Limitations of Local Price Cutting as a Barrier to Entry," *Journal of Political Economy* (August 1956), pp. 329–332. In addition, see John S. McGee, "Predatory Price Cutting: The Standard Oil (N.J.) Case," *Journal of Law and Economics*, Vol. 1 (October 1958), pp. 137–169, and the discussion of McGee's analysis in Chapter 3. Also see Roland H. Koller II, "The Myths of Predatory Pricing," *Antitrust Law and Economics Review*, Vol. 4 (Summer 1971), pp. 105–123.

60. Free market monopoly is consistent with consumer choice as long as markets are legally open to entry. To "monopolize" existing buyer preferences is not harmful and should not be illegal.

CHAPTER THREE

Monopoly Under the Sherman Act: From E. C. Knight (1895) to Standard Oil of New Jersey (1911)

The first legal action initiated under a new law to reach the Supreme Court is extremely important. Such a case is often a test of the applicability, and even the constitutionality, of a statute. Thus, the government suit brought under the Sherman Act against the American Sugar Refining Company in 1893, and decided by the Supreme Court in 1895, was crucial in many respects.[1]

THE E. C. KNIGHT CASE (1895)

The *E. C. Knight* case, however, proved to be a mild disaster for the U.S. Justice Department and for federal enforcement of the antimonopoly statute. A majority of the Supreme Court did admit that the acquisition of E. C. Knight Company and three other independent sugar refiners, by the American Sugar Refining Company did tend to create a monopoly in the manufacture of sugar, and did increase American's percentage share of the refined sugar market to 95 percent; and even though only one significant East Coast company remained in the market (Nash Spaulding & Company),[2] the Supreme Court determined that the "Sugar Trust" was not in violation of the Sherman Act. The justices reasoned that American's near manufacturing monopoly was not necessarily a monopoly or illegal restraint of interstate commerce, and that such manufacturing monopolies only incidentally and indirectly affected interstate trade and commerce.[3] Speaking for the majority, Justice Fuller concluded:

> The monopoly and restraint denounced by the Act are the monopoly and restraint of interstate and international trade or commerce, while the conclusion to be assumed on this record is that the result of the transaction complained of [the acquisitions] was the creation of a monopoly in the manufacture of a necessary of life. . . .[4]

> It does *not* follow that an attempt to monopolize, or the actual monopoly of, the manufacture was an attempt, whether executory or consummated, to *monopolize commerce*, even though, in order to dispose of the product, the instrumentality of commerce was necessarily involved. *There was nothing in the proofs to indicate any intention to put a restraint upon trade or commerce*, and the fact, as we have seen, that trade or commerce might be indirectly affected, was not enough to entitle complainants to a decree.[5]

As long as there had been no attempt to put an outside restraint upon trade or commerce, it appeared that the federal courts lacked any jurisdiction over manufacturing monopolies.

The Sugar Industry

Surprisingly, the changes in the refined sugar market after 1895 made the economic significance of the decision not to dissolve the Havemeyer "Sugar Trust" almost purely academic. With or without the courts, the competitive market forces within the sugar industry dissolved the near monopoly position of the Trust rapidly. American Sugar's relative share of domestic sugar refining slipped quickly and continuously from 95 percent in 1893 to just 25.06 percent by 1927. Indeed, after an alleged attempt to restrain production in 1893 and 1894, competition entered the refining market and reduced American Sugar's market share to 85 percent and its profit margins to pre-1893 levels. Thus, free-market competition neutralized the "power" of the Trust even before the *Knight* case had been decided.[6]

The reasons for the inevitable competition in the sugar market are not difficult to discover. The high domestic tariff, the more than available raw materials at historically low prices, the absence of exclusionary patents, the relatively easy manufacturing process, and the increasing significance of domestic beet sugar, simply made entry into the sugar refining industry easy and modestly profitable. Firms such as United States Sugar Refining, California & Hawaiian Sugar Refining, New York Sugar Refining, Arbuckle Brothers, Federal Sugar Refining, Warner, Revere, Cunningham Sugar Refining, Pennsylvania Sugar, Western Sugar Refining, Godchauz Sugars, W. J. McCahan Sugar Refining and Molasses, Savannah Sugar Refining, Imperial Sugar, and National Sugar Refining (25 percent owned by American Sugar Refining), and many others were all—at one time or another—active competitors of American Sugar, and many managed to survive and prosper. In 1920, for example, there were already 105 plants producing sugar from beets; beet sugar manufacture had come to represent almost 15 percent of the total refined sugar market by that date. In short, although the Sugar Trust dominated the industry momentarily, and although it did secure a stock interest in a few potential competitors, it was completely unable to foreclose the refined sugar market to competitive rival manufacturers.

Moreover, there is little statistical evidence that the American Sugar Refining Company was ever able to wield its alleged monopoly power in the sellers market for any extended period of time. Refined sugar sold at retail for more than 9 cents in 1880; 6.9 cents in 1890; 5.3 cents in 1895; 6.1 cents in 1900; 6.0 cents in 1905; and 6.0 cents in 1910. Wholesale prices per pound were 9.602 cents in 1880; 6.171 cents in 1890; 4.152 cents in 1895; 5.320 cents in 1900; 5.256 cents in 1905; and 4.972 cents in 1910. The theoretical margin between raw and refined sugar, out of which the refiner must make his profits, fluctuated from a high of 1.437 cents in 1882 (well before the "monopoly") to .720 cents in 1890; .882 cents in 1895; .500 cents in 1899; .978 cents in 1905; and .784 cents in 1910. The margin was lower in 1895 (when American Sugar did 95 percent of the sugar refining) than it was in 1910 (when they did less than 62 percent). Refined sugar prices were .852 cents lower in 1894 than they were in 1910. In conclusion, the failure of antitrust law to divest the Sugar Trust did not produce the all embracing, exploitative monopoly envisioned by economic theory, and any restraint of trade that did occur in sugar was due more to U.S. tariff policy than to free market monopoly power.[7]

It should be apparent that the Supreme Court was not interested in any conduct-performance information concerning the American Sugar Refining Company. An economic analysis of the tariff on sugar, entry conditions into refining, prices and outputs, and alleged predatory practices did not play any substantive part in the final court decision.

THE NORTHERN SECURITIES CASE (1904)

The *Northern Securities* case, decided by the Supreme Court in 1904, was a turning point in prosecuting monopoly under the Sherman Act.[8] A majority of the Supreme Court agreed that a holding company, Northern Securities

Company, that had acquired a controlling interest in two formerly "independent and competitive" interstate railroads, the Northern Pacific and the Great Northern, was necessarily a "trust" or a combination in restraint of interstate commerce. As Justice Harlan stated in the majority decision:

> No scheme or device could more certainly come within the words of the Act [Sherman] . . . or could more effectively and certainly suppress free competition between the constituent companies. This combination is, within the meaning of the Act, a "trust"; but if it is not, it is a combination in restraint of interstate and international commerce; and that is enough to bring it under the condemnation of the Act. The *mere existence of such a combination* and the power acquired by the holding company as its trustee, constitute a menace to, and a restraint upon, that freedom of commerce which Congress intended to recognize and protect, and which the public is entitled to have protected.[9]

Since the Sherman Act embraced all restraints of trade and not just unreasonable ones, and since the *Trans-Missouri Freight Association*[10] decision clearly established that agreements to restrain interstate commerce involving railroads fell within the Act's jurisdiction, Harlan concluded, as had the Circuit Court,[11] that the Northern Securities Company had violated the Sherman Act. Although Justice Brewer disagreed with part of Harlan's opinion, arguing that not all restraints of trade were made illegal by the Sherman Act, just unreasonable ones, he concurred in condemning Northern Securities as an illegal restraint that threatened to mitigate the benefits to the public of unrestricted competition.

The *Northern Securities* decision was not unanimous. There were two written dissents, one by Mr. Chief Justice White and another by Mr. Justice Holmes (Mr. Justice Peckham joined with both), and both challenged the reasoning of the majority decision. White argued simply that the ownership of stock of two competing railways was not interstate commerce. The expression, "interstate commerce," as established in *Gibbons v. Ogden*, implied "traffic, but it is something more, it is intercourse." But the issue in *Northern Securities* in White's view, did not involve traffic or intercourse, but ownership of property; and the ownership of stock in a state corporation was a state problem: "I think the ownership of stock in a state corporation cannot be said to be in any sense traffic between the states or intercourse between them."[12]

Justice Holmes was even more penetrating in his dissent. He, too, agreed that the effect of the stock ownership by Northern Securities on interstate commerce was "indirect" and "not shown to be certain and very great," and that if such a "remote result of the exercise of an ordinary incident of property and personal freedom is enough to make that exercise unlawful, there is hardly any transaction concerning commerce between the states that may not be made a crime by the finding of a jury or a court."[13] But even more significantly, Holmes argued that conspiracies under the common law "were combinations to keep strangers to the agreement out of the business."

> This restriction by contract with a stranger to the contractor's business is the ground of the decision in United States v. Joint Traffic Association, 171 U.S. 505, following and affirming United States v. Trans-Missouri Freight Association, 166 U.S. 290. I accept those decisions absolutely, not only as binding upon me, but as decisions which I have no desire to criticize or abridge. But the provision has not been decided, and, it seems to me, could not be decided without perversion of plain language, to apply to an arrangement by which competition is ended through community interest—an arrangement which leaves the parties without external restaint. That provision, taken alone, does not require that all existing competitions shall be maintained. It does not look primarily, if at all, to competition. It simply requires that a party's freedom in trade between the states shall not be cut down by contract with a stranger. So far as that phrase goes, it is lawful to abolish competition by any form of union.[14]

Thus, for Holmes, there could not be an illegal restraint unless an agreement existed with a "stranger" to restrict trade—competition. But no such arrangements had even been attempted in the Northern Securities case.[15] The inherent elimination of competition between any two parties (for example, between two competitive railroads) as a consequence of a voluntary merger or fusion, was thus perfectly legal. If this were not so, Holmes reasoned, "every such combination, as well the small as the great is within the Act"; and this would not be an attempt to regulate commerce, but rather, "an attempt to reconstruct society." But this the Congress had neither the legitimate power nor the inclination to do.[16]

Background to Northern Securities

Actually, both the majority and minority opinions in this case ignored (and as far as judicial precedent was concerned, it was quite proper to do so) the essential economic factors involved. For example, were the two railroads actively competitive with each other in the first place; how had competition performed; and, had their voluntary consolidation injured, or would it be likely to injure the public? As B. H. Meyer aptly put it: "It was assumed that competition had been stifled without first asking the question whether competition had actually existed; and whether, if competition could be perpetuated, the public would profit by it."[17]

In fact, the origins of the Northern Securities Company stem not from the fusion of two competitive railroads, but from a competitive business rivalry that existed between James J. Hill's Great Northern, J. P. Morgan's Northern

Pacific, and E. H. Harriman's Union Pacific.[18] While the Great Northern and Northern Pacific appear geographically to be alternative railroads between St. Paul and Seattle, intense price wars had ended, for various reasons, long before 1904. Meyer indicates that the roads had lived in "comparative peace" for at least twenty years.[19] Both railways had maintained joint rates, and the consequent backloading and even flow of freight realized from such arrangements had increased the efficiency and economy of each line, and allowed a generally low level of rates that would have bankrupted other roads.[20]

There were two factors that appeared to stand in the way of continued cost savings: a more reliable arrangement was necessary to insure the stability of the joint rates; and control of the strategically located Burlington railroad line was deemed crucial. The Burlington road stretched east from St. Paul to Chicago and tapped "the principal livestock markets, important cotton, coal and mineral areas of the United States."[21] It was a logical extension of the Hill–Morgan system, and in January 1901, negotiations began for the purchase of the line. Although Harriman requested to join the negotiations, his request was refused, and a month later the Burlington was sold to the Hill–Morgan interests.[22]

E. H. Harriman then began his famed Wall Street assault on the Northern Pacific itself. In an effort to get a controlling stock interest, the price of the Nothern Pacific's common was bid up from $144 per share to over $1000 in just four days.[23] Although Harriman did obtain a majority of the common and preferred stock, a technicality kept him from exercising control; and as far as the Hill–Morgan interests were concerned, from wrecking the economic advantages of their close association.[24] Thus, the holding company idea, Northern Securities, was a logical and necessary consolidation of properties to put the Hill–Morgan rail plans beyond Harriman's control.

> With the view of preventing the possibility of future "raids" upon the Great Northern and Northern Pacific stock and of fortifying these two roads and their connections in their competitive struggle with "the Suez Canal and the high seas and the entire world", the idea of a permanent holding company was invented. It has been persistently denied that the desire to restrain competition among constituent companies had anything to do with the organization of the Northern Securities Company.[25]

In short, the Northern Securities Company, incorporated in New Jersey in November 1901, did not actually restrain competition between two previously rival rail systems. Instead, as far as the individuals involved were concerned, it finalized an efficient and eminently sensible consolidation of rail properties. As evidence, perhaps, of the efficiency of the arrangement, rail rates on the Hill–Morgan lines continued to decline between November

1901 and 1903.[26] But economic facts and economic analysis played no role whatever in the final decision of the Supreme Court.

Buoyed by the *Northern Securities* decision, the Justice Department initiated a number of legal actions against large corporate holding companies. None was to prove more important than the criminal action filed in a St. Louis Federal Court on November 15, 1906, against the Standard Oil Company of New Jersey. This industry and this antitrust case are important for three reasons: first, the case set important precedents in judicial interpretations of the antitrust laws; second, the Standard Oil legend created or gave rise to "facts that everybody know" concerning the conduct and performance of large corporations; finally, a study of the petroleum industry will allow a reasonable discussion of the hypothesis that business monopoly is not a free-market problem at all, but arises through government and business intervention.

THE STANDARD OIL OF NEW JERSEY CASE (1911)

The modern petroleum industry began in 1846 when a Canadian geologist named Dr. Abraham Gesner discovered that oil could be distilled from coal, and that kerosene could be drawn off and used as an illuminant.[27] Several years later, a number of firms had entered the business of extracting oil from shale. The kerosene produced would not gum or smoke when burned in properly designed oil lamps; most importantly, the kerosene was relatively cheaper than existing illuminants. Whale or sperm oil, always in uncertain supply, frequently sold for over $3 a gallon and gas, though cheaper than sperm oil, was not universally available. Thus, when Benjamin Silliman, a Yale professor, confirmed for the Pennsylvania Rock Oil Company the potential value of some oil found floating on marshy creeks in Pennsylvania, the only commercial question left was: can oil be found in abundant supply? Colonel E. L. Drake, a 39-year-old drifter and ex-railroad conductor, supplied that answer in 1859 when he struck oil in Titusville, Pennsylvania. With Drake's well pumping 25 barrels a day, and with the early price of a barrel of crude oil at $20, the petroleum industry, and age, had begun.

The Petroleum Industry: 1860–1911

When the oil word leaked out, northwestern Pennsylvania was overrun with businessmen, speculators, misfits, horse dealers, drillers, and bankers. Dirt-poor farmers leased their land out at fantastic prices and oil rigs began to blacken the landscape. Existing towns were jammed full overnight, and new towns appeared almost as quickly. "Smellers" and oil "diviners" worked overtime in a frenzied effort to locate the mysterious deposits of black gold.

But getting a rig and sinking a hole on someone's leased land were only the beginning of the problem. The crude-oil flow had to be successfully controlled, and the threat of waste and fire was always high. Furthermore, the heavy, corrosive crude oil had to be stored and shipped somehow. The barrels of the day were too weak, so new barrels had to be devised. Teamsters had to drive animal teams through hip-deep mud, carrying barreled petroleum from well sites to Oil Creek, the nearest available transportation. The barrels were then floated on top of flatboats down the creek—when there was water. Periodically, freshets would be opened by lumber firms upstream (they usually extracted a toll of a few pennies per barrel), and river boat captains would skillfully guide the precious cargo towards the docks at Oil City. As might be expected, much of the oil did not arrive, and many lost their lives attempting to transport crude. However, there were eager buyers at Oil City, and the price for crude oil was good; thus, the first dribbles of oil soon became a swelling stream.

Investments in industries related to the fledging petroleum industry quickened. Railroad men smelled money in oil transport and quickly laid track to haul oil from northwestern Pennsylvania to Oil City and then to some early refineries. Barrel makers—some right by Oil Creek—tripled production, then tripled it again; but outputs still fell below demand and consumption. Mules and horses were precious, and courageous river boat captains were at a high premium. Barge companies acting as crude tankers quickly came into existence to move the crude from Oil City to refineries in Cleveland and Pittsburgh. A 2-inch wooden oil pipeline was constructed in 1865, only to be destroyed by suddenly unemployed bands of teamster boys; another built in the same year, destroyed in the same fashion, rebuilt, and then protected by Pinkerton's, proved successful. A metal drum called a tank car, into which petroleum could be pumped, and in which it could be stored and transported along a railroad track, was also pioneered in the same year. Crude oil became available in ample supplies and could be moved efficiently over land and water to its ultimate destination. The early stream of crude oil turned into a torrent.

The development of the industry was, predictably, a mixed blessing for the producers, especially for the small marginal operators. The profit-laden $20-per-barrel prices for early crude had soured quickly to $12; then to $2; and then in early 1862, to 10 cents.[28] Although the prices would recover somewhat in later years, the windfall profits vanished forever. The producers were harshly pushed back to reality by the laws of supply and demand. But the steady production, efficient transportation, and relatively low prices paved the way for another group of oil entrepreneurs—the refiners. It would be the refiners, and particularly the Standard Oil Company, that would turn petroleum into one of America's greatest growth industries.

The Petroleum Refiners.   By 1865 the development of the petroleum refining industry was well underway. The first region to develop refiners was the crude oil production region itself, and there were at least thirty independent refiners there.[29] But the costs of refining petroleum in northwestern Pennsylvania were high because of heavy charges for shipping machinery and sulfuric acid, and because land was expensive. Therefore, other areas that were better situated (in regard to cost) grew more quickly than the always marginal oil-region refiners. Pittsburgh, for example, fewer than sixty miles from Oil City, quickly developed into the refining capital of the industry. It was close to some good potential market areas (e.g., Philadelphia), and had good rail and water transport, and a cheap supply of coal and labor. By 1865, eighty refineries were manufacturing kerosene and related products from crude petroleum, and the sky over Pittsburgh was heavy with smoke.[30] There were other refineries in Baltimore, Philadelphia, and New York, and the industry was growing rapidly. Some sources estimate the total number of independent refiners at this point at about 250.[31] But the most interesting developments, as it turns out, were taking place in Cleveland, Ohio.

Though Cleveland had about fifty refineries by 1866, its strategic position in the refining industry had always been precarious. Cleveland was over 150 miles from the crude oil-producing region, and 600 miles from New York and the important eastern markets. Though it had an excellent location for reaching any western markets that might develop, its immediate future rested on the level of transportation rates.

If rates for shipping oil through the Erie Canal could be pushed down, and if rates over the two competitive railroads—the Atlantic and Great Western, and the Lake Shore Railroad—could be lowered and kept low, Cleveland refineries could be competitive with other refineries in the eastern markets. The key to efficiency and competition in the Cleveland area was transportation, and that key would unlock many of the major developments of the industry.

The Rockefeller Organization.   John D. Rockefeller was 23 years old and already a success in his own profitable commission business when he decided to risk $4000 in a speculative oil refinery in Cleveland. The firm quickly prospered under the technical direction of Samuel Andrews, and a second refinery was constructed in 1866. Later, Maurice Clark, one of the original partners in the firm, was bought out (for $72,500), and Rockefeller then brought in his brother, William—for entrepreneurial know-how—and the shrewd and wealthy Henry Flagler for additional capital. By 1868, Rockefeller's complete and undivided attention had turned to petroleum and to the profits that could be made by "penny-pinching."

The firm of Rockefeller, Andrews, and Flagler prospered quickly in the intensely competitive industry due to the economic excellence of its entire operations. Instead of buying oil from jobbers, they made the jobber's profit by sending their own purchasing men into the oil region. They also made their own sulfuric acid, barrels, lumber, wagons, and glue. They kept minute and accurate records of every item from rivets to barrel bungs. They built elaborate storage facilities near their refineries. Rockefeller bargained as shrewdly for crude as anyone has before or since; and Sam Andrews coaxed more kerosene from a barrel of crude than the competition could. In addition, the Rockefeller firm put out the cleanest burning kerosene and managed to profitably dispose of most of the residues, in the form of lubricating oil, paraffin wax, and vaseline. Thus, it was not surprising that by the late 1860s the firm was turning out the industry's best line of petroleum products at the lowest production costs, and that it managed to prosper even while the spread between crude and refined prices elsewhere in the industry decreased significantly. Rockefeller, the eternal optimist, expanded outputs while others were more conservative, and by 1870 the firm was the biggest refiner in Cleveland, and quite possibly in the country.

The Success of the Rockefeller Organization. In 1870 Rockefeller's share of total refined output was no more than 4 percent, and there might have been as many as 250 independent refiners in existence. By 1874, the Rockefeller company was refining almost 11,000 barrels a day, or about 25 pecent of estimated industry output, and had purchased 21 of its 26 Cleveland competitors.[32] By 1880, his total market share had climbed to between 80 and 85 percent, and the number of independent refiners had decreased to between 80 and 100.[33] During this chaotic period, Rockefeller had tried unsuccessful collusion with other refiners and railroads (the South Improvement Company), and had fought numerous battles with railroads to secure rebates (more on this below), and a final, expanded business war with the Empire Transportation Company and the Pennsylvania Railroad. At the decade's end, the Rockefeller organization emerged triumphant with significant interests in pipelines and tank cars, and an overwhelmingly advantageous bargaining position with some railroads. By 1880, John D. Rockefeller was the undisputed king of petroleum, and his position appeared quite invulnerable.

But how was all this success accomplished? How did Standard Oil of Ohio (the name had been adopted on incorporation in Ohio in 1870) increase its market share so rapidly? And why did many other firms sell out and allow the creation of an alleged near-monopoly in refining? To begin to answer these questions, it must be emphasized that the 1870s were a treacherous period for all speculative businesses, and particularly for the overbuilt oil refinery industry. The U. S. Treasury's deflationary policies (withdrawing greenbacks from circulation in an attempt to resume specie payment in the late 1870s) and the subsequent post-Civil War decline in general demand and prices, hurt all speculative businesses including, of course, oil refining. Prices for refined petroleum (kerosene) fell from over 30 cents a gallon in 1869, to 22 cents in 1872, and to 10 cents by November of 1874.[34] Many firms that had entered the industry during the Civil War period, left the market as the prices soured with no relief in sight. Other firms, though less opportunistic, were forced to sell out, since they were small, nonintegrated refiners that could not reduce their input costs as quickly as market prices declined. For these two reasons, a general reduction in the number of refiners would have been expected in this period with or without the presence of the Standard Oil Company.

Standard Oil of Ohio acquired many oil companies in the early 1870s, and the prices they paid for these properties were occasionally below the original cost. There is nothing suspicious about this, however. The value of almost all property, and particularly refinery property, had deflated in the 1870s as overproduction and deflation lowered exchange values. The original cost of a refinery in 1865 was irrelevant in 1875, since the market conditions were radically different. Standard Oil cannot be faulted for the fact that it paid 1875 market prices for properties that had lost substantial exchange value and, in many cases, were so inefficient that many marginal operators were subsequently closed down by Standard.

Moreover, rival refineries were often quite anxious to be purchased by Standard, and at "outrageous" prices. The story of George Rice does not appear atypical. In 1882, Rice attempted to bribe and blackmail Standard Oil into paying $250,000 for a refinery he had offered to sell them in 1876 for $24,000; in 1890, he wanted $500,000.[35] Other examples that are cited by John McGee indicate that this was a rather common practice.[36]

In addition, the technology and capital requirements of the industry were rapidly changing, and firms that proved too small to invent, innovate, or take advantage of scale economies, were destined to be of marginal importance. Destructive distillation (the cracking of crude) was introduced in 1875, and the minimum size of an efficient refinery was increased to over 1000 barrels a day. Moreover, large efficient refineries and related equipment were far more expensive than the simple stills of the 1860s. These greater capital requirements certainly limited the role of the very small operator. Actually, much of the crude oil refined in the late 1880s was a very poor, high-sulfur grade of petroleum that yielded less kerosene, and it was only handled efficiently because of the successful experiments of chemist Herman Frasch and the

$200,000 research gamble of the Standard Oil Company. Certainly, technological innovation and scale economies helped determine the structure of the petroleum industry.

Efficient operations in the 1870s meant tank cars, pipelines, adequate crude sources, cheap barrels, huge storage facilities, and export capabilities, all of which the Standard Oil Company had invested in heavily, and most of which the smaller competitors had not. The Standard Company has often been criticized for the fact that its competitors could not enjoy the efficiencies of a tank car fleet, access to cheap pipelines, and large storage facilities. But, surely, the fact that competitors would not or could not be as efficient as Standard in these areas was not Standard's responsibility. Was it unfair to buy or built pipelines and then employ them to obtain lower rates for railroad freight? Was it unfair to own tank cars and use them efficiently? Was it unfair to invest millions in storage facilities to take advantage of slight variances in the demand and supply of crude or refined petroleum? And was it unfair for Rockefeller to surround himself with singular men of exceptional "brainpower, astuteness, and foresightedness"? While competitors that could not or would not do these things might have regarded these activities as unfair, the ultimate justification of these policies was proven again and again in the market place: they lowered the costs of production and the price of the product and raised the profits of the Standard Oil Company.

Between 1870 and 1885, the price of refined kerosene dropped from 26 cents to 8 cents per gallon.[37] In the same period, the Standard Oil Company reduced the average costs per gallon from almost 3 cents in 1870 to 0.452 cents in 1885.[38] Clearly, the firm was relatively efficient, and a good share of that efficiency was transmitted profitably to the consumer in the form of lower prices for a much impoved product.

Rebates and the Railroads.   The issue of railroad rebates has provoked considerable controversy concerning the growth of Standard Oil. According to some critics, it was the receipt by Standard of unfair and discriminatory rebates that allowed it to triumph over competitors and nearly monopolize the petroleum industry.

A rebate is a price concession—usually secret—granted by a railroad to a shipper. Its immediate consequence is to lower transportation costs to that shipper. But to understand why rebates are granted and whether they are fair or not, it is necessary to understand the economics of railroading.[39]

Railroads are industries that typically have high fixed costs and low variable costs. Most of their expenses are fixed charges, such as interest and depreciation, that must be paid regardless of the volume of traffic. Thus railroads are always hungry for traffic, and their rate schedules often reflect this fact. Railroad rates, like all prices in a free market, are determined by competition. Since the variable costs associated with providing railroad services are low, railroad rates can range from well above average costs where they have little price competition, to rates that fall significantly below average costs where there is intense competition. Railroads charge what the traffic will bear, like any other business, and like almost any other business, the traffic will bear different rates at different times and places, depending on the degree of competition. Like any firm, it will pay a railroad, in the short run, to take additional freight business as long as the rate received covers out-of-pocket (i.e., variable) costs. Since average variable costs are low (especially if shippers cover some of them), prices on very competitive runs may fall very steeply, and almost to nothing. But some revenue, be it ever so little, is better than nothing, and railroads will charge low rates if they have to. Hopefully the deficit on below average-cost runs can be funded on runs where prices exceed average costs.

In the 1870s much of railroading was very competitive, especially that east of the Mississippi.[40] Many roads had overbuilt, and the post-Civil War deflationary period was one of intense and persistent rate competition. Though there were hundreds of voluntary pools, rail rates were generally down throughout the period. Railroad pools had attempted to fix and maintain prices, but the agreements often lasted no longer than the meetings needed to draw them up.[41]

Railroads went through the motions of drawing up formal rate schedules, but it was common knowledge that the book prices were the point at which bargaining began; shippers bargained for their own prices, and the relative strength of supply and demand (competition) determined the exact rate. Almost always the exact rate charged a customer was kept secret in order to prevent a destructive price war. Yet almost always the actual rates were revealed, as some shippers paying one rate attempted to compete in the same market with other shippers paying different rates.

For hundreds of years, competition in the marketplace had been limited by the extent of the market, and the market had been limited by transportation costs. Goods of considerable weight could not compete in faraway markets because the costs of transportation inflated the selling price. Only with the development of cheap transportation (canals, railroads, etc.), and then with competitive cheap transportation, could the rates on freight be bid down to allow competition between distinct cities. It was perfectly possible, therefore, to see railroad rates lower from say Cleveland to New York then from Titusville to New York, even though the former distance was one hundred miles longer than the latter: it all depended on the relative supply and demand conditions in both regions. In and of itself, distance, like technology, means little in economics; the value of services is determined by the relative strength of demand and supply at any given moment.

Because Cleveland shippers were in a better bargaining position than oil region shippers, their rail rates were usually lower. If the rates drifted down toward average variable costs, this only attested to the poor economic position of the railroads. If these rates were lower than the rates paid by oil region shippers, this was to be expected, and as far as overall competition in New York is concerned, to be applauded. If competition exists in the final product market, almost all rebates or discriminations ultimately generated increases in supply and lower prices.

There has been no discussion to this point as to whether firms deserve their rebate. For some economists, rebates are fair when, say, a 10 percent rebate actually represents a 10 percent "savings" to the railroad from handling a shipper's business. Two points are relevant here. In the first place railroads did realize cost savings, and these savings may have been considerable. Standard Oil, for example, furnished loading facilities and discharging facilities at great cost; it regularly and reliably provided a heavy volume of traffic (even one of Standard's severest critics admits that this led to "savings of several hundred thousand dollars a month in handling" for the railroads),[42] it provided terminal facilities and exempted the railroads from liability for fire by carrying its own insurance. Thus, Standard Oil might be said to have received a legitimate discount for realized economies.

But realized economies need have nothing directly to do with rebates; costs do not directly determine prices. If Standard Oil was, in fact, "paying for" a share of railroad's variable costs, so much the better, for the roads; the price necessary to secure Standard's business could fall even further than before. In fact, since Standard probably performed some of the railroad's variable expenses more efficiently than they did, the mechanism of rebate was certainly beneficial for both. Still, from any railroad's point of view, the dominating economic factor is volume. To secure additional volume, it may have to accept any rate higher than its average variable costs.

Standard's ability to threaten water shipment, pipeline shipment, or shipment along another railroad, was an important factor that lowered its rail rates. Since its shipments of oil were so important to the railroads, they could not afford to lose them; if the prices covered railroad variable costs, it still made sense to take the business. In short, Standard's price could be and was considerably different from the rates paid by other shippers, but the differences are not mysterious or regrettable; they are a consequence of railroad transportation economics and the competitive pressures of an open market.

Seen in this light, the "unfairness" of price discrimination is certainly debatable. What is unfair about securing all the advantages that are possible in a free and open competitive market? What is unfair about granting concessions to the biggest, most versatile shipper who can threaten a volume shift, and not to the small producer and shipper whose volume is far less significant? Much of the criticism of price discrimination is based on emotion, and is more concerned with the fate of particular competitors than with the way an open competitive process benefits the consumer.

Predatory Pricing.   Similar emotions still pevail over another of Standard's supposed unfair business practices: predatory price cutting. Predatory price cutting is the practice of deliberately underselling rivals in certain markets to drive them out of business, and then raising prices to exploit a market devoid of competition. Ida Tarbell immortalized the charge forever in Chapter 10 ("Cutting to Kill") of her *History of the Standard Oil Company*. If interested parties had taken the trouble to read that chapter, however, they would have discovered that Tarbell wrote more of railroad discrimination, Standard's efficient kerosene marketing system, and its morally questionable (to her) use of an elaborate industrial espionage system, than of any specific predatory practices. Nonetheless, such practices were (and remain) part of the Standard Oil legend.

Unfortunately for lovers of legends, this one has been laid theoretically and empirically prostrate. In a now classic article, John S. McGee theorized that Standard Oil did not employ predatory practices because it would have been economically foolish to have done so.[43] In the first place, McGee argued, such practices are very costly for the large firm; it always stands relatively more to lose since it, by definition, does the most business. Second, the uncertainty of the length of the forthcoming battle, and thus its indeterminate expense, must surely make firms wary of initiating a price war. Third, competitors can simply close down and wait for the price to return to profitable levels; or new owners might purchase bankrupt facilities and ready them to compete with the predator. Fourth, such wars inevitably spread to surrounding markets, endangering the predator's profits in his "safe" areas. And last, predatory practices already assume a "war chest" of monopoly profits to see the firm through the costly battles; firms apparently cannot initiate predatory practices unless they already possess monopoly power. But if this is true, firms cannot *gain* initial monopoly positions through predatory practices. To sum up McGee's reasoning, then, there are serious logical weaknesses in the assumption that large firms are motivated to engage in predatory practices.

The empirical evidence with respect to Standard Oil's practices reinforces these theoretical predictions. McGee concludes after sifting through almost 11,000 pages of the *Standard Oil* trial record, that:

> Judging from the Record, Standard Oil did not use predatory price discrimination to drive out competing refiners, nor did its pricing practice have that effect. Whereas there may be a very few cases in which retail kerosene peddlers or dealers went out of business after or during price cutting, there is no real proof

that Standard's pricing policies were responsible. I am convinced that Standard did not systematically, if ever, use local price cutting in retailing, or anywhere else, to reduce competition. To do so would have been foolish; and, whatever else has been said about them, the old Standard organization was seldom criticized for making less money when it could readily have made more.[44]

Thus, to conclude this section, Standard's position in oil refining grew rapidly because of the natural decline of small competitors; the increasing capital and innovation requirements of large-scale oil technology; the economic advantages achieved through intelligent entrepreneurship; the ownership of tank cars and pipelines; vertical integration into barrels, cans, glues, exporting; and the consequent lower transportation costs provided by the railroads. It did not grow from any general reliance on alleged predatory practices.

The Standard Oil Trust. The 1880–1895 period for the Standard organization was one of rapid expansion—particularly in Europe—continued integration both forward and backward, and experimentation with various institutional arrangements for increasing managerial efficiency. Choosing an effective legal structure was proving particularly bothersome. Almost all states, including Ohio, did not permit chartered companies to hold the stock of firms incorporated in other states. Yet Standard, by 1880, effectively controlled fourteen different firms, and had a considerable stock interest in about twenty-five others, including the giant National Transit Company. How were these companies to be legally and efficiently managed? In addition, Pennsylvania had just unearthed (with the help of Standard's competitors and some producers) an old state law that allowed a tax on the entire capital stock of any corporation doing any business within its borders; other states threatened to follow suit.[45] Thus, a new organizational arangement was mandatory to allow effective control of all owned properties and to escape confiscatory taxation without breaking the law.

Standard chose to resurrect an old common law arrangement known as the *trust.* In a trust, individuals pool their property and agree to have a trustee or trustee group manage that property in the interests of all the owners. Just as incorporation allows incorporators to pool their property and choose their directors and managers, trusts in the 1880s allowed the same convenience with entire corporate holdings. Thus, a trust was a modern holding company, but frequently without the formalities of legal incorporation and the necessity of any public disclosure.

The Standard Oil Trust was formed in 1882, though smaller informal trustee arrangements had existed before. The forty-two stockholders of the thirty-nine companies associated with Standard agreed to tender their stock to nine designated trustees; in return, the ex-stockholders received twenty trustee certificates per share of stock tendered. The original Standard Oil Trust was capitalized at $70 million, and John D. Rockefeller himself held over 25 percent. Rockefeller, his brother William, Henry Flagler, John D. Archbold, and five others then managed Standard's entire operations, setting up committees on transportation, export, manufacturing, lubricating, and other affairs to advise the executive committee.

This organizational arrangement functioned until March 1892, when the Supreme Court of Ohio ruled that the trust arrangement was illegal, and ordered Standard Oil of Ohio to withdraw from it. Seven years later the same men, with essentially the same firms, came together again to incorporate as Standard Oil of New Jersey, a legal holding company, and their goal of effective and legal multi-firm control over common properties was achieved.

In addition, substantive changes within the organization during this period were also significant. Standard closed down many smaller refineries and built large ones in their place. Various units of the refining empire were forced to compete with one another, and substantial cost savings were realized. Refinery output expanded rapidly and enormous expenditures had to be made for tanks and pipelines to hold and move this vast supply. Technological innovation was encouraged; for example, Standard developed machines that turned out 24,000 five-gallon tin cans daily by 1890. Even Standard's severest critic, Ida Tarbell, recognized much of this efficiency, and her glowing chapter, "The Legitimate Greatness of the Standard Oil Company," pays tribute to the commercial intelligence of the Standard organization. Though that chapter is filled with many excellent examples, one of the best—because it demonstrates the economics of integration—is the following:

Not far away from the canning works, on Newtown Creek, is an oil refinery. This oil runs to the canning works, and, as the newmade cans come down by a chute from the works above, where they have just been finished, they are filled, twelve at a time, with the oil made a few miles away. The filling aparatus is admirable. As the newmade cans come down the chute they are distributed, twelve in a row, along one side of a turn-table. The turn-table is revolved, and the cans come directly under twelve measures, each holding five gallons of oil—a turn of a valve, and the cans are full. The table is turned a quarter, and while twelve more cans are filled and twelve fresh ones are distributed, four men with soldering cappers put the caps on the first set. Another quarter turn, and men stand ready to take the cans from the filler, and while they do this, twelve more are having caps put on, twelve are filling, and twelve are coming to their place from the chute. The cans are placed at once in wooden boxes standing ready, and, after a twenty-four-hour wait for discovering leaks, are nailed up and carted to a nearby door. This door opens on the river, and there at anchor by the side of the factory is a vessel chartered for South America or China or where not—waiting to receive the cans which a little more than twenty-four hours before were tin sheets lying in flatboxes. It is a marvelous example of economy, not only in materials, but in time and in footsteps.[46]

By the late 1880s, the economies of integration that were so important to domestic operations were being transferred to foreign production and distribution, as well. In 1895, for example, Standard had seventeen manufacturing plants in Europe, hundreds of warehouse and depot facilities under lease, over 150 tank cars, and close to 5000 tank wagons for bulk shipment to retailers. Though it had considerable foreign competition, especially from Russian and British petroleum operations, the Standard Oil Company was a major factor in the development of foreign oil markets throughout the world.

Finally, during the 1880–1895 period, refined oil products increased in quality, and the nominal price to the consumer was reduced. Though Standard's share of the refining market declined only slightly (82 percent in 1895, compared to over 88 percent in 1879), the price of refined oil per gallon in barrels was reduced from 9.33 cents in 1880 to 8.13 cents in 1885 to 7.38 cents in 1890 and to 5.91 cents in 1897.[47] In addition, Standard's average refining costs per gallon fell to 0.29 cents in 1896.[48] Thus, at the very pinnacle of Standard's alleged industry control, the costs and the prices for refined oil reached some of their lowest levels in the history of the petroleum industry.

It is important to note, given subsequent legal events, that the long-run trend in outputs of various petroleum products was strongly upward throughout this period. If monopoly control implies anything, it implies the power to restrict the market supply and, consequently, to increase the market price. Yet Standard's price and output behavior is entirely consistent with what would have been expected under competitive conditions. For instance, between 1890 and 1897, Standard increased its kerosene production 74 percent, lubricating oil production 82 percent, and wax production by 84 percent.[49] In short, there was no restriction of supply, and monopoly prices were never realized, even during periods of relatively high market share. Standard was a large, competitive firm in an open, competitive market.

Changing Market Conditions: 1896–1911. Between 1896 and 1911, the petroleum industry began to change radically, and Standard Oil of New Jersey's position in the changing market became less and less secure. The most revolutionary change that occurred, and the one that fueled other changes, was the demand shift away from kerosene to other petroleum products. Kerosene sales leveled off as the competitiveness of gas and electricity cut deeply into a once solid growth area; correspondingly, lighter fuel oils, lubricating oils, and gasoline became significantly more important. Between 1899 and 1914, kerosene sales as a percentage of all refined petroleum produts declined from 58 percent to 25 percent, while fuel oil rose from 15 percent to 48 percent.[50] The kerosene age was over.

As new crude supplies in Kansas, Oklahoma, Texas, and California reached the market, new large, vertically integrated petroleum companies came into existence to direct the crude flow towards the new demand. For example, the Pure Oil Company was formed in 1895, and by 1904 it owned fourteen refineries, mostly in the oil region, 1500 miles of crude oil pipe line, and another 400 miles of pipeline for refined products; it handled 8000 barrels of crude a day, owned steamers and barges, and was capitalized at over $10,000,000.[51] Moreover, other firms were formed, such as Associated Oil and Gas (1901), Texaco (1902), and the giant Gulf Company (1907).[52] By 1908 there were at least 125 independent refineries in the United States, among them such companies as Sun Oil, Union Oil and the Tidewater Company; by 1911 there were at least 147.[53] The petroleum industry was exploding faster and in more directions than any one man or firm could predict or control. The open, competitive market was taking apart Standard Oil of New Jersey's market position. As the Hidys so neatly put it: "Thus even before the breakup of the combination, the process of whittling Standard Oil down to reasonable size within the industry was already far advanced."[54] Even though Standard was continuously increasing its output of petroleum products and its consumption of cude oil, its percentage of output and crude oil consumed decreased steadily throughout the period. Standard's share of the petroleum products market fell from approximately 88 percent in 1890, to 68 percent in 1907, and to 64 percent by 1911. And even though Standard consumed and refined increasing volumes of crude oil (39 million barrels in 1892; 52 million barrels in 1902; 65 million barrels in 1906; and 99 million barrels in 1911), its own oil production as a percentage of total market supply decreased significantly from 34 percent in 1898 to 20 percent in 1902 to but 11 percent in 1906.[55] Thus to seriously maintain that Standard was increasingly monopolizing the petroleum industry at the turn of the century, or that the antitrust suit against Standard, begun in 1906 was a legitimate response to almost complete monopolistic control, is patently absurd. The raw data of the period indicate no such increasing monopoly by Standard. Reasonable inferences, even from a neoclassical perspective, would be all the other way.

Nonetheless, the intellectual criticism of big business, and especially of Rockefeller and the Standard Oil Company, intensified. Though Standard had remained relatively clean of political scandal and was not the beneficiary of tariff protection, subsidy, or public land grants—as were the sugar and steel trusts—most of the journalistic muckrakers saved their best shots for the petroleum combination. Henry Demarest Lloyd set the tone of the era with his great populist polemic, *Wealth Against Commonwealth*, published in 1894. The Hearst papers, *Life, Collier's,* and *Harpers,* quickly discovered that antiwealth and particularly antimonopoly journalism paid off handsomely. And when Ida Tarbell's articles, titled, "The History of the Standard Oil Company," published during 1902 and 1903 in *McClure's*, became modern classics, popular antibusiness resentment reached its zenith. The fact that most of the attacks were personal, emotional, and even illogical was irrelevant; the fact that some of the attacks were ambiguously motivated (e.g., Ida Tarbell was the sister of William Tarbell, Treasurer of the Pure Oil Company) was ignored. Rockefeller and Standard Oil's silence on all criticism just fired the public indignation more. Between 1904 and 1906, at least twenty-one state antitrust suits were brought against Standard Oil subsidiaries in ten states.[56] And on November 15, 1906, the federal government filed its Sherman Act case and petitioned for the dissolution of Standard Oil of New Jersey.

The Lower Court Decision

Standard was convicted in the federal antitrust suit on November 20, 1909, and ordered dissolved back into its independent component parts.[57] The four court judges (Sanborn, VanDevouter, Hook, and Adams) all agreed that Standard violated the Sherman Act by forming a holding company in 1899, and that the holding company had not allowed any competition between the merged firms. Judge Sanborn stated that:

> By the trust of 1899, more than 30 corporations were combined with the principal company, and that corporation was given the power to fix the rates of transportation and the purchase and selling prices which all *these* companies should pay and receive for petroleum and its products throughout the republic and in the traffic with foreign nations. The principal company and many of the subsidiary corporations were many of them *capable of competing with each other in that trade, and would have been actively competitive if they had been owned by different individuals or different groups of individuals.* . . . The majority of the stock of the New York Company and of 18 other corporations engaged different branches of the production, manufacture, and sale of petroleum and its products was conveyed to the New Jersey Company in exchange for its stock, and the latter has ever since controlled and operated all these corporations and those which they controlled, *and has prevented them from competing with it or with each other.*[58]

Since "*any* contract or combination of two or more parties, whereby the control of such rates or prices is taken from separate competitors in that trade and rested in a person or an association of persons, *necessarily restricts competition* and restrains that commerce," and since Standard had necessarily formed such an "association," Standard had necessarily violated the Sherman Act:

[Since] the power to restrict competition in interstate commerce granted to the Standard Oil Company of New Jersey by the transfer to it of the stock of the 19 companies and of the authority to manage and operate them and the other corporations which they controlled was the absolute power to prevent competition *between any of these corporations* ... and the *necessary* effect of the transfer of the stock of the 19 companies to the holding company was, under the decision in the case of the Nothern Securities Company, direct and substantial restriction of that commerce, that transfer and the operation of the companies under it constituted a combination or conspiracy in restraint of interstate and international commerce in violation of the Anti-trust Act of July 2, 1890.[59]

Nowhere in the decision was there a discussion of the reasonableness or unreasonableness of Standard's competitive market practices. Nowhere was there any economic analysis of Standard's performance in the market. The determining issue was that the formation of the holding company in 1899 necessarily restrained trade *between the parties to the holding company*. As Judge Hook so neatly put it:

A holding company, owning the stocks of other concerns whose commercial activities, if free and independent of common control, would naturally bring them into competition with each other, is a form of trust or combination prohibited by Section I of the Sherman Act. The Standard Oil Company of New Jersey is such a holding company.[60]

Hence in 1909, the Sherman Act was being enforced literally, as it had been generally since 1904: trusts or holding companies necessarily restrained trade, and Standard was a holding company. In 1909, there was no explicit concern with intent or with substantive facts concerning conduct performance.

The Supreme Court Decision

On May 15, 1911, the decision against Standard was reaffirmed by the U.S. Supreme Court.[61] The general impression this decision left is that the Supreme Court set an important precedent when Justice White argued that not all restraints of trade or contracts or conspiracies were illegal and in violation of the Sherman Act, but only "unreasonable" ones.

Thus not specifying, but indubitably contemplating and requiring a standard, it follows that it was intended that the standard of reason which had been applied at the common law ... was intended to be the measure used for the purpose of determining whether, in a given case, a particular act had or had not brought about the wrong against which the statute provided.[62]

According to the logic of Justice White's position, no firm (including Standard Oil, presumably) was to be judged guilty of Sherman Act violations because of, let us assume, its dominant position in the marketplace or because it was simply a holding company. What supposedly was to be the crucial factor determining innocence or guilt was the reasonableness or unreasonableness of a firm's actions, or whether they were

> of such a character as to give rise to the inference or presumption that they had been entered into or done with the *intent to do wrong to the general public and to limit the rights of individuals,* thus restraining the free flow of commerce and tending to bring about the ends, such as *enhancement of prices,* which were considered to be against public policy.[63]

Justice White appears concerned with business acts that reveal an unmistakable intention to "wrong the public" or to "limit individual rights." If one discovered such acts and analyzed them, one could infer that the intent was to restrain trade and thus, to violate the law.

But a careful reading of the Supreme Court decision does not substantiate the widely held view that Standard Oil was convicted by employing "reason" as a standard in a careful examination of Standard's conduct performance. While White maintained that a "rule of reason" should apply to such activities, there is little to indicate that the Court actually applied any reasonable standard to Standard Oil's conduct performance. The application of such a standard would have required a careful and methodical sifting of all the conflicting evidence concerning rebates, high oil prices, railroad discriminations, predatory practices, the setting up of bogus independents, industrial espionage, and other alleged "unfair" competitive practices, as mentioned in the government's long petition. Yet no such "sifting" was detailed in the Supreme Court decision (nor, of course, in the lower court decision) and, consequently, no specific finding of guilt was made with regard to any of these allegations. We are simply told, with regard to these "acts," that

> no disinterested mind can survey the period in question without being irresistibly driven to the conclusion that the very genius for commercial development and organization which it would seem was manifested from the beginning *soon begot an intent and purpose to exclude others* which was frequently manifested by acts and dealings wholly inconsistent with the theory that they were made with the single conception of advancing the development of business power by *usual* methods, but which, on the contrary, necessarily involved *the intent to drive others from the field and to exclude them from their right to trade,* and thus accomplish the mastery which was the end in view.[64]

But how can a "disinterested mind" be driven "irresistibly" to a "conclusion" without facts, and without economic analysis applied to those facts?

What are these "usual methods" of business development that the Court refers to, and are Standard's "unusual" methods to be judged automatically unreasonable because they are not "usual"? How did Standard Oil exclude competitors "from their right to trade," and were these "unreasonable" exclusions? Had the "acts" worked an "injury to the public"? Had Standard Oil raised its prices, restricted outputs, repressed technoloical change, produced shoddy products, and driven its competition from the market through predatory practices? These are crucial questions that a "rule of reason" would provoke in many subsequent cases. But these issues were not analyzed fully in the *Standard Oil* decision.[65]

Now the conduct performance record of the industry indicates that petroleum prices fell, costs fell, outputs expanded, product quality improved, and hundreds of firms at one time or another produced and sold refined petroleum products in competition with Standard Oil. Many competitors, of course, had left the market for one reason or another. Many sold out to the Standard organization, and many were glad to; but surely, their right—and the subsequent rights of any other refiner to compete and trade—were not involved or infringed. The oil markets were legally open, and Standard was not able to obtain artificial or political exclusions. All firms had the right to trade; whether they were equipped to trade efficiently in competition with the Standard organization, and did trade efficiently, are other questions. If they were excluded because they did not have tank cars, pipelines, barrel factories, can factories, exporting firms, proper locations, crude supplies, storage facilities, and the consequent ability to obtain rebates from the railroads when necessary, their right to trade is not at issue. They were excluded because they could not match the economic advantages of Standard Oil. Efficiency is always exclusionary of less efficient competitors, but such exclusions are the very purpose of a competitive process. The significant point here is that the Supreme Court did not analyze these issues.

How then was Standard Oil of New Jersey convicted? On what basis was the firm found guilty of violating the Sherman Act? After Justice White had detailed his rule of reason, he turned to an examination of "the facts and the application of the statute to them." Beyond dispute were: (1) "The creation of the Standard Oil Company of Ohio"; (2) "the organization of the Standard Oil Trust in 1882"; and (3) "the increase of the capital of the Standard Oil Company of New Jersey and the acquisition by that company of the shares of the stock of the other corporations in exchange for its certificates."[66]

Now this latter aggregation of a "vast amount of property and the possibilities of far-reaching control" over the trade and commerce in petroleum and its products "*operated to destroy the 'potentiality of competition' which otherwise would have existed. . . .*" The lower court had concluded that Standard thus violated Sections 1 and 2 of the Sherman Act. Justice White saw "no cause to doubt the correctness of these conclusions."[67]

But what were the conclusions and how were they arrived at? Was Standard guilty simply because it had formally created a holding company in 1899, made up of properties allied to it since the early 1880s, and that this holding company had destroyed the "potentiality of competition" in the petroleum industry? Moreover, was the Court simply concluding that the destruction of potential competition between the now merged firms automatically constituted an illegal restraint of trade, just as the lower court had done? White attempted to explain why the Supreme Court had affirmed the lower court decision.

> Because the unification of power and control over petroleum and its products which was the *inevitable* result of the *combining in the New Jersey corporation* by the increase of its stock and the transfer to it of the stocks of so many other corporations, aggregating so vast a capital, gives rise, *in and of itself*, in the absence of countervailing circumstances, to say the least, to the *prima facie* presumption of intent and purpose to maintain the dominancy over the oil industry, not as a result of *normal methods of industrial development, but by new means of combination.* . . .[68]

Now this is hardly a sophisticated rule-of-reason approach. White simply reiterated that the creation of the holding company in 1899, or the formal merger of firms allied with Standard Oil for almost twenty years (the "new means of combination"), was in and of itself *prima facie* proof of intent and purpose to monopolize, and that this "unification of power and control over petroleum" was an inevitable result of the combination. But it should be apparent that this reasoning is thoroughly circular. Later, he added that "the exercise of the power which resulted from that organization fortified the foregoing conclusions," since

> the acquisition here and there which ensued of every efficient means by which competition could have been asserted, the slow but resistless methods which followed by which means of transportation were absorbed and brought under control, the system of marketing which was adopted by which the company was *divided into districts and the trade in each district in oil was turned over to a designated corporation within the combination, and all others were excluded,* all lead the mind up to a conviction of a purpose and intent which we think so certain as practically to cause the subject *not to be within the domain of reasonable contention.*[69]

But surely, the reasonableness of Standard's acquisitions can be debated (it was debated during the trial), and surely it is not always unreasonable for a holding company to designate the selling markets of its *own* subsidiaries and to exclude all others. Though these activities might not have been normal or usual for the day, they presumably were not—under a rule of reason—to be considered inherently unreasonable. And finally, it must be the strangest feat of judicial logic in memory to argue that a rule of reason applied to Sherman Act allegations, and then to have dismissed the entire subject with reference to Standard Oil as practically "not within the domain of reasonable contention."

In conclusion, while the essence of a conduct performance rule of reason may have been suggested in the *Standard Oil* case of 1911, there is little, if any, concrete evidence that it was carefully applied in that case. No economic analysis of Standard Oil's conduct and performance in the period under consideration was made by the Court to determine whether its business activities were reasonable. Standard was convicted and partially dissolved in 1911, but an economic analysis of its conduct performance had little, if anything, to do with that decision.

INTERVENTION IN THE PETROLEUM INDUSTRY

The early years of the petroleum industry just reviewed are remarkable in that they represent a virtual textbook example of a free and competitive market. There was relatively little governmental regulation or subsidization during this period (no price controls, tariffs, allocation controls, or quotas) and, not coincidentally, the industry experienced a remarkable growth and development. As we have seen, outputs of kerosene and related products were enormously expanded and prices were reduced during most of the period. And even though these years of intense development were dominated by Standard Oil of New Jersey, the corporation was unable to prevent the entry and growth of many competitors (e.g., Shell, Gulf, Texaco, Sun) or prevent a substantial decline in its own considerable market share. In short, the early years in petroleum were both relatively unregulated and competitive, with no apparent monopolistic abuse of either consumers or competitors.

Increasingly after 1911, there was active governmental intervention in the petroleum industry, and the industry itself, as well as the state, must bear a responsibility for that interventionism. Historically a substantial amount of petroleum regulation and legislation was supported, in whole or in part, by various segments of the industry in an attempt to further short-run business objectives. Unable to achieve monopoly power in a free market, various industry representatives and trade associations sought to transform the free petroleum maket into a regulated and controlled market. Not surprisingly, the regulated petroleum market has been less than efficient, and has involved both a substantial loss of freedom and a costly misallocation of resources. It is not at all unexpected to economists that just such continued intervention eventually produced the energy crisis of the 1970s and 1980s.

The World War I Years

The laissez-faire era for petroleum ended rather abruptly during World War
I. The war needs of the United States and the Allies were such, it was maintained, that large and steady amounts of diesel fuel (the U. S. Navy was consuming almost 6 million barrels a year by 1918) had to be produced and di-
verted to wartime purposes. Similar reallocations of strategic resources were
taking place throughout the oil industry (and, indeed, throughout the economy), and important executives in the industry agreed to cooperate with the
government in the emergency wartime planning.

Most of the wartime planning arrangements in petroleum were assigned to
the Commodities Section of the Petroleum War Services Committee and to
the Oil Division of the United States Fuel Administration. Revealingly, the
chairman of the War Services Committee was A. C. Bedford, president of
the world's largest oil firm, Standard Oil of New Jersey; and the director
of the Oil Division was a California petroleum engineer (and protégé of Herbert Hoover), Mark Requa.[70] Bedford's appointment was in itself quite a remarkable development since, as historian Carl Solberg has written, only "six
years after the dissolution (of Standard Oil) its chief executive officer was in
Washington helping direct industry's cooperation with government."[71] Even
more interesting, perhaps, is the fact that when the War Services Committee
was dissolved at the end of the hostilities, Bedford became the chairman of
the newly formed trade association, the American Petroleum Institute. API
was created, in its own words, "to afford a means of cooperation with the government in all matters of national concern."[72] Thus in the short space of less
than a decade, petroleum industry and federal government relations had
taken a 180-degree turnabout from noninterference, even apathy, to vigorous
"cooperation" (one might say, collusion) and accommodation.

Scholars are unanimous in describing these wartime arrangements as cooperative, as a unique experiment in government and central industry planning.[73] The Oil Division of the U. S. Fuel Administration in cooperation
with the War Services Committee, was responsible for determining oil production and for allocating crude supplies among various refiners. In short,
these governmental organizations, with the coordinating services of leading
business interests, had the legal power to operate the oil industry as a cartel,
eliminating what was described as "unnecessary waste" (competition), and
making centralized pricing and allocative decisions for the industry as a
whole. Thus, the wartime experiment in "planning" (i.e., planning by political agents to satisfy political interests rather than by consumers, investors,
and entrepreneurs to meet consumer demand) created what had previously
been unobtainable: a governmentally sanctioned cartel in oil.

The Post-War Years and Depression

When the war ended, a strong sentiment among oil industry leaders existed for continuing the War Services Committee's policy of cooperation and supervised competition toward the petroleum industry. For example, most influential oil spokesmen heartily approved of President Coolidge's Federal Oil Conservation Board created in 1924, and most endorsed that board's early recommendations for compulsory withholding of oil resources and state prorationing of oil.[74] The American Petroleum Institute consistently advocated enforced cooperation among oil companies and various regulatory schemes to limit production.[75] A majority of the API directors led by the outspoken Henry Doherty of Cities Service Company favored federal regulation of production in 1927.[76] More explicitly interventionist, the Independent Petroleum Association of America (IPAA) did not even pretend to hide behind the mantle of free enterprise. They consistently advocated strong state regulatory control over crude oil production and a tariff on foreign crude oil, and even sanctioned the declaration of martial law and the use of National Guard troops in order to enforce state prorationing (state quotas on production) by armed force in Texas and Oklahoma during the early 1930s. (Much to the delight of the independents, by the way, some eastern Texas crude oil prices rose from 10 cents a barrel in August 1931 to 85 cents a barrel in June 1932).[77]

But it was during the Depression of the 1930s, and particularly with respect to the National Recovery Act (NRA) of 1933, that all measure of pretense concerning free enterprise was abandoned by oil businessmen.[78] Under the Act's separate oil-code section, which was actually written by the American Petroleum Institute, the production of crude oil was to be coordinated by law with demand. State prorationing laws were to receive federal support. Interstate and foreign shipments of oil were restricted by quotas that were to be determined by Secretary of the Interior Ickes and a Petroleum Administrative Board. The Reserve Act of 1932 had already imposed import duties on crude and even higher duties on refined products mostly at the urging of the IPAA. By the end of 1933, in sum, important government and business interests had succeeded in cartelizing domestic petroleum production.

There were four problems that would have made the producer cartel unstable and they were all eventually accommodated. In 1935 the Interstate Compact to Conserve Oil and Gas was created (C. B. Ames of Texaco had been a leading industry advocate of this legislation) to coordinate and dovetail decisions on proration in the various states. Following this, when the Supreme Court swept away the entire National Industrial Recovery Act (NRA) in 1935, the Congress—without hearings—passed Texas Senator Connally's bill (dubbed the Connally "Hot Oil" Act) that made it illegal to transport interstate oil produced in violation of state proration requirements. And finally the courts, including the Supreme Court, declared state proration to be perfectly constitutional, since its announced intent was conservation of resources in the "public interest," with only an alleged incidental effect on price.

The final loophole in the domestic crude oil cartel was closed by President Eisenhower in 1959. At the intense urging of small independent crude oil producers, mandatory import quotas were imposed on foreign crude oil. Import controls were also endorsed by API and the National Petroleum Council.[79] Thus the last vestige of a dwindling laissez-faire in crude oil production and selling was eliminated, and the industry–government arrangement legitimizing control over crude oil supplies was virtually complete.

World War II and Mideast Oil

World War II and the immediate post-war period were years of intense cooperation and accommodation between the petroleum industry and government. Wartime emergency regulation recreated the militarist central planning and allocation system of World War I. Further, the federal government directly supported the oil industry's war effort with generous tanker subsidies, important pipeline construction, and various other direct and indirect subsidies. In the immediate post-war period, under the auspices of Marshall Plan reconstruction, a substantial portion of the European recovery aid from United States taxpayers went directly to pay for oil shipped by large American oil companies exploiting "concessions" in several Persian Gulf countries.[80] The oil often was sold profitably at prices based on the higher Texas crude oil rates, and not on local market conditions.

Government and industry worked together abroad during those years to control foreign oil sources, especially in the Middle East. With U. S. State Department assistance, foreign oil concessions were gained by American oil companies in many important Persian Gulf oil countries. This development was encouraged for a variety of reasons. In the first place, the domestic proration cartel required worldwide supply control, and foreign supplies were cheap and the wells incredibly prolific. Second, after 1950, "royalty payments" to foreign governments became "taxes" in the lexicon of the Internal Revenue Service, and these were deductible dollar-for-dollar from domestic tax obligations; such a development encouraged foreign oil investments. And finally, the U. S. military's strategic thinking in the post-World War II period was to "secure cheap foreign oil under American control" and, accordingly, conserve domestic supplies of crude for "national security" purposes. Thus, not surprisingly, the strategy and policy objectives of the government and the oil industry with respect to foreign oil were in remarkable coincidence during this period. And with world oil supplies under fairly tight control, the nominal price of crude oil remained remarkably, and uncharacteristically, stable between 1947 and 1967.

The Late 1960s and Beyond

The era of stability in oil prices ended abruptly toward the end of the 1960s. There were many reasons for this development, and some are clearly related to the previous discussion. For example, after 1969—and especially at the time of the OPEC boycott period in late 1973—it became increasingly evident that American oil companies had lost their nearly unilateral power to determine production levels and prices for foreign crude oil.

Although American companies held important concessions abroad, host foreign governments increasingly decided to withdraw a portion, and then eventually all, of these so-called concessionary privileges. They demanded and received an increase in their oil royalties, and then, in many important producing areas (Saudia Arabia in particular) assumed strong national control over crude oil production. Thus, lacking defensible property rights, the American oil companies proceeded to lose control over resources which they had never really owned in the first place. The result was a sharp increase in the posted price for foreign oil and the beginning of what the public has called the energy crisis.

Two additional factors which led to higher oil prices were the explosive domestic inflation fueled by the Federal Reserve, and the higher costs imposed on the oil industry by anti-pollution laws and a concern for a cleaner environment. In the short period from 1967 to 1971, emission-control equipment on automobiles sharply increased gasoline consumption; the Alaskan pipeline was delayed for 5 years due to environmentalist legal challenges; the oil well spill off Santa Barbara in 1969 prompted a four-year moratorium on California offshore drilling, and a two-year federal moratorium; oil refinery construction was repeatedly delayed, or abandoned altogether, because of environmentalist concern; and, most importantly, the Clean Air Act and various state laws restricting sulfur emissions prompted a massive industry shift from cheaper, high-sulfur ("dirty") fuel oil to low-sulfur oil, especially by electric utilities in the Northeast.[81]

It is not being suggested here that this concern for a cleaner environment was or is misplaced; far from it. Rather, this sharp shift in environmental concern in the late 1960s tended to increase the demand, decrease the supply, and otherwise increase the explicit cost and price of oil and oil products.

Even more deeply, perhaps, this environmental concern can be understood as a political backlash against the cavalier views on pollution held by many

industry spokesmen up to that time. Pollution, after all, is a nonvoluntary exchange that, like theft, violates the fundamental assumption of the market
economy; that is, the sanctity of property rights. It is a market "intervention"
in precisely the same respect as the other interventions that have been reviewed: It tends to promote the interests of some at the expense of others.
Unfortunately, the present environmental regulations are not based on property rights. Rather than instituting property rights in water, land, and other
resources in conjunction with a system of common law torts for rights violations, the present restrictions on pollution activity are political and bureau-
cratic, and hence subject to the prevailing political winds, which may well be
antienvironmental in the future.

Price Regulation and Allocation Controls: The Energy Crisis

Natural gas prices at the wellhead came under Federal Power Commission
(FPC) regulation beginning in 1954 with the *Phillips* decision, and rates were
effectively frozen at 1960 levels during the entire decade of the 1960s. Prices
for crude oil produced domestically were regulated under the Nixon controls
of August 1971, and were first controlled by the Federal Energy Administration (FEA) and then by the Department of Energy. As a direct result of the
price regulation, both interstate natural gas and "old" domestically produced
oil sold well below free market or world market prices for decades.

Price-fixing in crude oil and natural gas during this inflationary period resulted in predictable consequences.[82] Natural gas shortages in the interstate
pipelines brought about by governmental price-fixing prompted the rationing
and federal allocation of natural gas. Shortages in domestic crude prompted
refiners to increase their demand for imported crude oil which propped up
the OPEC pricing system. In addition, regulation of the price of crude oil affected some refiners more severely than others, and resulted in important
competitive difficulties in the marketplace. Historically many independent refiners had relied on cheap foreign crude in order to compete with larger companies that had their own domestic suppliers. In the 1970s, however, as foreign crude prices skyrocketed and domestic prices remained regulated,
independent refiners and marketers began to complain bitterly that the crude
cost differentials made effective competition with the larger companies all but
impossible. Thus to remedy the competitive inequities produced by its own
crude-oil price regulation, the FEA instituted various buy–sell and entitle-
ment programs to insure independent refiners access to crude oil at "fair"
prices.

There is little direct evidence that the oil or natural gas industry favored
the initial system of price controls; indeed, there is some evidence that certain

segments of these industries bitterly opposed early regulation.[83] What does seem certain in oil, however, is that after the regulation was in place for some months, important independent oil refiners and marketers began to lobby frantically for an extension and continuation of the control program, and for modifications that would enhance their ability to maintain or increase their market share vis-à-vis the major oil companies.[84] Led in their interventionist efforts by the Independent Refiners Association of America, industry representatives testified before various congressional committees that the very survival of the independent refiner and marketer depended mightily upon continued "government action to allocate crude oil and petroleum products."[85] And although some oil men occasionally gave lip service to the desirability of a return to the free market, such visions were framed in very long-run terms; in the short run, the talk was of "working within the control system," offering "improvements" in the regulations, and fighting to keep those parts of the system that benefited specific companies or specific segments of the industry.

One example was the almost classic interventionist debate that occurred over the so-called small-refiner bias in the entitlements program administered by the FEA.[86] The Justice Department itself had maintained that the small-refiner entitlements bias represented an enormous subsidy to small refiners, amounting in the first six months of 1976 to some $211 million. Yet Frank Woods, Jr., chairman of the American Petroleum Refiners Association, and Jason Dryer, executive secretary of the Independent Refiners Association of America, testified before the FEA that the small-refiner "bias" ought to be continued in the interests of "fair competition" with larger and more efficient refiners. Several small refiners that directly benefited from the entitlements bias also strongly supported the continuation of the subsidy program. The larger refiners, as might be expected, opposed the continuation of the entitlements bias and, indeed, of the entire entitlements program itself.

The same sort of industry split occurred in the late 1970 with respect to the continuation of the FEA's mandatory "buy–sell" program.[87] Crude-oil sellers and the Justice Department argued that the program ought to be abandoned, since the conditions that gave rise to it—the 1973 oil embargo—had clearly ended. Crude-oil buyers, on the other hand, argued before the FEA that the program had to be continued. The Independent Refiners Association of America went on record as strongly favoring continued government allocation of crude oil. Though forced to admit that small refiners had physical access to crude, they maintained that such refiners still did not have "adequate access in economic terms." Further, they argued that since the supplies of domestic crude were shrinking, the buy–sell arrangements for foreign oil would become even more necessary—even "critically important"—as time went on.

Interventionist politics has not, of course, been a monopoly of small refiners or trade associations that represent their interests. The larger refiners and the more prestigious trade associations have habitually supported particular governmental energy controls, ERDA (Energy Research and Development Administration) subsidies for energy development, forced conservation, the synfuels program, and import restrictions. Thornton Bradshaw, formerly president of ARCO, repeatedly championed governmentally enforced "conservation," and was totally explicit in recommending permanent national planning in energy.[88] During the 1973–1974 oil boycott period, some leading oil executives from Texaco, Exxon, and ARCO supported stern federal "conservationist" measures, including gasoline rationing.[89] The American Petroleum Institute, supposedly committed to an unregulated market in petroleum as a long-run goal, has repeatedly adopted public positions at variance with the alleged commitment.[90] The same can easily be said of several other trade associations in petroleum, such as the Kansas Independent Producers, the Texas Independent Producers and Royalty Owners Association, and the National Congress of Petroleum Retailers.[91] All have given lip service to popular support for a full restoration of the free market while at the same time recommending continued controls or regulations designed to further their own self-interest or the self-interest of their members.

The predictable result of this interventionist process was the piecemeal creation of a crazy-quilt system of regulatory privileges and punishments that made no economic sense whatever, but necessarily generated great uncertainty and a vast misallocation of energy resources.[92] In short, business and government interventionism led inexorably to the energy crisis of the 1970s and early 1980's.

Conclusion

The antitrust implications of this extended legal and historical analysis should be apparent. Monopoly power in the petroleum industry—to the extent that it does exist—is not the inevitable product of any free-market process, but has resulted from specific instances of business and government interventionism. In the absence of interventionism, petroleum markets would have been competitive and coordinated, and resources would have been allocated efficiently from a consumer perspective. But as the markets became increasingly subsidized and regulated, the mutual gains and advantages associated with open competition were strikingly diminished. It should be apparent that a thorough and complete deregulation—and not any sort of antitrust policy—is the appropriate public response for restoring a competitive market in petroleum and in natural gas.

NOTES

1. *United States v. E. C. Knight Co.*, 156 U.S.1 (1895).

2. Elliot Jones, *The Trust Problem in the United States* (New York: The Macmillan Co. 1923), p. 44.

3. Donald Dewey, *Monopoly in Economics and Law* (Chicago: Rand McNally and Company, 1966), p. 214.

4. *United States v. E. C. Knight Co.*, 156 U.S., 328–329.

5. *Ibid.*, p. 331 (emphasis added).

6. *Sugar Institute et al. v. United States*, 297 U.S. (1936) 533, 565. I am indebted to Yale Brozen for calling my attention to the rapid decline in American Sugar's market share in the 1890s.

7. Price information is taken from Elliot Jones, *The Trust Problem in the United States* (New York: The Macmillan Company, 1923), p. 117. Additional information can be found in Joshua Bernhart, *The Sugar Industry and the Federal Government* (Washington, D.C.: Sugar Statistical Service, 1948), p. 21. For a revisionist history of the Sugar Trust with specific emphasis on the relationship between market concentration and tariff policy, see Richard Zerbe, "The American Sugar Refining Company, 1887–1914: The Story of a Monopoly," *Journal of Law and Economics*, Vol. 12 (Oct. 1969), pp. 339–375.

8. *Northern Securities Co. et al. v. United States*, 193 U.S. 197 (1904).

9. *Ibid.*, p. 327 (emphasis added).

10. 166 U.S. 290 (1897).

11. 120 Fed. Reporter 721, 724.

12. 193 U.S. 369.

13. *Ibid.*, pp. 402–403.

14. *Ibid.*, pp. 405–406.

15. *Ibid.*, p. 409.

16. *Ibid.*, p. 411.

17. Balthasar Henry Meyer, "A History of the Northern Securities Case," in *Wisconsin University Bulletins*, Vol. I (1904–1906), p. 305. The trial court had raised, but had dismissed, these issues. See *ibid.*, pp. 273–274.

18. Dewey, *op. cit.*, pp. 214–216.

19. Meyer, *op. cit.*, p. 227.

20. *Ibid.*, p. 228.

21. *Ibid.*, p. 227.

22. *Ibid.*, p. 231.

23. Dewey, *op. cit.*, pp. 214–215.

24. Meyer, *op. cit.*, p. 235.

25. *Ibid.*, p. 236.

26. 193 U.S. 238.
27. For general discussions of the beginnings of the petroleum industry, see J. Stanley Clark, *The Oil Century* (Norman: The University of Oklahoma Press, 1958); Albert Z. Carr, *John D. Rockefeller's Secret Weapon* (New York: McGraw-Hill, 1962); Jules Abels, *The Rockefeller Billions* (New York: Macmillan Company, 1965); Ralph and Muriel Hidy, *Pioneering in Big Business, 1882-1911: History of the Standard Oil Company (New Jersey)* (New York: Harper and Row, 1955); Harold Williamson and Arnold Daum, *The American Petroleum Industry* (Evanston, Ill.: Northwestern University Press, 1959); Ida Tarbell, *The History of the Standard Oil Company* (New York: Peter Smith, 1950); Allan Nevins, *Study in Power: John D. Rockefeller*, 2 Vols. (New York: Charles Scribner's Sons, 1953); and John Chamberlain, *The Enterprising Americans: A Business History of the United States* (New York: Harper and Row, 1963), pp. 146-155.
28. Tarbell, *op. cit.*, p. 383.
29. Abels, *op. cit.*, p. 51.
30. *Ibid.*
31. *Ibid.*, p. 65. *The Petroleum Almanac* (New York: National Industrial Conference Board, 1946) lists 170 "establishments" in 1869. See p. 87.
32. Abels, *op. cit.*, p. 83.
33. *Ibid.*, pp. 106-108. Also, see Williamson and Daum, *op. cit.*, p. 471.
34. Tarbell, *op. cit.*, p. 384.
35. Abels, *op. cit.*, p. 201.
36. John S. McGee, "Predatory Price Cutting: The Standard Oil (N.J.) Case," *Journal of Law and Economics*, Vol. 1 (October 1958), pp. 144-148.
37. Tarbell, *op. cit.*, pp. 384-385.
38. Abels, *op. cit.*, p. 98. And this might have been as much as 60 percent less than the industry average; see Williamson and Daum, *op. cit.*, pp. 483-384.
39. An excellent and brief discussion of the issues involved here appears in Alfred D. Chandler, Jr., ed., *The Railroads: The Nation's First Big Business: Sources and Readings* (New York: Harcourt, Brace and World, 1965), pp. 159-172.
40. Louis M. Hacker, *The World of Andrew Carnegie: 1865-1901* (Philadelphia: J. B. Lippincott, 1968), pp. 206-210.
41. Gabriel Kolko, *Railroads and Regulation, 1877-1916* (Princeton: Princeton University Press, 1965), Introduction and Chapter One.
42. Matthew Josephson, *The Robber Barons* (New York: Harcourt, Brace and Company, 1934), p. 113.
43. McGee, *op. cit.*, pp. 137-169.
44. *Ibid.*, p. 168.
45. Abels, *op. cit.*, p. 154.
46. Tarbell, *op. cit.*, pp. 240-241.
47. *Ibid.*, p. 385.

48. Hidy and Hidy, *op. cit.*, p. 422.

49. *Ibid.*, p. 289.

50. Clark, *op. cit.*, p. 127.

51. *Ibid.*, p. 123.

52. Gabriel Kolko, *The Triumph of Conservatism* (New York: The Free Press of Glencoe, 1963), pp. 40–42.

53. *Ibid.*, p. 40. Also, see McGee, *op. cit.*, p. 156, and *The Petroleum Almanac*, p. 87.

54. Hidy and Hidy, *op. cit.*, p. 477.

55. *Ibid.*, p. 407.

56. *Ibid.*, p. 683.

57. *United States v. Standard Oil Company*, 173 Fed. Reporter 179.

58. *Ibid.*, p. 185 (emphasis added).

59. *Ibid.*, pp. 189–190 (emphasis added).

60. *Ibid.*, p. 193.

61. *Standard Oil Company of New Jersey v. United States*, 221 U.S. 1.

62. *Ibid.*, p. 60.

63. *Ibid.*, p. 58 (emphasis added).

64. *Ibid.*, p. 76 (emphasis added).

65. Though a great portion of the actual trial was taken up with these charges, Standard Oil offered rebuttal on all points. See Hidy and Hidy, *op. cit.*, pp. 693–697.

66. 221 U.S. 70.

67. *Ibid.*, p. 74 (emphasis added).

68. *Ibid.*, p. 75 (emphasis added).

69. *Ibid.*, pp. 76–77 (emphasis added).

70. Gerald D. Nash, *United States Oil Policy, 1890–1964* (Pittsburgh: University of Pittsburgh Press, 1968), p. 30.

71. Carl Solberg, *Oil Power* (New York: Mason Charter, 1976), p. 73.

72. Quoted in D. T. Armentano, "Petroleum, Politics, and Prices" *Reason* (June 1974), p. 10.

73. See, for instance, Nash, *op. cit.*, pp. 24–38.

74. *Ibid.*, pp. 84–85.

75. Erich W. Zimmerman, *Conservation in the Production of Petroleum: A Study in Industrial Control*, Petroleum Monograph Series, Vol. 2 (New Haven: Yale University Press, 1957), p. 115.

76. Nash, *op. cit.*, p. 91.

77. *Ibid.*, p. 118.

78. For a review of production controls in petroleum, see Stephen L. McDonald, *Petroleum Conservation in the United States* (Baltimore: The Johns Hopkins

Press, 1971); or see Wallace Lovejoy and Paul Homan, *Economic Aspects of Conservation Regulation* (Baltimore: The Johns Hopkins Press, 1967).

79. Robert Engler, *The Brotherhood of Oil: Energy Policy and the Public Interest* (Chicago: University of Chicago Press, 1977), p. 96.

80. Solberg, *op. cit.*, p. 181.

81. *National Petroleum News* (December 1973), p. 32. See also *National Petroleum News Factbook* (New York: McGraw-Hill, mid-May, 1973), p. 77.

82. For a review of the economic effects of regulation in petroleum see Walter Mead, "Petroleum: An Unregulated Industry?" in *Energy Supply and Government Policy*, Robert Kalter and William Vogely, eds. (Ithaca: Cornell University Press, 1976). See also Edward Mitchell, *U.S. Energy Policy: A Primer* (Washington: American Enterprise Institute for Public Policy Research, 1974); and Paul MacAvoy, "The Regulation Induced Shortage of Natural Gas," *Journal of Law and Economics*, Vol. 14 (April 1971).

83. For the gas and oil industry's opposition to wellhead pice controls in the *Phillips* case, see Robet Engler, *The Politics of Oil* (Chicago: University of Chicago Press, 1967), pp. 130–131.

84. See, for instance, the testimony of Ashland Oil, *Oversight-Mandatory Petroleum Allocation*, Hearings before the Committee on Interior and Insular Affairs, U.S. Senate, 93rd Congress, 2nd Session (Washington: 1974) Part 1, pp. 102 ff. Also see Robert Engler, *The Brotherhood of Oil*, p. 253.

85. *Oil and Gas Journal*, Vol. 72, No. 25 (June 24, 1974), p. 90.

86. *Oil and Gas Journal* (March 21, 1977), pp. 70–71.

87. *Oil and Gas Journal* (April 25, 1977), p. 84.

88. Thornton Bradshaw, "My Case for National Planning," *Fortune* (February 1977).

89. *Oil and Gas Journal*, Vol. 71, No. 49 (December 3, 1973), p. 13.

90. API has, for instance, supported some import controls. See Robert Engler, *The Brotherhood of Oil*, p. 90.

91. *The Oil Daily* (April 13, 1977), p. 8. See also *Oil Gram* (December 15, 1976).

92. Kenneth Arrow and Joseph Kalt, "Why Oil Prices Should be Decontrolled," *Regulation* (September/October 1979), pp. 13–17.

CHAPTER FOUR

Monopoly in Business History: From American Tobacco (1911) To Telex–IBM (1975)

Orthodox competition theory suggests that consumers can be injured in open markets by business organizations that acquire and exercise monopoly power. In addition, there are alleged to be social welfare losses when monopoly misallocates resources relative to some optimal resource employment that occurs under perfectly competitive conditions. Finally, firms with monopoly power might subvert the public interest through either a retardation of technological development or through wasteful expenditures on non-price competition.

It has already been argued that such a theory of business power is seriously flawed, and that no such behavior ought to be in evidence in an unregulated market. We now turn to an examination of some additional classic monopoly cases, in order to determine whether there is evidence that unregulated business organizations abuse the public interest from an instrumentalist perspective. We recognize that, in a strict sense, cases cannot prove or disprove any economic theory. The cases are presented only with the understanding that they can be illustrative of the theoretical forces at work in a competitive market.

THE AMERICAN TOBACCO COMPANY CASE (1911)

The Cigarette Industry in America

Although cigarettes appeared in America in the early 1850s and were unpopular enough with the government to rate their own special penalty tax of up to $5 per thousand by 1868, there was hardly what could be termed a "cigarette manufacturing industry" prior to 1880.[1] Up to that point, the cigarette business had been concentrated in the New York City area where many small firms employed immigrant labor to hand roll mostly blends of Turkish tobaccos. The raw material was relatively expensive and the hand-rolling operation was relatively inefficient; also, there appeared to be great popular reluctance to smoking the small cigarettes, especially the manufactured variety. Consequently, the outputs and markets for cigarettes were severely limited. Total output of all domestically produced cigarettes was never more than 500 million in any one year prior to 1880.[2]

But the rapid shift in public taste to Virginia tobacco blends, the adoption of machinery for manufacturing cigarettes, and the extensive use of advertising to popularize particular brands or blends of tobaccos, changed the industry radically in the 1880s.

Machines that manufactured cigarettes quickly were rapidly being improved, reducing the costs of production and placing a profit premium on mechanization. Labor costs were reduced from 85 cents per thousand without machines to 2 cents per thousand with machines.[3] While an expert hand roller could make approximately 2000 "smokes" a day, a properly operating cigarette machine could produce 100,000.[4] A few leased cigarette machines—particularly the Bonsack model—could, in a very short time, generate the entire yearly output of any small cigarette firm. Thus with the introduction of machines, the optimum size of an efficient cigarette firm was increased manyfold, and the industry emphasis shifted to creating and expanding the demand for particular brands of cigarettes. Advertising and marketing expenditures began in earnest in the late 1880s, and it was not at all surprising to find five large firms doing most of the trade in manufactured cigarettes by 1889. Though there were hundreds of small cigarette producers in that period, the firms of Goodwin and Co., William S. Kimball and Co., Kinney Tobacco, Allen and Binter, and the W. Duke & Sons Co. came to dominate the young industry, and together they did an estimated 90 percent of total domestic cigarette sales.[5]

The American Tobacco Company

The name of James B. Duke is synonomous with cigarettes and with the rapid development of the tobacco industry in this country. Though a relative newcomer to the cigarette industry (he had entered in 1881), Duke quickly pushed his firm into industry leadership by rapidly mechanizing his operations, and by spending large amounts of money on advertising to increase the demand for his products.[6] Duke took huge newspaper ads and rented billboard display space to push "Duke of Durham" and "Cameo" brands. He placed redeemable coupons inside his newly innovated cigarette boxes to popularize "Cross Cut" and "Duke's Best." He also enticed jobbers and retailers with special bonus plans and gimmicks if they would handle and promote his products. This unusual marketing approach proved extremely successful, and by 1889, Duke's cigarette firm sold over 30 percent of the total industry output, and the company was netting almost $400,000 a year on gross sales of $4.5 million. Duke's firm was easily the largest and most profitable firm in the manufactured-cigarette industry, and appeared to be growing far more quickly than its rivals.

In January 1890, the five leading cigarette firms merged, forming the American Tobacco Company, and installed J. B. Duke as president. Although competition between the leading firms had been severe in the late 1880s, there is little direct evidence that the combination was the exclusive consequence of a "destructive trade war," as some accounts suggest.[7] Rather, the merger was the inevitable consequence of the economics of the cigarette industry.

The cigarette industry in 1890 was potentially very profitable. The price of leaf tobacco, the raw material, was now historically modest (about 4¢ per pound); the costs of manufacture—even with less than an optimal utilization of equipment—were low; and the existing market prices for cigarettes were already enough to allow adequate returns. Two difficulties appeared to cloud the potential profit picture of the industry: maximum utilization of the most efficient machinery to reduce the cost-per-unit to a minimum; and a severe reduction in total advertising expenditures as a percentage of total output or sales.

A corporate consolidation provided both of the last mentioned economies. Consolidation would allow concentration on those tobacco blends that could be produced most efficiently. Consolidation would also allow substantial economies of scale to be realized in advertising expenditures. Thus, production and selling expenditures could be lowered per unit of output, and profits could grow accordingly. A combination or trust of smaller cigarette firms was, thus, a natural and predictable economic arrangement, since it was more efficient than the formerly decentralized market structure.

To increase its profits still further, American Tobacco also diversified into a number of related product areas. Diversification was to be expected, since cigarettes, although profitable, represented only 3 percent to 5 percent of the entire tobacco industry sales in 1890.[8] Also, the public's changing tastes rapidly made particular brand names and even whole products obsolete, and made any specialization extremely dangerous.[9] Furthermore, there was reportedly a distinct prejudice against machine-made cigarettes, and sales simply did not expand as rapidly as anticipated. While American Tobacco had produced slightly more than 3 billion cigarettes in 1893, they produced only

3.4 billion in 1899, and fewer than 3 billion annually between 1900 and 1905; American's production of cigarettes in 1907 was only 3.9 billion. Moreover, American's share of domestic cigarette sales steadily declined from over 90 percent in 1890, to 74 percent in 1907.[10]

American Tobacco's diversification and growth in the tobacco industry was accomplished through the purchase of existing firms with cash or stock. It is estimated that American may have purchased as many as 250 firms between 1890 and 1907.[11] Some of these acquisitions were competitive cigarette manufacturers, though the bulk of them were not. Most of these acquisitions were made, apparently, to acquire a successful brand name, since brand-name loyalty was the most important asset of any tobacco firm.[12]

The bulk of American Tobacco's acquisitions were firms producing noncigarette tobacco products. For example, diversification into firms that made smoking tobacco, snuff, plug chewing tobacco, and cheroots was begun as early as 1891. These tobacco products were noncompetitive with cigarettes and with each other, had their own particular markets, and used their own particular kinds of leaf tobacco.[13] In 1898, after many years of competitive low-price rivalry,[14] American purchased the leading plug manufacturers, including, at a later date, the large and imporant Ligget and Myers Company. These acquisitions were subsequently organized into the Continnental Tobacco Company, partially owned and completely controlled by Duke and American Tobacco interests. Shortly thereafter, in March 1899, the Union Tobacco Company—manufacturer of the famous "Bull Durham" smoking tobacco—was purchased. The American Snuff Company was then organized in March 1901, with a paid-in capital of $23 million, and the stock was paid out to the three leading, formerly independent snuff manufacturers. The American Cigar Company was also formed in 1901 and became the largest firm in that sector of the tobacco market. In addition, American Tobacco purchased licorice firms, bag firms, box firms, firms that made cigarette machinery, tin foil, and processed scrap tobacco. By 1902, American Tobacco was manufacturing and selling a complete line of tobacco and tobacco-related products, including over 100 brands of cigarettes and over 60 percent of the nation's smoking and chewing tobacco, about 80 percent of the nation's snuff, and 14 percent of its cigars. And when the newly organized Consolidated Tobacco Company, the Continental Tobacco Company, and the American Tobacco Company all merged in October 1904, to form the new American Tobacco Company, popularly called the Tobacco Trust, the last phase of the diversification and consolidation of tobacco properties by Duke was complete. The American Tobacco Company was now a major factor in all phases of the tobacco industry domestically and internationally (although relatively weak in cigars), and its market position would be generally maintained until its dissolution by the courts in 1911.

Acquisitions of the 1890–1910 Period. Though American Tobacco did acquire many firms in all phases of the tobacco business between 1890 and 1910, the total number of their acquisitions must be put in relative perspective. While over 200 acquisitions appears high, and creates the impression that only a few independent tobacco firms remained, the tobacco industry contained thousands of independent firms in the period under consideration. While American Tobacco did the great bulk of its production in a few large manufacturing plants, thousands of smaller independent firms sold their products at a profit in the open market in competition with the Trust.

For example, as many as 300 independent cigarette manufacturers may have existed in 1910.[15] Similarly, while the Trust produced a great percentage of the nation's output of smoking tobacco in fewer than 25 plants, there were as many as 3000 plants manufacturing smoking tobacco in 1910.[16] In addition, the Trust accounted for only seven of the nation's estimated seventy snuff manufacturing plants.[17] And finally, the American Cigar Company operated just twenty-nine manufacturing plants in 1906, while the cigar industry may have contained upwards of 20,000 independent firms.[18] Thus the tobacco industry contained thousands of firms in spite of the acquisition activities of the American Tobacco Company.

The major reason for the numerous amount of rival sellers is not difficult to discover. With or without the Trust, entry into tobacco manufacture was relatively easy. The raw material was available at competitive market rates, and the Trust itself owned no tobacco land whatsoever. Any organization that wanted to compete in the market could purchase the available raw materials and attempt to sell its finished products. In addition, the Trust possessed neither discriminatory transportation rates nor rebates,[19] nor any superior production method protected by patent.[20] Thus, it was not surprising to find thousands of independent firms in an industry where neither the raw material nor the efficient means of production were, or could have been, monopolized.

The major reason for American Tobacco's policy of acquisitions is not difficult to discover either: It made good economic sense. For example, some critics have argued that American Tobacco acquired firms and subsequently shut them down.[21] The crucial point, of course, is that American concentrated tobacco production—and particularly cigarette production, with only two large plants, one in New York and one in Richmond—to achieve quite obvious and substantial scale economies.[22] Most of the facilities obtained through merger were mechanically inefficient and had been acquired to secure the immensely more valuable competitive brand name of some tobacco product. Once procured, the product itself could be produced more efficiently in American Tobacco's own larger, more efficient facilities. Thus, it made good sense and good economics to close down marginally efficient manufacturing operations, and no tears need be shed for the dismantled factories. Certainly there is no evidence that any of the former owners shed such tears, since American Tobacco's merger terms (stock in the Trust or cash) were generous. Thus, the rival companies were not gained just to shut down their plants.

Other economies associated with this acquisition policy were achieved in important, though not so obvious, ways. For example, American Tobacco's huge production made the ownership of its own foil, box, and bag firms almost mandatory; and the advantages and savings to be realized by accurate and continuous deliveries of these products were substantial. Its acquisition of MacAndrews & Forbes and Mell & Rittenhouse—the two leading manufacturers of licorice paste—was predicated on just such cost savings, and on the fact that the Japanese–Russian War threatened Near East licorice supplies and, consequently, American Tobacco's expansion of plug tobacco which contained licorice as one of its ingredients.[23] Independent foil, box, and bag firms still remained in the market place, and at least four other manufacturers sold licorice paste independently of the American Tobacco firms. There is no evidence that American's paste firms would not sell to anyone that demanded licorice at going market prices. Thus, the vertical integration activities of American Tobacco appeared economically sensible and certainly cannot be condemned, in the face of open, competitive markets, as a restraint of trade.

American Tobacco's integration into distribution also realized cost savings. With the virtual elimination of the middleman, the tobacco jobber's not unhealthy margin could be realized by the tobacco manufacturer.[24] Wholly owned retail establishments could also market particular brands more effectively and would themselves become an important advertising and marketing innovation. American Tobacco's United Cigar Stores, the most famous and effective tobacco product's retail chain—with over 1000 stores by 1910 and at least 300 in New York City alone—was certainly innovative in this respect.

There were still other, more subtle economies. Given the location of American Tobacco's facilities, a certain amount of inefficient cross-hauling or cross-freighting was automatically eliminated: American Tobacco could fill orders for finished tobacco products from a number of different manufacturing locations.[25] In those modernly equipped factories labored nonunion help, and this saved American from 10 to 20 percent on its wage expenses vis-a-vis most of its competitors, who employed Tobacco Workers' Union labor.[26] The Tobacco Trust could and did demand prompt settlement of all outstanding accounts (30 days), while it was quite common for smaller manufacturers to wait from two to four months for payment.[27] It could employ fewer salesmen per product, since many of its brands were long established; orders were often even filled by mail without agents of any sort.[28] And lastly, it could and did employ some of the industry's keenest managerial talent,[29] who in turn proceeded to implement and extend the potential efficiencies and economies discussed above.

Policies Toward Consumers and Competitors.   But while the American Tobacco Company enjoyed an increased efficiency, what became of the tobacco consumer and the Trust's competitors? Did American Tobacco simply act like a neoclassical monopolist and restrict output and increase prices? Or did American act like a predatory monopolist and use its market power to lower prices and, consequently, drive its competition from the market? Or did it "limit price" to deter entry and competition?

Actually, there is little evidence that American Tobacco followed any of these monopolistic-like practices: it neither restricted outputs nor engaged, as a general rule, in predatory pricing practices designed to eliminate the competition.[30] For example, American Tobacco's cigarettes (per thousand, less tax) sold for $2.77 in 1895, $2.29 in 1902, and $2.20 in 1907; fine-cut (per pound, less tax) sold for 27 cents in 1895, 33 cents in 1902, and 30 cents in 1907; smoking tobacco sold for 25 cents (per pound, less tax) in 1895, 26.7 cents in 1902, and 30.1 cents in 1907; plug sold for 15.5 cents (per pound, less tax) in 1895, 27.7 cents in 1902, and 30.4 cents in 1907; and little cigars sold for $4.60 (per thousand, less tax) in 1895, $4.37 in 1902, and $3.60 in 1907.[31] In the same period (1895–1907), the price of leaf tobacco per pound rose from 6 to 10.5 cents.[32] Thus, the pricing record indicated above for tobacco products was accomplished during a period when the price of the essential raw material had increased approximately 40 percent.

Predatory practices are expensive and it is not usually profitable to attempt to eliminate competition through this technique. This would be especially true in an industry where market entry was relatively easy, where nonprice competitive factors were crucial, and where there were hundreds, even thousands, of competitive sellers already in existence. Such a general policy on the part of American Tobacco would have been foolish and foolhardy, and no such general policy was attempted. Although there may have been some isolated instances where price-cutting played an important role in merger or consolidation, such practices were not the general rule.[33]

The American Tobacco Decision

The comments and analysis above concerning American Tobacco's industrial efficiency and price policy are certainly not original with this account. The same observations can be discovered in a reading of a Circuit Court decision (*U.S. v. American Tobacco*, 164 Federal Reporter 700, 1908), in which it

was determined that American Tobacco had violated the Sherman Antitrust
Act. Although Judge Lacombe found American guilty of violating the Sherman Act, he stated, with respect to the economic issues involved, that:

> The record in this case does *not* indicate that there has been any increases in
> the price of tobacco products to the consumer. There is an *absence* of persua-
> sive evidence that by unfair competition or improper practices independent
> dealers have been dragooned into giving up their individual enterprises and
> selling out to the principal defendant . . . During the existence of the American
> Tobacco Company new enterprises have been started, some with small capital,
> in competition with it, *and have thriven.* The price of leaf tobacco—and raw
> material—except for one brief period of abnormal conditions, has steadily *in-
> creased,* until it has nearly doubled, while at the same time 150,000 additional
> acres have been devoted to tobacco crops and the consumption of leaf has
> greatly increased. Through the enterprise of defendant and at a large expense
> new markets for American tobacco have been opened or developed in India,
> China, and elsewhere.[34]

Judge Noyes, while concurring with Judge Lacombe in American Tobacco's
legal guilt, also appeared to concur in the economic issues involved.

> Insofar as combinations result from the operation of economic principles, it
> may be doubtful whether they should be stayed at all by legislation . . . It may
> be that the present antitrust statute should be amended and made applicable
> only to those combinations which unreasonably restrain trade—that it should
> draw a line between those combinations which work for good and those which
> work for evil. But these are all legislative, and not judicial, questions.[35]

It was Judge Ward (dissenting), however, who crystalized the important economic issues in this case.

> So far as the volume of trade in tobacco is concerned, the proofs show that it
> has *enormously increased* from the raw material to the manufactured product
> since the combinations, and, so far as the price of the product is concerned,
> that it has *not been increased* to the consumer and has varied *only* as the price
> of the raw material of leaf tobacco has varied.

> The purpose of the combination was not to restrain trade or prevent competi-
> tion . . . but, by intelligent economies, to increase the volume and the profits of
> the business in which the parties engaged.[36]

> A perusal of the record satisfied me that their [American Tobacco's] purpose
> and conduct were not illegal or oppressive, but that they strove, as every busi-
> nessman strives, to increase their business, and that their great success is a natu-
> ral growth resulting from industry, intelligence, and economy, doubtless largely
> helped by the volume of business done and the great capital at command.[37]

Yet, although three of the four judges admitted that there was solid evidence to indicate that American Tobacco was efficient, had not raised prices, had expanded outputs, and not depressed leaf prices, and had not "dragooned" competitors, Judge Coxe joined Judges Lacombe and Noyes in concurring that American Tobacco had violated the Sherman Act. Clearly, the conduct and economic performance of the dependent had nothing whatever to do with this decision. American Tobacco was convicted in spite of its economic record because its mergers and acquisitions inherently restrained trade between the now merged or acquired firms, and that violated the Sherman Act as interpreted in 1908. Judge Lacombe made the majority's position explicit:

> [E]very aggregation of individuals or corporations, formerly independent, *immediately upon its formation terminated an existing competition*, whether or not some other competition may subsequently arise. The act as above construed [Sherman Act] prohibits *every* contract or combination in restraint of competition. Size is not made the test: two individuals who have been driving rival express wagons between villages in two contiguous states, who enter into a combination to join forces and operate a single line, restrain as existing competition . . .

> Accepting *this* construction of the statute, as it would seem this Court must accept it, there can be little doubt that it has been violated in this case. . . .the present American Tobacco Company was formed by subsequent merger of the original company with the Continental Tobacco Company and the Consolidated Tobacco Company, and when *that merger* became complete two of its existing competitors in the tobacco business were eliminated.[38]

It was irrelevant to inquire into the economic benefits of the combination, argued Judge Lacombe. It was "not material" to consider subsequent business methods or to judge the effect of the combination on production or prices. The fact that American Tobacco had not abused competitors, tobacco growers, or consumers was "immaterial." The only issue that was material was that "each one of these purchases of existing concerns complained of in the petition was a contract and combination in restraint of competition existing *when it was entered into* and *that* is sufficient to bring it within the ban of this drastic statute."[39] And thus the three Circuit judges (with Judge Ward dissenting) ruled that the American Tobacco Company must be dissolved.

The Supreme Court Decision

The Supreme Court decision written by Justice White in 1911 is a virtual replay of the *Standard Oil* decision of the same year.[40] White suggests that a "rule of reason" be applied to the undisputed facts concerning the activities of the American Tobacco Company.[41] But again, that "rule of reason" does

not include a careful economic analysis of American Tobacco's conduct performance in the period under consideration. All that the Supreme Court did
was to detail the history of the tobacco industry between 1890 and 1907,[42]
and infer from these undisputed facts that the intent and "wrongful purpose"
of American Tobacco must have been to achieve a monopolistic position in
the tobacco industry.[43] This conclusion was "inevitable," said White,[44] and
could be "overwhelmingly established" by reference to the following facts:
(1) the original combination of cigarette firms in 1890 was "impelled" by a
trade war; (2) an "intention existed to use the power of the combination as a
vantage ground to further monopolize the trade in tobacco," and the power
was used, that is, the "plug and snuff wars"; (3) the Trust attempted to con-
ceal the extent of its control with secret agreements and bogus independents;
(4) American Tobacco's policy of vertical integration served as a "barrier to
the entry of others into the tobacco trade"; (5) American Tobacco expended
millions of dollars to purchase plants, "not for the purpose of utilizing them,
but in order to close them up and render them useless for the purposes of
trade"; and (6) there were some agreements not to compete between American and some formerly independent tobacco manufacturers.[45] With these
"facts" in mind, the conclusion was inevitable:

> Indeed, when the results of the undisputed proof which we have stated are fully
> apprehended, and the wrongful acts which they exhibited are considered, there
> come *inevitably to the mind the conviction that it was the danger which it was
> deemed would arise to individual liberty and the public well-being from acts
> like those which this record exhibits,* which led the legislative mind to conceive
> and enact the anti-trust act . . .[46]

But as has been demonstrated in our review of the history of the American
Tobacco Company, whether such acts are a danger to individual liberty and
to the public well-being *is* a matter of dispute. To inevitably deduce, for example, that purchasing plants and closing them down endangers liberty or
the public well-being, without an economic analysis of the costs and benefits
of such an action, is an unwarranted and faulty inference. If the agreements
to secure these plants were voluntarily arrived at, then individual liberty was
not endangered. If the plants closed down by American Tobacco were inefficient, and if the tobacco products continued to be produced at larger, more
efficient factories, then the danger to the public well-being is not obvious.
The same kind of questions can be raised about the rest of the "undisputed
facts" and "inevitable inferences" in this classic case.

Unfortunately the Supreme Court did not choose to analyze rigorously the
economic issues involved, nor did it choose to employ the rule of reason as an
economic standard to see whether the public well-being had been harmed in

a neoclassical sense. Such an analysis, if performed, would have involved a discussion of prices, outputs, cost savings associated with merger, the growth of competitors (especially in cigarette manufacture), and a host of related issues; no such analysis is discovered in this decision. American Tobacco was convicted of violating the Sherman Act because its acts, contracts, agreements, and combinations were of such "an *unusual* and *wrongful* character as to bring them within the prohibitions of the law."[47] The Circuit Court was directed to devise a plan for partially dissolving the holding company and re-creating a new decentralized market structure that would not violate the monopoly law.

THE UNITED STATES STEEL CORPORATION CASE (1920)

The United States Steel Corporation was formed on April 1, 1901, when ten formerly independent steel companies (three steel producers and seven steel finishers) and one other company (which owned the Mesabi ore mines, some railroads, and some ore-carrying ships) came together to form America's first $1 billion company. The holding company had impressive dimensions (44 percent of the nation's ingot capacity; 66 percent of the nation's total output of steel products), and although its principal architects (Morgan, Carnegie, and Moor) talked of increased industrial efficiency and lower prices, everyone else talked of monopoly and monopoly power.

The Iron and Steel Industry in America

There had been little talk of monopoly in the competitive and decentralized iron and steel industry prior to 1890. On the contrary, the industry and its growth had been the personification of the American industrial dream.[48] From the small forges and pig iron furnaces of the 1850s, it had developed into one of the country's most capital-intensive and progressive industries. Outputs climbed rapidly from 69,000 tons in 1870 to 1.3 million tons in 1880, and 10 million tons in 1900 and twice the British output in that year. Steel rail production increased from 84,000 tons in 1872 (when 800,000 tons of iron rail had also been made), to 291,000 tons in 1875, and over 3 million tons in 1900 (when no iron rail was made).[49] Consequent with the huge output increases, the price of steel rail tumbled from $106 in 1870 to but $17 a ton in 1898.[50] The price and output record on other steel products was similarly impressive.

This remarkable increase in production and decrease in selling price was a direct function of relatively open markets and free competition. The most effective way to illustrate the competitive process is to review the history, progress, and success of one of the industry's most efficient organizations, originally called the Edgar Thompson Company, later known as the Carnegie Company.

The Edgar Thompson Company

In 1873, Andrew Kloman, Henry Phillips, David McCandless, John Scott, David Stewart, William Shinn, and Tom Carnegie each subscribed $50,000, while William Coleman subscribed $100,000, and young Andrew Carnegie put up $250,000 towards the construction of a major steel works on a 107-acre plot of land called Braddocks Field, about 12 miles from Pittsburgh. The men involved in the speculative undertaking were an odd mixture of iron and steel experience, railroad knowledge, and financial interests. Kloman, Phillips, and Coleman were iron and steel men, with over 100 years of metal-making experience between them in their respective areas; McCandless was a prominent Pittsburgh merchant and vice-president of the Exchange National Bank; Stewart was president of the Pittsburgh Locomotive Works; and Scott was a director of the Allegheny Valley Railroad. These men became convinced that the success of the "Bessemer process" for making steel in England, could be duplicated with even more profitability in Pittsburgh. Mr. A. L. Holley—who had already negotiated the original Bessemer patents in 1864, and erected the first American hearths in Troy, New York—was commissioned to lay out the most efficient mill possible, and one capable of producing up to 75,000 ingot tons a year. On September 1, 1875, the first steel rail made at the newly completed steel works was forged; and the Carnegie dominated firm, with strong ties to the Pennsylvania Railroad, was on its way.

Two years after the Edgar Thompson Company was completed, ingot production exceeded rail mill operations and new uses for fabricated steel were pioneered. For example, billets of high-carbon steel were shaped into buggy springs; axle steel replaced crucible steel for railroad cars; and thin steels were developed for plow shares, stovepipes, and cartridge cases. The increasing demand for ingot and steel products prompted the building of a number of pig iron furnaces, and these furnaces turned out to be extremely efficient. In April of 1880, for example, a Thompson furnace produced 2723 tons of pig iron, while consuming 2536 pounds of coke per ton of iron produced. A decade later, 10,075 tons of pig iron could be produced with only 1,847 pounds of coke per ton. And in December 1902, over 17,000 tons of pig iron could be made with but 1,875 pounds of coke per ton.[51]

The technological development in ingot and steel rail production was similarly impressive. By 1880, the Thompson Company could pour over 10,000 tons of steel ingot a month, and an equal tonnage of steel rails could also be accomplished. By November 1881, the figures for ingot and rail were 16,000 and 13,000 tons per month respectively, and the Thompson Company had surpassed the monthly outputs of the Troy, Harrisburg, North Chicago, and Cambria steel producing areas.[52]

In the years that followed, the company expanded operations internally, purchased other steel properties (the Homestead mills in 1883 and the Duquesne mills in 1890), and engaged in extensive vertical integration. Great ore mines on Lake Superior were leased; railroad and steamship interests were obtained; and harbors were built and operated by the company itself. By 1900, the Carnegie Company (the name had been changed in 1881) controlled every movement of its own materials, from the initial mining and transporting of the iron ore to the finishing and shipping out of the iron rail, and the organization was easily one of the most impressive industrial organizations in the world.

In sum, the competitive vigor and economic progressiveness of the steel industry—as represented by its leading firm—was unquestioned. The industry, though geographically concentrated in a few major market areas, contained hundreds of producing firms that actively engaged in price and non-price competition. Gentlemen's agreements and pools to reduce price competition had been attempted, but they had all been short-lived and they had all collapsed.[53]

The formation of Federal Steel, National Steel, National Tube, American Bridge, and the American Sheet Steel Company in the 1898–1900 period, however, raised competitive eyebrows. These new incorporations were formed by the combination of smaller, regional steelmakers or fabricators, and although the combinations appeared economically logical, it also appeared that such combinations could reduce competition in the steel industry. And when these firms, the giant Carnegie Company steel works, and eight other major steel firms all combined to become the giant holding company, United States Steel Corporation, in 1901, the insinuation that competition would be lessened considerably was a distinct possibility. Thus, there was little surprise when on the heels of success in *Standard Oil* and *American Tobacco*, the Justice Department brought civil suit against U.S. Steel, claiming repeated violations of the Sherman Act and asking divestiture as a remedy.

The District Court Decision

Had United States Steel unreasonably restrained trade or commerce in the steel industry, and had it monopolized or attempted to monopolize the market in steel and steel products between 1901 and 1911? The U.S. District Court of New Jersey on June 3, 1915,[54] answered no on both counts, and the Supreme Court agreed in a close 4–3 decision some years later.[55] Although

Supreme Court Justice McKenna found U.S. Steel of "impressive size" and "equal or nearly equal to them [competitors] all . . . its power over prices was not and is not commensurate with its power to produce . . . we must adhere to the law, and the law does not make mere size an offense. It, we repeat, requires overt acts . . ."[56] Since the majority on the Supreme Court in 1920 had found no "overt acts" that violated the statute, the corporation was not guilty.

Unlike the oil and tobacco cases previously discussed, the *U.S. Steel* case was heard and decided on the relevant conduct performance facts surrounding competition in the steel industry between 1901 and 1911. For example, in the lower court decision of 1915, District Judge Buffington[57] (with Judges Wooley, Hunt, and McPherson concurring)[58] explained that U. S. Steel's position in the steel market between 1901 and 1911 had declined in relative percentage terms in every important iron–steel product category except pig iron; there its percentage had increased slightly from 43 percent in 1901 to 45 percent in 1911.[59] But in the crucial area of "finished rolled product," for instance, U.S. Steel's share of the market had declined from 50.1 percent in 1901, to 46 percent in 1911; in steel ingot production, it had dropped from 66 percent to 54 percent; and in wire nails, it had fallen from 67 percent to 55 percent. In addition, continued Buffington, U.S. Steel's competitors managed to produce 78 percent of all domestic wire netting, fencing, and other wire products, and almost 70 percent of the nation's structural steel that was used in bridges, buildings, and auto frames. In sum, a full 60 percent of all the iron and steel products sold domestically in 1911 were produced by at least eighty business organizations that were competitive with the United States Steel Corporation.[60] Firms like Bethlehem, Pennsylvania, Inland, La-Belle, Jones & Laughlin, Cambria, Colorado, Republic, and Lackawanna grew rapidly between 1901 and 1911. Bethlehem, Inland, LaBelle, and Jones & Laughlin had increased their production 3778.7 percent, 1495.9 percent, 463.3 percent, and 206.7 percent, respectively, in the period 1901 to 1911.[61] The U.S. Steel Corporation, on the other hand, had increased its total output less than 40 percent, and its relative position in the domestic market had accordingly declined.[62] As far as Judge Buffington was concerned, the giant steel firm had not monopolized the steel industry's output, and the trends in the industry were all going in the other direction.

The court's position on a possible iron ore monopoly by U.S. Steel was also distinctly clear. U.S. Steel Corporation had no ore monopoly, and "there is no basis on which to attempt ore monopoly."[63] The court was careful to note that all of U.S. Steel's major competitors (notably companies such as Pennsylvania, Maryland, and Bethlehem) had adequate ore supplies that were independent of the U.S. Steel-dominated Lake Superior fields. For example, the court pointed out that rich iron ores were readily available from the great Cornwall beds of Eastern Pennsylvania, or from the Adirondack regions of New York, or from Sweden, Chili, and Cuba. In addition, steel-producing plants on the Pacific Coast had access to pig iron produced and shipped from China and India, and at prices that were more than competitive with eastern mill quotes, including rail freight.[64] In no sense, therefore, was U.S. Steel's position in iron ore or pig iron a detrimental factor to competitive steel industry expansion anywhere in the country.[65]

The court also dismissed the notion that any firm, including U.S. Steel, had the market power to initiate a "ruinous trade war" in the steel industry during the period under consideration. An attempt at selective predatory price cutting would have, according to Judge Buffington, "owing to the sensitiveness and interrelated character of the steel markets, result(ed) in forcing the company that was thus ruinously selling in any particular market or locality to in the same way ruinously lower its prices in *every* other community."[66] But this sort of business conduct (as explained in the Standard Oil and American Tobacco discussions) would threaten to ruin the large firm that had initiated the price reduction. As an empirical clincher, no competitor testified that any such business action had occurred in the period between 1901 and 1911.[67]

One of the most interesting discoveries in the District Court decision is that there was little evidence that U.S. Steel, or the steel industry itself, was able to charge arbitrary monopoly prices, or increase prices by arbitrarily restraining demanded outputs.[68] On the contrary, Judge Buffington noted that there were significant increases in production and reductions in many important steel product prices between 1901 and 1911. For example, wire nail prices fell from $51 to $36; steel bar prices declined from $33 to $25; steel beams went down from $36 to $27; and billets dropped from $27 in 1901 to $24 in 1911. In fact, U.S. Steel's prices on all fabricated products sold domestically declined 19 percent between 1904 and 1912; its prices on all other goods sold fell an average of 11 percent in the same period. And these price decreases occurred at a time when freight rates on coke and limestone had increased more than 10 percent, and wages for steel workers had risen more than 25 percent.[69] Thus pricing in the steel industry certainly appeared to be determined by competition, and there was no acceptable evidence of any general monopoly power over prices or over competitors. As Judge Buffington put it:

The testimony of these men [the competitors of U. S. Steel]—and there is no testimony to the contrary—is that the iron and steel trade in the various products of the steel corporation is and has been open, competitive, and uncontrolled, and that *all* engaged therein have free will and control in selling at their own prices.[70]

And finally as to earnings, the United States Steel Corporation's net return on investment in the period 1901 to 1911 averaged 12 percent.[71]

But what of the famous and much publicized "Gary Dinners"?[72] Though the District Court did admit at one point that the meetings between U.S. Steel and some of its competitors to discuss price and other common interests amounted "to a combination or common action forbidden by the law," they also noted that: (1) the meetings had been started *late* in the period under consideration (November 1907) and had been continued for only fifteen months; (2) their meetings had been the "only instance" of such cooperation and the "whole movement was exceptional"; and (3) the participants in the movement had not meant to act illegally and the whole system had been abandoned before the initiation of the Sherman Act case.[73] Most importantly, however, "a large section of the trade paid little attention, if any, to this effort at cooperation," and "consumers who testified had no difficulty buying at rates sensibly below the prices thus referred to."[74] Thus, the practical economic significance of the "cooperative dinners" was certainly questionable. While the pricing philosophy of the U.S. Steel Corporation may have encouraged price stability in the industry, or at least tempered the usually violent swings in prices in the short run (customers testified at court that this was generally a desirable policy), there is little reason to conclude that any steel prices were "fixed," or that independent pricing decisions by individual competitors based on their own estimation of supply, demand, and competition had been abandoned. Certainly the economic performance of the steel industry in this period would not lead inevitably to that conclusion.

Because of the conduct performance information discussed above, and because U.S. Steel was a major factor in the world steel trade, the District Court and the Supreme Court refused to find the Steel Company guilty of violating the Sherman Act. In 1920 at least, and at last, corporate size itself was no legal offense.

THE ALCOA CASE (1945)

On April 23, 1937, in the Federal District Court for the Southern District of New York, the federal government brought a lengthy antitrust complaint against the Aluminum Company of America, seeking the dissolution of that company as a relief to the petition. Four years, 155 witnesses, 1803 exhibits, and 58,000 trial court pages later, District Court Judge Francis G. Caffey, in an unusual nine-day oral presentation, cleared the firm of all wrongdoing, though he reserved judgment on two counts.[75] The government had made nearly 140 separate charges involving antitrust violations, supposedly ranging from Alcoa's monopolization of bauxite deposits, water power sites, aluminum castings, alumina and virgin ingot aluminum, to the conscious "squeezing" of fabricators and repeated conspiracy with other (foreign) aluminum firms. Judge Caffey found the firm innocent of all the monopoly and conspiracy charges and dismissed them. On appeal by the government to a special Appeals Court acting in lieu of the U. S. Supreme Court, Judge Learned Hand, speaking for the majority, reversed one of Caffey's judgments and found Alcoa guilty of illegally monopolizing virgin ingot aluminum.[76] To comprehend this complex case and the two different judgments, one must place them in the context of the aluminum industry prior to 1937.[77]

The Aluminum Industry in America

Although the element aluminum was discovered and named by Sir Humphrey Davy in 1807, and although Frederic Wohler improved a chemical process whereby pinheads of the new metal could be obtained, it was 21-year-old Charles Hall who discovered (1886) and patented (1889) the first commercially successful method for making aluminum: the electrolysis of a molten alumina solution dissolved in cryolite. Hall, after an intensive search, interested Captain Alfred E. Hunt in the commercial possibilities of the process, and a $20,000 pilot plant called the Pittsburgh Reduction Company was constructed in Pittsburgh in 1888. Hall and Arthur V. Davis, fresh from Amherst College (and later Chairman of the Board of Alcoa), were among the young men who manned the plant day and night, and both helped store the initial tiny outputs of aluminum in the office safe every night for safekeeping. As must be evident, the entire operation was purely speculative.

In 1888 there were no known end uses for the shiny, light metal and no customers. Although the metal had easily recognized industrial possibilities, it was at that time an extremely expensive and scarce material. The first prices for aluminum ingot in the open market ranged between $5 and $8 per pound in 1887. In early 1888, Hall and his co-workers could squeeze no more than 10 pounds of metal a day from the entire operation. The crucial raw material alumina was relatively expensive, and cheap continuous electrical supplies (10 kilowatts of electric power per pound of aluminum produced were required) were simply not available; the original Pittsburgh plant made its own electric power. Aluminum would only become commercially successful if the raw materials could be obtained cheaply, making the price of aluminum competitive with substitute materials.

Through much entrepreneurial effort, outputs of aluminum increased to 50 pounds a day by 1889; over 1000 pounds a day in 1892; and 8000 pounds a day by 1897. In a like fashion and coincident with the same business philosophy, prices of ingot per pound fell from $5 in 1887, to $3 in 1889, to 50 cents in 1899, to 38 cents in 1910. The price of aluminum ingot per pound

(New York) in 1937 was 22 cents, and it fell to 15 cents in 1941. The output increases and price decreases were sustained by extensive explorations and developments of bauxite deposits in Arkansas. Cheap water power sites were secured, and dams and power stations were constructed to generate billions of kilowatts of cheap power; long-term supply contracts with the Pennsylvania Salt Manufacturing Company for steady supplies of alumina were initiated; and end uses for the metal in the wire industry, for surgical instruments and other medical apparatus, and for fabrication into cooking utensils were all developed and promoted by Alcoa. In 1937, the Aluminum Company of America was producing 500 million pounds of metal per year and consuming almost 22 billion kilowatts of electricity in the process.

The Pittsburgh Reduction Company's original patent on the Hall electrolysis process ran from 1889 to 1906. Through a complex set of patent infringement suits, claims, and counter claims, Alcoa managed to extend the legal monopoly on the method for making aluminum until 1910. This four-year extension was accomplished in 1903 when Alcoa purchased the exclusive rights to the "Bradley patents" (which concerned the *heating* of the alumina solution with electricity) from a firm called Cowles Brothers. The patent squabble between Alcoa and Cowles had begun in 1891, when Cowles Brothers (for whom Charles Hall had been employed for two months in 1886) began producing aluminum with the electrolysis method that Hall had patented. The Pittsburgh Reduction Company quickly sued Cowles and won a patent infringement decision in 1893; on appeal, however, the judgment was reversed in 1903. The difficulties involved were that while Hall apparently did have a valid patent on the electrolysis process, the Bradley patents owned by Cowles Brothers dealt with the heating of the alumina solution with electricity and it was also judged valid. Both patented processes were necessary to reduce aluminum commercially—yet the respective patents were the legitimate property of two different firms. Not surprisingly, Cowles Brothers sold the Bradley patents to Pittsburgh Reduction for $1,500,000, some stock, and options to purchase ingot at below-market prices. Thus in 1910, Alcoa was the sole producer—by law and legitimate patent—of primary aluminum, and had been in that business without direct domestic competition for over twenty years.

The 1910–1937 Period

Between 1910 and 1937, various groups tried, unsuccessfully, to enter the business of producing primary aluminum. For instance, a firm called the Southern Aluminum Company had begun construction of a modest reduction works complex in North Carolina in 1912. Southern had French financing, had acquired bauxite deposits, and was nearing the completion stage of its reduction facility, when work was suspended at the outbreak of World War I. Attempts to secure domestic financing failed and the firm was sold eventually to the only interested buyer—the Aluminum Company of America. The story is described in greater detail later in this chapter.

In addition to the Southern Aluminum Company, exploratory investigations concerning the economic feasibility of primary ingot production were begun by a Mr. Lloyd Emory for the wealthy Milwaukee brewing family, the Uihleins, by J. B. Duke, the multimillionaire tobacco and utility entrepreneur, and possibly even by the Ford Motor Company. Certainly all of these groups possessed the financial capital to compete with Alcoa, if they had decided to compete; yet all these explorations were terminated in the planning stage. While hundreds of firms flowed easily into the various fabrication areas for aluminum and aluminum alloyed products, no new domestic virgin ingot competitor dared challenge the preeminent position of the Alcoa Company.

Why no competitors in primary ingot? Simply put, Alcoa had no direct competition for one essential reason: no competitor could expect to match, much less excel, its economic performance during this period. In 1937, Alcoa was producing slightly under one-half billion tons of metal and selling it for 22 cents a pound; its average rate of return on capital investment was 10 percent in the period 1912–1936. It had pioneered an extensive research and development facility that had provided crucial technical breakthroughs in aluminum and related products. For example, Alcoa's research was responsible for major innovations in the processes for the recovery of alumina from fairly low-grade ores, and for the obtaining of 99.99 percent pure aluminum in the electrolysis process. In addition, Alcoa developed dozens of methods to increase the strength and anticorrosiveness of the metal and many alloys used for rolling, forging, and making castings. In short, users of ingot or sheet, and ultimately the consumers of fabricated products made from aluminum by Alcoa, were being served at degrees of excellence, prices, and profit rates that no one could equal or exceed. The risks of direct competition in primary ingot production vis-à-vis the possible gains were simply too great and, rather wisely, potential investors and entrepreneurs took their funds and talents elsewhere. To have attempted to compete with a firm like Alcoa in the 1912–1936 period would likely have been unprofitable and, consequently, an economic mistake. It is not surprising, nor regretable, that Alcoa retained its singular position in domestic primary aluminum ingot production.

But if this analysis is correct, what of the government's many charges in the 1937 Sherman Act case? Did Alcoa exclude competitors by preempting or monopolizing bauxite deposits, water power sites and alumina? Had Alcoa conspired to fix prices with a foreign cartel of producers? Had Alcoa acted monopolistically and illegally restrained trade, and was its position in the aluminum industry a function of illegal monopolization? For an understanding of these conduct-performance issues, one should properly turn to the District Court decision where these charges, and many others, were thoroughly investigated.

The District Court Decision

District Court Judge Caffey began his examination of the charges against Alcoa by noting that Alcoa had been in court before on similar charges. In 1912, Alcoa had accepted a consent degree and had agreed not to enter into restrictive covenants with suppliers or with foreign aluminum producers; Caffey noted that Alcoa had already abandoned such agreements prior to the beginning of that legal proceeding. In another, more complex legal action brought by the Federal Trade Commission in 1925, the FTC examiner found heavily in favor of Alcoa. Since the issues examined and decided in that lengthy hearing (10,000 pages of testimony) were similar to those enumerated in the government's latest petition, Judge Caffey thought it relevant to present a review of eight of the examiner's major findings. The FTC examiner's report was dated December 16, 1929, and stated:

1. The record also shows that respondent (Alcoa) never attempted to monopolize the scrap market; that it is impossible to do so, the scrap market being so scattered and diversified and in such great available quantities that one concern, no matter how large its purchases, could never corner the said market.

2. Respondent has no monopoly on bauxite (the ore of aluminum); there being sufficient supplies of bauxite in the world, exclusive of respondent's holdings, available for many generations to come.

3. Respondent has no monopoly on water power; its holdings now being only a small percent of the available water power in the world.

4. The respondent does not now nor has it ever attempted to control or dominate the policy of the Aluminum Goods Manufacturing Company.

5. Respondent has never attempted to control and does not now control the market for foreign aluminum in the United States.

6. That foreign aluminum is imported into the United States and competes with respondent in the sale of virgin aluminum ingots.

7. There is no arbitrary or direct differential between the purchase price of scrap aluminum and the selling price of virgin aluminum. The purchase price of scrap depends upon the law of supply and demand.

8. That respondent has never had a monopoly of the sand castings industry of the United States.[78]

While Caffey admitted that the examiner's report of 1929 could not legally bear directly on the present proceedings, he thought it considerably important that "on some of the exact issues now facing me the Commission found squarely in favor of Alcoa."[79]

Judge Caffey then turned to a consideration of the first government allegation. The initial charge of illegal monopolization rested on a paragraph in the 1903 patent agreement between Alcoa and Cowles Brothers which referred to the fact that Cowles had agreed not to engage in the manufacture of aluminum by "electrolysis from a fused bath" in the period 1903–1910. This "restrictive agreement," however, only restated the legal fact that Alcoa had by then acquired legitimate exclusive right to all the Bradley patents (see page 102) and could legally prevent anyone, including Cowles Brothers, from engaging in alumina electrolysis. Caffey noted that the government itself had already admitted that, prior to 1909, Alcoa had obtained a legal and lawful monopoly through patent holdings.[80] He therefore dismissed the charge that the "restrictive" contract was evidence of illegal monopolization.[81]

Caffey then turned to the charge that Alcoa had gained and maintained a monopoly over bauxite and had excluded others from a "fair opportunity" to engage in interstate trade and commerce in that article. Unfortunately the only two witnesses that the government could produce to affirm the bauxite monopoly charge admitted, under oath, that they were neither qualified to furnish such information nor had their respective "searches" into available bauxite deposits been more than what the court labeled "superficial."[82] Curiously enough, as it turns out, both witnesses (Mr. Uihlein and Mr. Haskell) had been the respective parties who had made inquiries into bauxite deposits for the Uihlein family and J. B. Duke.

In contrast to the assertions of these men, Dr. Branner, the state geologist of Arkansas, testified that Alcoa owned approximately 48 percent of the probable deposits of bauxite of aluminum ore quality in Arkansas, and that parties other than Alcoa owned 52 percent. The testimony of Dr. Branner was confirmed by Alcoa's geologist, Mr. Litchfield. Both admitted that bauxite was available in six other states and, according to the court, "outside the United States, the supply of bauxite is practically inexhaustible." Judge Caffey concluded:

> The testimony given by these two experts was quite extensive and quite thorough. It occupied approximately 1900 pages of the record. These are pages 36464 to 38447, except for 53 pages covering the testimony of an out-of-town witness, which was quite brief. And, so far as I can see, the testimony of the government in regard to the amount of aluminum grade bauxite in Arkansas completely fails to sustain its contention. I think the testimony of the two experts is the best we can get and is the kind of testimony which we must rely on if we are to have any information at all on a subject like this.

My conclusion, therefore, as to bauxite, is that the government has not proved its allegation in support of its charge of monopolization with respect to bauxite.[83]

Judge Caffey next turned his attention to an examination of Alcoa's alleged water power or water power "sites" monopoly. Citing statistics published by the Federal Power Commission, he showed that Alcoa not only produced an insignificant amount of the entire nation's electrical energy, but that it owned only five undeveloped water power sites out of an FPC-compiled list of 1883.[84]

It is plain that the amount of power developed or potential and fit to produce aluminum, owned by Alcoa, is but an insignificant portion of the total available in the United States. In other words, the charge against Alcoa of monopolization of water power in the United States is entirely without foundation.[85]

Moreover, if Alcoa had not monopolized bauxite and had not monopolized water power sites, the only essential raw materials necessary to produce aluminum, by the government's own admission, "it may well be argued that the issue of monopolization is at an end in this case."[86]

The issue of monopolization was not at an end, however. Caffey next went on to consider the government allegation that Alcoa had monopolized alumina (AL_2O_3). He remarked that the patented Bayer process for making alumina from bauxite had expired in 1903, and that anyone could produce and sell alumina in the United States after that "without any obstruction by patent or otherwise."[87] Alcoa, before 1903, had purchased all of its alumina requirement, and mostly from the Pennsylvania Salt Company. After 1903, Alcoa manufactured some of the substance itself though it still relied on Pennsylvania Salt for many years afterward. By 1937, however, Alcoa was making all the alumina used to make primary aluminum—which was a necessary fact, since it was the only domestic producer of primary aluminum. Indeed, by that time, it was making more alumina than it required for its own reduction activities. Figures presented at the trial indicated that in the 1928–1938 period, Alcoa consumed 78 percent of its alumina production and sold the rest. Additional figures demonstrated that the Pennsylvania Salt Manufacturing Company supplied approximately 33 percent of the alumina available to nonproducers of aluminum; the total of alumina available to non-Alcoa interests for that ten-year period had been slightly less than 251 million pounds. In that period, Caffey pointed out, any other chemical company in the country could have produced alumina from bauxite, and probably would have, "if the price which they could get for it were sufficiently inviting."[88] In conclusion, Caffey ruled that the government had "entirely failed to prove any of its charges regarding alumina."[89]

The next charge examined by Caffey concerned Alcoa's admitted position in virgin or primary ingot aluminum. In a sense, this was the easiest and yet most confusing issue of all. It was beyond dispute that the Aluminum Company of America was the sole domestic manufacturer of primary aluminum: This fact had been readily admitted by the defendant, and there was no controversy about that. What was at issue, however, was: 1) did such a monopoly position violate Section 2 of the Sherman Act, and 2) did Alcoa illegally exclude others from primary aluminum production?[90]

With regard to the first question, Judge Caffey's analysis is extremely interesting and important, as subsequent judicial analysis at the Appeals Court would prove. It would be wise to quote him exactly:

> On principle it seems to me that it would be little short of absurd to construe Section 2 without qualification to mean that production of the entire output in the United States of a particular article, or of any article, or that the possession or sale of it by the producer, *without other complaint or criticism of his conduct*, would constitute monopolization of the article. I think that such an interpretation would be wrong. I think it would be wrong, among other things, because if adopted the statute so interpreted thereby would provide punishment for what others than the producer (even though wholly unrelated to and disconnected from him) might do or had done.[91]

Caffey then created a hypothetical example to illustrate his point. He assumed that two producers, A and B manufactured the same article and sold it in the same areas. Over time, producer A, because it could produce and sell the item cheaper than producer B, came to acquire all of B's customers. As a consequence, producer A did 100 percent of the business in the article. Was producer A now "monopolizing" in violation of the Sherman Act? Caffey answered his own rhetorical questions:

> . . . if the theory of the government, stated by its counsel, as to what Section 2 of the Sherman Act means be accepted, then obviously A would be punished for what B, or what B's customers, or what B and his customers had done.

> So far as I can discover the Supreme Court has never given the slightest support to such an interpretation as the government advocates.[92]

What previous Court precedents had implied, Caffey stated, was that the "unexerted power to control is not an offense"; thus, Section 2 could not be so construed as to condemn a sole producer that had gained and held its monopoly position fairly in an open market.[93] To defend this interpretation, Caffey noted that the Congress, in drafting Section 2, had been careful to use verbs, not nouns, to describe the conduct that it meant to make illegal: "every person who shall monopolize, or attempt to monopolize . . ." Moreover, an examination of the *Congressional Record* of 1889 revealed that during the Sherman Act hearings, Senator Kenna and Senator Edmunds had debated the issue of obtaining a "legitimate" monopoly position in a market. That particular debate, Caffey continued, showed clearly that the "offense of monopolization cannot be established unless there be proved, as one of the constituents, the element of exclusion."[94]

But what of exclusion? Had Alcoa unlawfully excluded competitors or potential competitors from primary aluminum manufacture? The only example of exclusion put forth by the government at the trial concerned the case of the Southern Aluminum Company.[95] The French Aluminum Company of France had begun construction of an aluminum facility in North Carolina in 1912, but had been forced to suspend further construction with the outbreak of World War I in August of 1914.[96] Thereafter, repeated attempts were made by Southern to negotiate the sale of the uncompleted properties to the Alcoa company. The court record made it clear, Caffey stated, that it was Southern's lawyers that pressed and pursued the matter for almost a year, until the sale was actually made at a price equal to Southern's costs to that date. The entire matter was reviewed favorably by the Justice Department on September 3, 1915, and the transaction was finalized on November 23, 1915.[97] Thus, the charge that Alcoa "excluded" competition by purchasing the Southern Aluminum Company—and supposedly at a price that greatly exceeded its value—turns out to be groundless. In fact, Alcoa purchased, with much insistence from Southern at cost, a substantially uncompleted complex (the dam was only one-eighth finished) which it proceeded to radically redesign and complete at its own considerable expense.[98] In summary, Alcoa neither illegally monopolized nor illegally excluded others from the right to trade; or as Caffey put it: "In no respect, related to the production or selling of virgin aluminum, has it been shown that Alcoa violated Section 2 of the Sherman Act."[99]

At this point in the judgment, Judge Caffey called attention to the fact that ingot aluminum produced by Alcoa was not without competition from a variety of sources. For example, he noted that imported primary ingot competed with Alcoa's ingot; "scrap" or "secondary" aluminum, which was chemically the same as primary ingot, actively competed; and steel, nickel, tin, zinc, copper, and lead were all the "chief industrial competitors of aluminum."[100] The scrap and secondary markets were of particular interest, for there it could be "established without contradiction that, through use of well known processes . . . aluminum of every grade can be produced of the same chemical composition as if it had been produced from virgin aluminum and some factories claim that they can produce from secondary aluminum all the commodities that can be produced from primary aluminum . . . which includes aluminum of 99.75 percent purity."[101] And it was there that 125 million pounds of scrap and secondary aluminum had been produced and sold in 1937 at prices competitive with primary ingot. In fact, on a few occasions, and "under appropriate market conditions, secondary aluminum is sold at prices higher than the price of primary aluminum."[102] Thus, if the issue was a relevant one, primary ingot faced competition from a variety of close substitutes, even though Alcoa was admittedly the only domestic primary aluminum manufacturer at the time of the trial.

The rest of the government's charges, relating to Alcoa's supposed monopolization of aluminum castings, cooking utensils, pistons, extrusions and structural shapes, foil, and miscellaneous fabricated articles, were all dismissed by Judge Caffey, while final consideration of the charges dealing with "sheet" and "cable" were delayed. In summary, the Judge concluded the entire area of monopolization by stating that "*none of the monopolization charges has been satisfactorily proved* and that in regard to them the Government has not shown that it is entitled to any relief."[103]

Much had been made of Alcoa's supposed conspiracy with a cartel of European firms and the second part of Judge Caffey's decision dealt with these allegations. The government had charged, among other things, that Alcoa conspired directly, and through Aluminum Ltd., with several European firms, and *The Alliance* to limit output, raise price, and restrict the importation of aluminum and aluminum products. Though the government had once admitted that "conspiracy constitutes only 5 percent of this case,"[104] Caffey devoted a full fifty pages of text to the charges and countercharges. After thoroughly examining all of the charges relating to the supposed "sundry conspiracy" he concluded:

> In consequence, I conclude that the government has *failed* to establish the charge of conspiracy between Alcoa and European producers of aluminum or Aluminum or either or any of them.

> I further conclude that the Government has *failed* by credible evidence to show that either 1) there was ever a conspiracy between Alcoa and Aluminum or 2) that since January 23, 1915, there has ever been a conspiracy between Alcoa or any of the other foreign producers to fix prices or to restrict importations or to limit the quantities of production or to allocate customers or shipments to customers of aluminum or aluminum products of any kind.[105]

The final part of the court decision dealt with "other misconduct" of Alcoa, specifically the allegation that Alcoa charged "extortionate prices" and thus made "exorbitant" profits.[106] Although Caffey admitted that neither allegation, even if sustained by evidence, was itself a violation of the Sherman Act, and that he had already ruled against the government "on all the issues raised by the bill involving monopolization and, therefore, against all those involving prices or profits," he proceeded to examine the relevant price–profit information. Alcoa had submitted evidence that its average rate of return on investment for the period 1887–1937 was 9.96 percent; the government's figure for the same period was "a small fraction in excess of 10 percent."[107] Since the court dismissed the relevancy of examining profit rates on particular items or profit rates in particular years, it concluded that as a general matter Alcoa had not "exacted extortionate prices" nor "been shown to have made exorbitant profits."[108]

To summarize and conclude the entire proceeding, Judge Caffey had examined and dismissed the entire government petition with regard to illegal monopolization, conspiracy, and "other misconduct." He had not found sufficient proof to sustain any of the government's charges and allegations against the Aluminum Company of America. On October 10, 1941, Caffey ruled Alcoa innocent of violating the Sherman Act.

The Appeals Court Decision

Judge Caffey had expected an appeal from the losing party in this complex case, and such an appeal was forthcoming by the government. The Supreme Court, however, was unable to hear the appeals case because four of its justices had previously participated in antitrust actions against Alcoa when they had been with the Justice Department. After more than two years of delay, Congress passed a special act on June 9, 1944, allowing a U. S. Circuit Court of Appeals to hear the government's appeal and act as a "court of last resort." Judges Learned Hand, Augustus N. Hand, and Thomas Swain were selected to preside in the appeals case, and Judge Learned Hand delivered the decision.[109]

The government's appeal and the emphasis in the Appeals Court decision clearly centered on one issue—Alcoa's "monopolization" of the virgin ingot aluminum market. Although District Court Judge Caffey had examined and dismissed that charge on at least three grounds,[110] the Circuit Court of Appeals argued on more narrow grounds that Caffey's analysis of Alcoa's market share was incorrect. Caffey had suggested, as part of his argument, that if one excluded the primary ingot that Alcoa fabricated itself, and included scrap or secondary aluminum ingot, Alcoa's share of the aluminum ingot market was approximately 33 percent, and not enough for monopolization per se. Judge Hand argued, instead, that it was improper to exclude Alcoa's own fabricated ingot since Alcoa's fabrication "*pro tanto* reduce(s) the demand for ingot itself," and thus affects the primary ingot market and ingot price.[111] In addition, secondary ingot should not be included (even though he stated that "at any given moment . . . 'secondary' competes with 'virgin' in the ingot market"),[112] since Alcoa's monopoly over virgin ingot in the present allows an influence over all "future supply of ingot" including, necessarily, secondary ingot. Thus, Hand reduced the relevant market under consideration to virgin ingot aluminum, and concluded, not surprisingly, that Alcoa "monopolized" it with 90 percent control (10 percent was imported primary ingot).

To arrive at such a conclusion, the court bent or broke familiar legal and economic guidelines as to the meaning of "monopolize" and to the "relevant market" under consideration. A relevant market for a product "should include all firms whose production has so immediate and substantial an effect on the prices and production of the firms in question that the actions of the one group cannot be explained without direct reference to the other. One should include in a market all firms whose products are, in fact, good and directly available substitutes for one another in sales to some significant group of buyers, and exclude all others."[113] Secondary or scrap was chemically and economically competitive with virgin and, therefore, a part of the relevant market for aluminum ingot. Just as clearly, Alcoa's fabricated ingot was not available for "marketing" and, therefore, not part of the aluminum ingot market. To exclude scrap and include "own-use" ingot was an arbitrary construction, which proves only that markets defined narrowly enough can make a monopoly out of any firm. Alcoa was not monopolizing even in Hand's terms, any reasonably defined market.

Judge Hand also rebuked Caffey for placing any relevance on the fact that Alcoa had not "monopolized," since its net return was calculated at only 10 percent. Hand stated that "the whole issue is irrelevant anyway, for it is no excuse for 'monopolizing' a market that the monopoly has not been used to extract from the consumer more than a 'fair' profit. *The Act has wider purposes.*"[114] Since Congress "did not condone 'good trusts' and condemn 'bad' ones, it forbade all," and since the court had already proven that Alcoa's share of the market was enough for it to qualify as a trust or monopoly, the exercise of monopoly power was irrelevant to the issue. Alcoa was a competent, ingenious firm—no one disputed that; in fact, the court's praise was almost embarrassing at points.[115] But Alcoa monopolized, and that was the only legitimate legal concern.

But was Alcoa's monopoly "thrust upon" the firm?[116] Was it the "passive beneficiary" of a monopolistic position earned legitimately in the market? Supposedly, according to Hand, the court would not indiscriminately condemn a single producer that had gained its position "merely by virtue of his superior skill, foresight, and industry."[117] Yet, in the next breath, Alcoa's superior skill, foresight, and industry were condemned as "exclusionary" and illegal.[118] Hand stated that Alcoa "forestalled" competition by stimulating demand and then efficiently supplying a demand "it had evolved"; it correctly anticipated increases in demand for ingot and then "doubled and redoubled" its capacity to fill that demand; it embraced every new opportunity with a "great" organization manned with elite business personnel. That Alcoa meant to keep its market position through such efforts and violate the Sherman Act was an obvious conclusion for Judge Hand and the Circuit Court of Appeals.[119]

That Alcoa's industrial efficiency was being condemned was just as obvious. In fact, Hand's analysis inverts Judge Caffey's theory of exclusion. By making business efficiency "exclusionary" and a restraint of trade, antitrust has now been literally turned on its head, condemning those practices it was allegedly designed to promote. Thus Alcoa was convicted of being the efficient single supplier in an artifically defined relevant market.

Not unreasonably, the court refused to dissolve "an aggregation which has for so long demonstrated its efficiency . . ."[120] Instead it hoped that the government owned aluminum properties that had been constructed for the war effort would be disposed of in a fashion that would create competition in the aluminum industry. Subsequently, many of the government aluminum reduction plants were sold to Reynolds Metal and Kaiser Aluminum. In 1948 both the government and Alcoa petitioned for a reopening of the case: the government was not satisfied with the competitive market structure and wanted divestiture of much of Alcoa's properties; Alcoa wanted Judge Hand's "guilty of monopolization" decision rejected because of the existence of Reynolds and Kaiser. Again, as in the Caffey trial, Judge Knox (Caffey had retired in 1947) of the New York District Court ruled against the government petition on almost every count.[121] Knox praised Alcoa for its war efforts, for its royalty-free licensing of patents, for a record free of unfair competition of any kind, and concluded that competition was quite vigorous in the aluminum industry. He thus rejected the divestiture petition. Although no specific finding of illegal activity, collusion, or conspiracy were proved, he did order ingot stockholders in both Alcoa and Aluminum, Ltd. to divest themselves of one or the other. On January 16, 1951, Judge Knox accepted a stock disposal plan and the thirteen-year court battle involving Alcoa came to an end.

THE UNITED SHOE MACHINERY CORPORATION CASE
(1953, 1968)

The United Shoe Machinery Company was begun in January 1899, when four formerly independent shoe machine firms formed the company. On May 2, 1905, the United Company, containing the once independent shoe machine manufacturers, formally incorporated in the State of New Jersey as United Shoe Machinery Corporation, with corporate headquarters and essential manufacturing facilities at Beverly, Massachusetts. After still another reorganization in 1917, United Shoe Machinery had attained a position in the shoe machine manufacturing industry such that it leased or sold approximately 85 percent of the nation's shoe machinery. Although at least ten other shoe machinery firms sold or leased equipment throughout the period, United maintained its 1917 market share for the next thirty years.[122]

Prior to 1947, United Shoe had been in the courts twice on similar charges. In a 1918 Sherman Act case,[123] the government had sought to dissolve the reorganized shoe machinery corporation, since it dominated that industry and was allegedly extending its market control through various tying arrangements with customers. The Supreme Court, however, did not agree with the government's arguments and released the firm under the theory that efficient firms using legitimate patents do not necessarily violate the Sherman Act, even though they may dominate their industry. In a second case decided in 1922,[124] Section 3 of the Clayton Act was successfully used to purge some of the "restrictive" and "tying" features from United's leasing contracts; the leasing system itself and the dominant market position of United in that industry were accepted and left intact. In December of 1947, a third antitrust action was launched under Section 2 of the Sherman Act,[125] in still another attempt to end United's alleged "monopoly" in shoe machinery and its "exclusionary" business practices.

United Shoe Machinery and the Courts

The District Court decision written by Judge Wyzanski in 1953 began with a brief discussion of the shoe machinery industry and United's position within it.[126] Through a set of tables indicating the number of machines leased or sold by United, compared to the rest of the leases and sales made by other shoe machinery manufacturers, Wyzanski estimated United's share of the machinery market to be between 75 and 90 percent.[127] This position was attributable, Wyzanski said, to the firm's original construction creating the United Shoe Machinery Corporation in 1905 and reorganized in 1917, to the company's "superior products and services," and to certain business practices, notably the leasing system. Now, since the first factor had been thoroughly investigated, reviewed, and dismissed in 1918, the only relevant issues at this trial were to be United's supposed efficiency and United's supposed exclusionary leasing system.

The court's first action was to dismiss the government's contention that the purchase of some firms by United Shoe Machinery since 1917 had violated the antitrust laws. Although there had been thirty-odd acquisitions valued at 3.5 million dollars between 1916 and 1938, Wyzanski concluded that "they have not been one of the principal factors in enabling defendant to achieve and hold its share of the market."[128] In a like manner, he summarily dismissed the government allegations of anticompetitive effects of certain "restrictive agreements" between United and other firms.[129]

The District Court then considered United Shoe's leasing policies and agreements. United manufactured 342 different types of shoe machines in 1947: 178 of these machines were available on a lease basis only, 42 were available on an outright sale basis only, and the other 122 shoe machines could be sold or leased, depending on the preferences of the customer.[130] Although almost 50 percent of all United's machines could be sold, it was the other 50 percent that could be leased, and particularly the 178 machines that could only be leased, that was of particular concern to the court.

Leasing shoe machinery was the accepted practice in the shoe industry, had been since the Civil War, and was used by United's important competitors. The court emphasized that the practice of leasing shoe machinery had made entry into shoe manufacturing easy (there were 1462 shoe firms in 1947, an increase of almost 500 over 1937),[131] and that small shoe manufacturers could grow quickly under the leasing system, with small capital expenditures.[132] The court also noted that the leased machines from United Shoe performed excellently and were serviced by United's 1500 roadmen "promptly, efficiently and courteously."[133] Furthermore, the general rates for leasing machines had been uniform and fair, and the 1220 factories that employed United equipment had shown no expressed dissatisfaction with the system, whatsoever.[134]

The leasing system also worked successfully for United Shoe Machinery, since it greatly stabilized revenues—unusual for a capital goods firm—allowed constant contact with shoemakers and their particular machinery needs, and consequently spurred expenditures for research and development to produce and market more efficient machines for shoe manufacturers. On the whole the court concluded, United Shoe and its customers were quite satisfied with the leasing arrangements.[135]

There was also no general dissatisfaction concerning United's pricing policy. The nine examples of pricing conduct detailed by the court demonstrated only that United reduced its rates in the face of competitive challenges, and that its general rates throughout the period under discussion had hardly been excessive. In addition, the firm had not sold below cost—as the government had alleged—nor engaged in "predatory price cutting" or coercive practices of any kind.[136] As a result, its pricing policies had not generated any monopoly return. Judge Wyzanski concluded that "United's book earnings on its total operations 1925–1949 were about 10 percent net, after taxes, on invested capital."[137]

Furthermore, the court strongly praised United's research facility ("United has a research organization of efficiency, intelligence and vision"),[138] and the fact that it explored "every branch of science and every modern scientific device which could be brought to bear upon the problems of shoe making."[139] Moreover, United's fundamental research had been turned quickly into technological developments and "has *not* been slowed down or withheld . . . until competition appeared, or until the demand for its own models abated. It has not shelved developments."[140] The court concluded that there was no reliable evidence that United repressed invention or innovation (United held almost 4000 patents) nor had it "refused any reasonable offers for licenses made by others."[141]

But if all the above information is to be accepted, what was wrong with the United Shoe Machinery Corporation? If its prices were competitive, nondiscriminatory, and nonpredatory; if its services were excellent; if its research complex was famous throughout the world; if it had not repressed innovation; and if its net profits had averaged 10 percent on capital, then where was the monopoly power and the restraints of trade? To discover the alleged restraints one must return, with the court, to an analysis of the leasing agreements.

The government had alleged, and the court accepted, that the standard, ten-year leasing contract in the shoe machinery industry was just too long.[142] Too long for whom? Shoe manufacturers that leased machines from United had not requested a reduction in the leasing period. In fact, it had been their combined pressure that had raised the standard contract leasing period from seven years to ten years in the 1922 antitrust proceedings against United Shoe.[143] Long-term leasing was economically advantageous to United Shoe and to its customers, and provided few difficulties for the parties involved. It was, however, the competitors and the potential competitors of United Shoe Machinery that were put at a disadvantage by the long lease periods. With ten-year leases, Wyzanski stated, "a competitor may not get a chance to have his machine adequately tried out by a shoe manufacturer."[144] The fact that all of the leases eventually ran out, or could be terminated, or that "competitive" machinery could be tried out by firms employing United Machinery during "experimental periods,"[145] did not sway the court from its position that the leasing period must be shortened so as to increase "competition."

The next issues in the leasing contracts were more serious and concerned United's policy of requiring that the lessee "shall use the leased machinery to its full capacity upon all footwear . . ."[146] and that machines returned before the expiration of the contract leasing period was subject to a "return charge."[147] The "full capacity" clause implied that United could penalize lessees who employed non-United shoe machinery in their shoe manufacture. The return charge implied that firms that returned leased machinery before the expiration dates paid a pro-rata return charge; firms that replaced the returned machine with another United shoe machine paid a smaller "return charge" than those shoe manufacturers that intended to replace United's machines with shoe machinery of "outside manufacture." This "variation" in assessments was accomplished by applying the credits from an amortization plan or deduction fund to which the lessee contributed, towards the deferred payment or return charge when United machines were replaced with other United machines. The court regarded this as a "discriminatory" practice and not merely one defendable on revenue grounds. "The discrimination is designed to operate as, and does operate as, a method of excluding from the shoe factories shoe machinery competitive with United's."[148] Supposedly, there were ninety such instances of full capacity or return charge tactics to deter competition; the court listed eight, and even the president of United Shoe Machinery admitted during the trial that the practice deterred factories from employing competitive machines.[149]

And so it did, somewhat. But are we to infer that a significant proportion, indeed the dominant position of United Shoe Machinery, was attributable to this particular practice? Hardly; at best, this "discrimination" would have been a slight deterrent to the adoption of competitive machines.[150] If the competitive shoe machines were of higher quality, cheaper, or more reliable, then they certainly would have been adopted despite the return charge, and in increasing numbers, at the termination of the leasing period. That such was not the case implies that it was not unfair exclusion or discrimination that limited sales by competitors, but the overwhelming fact that United Shoe Machinery offered superior experience, terms, services, and "a long line of machine types while no competitor offers more than a short line."[151] Simply put, United Shoe was more efficient than its competition.

The District Court's examination of United's machine repair system confirmed the view expressed above. Judge Wyzanski regarded United's free repair maintenance system—or, more exactly, including repair in the original leasing contract without separate charge—as "exclusionary" because it made it difficult for both large independent repair companies to come into existence, and for foreign machine makers to compete without offering similar repair services.[152] Again, the court displayed a notable degree of concern and sympathy for firms as yet "unborn," and for other business organizations that had difficulty competing with United Shoe because they could not, admittedly, offer comparable terms. In Judge Caffey's terms, firm A was again being chastised for what firm B or B's customers had done or had failed to do. The interests of the existing shoe machinery lessee and, ultimately, of the consumers of shoes themselves, were ignored throughout this case.

As a final example of exclusion, the court pointed out that "United's lease system makes impossible a second-hand market in its own machines," and thus excludes potential competition.[153] Though not even an accurate statement, since at least 164 shoe machines could be purchased and ultimately appear in a second-hand market,[154] Judge Wyzanski in effect condemned

United for not making it easier for competitors or potential competitors to compete with it. Since it is extremely doubtful that the court would have considered a second-hand market in shoe machinery "competitive" anyway—shoe machinery becomes technologically dated and obsolete quickly—the entire issue is economically trivial. It does serve to demonstrate, however, that concern for the difficulties of competitors far outdistanced concern for the competitive process or the consumer in this trial.

The rest of the District Court decision concerned United's alleged attempt to monopolize the trade and commerce in "shoe factory supplies." Fourteen such supplies—ranging from shoe boxes to clicking dies—were examined by the court and, in most of these cases, "it is too plain for argument that United has not achieved a share of the market which *prima facie* indicates a monopoly."[155] What was indicated was that United did a substantial share of the business in some of these supplies because United had regular contact with 85 percent of the shoe manufacturing industry. As the court put it:

> Customers already know United, have current relations with it, trust it generally, believe it able to specify, select, or manufacture suitable supplies, and are aware that because of the lease provisions United is, as it were, a partner interested in the effective functioning of the machines.[156]

But was United's success in the supplies area due in any way, as the government had alleged, to predatory practices or to coercion? The court thought not and dismissed the charges in this area. ". . . there's *nothing whatsoever* to the government's allegations that customers are coerced, or are subservient, or a captive, or are deliberately mislead by United's representatives."[157] Yet, after the court admitted that United functioned efficiently and in a nonpredatory manner in these supply areas, it abruptly ordered divestiture of United's nail, tack, and eyelet subsidiaries.[158]

In conclusion, the court determined that specific provisions of United's standard leasing contract were restraining competition in violation of Section 2 of the Sherman Act. The full-capacity clause and return charge were not "practices which could be properly described as the inevitable consequence of ability, natural forces, or law." Instead, they were business practices that "unnecessarily exclude actual and potential competition (and) restrict a free market."[159] Hence, the court ordered United Shoe to purge the restrictive features:[160] the maximum standard leasing contract was reduced arbitrarily to five years; the full capacity and return charge system was modified to make it non-discriminatory; service charges were ordered separated from leased machine charges; and any shoe machine that United leased, it also had to offer for direct sale on substantially comparable terms. In addition, the court ordered United to license out all patents at uniformly reasonable rates and not to purchase any shoe or shoe machinery manufacturer if the transaction exceeded $10,000; nor were they to purchase any second-hand shoe machinery "except for experimental or like purposes."[161] The court argued that saddling United with special restrictions not faced by other shoe machinery manufacturers was necessary to "root out monopolization." It was further argued that these restrictions were not themselves "discriminatory," since United was already in a class by itself; indeed these provisions would help put United back in the same class with its "competitors."

To add insult to injury, the Justice Department appealed the lower court decision to the Supreme Court in 1967. They argued that Judge Wyzanski had not gone far enough and that even though United's market share had declined from 85 percent in 1953 to 60 percent in 1967, it still monopolized in violation of the law. The Supreme Court agreed in 1968, and ordered a lower court to work out a divestiture of a significant share of United Shoe's machinery business.[162] United was ultimately ordered to divest itself of shoe machines, manufacturing assets, and patents that had accounted, in 1968, for $8,500,000 in domestic revenues. Further, United was ordered to provide service and parts for the divested independent "competitor" (the firm was called the Transamerican Shoe Machinery Corporation), provide for the licensing of all of its own patents at a "reasonable royalty," and, the ultimate absurdity, refrain from active competition with the divested machine models for a period of five years.

THE DUPONT CELLOPHANE (1956) AND TELEX–IBM (1975) CASES

The Cellophane Case

In the duPont *Cellophane* case both the District Court[163] and the U. S. Supreme Court[164] agreed that duPont did not possess monopoly power in cellophane and did not control the relevant market. DuPont convinced the courts that cellophane was "reasonably interchangeable" with other so-called "flexible wrapping materials" produced and sold by hundreds of other firms, and that cellophane's share of that relevant market was only 17.9 percent—not nearly enough for illegal monopolization. In addition, the courts were persuaded that duPont acted like a competitor in the market with respect to cellophane, since it engaged in intensive research, sharply lowered its costs of production, improved the quality of its product, and progressively reduced the price of cellophane from $2.51 per pound in 1924 (poor quality cellophane) to 38 cents per pound in 1940 (high quality cellophane). Accordingly sales of moisture-proof cellophane increased from $603,222 in 1928 to $89,-850,416 in 1950.

In addition, and importantly, the courts conceded that duPont did not have the market power to exclude competitors or foreclosure potential competitors from entering the market for flexible wrapping materials and expanding their business. DuPont had, to be sure, made a liberal return on its investment in cellophane (15.9 percent net after taxes, 1937–1947), but such profits, in the absence of illegal monopolization, were not evidence of any violation of the law. And finally, although a minority of the Supreme Court, and some economists, were convinced that duPont's performance was indicative of rational monopolistic behavior,[165] a majority of the Supreme Court was not so convinced, and dismissed the case against duPont.

Although duPont's economic performance does appear consistent with competitive behavior, two special factors cloud an unambiguous judgment in duPont's favor. The first is that moisture proof cellophane was under patent protection from 1929 through 1946; cellophane was a legal monopoly, as even the lower court had admitted.[166] The second factor is that duPont had lobbied hard (in the late 1920s) for an increase in the tariff on imported cellophane from 25 percent to 60 percent *ad valorem*. And even though the Tariff Act of 1930 lowered the effective rate to 45 percent *ad valorem* (about 40 cents per pound), import competition was affected substantially and was never really a problem after that.[167] Thus, although duPont's economic performance vis-à-vis buyers was excellent, governmental interference (at duPont's insistence) with competitive entry did artifically restrain trade somewhat. In retrospect, the Department of Justice might have more appropriately sued the Patent Office and U. S. Customs rather than duPont for "monopolization."

The Telex–IBM Case (1975)

In the lower court decision on the *Telex–IBM* case (1973),[168] Judge Christensen concluded that International Business Machines Corporation—the world's largest manufacturer of general purpose computer systems, with gross revenues of $9.5 billion in 1972—had attempted to destroy its so-called "plug compatible" competitors, specifically the Telex Corporation, in violation of antitrust law. Christensen had been convinced that IBM monopolized "markets" for EDP (electronic data processing) equipment that interconnected with IBM equipment, and that they had gained that monopoly through specific predatory practices. Therefore, he ordered that Telex should be awarded $352 million treble damages (later reduced to $259 million). An Appeals Court reversed the decision in 1975, however, and dismissed the damage award entirely.[169]

Telex was a major independent manufacturer of add-on memory cores and magnetic disc storage devices that they designed to be "plugged" into IBM computer systems. They competed in the EDP market by offering such devices to IBM equipment users at reduced rates, and the company grew accordingly to have sales of $68 million by 1973. Early in the 1970s, however, IBM, after losing significant amounts of business to the peripheral computer companies, decided to meet the competition by reducing prices, innovating a more sophisticated technology (incorporating that technology in the main processing unit), and encouraging users of its equipment to sign long-term leases at favorable rates. And while Judge Christensen had determined that such practices were "predatory" and exclusionary, the Appeals Court determined, instead, that they were "valid competitive practices."[170] In addition, the Appeals Court argued that the lower court's definition of the relevant market was simply too narrow since, as in the duPont *Cellophane* case, that definition had excluded the products of companies that were "reasonably interchangable" with Telex equipment.[171] Thus in some of the recent monopoly cases decided, especially at the Appeals Court level, there appears to have been some movement away from the extreme position adopted in the *Alcoa* and *United Shoe Machinery* cases.[172]

CONCLUSIONS

It should be apparent from these corporate histories and antitrust cases that the conduct and performance presumptions of neoclassical monopoly theory simply have not been borne out. All of the corporations examined in these classic cases had expanded outputs, reduced prices, and engaged in important technological innovation, entirely consistent with competitive behavior and efficient performance. The corporations did not acquire monopoly power in the marketplace nor were they able to exercise any such power. And any restrictions of the competitive process that can be discovered in these cases are to be associated with governmental action (patents and tariffs) and not with purely free market activity.

Yet, as we have seen, the courts often drew incorrect conclusions concerning corporate behavior from familiar assumptions about corporate size and market share. In many of the cases the courts manipulated relevant markets, ignored existing substitutes, placed importance on the degree of concentration in the market, disregarded conduct performance information, and showed an almost total ignorance of the concept of efficient resource allocation. Efficient firms were a threat because they were efficient. Investing in productive facilities to supply future demands "pre-empted" potential rivals.

Offering a full line of machinery was "unfair," since no competitor could offer more than a short line of equipment. Purchasing power plant sites and developing them was "exclusionary." Offering free service "restricted" competitive entry and restrained competition. And retaining a high market share—a most extraordinary business accomplishment in a free market—was to monopolize and to violate the antitrust law. Clearly, the courts were led into serious economic mischief by an incorrect theoretical perspective, and it is that perspective that must be rejected before substantial changes in public policy become politically realistic.

NOTES

1. For information concerning the tobacco industry prior to 1911, see Meyer Jacobstein, "The Tobacco Industry in the United States," *Columbia University Studies*, Vol. 26 (1907); Richard B. Tennant, *The American Cigarette Industry* (New Haven: Yale University Press, 1950); William H. Nicholls, *Price Policies in the Cigarette Industry*, Nashville: The Vanderbilt University Press, 1951). John W. Jenkins, *James B. Duke: Master Builder* (New York: George H. Doran Company, 1927); P. G. Porter, "Origins of the American Tobacco Company," *Business History Review*, Vol. 43 (Spring 1969), pp. 59–76.

2. Tennant, *op. cit.*, p. 15.

3. Tennant, *op. cit.*, pp. 17–18. Some accounts say costs were reduced to 8 cents per thousand. See Porter, *op. cit.*, p. 69.

4. Jenkins, *op. cit.*, p. 66.

5. Tennant, *op. cit.*, pp. 19–25.

6. Jenkins, *op. cit.*, pp. 73–84.

7. Nicholls, *op. cit.*, p. 26, states flatly that the American Tobacco Company was formed in 1890 following an expensive business war begun by James B. Duke. But neither the *Report of U.S. Commissioner of Corporations*, Vol. 1 (Feb. 1909), which Nicholls indicates was his source, nor the court decision against American Tobacco in 1908, appear to bear this out. See William Z. Ripley, *Trusts, Pools and Corporations*, rev. ed. (Boston: Ginn & Company, 1916), pp. 269–70; and see 164 Fed. Reporter 722. For a discussion of the negotiations between the companies that created American Tobacco see Porter, *op. cit.*, pp. 71–73.

8. Even in the 1900–1904 period, cigarettes by weight represented only 2 percent of all tobacco products consumed. See Nicholls, *op. cit.*, p. 7. Cigarettes did not achieve any sort of national popularity until after World War I.

9. Jenkins, *op. cit.*, pp. 91–92.

10. *U. S. Research and Brief*, 221 U.S. 106, Appendix F, p. 318. Also see Jones, *The Trust Problem in the United States* (New York: The Macmillan Com-

pany, 1923), p. 140. Higher percentage figures in some accounts (83 percent is a common figure for 1907; see Nicholls) measure American's share of total output rather than output for domestic consumption.

11. Tennant, *op. cit.*, p. 27.

12. Jenkins, *op. cit.*, p. 149.

13. *Transcript of Record,* 221 U.S. 106. Vol. 1, p. 254.

14. It was not established at court that American Tobacco started this price war; see 164 Fed. Reporter 723, and 221 U.S. 160.

15. See Nicholls, *op. cit.*, p. 17. Jones mentions 528 independent plants in 1906; see Jones, *op. cit.*, p. 146.

16. Nicholls, *op. cit.*, p. 15.

17. *Ibid.*

18. *Ibid.*, p. 13. Also, see Ripley, *op. cit.*, p. 295.

19. 221 U. S. 129.

20. Jacobstein, *op. cit.*, p. 101.

21. Clair Wilcox, *Public Policies Toward Business,* 3rd ed. (Homewood Ill.: Richard D. Irwin, 1966), p. 139, says that one of American's "unfair" methods of competition was buying plants to shut them down.

22. *Transcript of Record,* 221 U. S. 106, Vol. I, pp. 208–211.

23. *Ibid.*, pp. 227–231.

24. Tennant, *op. cit.*, pp. 51–52.

25. Jacobstein, *op. cit.*, p. 126.

26. *Ibid.*, pp. 125–126.

27. *Ibid.*, p. 127.

28. *Ibid.*, p. 128.

29. *Ibid.*, p. 123.

30. Tennant, *op. cit.*, pp. 49–57.

31. *U. S. Research and Brief,* 221 U.S. 106, Appendix P, p. 329.

32. Tennant, *op. cit.*, p. 53.

33. The "plug war" (1894–1898) is probably the most famous example. During this "war," American sold plug at a loss until the large independent plug manufacturers defaulted. The "independents" came together to form the Continental Tobacco Company, whose president was James B. Duke.

But some additional facts complicate an easy interpretation of this "war." In the first place, it was not established that American started the plug war. Secondly, the price reductions were limited to only a few "fighting brands"; while American Tobacco lost money on plug, all the large independent plug manufacturers continued to earn a profit. Finally, plug sales increased from 9 million pounds in 1894 to 38 million pounds in 1897. See Tennant, *op. cit.*, p. 29.

34. 164 Fed. Reporter, pp. 702–703 (emphasis added).

35. *Ibid.*, p. 712.

36. *Ibid.*, p. 726 (emphasis added).
37. *Ibid.*, p. 728.
38. *Ibid.*, p. 702 (emphasis added).
39. *Ibid.*, p. 703 (emphasis added).
40. *United States v. American Tobacco Company*, 221 U. S. 105.
41. *Ibid.*, pp. 155, 178–179.
42. *Ibid.*, pp. 155–175.
43. *Ibid.*, pp. 181–184.
44. *Ibid.*, p. 182.
45. *Ibid.*, pp. 182–183.
46. *Ibid.*, p. 183 (emphasis added).
47. *Ibid.*, p. 181 (emphasis added).
48. There are some excellent works on the early history of the iron and steel industry. For a classic account, see James Howard Bridge, *The Inside History of the Carnegie Steel Company* (New York: The Aldine Book Company, 1903). For excellent recent accounts, see Louis Hacker, *The World of Andrew Carnegie: 1865–1901*, (Philadelphia and New York: J. B. Lippincott Company, 1968), esp. pp. 337–439; and Joseph Frazier Wall, *Andrew Carnegie* (New York: Oxford University Press, 1970).
49. Hacker, *op. cit.*, p. 342.
50. Bridges, *op. cit.*, p. 83.
51. *Ibid.*, p. 90.
52. *Ibid.*, p. 93.
53. Walter Adams, *The Structure of American Industry* (New York: The Macmillan Company, 1950), p. 147. Also, see Hacker, *op. cit.*, pp. 361–362.
54. *United States v. United States Steel Corporation*, 223 Fed. Reporter, 55.
55. *United States v. United States Steel Corporation*, 251 U. S. 417 (1920).
56. *Ibid.*, p. 433.
57. Judge Buffington's decision is reprinted in Ripley's, *Trusts, Pools and Corporations*, pp. 97–184. All following references to Ripley are to that decision reprint.
58. 223 Fed. Reporter, 57.
59. Ripley, *op. cit.*, p. 106. See also 223 Fed. Reporter, pp. 65–67.
60. Ripley, *op. cit.*, pp. 102–103.
61. *Ibid.*, p. 103. Also, see 223 Fed. Reporter, 68.
62. *Ibid.*
63. Ripley, *op. cit.*, p. 106.
64. *Ibid.*, p. 111.
65. 223 Fed. Reporter, 68–70.
66. Ripley, *op. cit.*, p. 113.

67. *Ibid.*, p. 114.

68. 223 Fed. Reporter, 80–89. For a contrary view see D. Parsons and E. Ray, "The United States Steel Consolidation: The Creation of Market Control," *Journal of Law and Economics*, Vol. 18, No. 1 (April 1975), pp. 181–219. Parsons and Ray argue, among other things, that U.S. Steel's monopoly power may have stemmed from its control of high-grade iron ore. And yet, as we have just noted, the court easily rejected such a presumption.

69. *Ibid.*, p. 81.

70. *Ibid.*, p. 82.

71. Jones, *op. cit.*, p. 211.

72. 223 Fed. Reporter, p. 154–61.

73. Gary had publicized the meetings by inviting the steel trade journals, the newspapers, and even the Justice Department itself. See Gabriel Kolko, *The Triumph of Conservation: A Reinterpretation of American History, 1900–1916* (New York: Free Press of Glencoe, 1963), p. 35.

74. 223 Fed. Reporter, p. 161 (emphasis added).

75. *United States v. Aluminum Company of America et al.*, 44 F. Supp., 97–311.

76. *United States v. Aluminum Company of America*, 148 F. 2d 416 (1945).

77. For a general discussion of the beginnings of the aluminum industry, see Charles C. Carr, *Alcoa: An American Enterprise* (New York: Rinehart & Company, Inc., 1952); D. H. Wallace, *Market Control in the Aluminum Industry* (Cambridge, Mass.: Harvard University Press, 1937).

78. *United States v. Aluminum Company of America et al.*, 44 F. Supp. 107.

79. *Ibid.*, p. 107.

80. *Ibid.*, p. 115.

81. *Ibid.*, p. 116.

82. *Ibid.*, p. 117.

83. *Ibid.*, pp. 120–121.

84. *Ibid.*, p. 123.

85. *Ibid.*, p. 124.

86. *Ibid.*, p. 144 (emphasis added).

87. *Ibid.*, p. 145.

88. *Ibid.*, p. 146.

89. *Ibid.*, p. 150.

90. *Ibid.*, p. 151.

91. *Ibid.*, p. 154 (emphasis added).

92. *Ibid.*, pp. 154–155.

93. *Ibid.*, p. 155.

94. *Ibid.*, p. 161 (emphasis added).

95. *Ibid.*, p. 161.

96. The French Government forbade the transfer of funds from France to continue the American operation. See *Ibid.*, pp. 161–162.

97. *Ibid.*, pp. 162–163.

98. *Ibid.*, p. 163.

99. *Ibid.*, p. 165.

100. *Ibid.*

101. *Ibid.*, p. 305.

102. *Ibid.*

103. *Ibid.*, p. 224 (emphasis added).

104. *Ibid.*, p. 225.

105. *Ibid.*, pp. 285–286 (emphasis added).

106. *Ibid.*, p. 286.

107. *Ibid.*, p. 298.

108. *Ibid.*, p. 304.

109. *United States v. Aluminum Company of America*, 148 F. 2d 416 (1945).

110. See 44 F. Supp. 150–165.

111. 148 F. 2d, p. 424.

112. *Ibid.* For an "analysis" of the second-hand market in aluminum, see Darius W. Gaskins, Jr., "Alcoa Revisited: The Welfare Implications of a Secondhand Market," *Journal of Economic Theory*, Vol. 7 (March 1974), pp. 254–271.

113. Henry Adler Einborn and William Paul Smith, eds., *Economic Aspects of Antitrust* (New York: Random House, 1968), p. 9.

114. 148 F. 2d, p. 427 (emphasis added).

115. *Ibid.*, pp. 430–431.

116. *Ibid.*, p. 429.

117. *Ibid.*, p. 430.

118. *Ibid.*, p. 430–431.

119. *Ibid.*, p. 432.

120. *Ibid.*, p. 446 (emphasis added).

121. *United States v. Aluminum Company of America*, 91 F. Supp. 333.

122. For background information concerning the shoe industry, see *United States v. United Shoe Machinery Corporation*, 110 F. Supp. 295 (1953), and Carl Kaysen, *United States v. United Shoe Machinery Corporation* (Cambridge, Mass.: Harvard University Press, 1956), pp. 1–24.

123. 274 U.S. 32.

124. 258 U.S. 451.

125. 110 F. Supp. 295 (1953), affirmed *per curiam*, 347 U.S. 521 (1954).

126. *Ibid.*, pp. 304–306.

127. *Ibid.*, p. 307. Dry thread sewing machines, though admittedly able to be substituted for United's machines, were excluded from the definition of the "mar-

ket" since United did not make any! See Lucille Keyes, "The Shoe Machinery Case and the Problem of the Good Trust," *Quarterly Journal of Economics*, Vol. 68 (1954), pp. 294–295.

128. 110 F. Supp. 312.

129. *Ibid.*, pp. 313–314.

130. *Ibid.*, p. 314.

131. *Ibid.*, p. 301.

132. *Ibid.*, p. 323.

133. *Ibid.*, p. 322.

134. *Ibid.*, pp. 322–323.

135. *Ibid.*, p. 323.

136. *Ibid.*, pp. 325–329.

137. *Ibid.*, p. 325.

138. *Ibid.*, p. 330.

139. *Ibid.*

140. *Ibid.*, p. 332.

141. *Ibid.*, p. 333.

142. *Ibid.*, p. 324.

143. *Ibid.*

144. *Ibid.*, p. 324 (emphasis added).

145. *Ibid.*

146. *Ibid.*, p. 320.

147. *Ibid.*

148. *Ibid.*, p. 321.

149. *Ibid.*

150. Carl Kaysen, *op. cit.*, devotes pp. 64–69 to this issue. Although he cautiously concludes that the long lease period and the return charge were "substantial" deterrents to competition (p. 68), his examples, though admittedly fragmentary, are far from convincing. Of 299 machines returned and replaced with competitive machines, 229 were returned to United *without charge!* The other 70 machines returned involved an average cash outlay of $300 per machine (p. 67).

151. 110 F. Supp. 343.

152. *Ibid.*, p. 325.

153. *Ibid.*

154. *Ibid.*, p. 314.

155. *Ibid.*, p. 335.

156. *Ibid.*, p. 336.

157. *Ibid.* (emphasis added).

158. *Ibid.*, pp. 352–354.

159. *Ibid.*, pp. 344–345.
160. *Ibid.*, pp. 351–354.
161. *Ibid.*, p. 354.
162. *United States v. United Shoe Machinery Corp.*, 391 U.S. 244 (1968). See also "Antitrusters Acquire a Hefty Fist," *Business Week* (May 25, 1968), p. 39.
163. *United States v. E. I. duPont de Nemours & Co.*, 118 F. Supp. 41 (1947).
164. *United States v. E. I. duPont de Nemours & Co.*, 351 U.S. 377 (1956).
165. George W. Stocking and Willard F. Mueller, "The Cellophane Case and the New Competition," *American Economic Review*, Vol. 45, No. 1, (March, 1955) pp. 31–63. For a recent (unconvincing) argument that the government action itself increased "competition" see Don E. Waldman "The duPont Cellophane Case Revisited: An Analysis of the Indirect Effects of Antitrust Policy on Market Structure and Performance," *The Antitrust Bulletin*, Vol. 25, No. 4 (Winter 1980), pp. 805–830.
166. *Ibid.*, pp. 39–40.
167. *Ibid.*, pp. 34–35.
168. *Telex Corp. v. International Business Machines Corp.*, 367 F. Supp. 258.
169. *Telex Corp. v. International Business Machines Corp.*, 510 F. 2d 894. The Appeals Court also affirmed the lower court finding that Telex was liable to IBM for theft of trade secrets. Telex was ordered to pay $17.5 million in compensatory damages.
170. *Telex Corp. v. International Business Machines*, "Brief in Opposition to Petition for a Writ of Certiorari," Supreme Court of the United States (October Term, 1975), pp. 30–32.
171. *Ibid.*, pp. 21–22.
172. In the *Berkey Photo–Kodak* appeal, for example, the court reversed part of the trial court decision against Kodak, and held that the superior performance associated with product innovation must not be considered illegal under the antitrust laws. See *Berkey Photo Inc. v. Eastman Kodak Company*, 603 R 2d 263 (1979).

POSTSCRIPT: SHARED MONOPOLY IN CEREALS?

Although some commentators have suggested that antitrust has mended its ways, the Federal Trade Commission prosecution of the leading ready-to-eat (RTE) cereals companies resembles business as usual.[1]

The cereals industry conveniently contains all the ingredients relevant to the orthodox and mistaken theory of monopoly power. The industry is "concentrated," with the four largest firms selling 90 percent of the so-called ready-to-eat cereals market. Concentration has stayed persistently high for many decades. The firms reportedly avoid price competition and almost always follow the industry leader (Kellogg) when changing their market prices. The profits of the companies have stayed persistently higher than the normal or competitive return on investment. Finally, and most importantly, the dominant firms maintain their market position by introducing dozens of new cereal types ("brand proliferation"), which has had the alleged effect of foreclosing new entry into the market and thus restricting competition in violation of the law. The remedy sought for such antisocial behavior is to force the three leading companies to split off three new competitors, and compulsorily license out all of their trademarked cereal brands (royalty free) to any companies currently excluded from the market.[2]

The extreme emphasis in this case on product differentiation as a barrier to entry is certainly not accidental. For decades students of industrial organization and antitrust policy have been told by respected theorists that product differentiation (and most often a "frivolous" differentiation) is an important barrier to effective competition, and is primarily responsible for inefficiency and welfare loss. We should not be surprised that such theories have finally been taken seriously by those officials now responsible for public policy in this area.

Product Differentiation

The argument that product differentiation misallocates resources by deterring entry and competition has arisen in previous antitrust cases, but it has never been the central issue—indeed the only issue—as in the RTE cereals case. The FTC argument (actually the argument of Professor Richard Schmalensee), is that brand proliferation by the existing companies so "crowds" the "product space" that there is virtually no room for additional brands by new entrants.[3] New entrants are deterred from entering the market since the risk of failure of a new brand is high, and the brand-specific fixed costs (especially advertising) are considerable. Thus continuous brand introductions by the existing companies excludes competition and forecloses the market to new competition. Even though the leading companies continue to earn monopoly profits, entry is effectively barred.

Although this argument may appear plausible, it is riddled with difficulties. Putting aside for the moment the issue of monopoly profits and the fact that cooked cereal, frozen waffles, and other breakfast substitutes were excluded by the FTC from the relevant market, the behavior of the existing companies is certainly compatible with intensely competitive market behavior. Indeed, the FTC is not objecting to monopoly, but to the rigors of the competitive process in the RTE cereals market. For instance, we are told by the FTC that it costs millions to introduce a new cereal. We are told that the risk of introducing any single new brand is extremely high. We are told that the existing companies introduce many new brands (84 between 1952 and 1973) and fill product "holes" quickly, so quickly in fact that new business organizations cannot possibly respond.[4] And finally we are told that all of this entrepreneurial activity is ultimately exclusionary of competition.

If all of this sounds familiar, it should, since it is a variation of Judge Hand's arguments in *Alcoa* (1945).[5] To review briefly, Hand argued that Alcoa "pre-empted" competition by investing in productive capacity and expanding its outputs of aluminum ingot before potential competitors could or would. Alcoa forestalled competition by purchasing water power sites and developing them such that its own industrial efficiency was improved. Alcoa anticipated increases in the demand for its products and efficiently fulfilled that increased demand, employing superb management and an elite personnel. But all of this was not inevitable, concluded Hand. Alcoa's behavior indicated that it meant to maintain its near monopoly position in the market by engaging in those specific exclusionary practices.

The fact that these so-called exclusionary practices in *Alcoa* were all efficient practices, and productive of economies and benefits, has now been widely admitted within antitrust circles. Yet the exclusions in the present cereals case do not differ in substance from the exclusions in *Alcoa*. After all, the cereal companies were not reducing output and repressing innovation. They were admittedly engaged in activities aimed at holding or increasing their market share, and these activities involved introducing and advertising new products (or variations of older products), and expanding the production of those products. That such activity was often accomplished successfully in the face of great market uncertainty is the very essence of the FTC complaint and the very heart of the matter.

If the cereals firms had misinterpreted consumer demand and not introduced new brands, they would have lost market share and there would have been no FTC case. If the firms had misidentified consumer demand and introduced the wrong brands, they would have lost market share and there would have been no FTC case. If the firms had failed to advertise and market their products successfully, there would have been no FTC action. In short, it is the success of private planning and production that is at issue in this case, just as it was in the *Alcoa* case, and no bias against sugar cereals or child-directed television advertising ought to divert our attention from this essential issue.

Profits and Resource Allocation

For some economists, and even for some of the critics of current antitrust policy, the fact that new entry into RTE cereals has been relatively modest, and the fact that profits for the leading companies has stayed persistently high, presents some serious difficulties. Why they ask, if the industry is allegedly competitive, do profit rates stay far above normal for extended periods of time? And is not such profit performance an indication of monopoly and resource misallocation?

The first point to be made is that even neoclassical competition theory admits that disequilibrium profits need *not* be normal. It is only in the long-run competitive equilibrium that firms should earn a competitive rate of return. And since cereal outputs are expanding and new products are constantly being developed, it is obvious that the industry has not yet reached any final equilibrium. Thus "high" profits, even from the perspective of the critics, do not unambiguously indicate any resource misallocation.[6]

Moreover, there is no reason to expect any rivalrous process, especially one involving highly differentiated consumer goods, to *ever* reach an equilibrium with normal profits. Although equilibrium is admittedly a useful pedagogical notion, economists should not get carried away and expect such theoretical constructs to actually exist in reality. They are taking their theoretical models far too seriously and as a consequence are committing grave methodological errors. Unfortunately these methodological errors may have rather serious public policy implications in this instance.

Finally, the cereal companies maintain convincingly that if their assets are revalued at replacement cost, their corresponding rate of return on investment is hardly excessive. On that basis, Kellogg, the most profitable of the companies, earned a modest 11.7 percent on investment between 1958 and 1970.[7]

Entry

There are several additional points to be made with respect to market entry into the cereals industry. The first is that entry need not be accomplished by totally new firms but can encompass expansions in capacity by existing companies.[8] The FTC insists on using the term "entry" in a manner which is not even consistent with traditional neoclassical practices. Since capacity in the cereals industry has increased in response to increases in demand, there certainly has been entry although it has not been the sort of entry (high-cost, new-firm entry) that the FTC would seem to prefer.

But even admitting that new entry has been limited is admitting too much. For the fact remains that there has been new entry into the industry, although much of the entry has occurred in special product areas. Indeed, Quaker Oats was dropped from the FTC case precisely because it had entered the market and expanded its market share so rapidly. All of the alleged

FTC "barriers to competition" were not enough, it seems, to prevent successful market entry and competition in natural cereals. Why this "competition" fails to destroy the entire logic of the FTC case against the big cereal companies is not immediately obvious.

Finally, the FTC has argued that the high profits cannot be explained as a return to high risk since the cereals industry, as indicated by the historical stability of its earnings, is hardly a high-risk industry. Yet earnings are stable despite the high risk associated with brand introductions precisely because the large companies are able to invest in a portfolio of brands, and thereby spread the risk of any single brand failure.[9] From the perspective of the potential small entrant, the industry is extremely risky and entry is, accordingly, deterred. It is uncertain consumer preferences, substantial scale economies, and modest profits that deter entry into the RTE cereals industry. The profits would have to be even higher, perhaps far higher, to encourage entry into most of the RTE brand areas. Rather than charge that profits are exorbitant, the FTC should more logically have argued that cereal profits were kept artificially low, given the risk, to discourage entry and competition.

In short, the RTE cereals case is another antitrust disaster in the making. It is both a travesty of justice and an abuse of sound economic principles and reasoning. But all of this is unlikely to deter the FTC persecution and the ultimate examination of these issues in court. By 1984, if we are lucky, we may find out whether selling Cocoa Puffs and Capt'n Crunch at a profit is really in the public interest.[10]

NOTES

1. This appendix is excerpted from my article, "Competition, Antitrust, and the Ready-to-Eat Cereals Case," *Policy Report*, Vol. 3, No. 2 (February 1981), pp. 1–5. The FTC complaint against Kellogg, General Mills, General Foods, and Quaker Oats was Docket No. 8883 and was filed April 26, 1972. (The Quaker Oats Company has since been dropped from the complaint.)

2. These assorted findings of "fact" are all contained in the four-volume FTC Staff Report titled, "Complaint Counsel's Proposed Findings of Fact, Conclusions of Law, Order, and Supporting Argument," September 30, 1980 (available from the FTC for $82.28).

3. FTC Staff Report, *ibid.*, pp. 256–392.

4. *Ibid.*, especially pp. 249–250.

5. *U.S. v Aluminum Company of America*, 148 F. 2d 416 (1945).

6. Kenneth Clarkson, "Are Corporations' Rates of Return Excessive?" in *The Attack on Corporate America*, ed. M. Bruce Johnson (New York: McGraw Hill Book Company 1978), pp. 267–271.

7. Tom Bethell, "Breakfastgate" The FTC v. the Cereal Companies," *Policy Review*, Vol. 16, (Spring 1981), p. 24.

8. Yale Brozen, "Competition, Efficiency, and Antitrust," in Yale Brozen, ed., *The Competitive Economy: Selected Readings* (Morristown, N.J.: General Learning Press, 1975), p. 11.

9. I am indebted to Professor Bud Herrmann, University of Hartford, for this insight.

10. Whether these issues will be resolved in court is now highly problematical. As this manuscript goes to press Federal Trade Commission administrative judge Alvin Berman has ruled that the cereal companies engage in "intense, unrestrained and uncoordinated competition" and has recommended that all charges against the companies be dropped. See *Wall Street Journal* (September 11, 1981), p. 7.

CHAPTER FIVE

Price Conspiracy and Antitrust Law

While some landmark monopoly cases have at least enjoyed the pretense of a rule of reason approach, price-fixing conspiracies have been judged illegal per se as early as 1898. Since the turn of the century, the courts have asserted that horizontal agreements to fix prices and restrict outputs inherently violate the Sherman Act, and that there can be no question of reasonableness with respect to such agreements.

A THEORY OF PRICE COLLUSION

The traditional rationale for a per se approach to price-fixing agreements depends upon familiar neoclassical assumptions. If collusive agreements are effective, and if the overall performance of business during collusion is inferior to what it would have been without collusion, then the power to fix prices and restrict production might well be condemned. According to this line of reasoning, the power to effect a price conspiracy would become the power to misallocate resources and reduce social welfare. Since there is a high probability that consumers and society would be injured by such agreements, a minute inquiry into the sundry details of any particular conspiracy would be superfluous.

If these collusive agreements are not effective, however, or if there are non-price-competitive factors that outweigh the welfare losses associated with conspiracy, a per se approach to such agreements can be misleading, even from a neoclassical perspective. One could argue the relative costs and benefits of collusion when non-price-competitive factors are important, or when the explicit alternative to conspiracy is either multiple bankruptcies, merger, or government regulation. Finally, as argued in Chapter 2, it is not scientifically demonstrable from a subjectivist perspective that social efficiency and welfare are reduced whenever market outputs are voluntarily restricted.[1]

The Difficulties of Collusion

An agreement by business organizations to restrict output and raise market prices could be profitable, under appropriate conditions. Theoretically the firms would sell less, charge more, and reap the monopoly bonuses associated with collusion. Or alternatively, a collusive agreement might bind the participants to submit noncompetitive bids at a public letting; one of these firms would be preselected to get the business. In short, collusion intends to restrict competition between firms, to their mutual benefit.

But what are the appropriate conditions for effective collusion and under what circumstances are these conditions likely to be fulfilled? The dominant presumption for some time has been that successful price collusion would be common in the American business system without antitrust prohibition. The intent of the following discussion is to challenge such a presumption and suggest, instead, that there are inherent economic factors which would tend at all times to limit the success, and hence the significance, of price-fixing agreements in a free market. It is to be assumed that the firms under discussion desire to reduce competition. What is being challenged here is their ability, in open markets, to effectuate such a situation.

Substitutes. The responsiveness of the amount purchased to price changes (termed *elasticity*) is of critical importance when considering the potential effectiveness of price-fixing agreements. If, for example, the commodity to be price-fixed has few good substitutes in the short run, an increase in its price may increase the total revenues of the conspiracy and make price collusion financially rewarding. But if, as more often is the case, there is a plentiful array of products that might be substituted for the commodity that is being price-fixed, the higher price may simply push marginal buyers to the relatively cheaper substitutes, and thus lower total conspiracy revenues.

This consequence will encourage firms to break the agreement to maintain a uniform price since the agreement does not, apparently, work in their economic interest. Certainly some firms will be relatively worse off with respect to substitute competition than others, and would be the first to feel the pinch of a revenue squeeze and the first to consider a policy of selective price reductions. Thus, the threat of substitute competition may make price conspiracy difficult to organize in the first place, or can lead to competitive price reductions that break the agreements apart.

Changes in Demand. A slight reduction in overall demand for the price-fixed commodity may tend to weaken the price agreement; business recession is the natural enemy of successful price collusion. A decrease in demand at fixed prices will dramatically curb market sales, and the temptation to ease the sales decline with a price reduction will be strong, especially for the low-profit firms involved. Since all firms differ in financial strength, and in their willingness to ride out a demand decline, there must be such temptations and such pressures. If the relatively weaker firms cut prices in an attempt to increase or maintain their sales, the formal price-fixing agreements tumble.

Output Agreements.   Firms that agree to maintain prices in the face of declining demand usually agree to some collusive marketing arrangement. Under these arrangements particular firms may be selected to get particular jobs, or some particular percentage of industry output. This part of the conspiracy is crucial since it must produce proper revenues to each firm involved, else one or more of the conspirators will "chisel" prices to "steal" orders. However these marketing arrangements are all but impossible to police or sustain for any extended period of time. Will the present market shares be maintained? And if they are maintained, how long will they last? What arrangements will exist for altering the status quo? Will a smaller firm attempt to cut the conspiracy price when it feels that its allotted share or territory is too restrictive, and no operational procedures for change exist? And what about new firms attracted to the market by the higher-than-competitive prices? By definition, they have no allotted outputs or selling territories. Will they be content to just take a slice of the existing action? But which of the existing sellers in the conspiracy is to give up sales to make room for the newcomer? The inevitable tendency of output restrictions is to frustrate aggressive sellers and attract new producers, and weaken any existing agreement to restrict output.

Costs.   Let us assume the existence of a manufacturing firm whose average production and selling costs per unit decline as output increases. There are certain economies associated with larger outputs; spreading the fixed overhead and purchasing supplies in larger quantities can lower average costs per unit of output, and make larger outputs cheaper to produce and sell than smaller outputs. The significant point for this discussion is that firms that restrict output as part of a price conspiracy invariably limit their ability to realize such economies. Hence, some profits will be sacrificed unless the extra revenue associated with the conspiracy exceeds the higher per unit costs associated with the output restriction.

This consideration must surely make high-overhead-cost firms hesitant to join such restrictive agreements. Further, smaller firms will be anxious to increase, not decrease, their output in order to enjoy the savings associated with larger scale output. To compete with larger, more efficient firms in the future may make this output expansion and cost savings mandatory. Thus, price-fixing and output agreements must be difficult to conclude when firms find it cost advantageous to increase, not decrease, their sales.

Imports.   As long as international markets are free, and it is within U.S. authority to reduce or eliminate quotas and tariffs on all goods, a domestic price-fixing conspiracy is limited by foreign competition. When imported goods are price competitive, domestic price-fixing agreements are inherently unstable. A world-wide price and output conspiracy is possible, but almost all such arrangements have existed and functioned successfully in the past only with active governmental support.

Honesty and Trust.   Honesty and trust between the firms involved in conspiracy is crucial to its successful operation. If one of the conspirators thinks, or is led to think, that anyone else is not living up to the price-output agreements (and they will have to police their own agreements), then price cutting is likely. And since it is difficult to turn down old customers and their price requests, and difficult not to discount from book price when demand is flat and backlog falling, and since all firms understand this, the suspicion of secret price concessions will always be strong. Furthermore, since firms don't trust one another in open competition, it is difficult to understand why they would suddenly trust one another during periods of collusion.

Differentiated Products.   Other things being equal, it can be expected that price-fixing would be more difficult in industries where the products being sold are highly differentiated. Firms selling homogeneous products (e.g., cement) concentrate most of the competitiveness of their output in one bit of significant data: price per unit weight. In theory, a price-fix on homogeneous products would, therefore, be relatively simple since the range of competitive variables is manageable. The greater the number of competitive variables or the less important unit-price becomes, however, the greater the difficulty that a simple price conspiracy could function in the interests of the parties involved. Consumer goods industries, with their usual emphasis on diversity and differentiation, would appear to be poor candidates for successful price collusion.

Transportation Costs.   Local or regional price conspiracies are delimited by transportation charges from areas where price competition is still open. For example, to fix the price of septic tanks in area A, the area A septic tank sellers would have to take into account the fact that sellers in area B could begin to compete, and thus weaken the conspiracy, whenever production costs plus transportation approach the price-fix. Thus if the manufacturing costs for all the area sellers were roughly similar, the price-fix in area A would be limited by the freight rates between area A and the nearest competitive market. Put slightly differently, if transportation costs between markets were low relative to final price, a local price conspiracy would find it difficult to increase and fix prices for any extended period of time.

Summary

In short, it is probable that private price-fixing agreements would be unstable when substitute competition is important, demand is falling, aggressive sellers are not a party to the conspiracy, production quotas are to be agreed upon, larger outputs are cheaper per unit than smaller outputs, imports are an important part of market competition, mutual distrust and suspicion abound, buyers are in a position to bargain, products are widely differentiated, and where transportation costs are negligible between relevant markets. Any of these factors might be enough to limit successful price collusion. And since a great many markets, at one time or another, display these various conditions, it appears reasonable to assume that generally successful collusion would be of minor proportions, even without antitrust prohibition.

Price Agreements and Social Welfare

To this point in our discussion we have assumed, consistent with the standard neoclassical perspective, that horizontal price agreements are socially undesirable. Yet neoclassical analysis has devoted scant attention to the benefits that might be associated with such agreements. The general presumption in the literature is that there are no social benefits, or that the benefits are so miniscule that they can be safely ignored.[2] In the section below we will speculate that there may be benefits associated with price agreement and that they may be substantial. This is not to argue for a "rule of reason" in price-fixing cases, which it seems would be justified from a neoclassical perspective, but to hold, instead, consistent with the subjectivist theory of efficiency outlined in Chapter 2, that all voluntary agreements are explicit evidence of an attempt to increase efficiency, and ought to be allowed. Moreover, while price agreements may offend one's sense of morality, just as lying and being a "bad sport" might, they are clearly not a property rights violation.[3] It can be maintained, therefore, that such agreements have as much right to exist in a free society as do unpopular agreements to, say, publish pornographic material or sell laetrile.

From a neoclassical perspective there are several reasons why price agreements could be considered beneficial and why prohibiting them could be considered inefficient. The first reason that comes to mind is that the agreements themselves always signify unambiguous evidence of benefit (utility) to the parties involved. We know that the parties to the agreement expect to benefit—else why did they make the agreement? On the other hand, we do not know if there is a loss to society as a whole, since costs are ultimately subjective and incapable of aggregation and exact measurement.[4] Thus we could always assert that in our judgment the benefits exceed any possible costs, and not vice versa, as neoclassical analysis has consistently assumed.

An additional social benefit associated with collusive agreements is that they may save independent firms from bankruptcy or merger. In the latter situation, merger is always a permanent reduction in competition from a neoclassical perspective, and prices are forever fixed after the consolidation. Under price-fixing agreements, it will be recalled, the arrangements are always tenuous and tend to break apart naturally in open markets. So the prohibition of any horizontal price agreement may encourage firms to create an organizational structure (merger) that is less competitive, in a neoclassical sense, than the activity prohibited. How this promotes the public interest, even from a utilitarian perspective, is not immediately obvious.[5]

Price agreements and output restrictions may also be initiated for perfectly respectable consumer welfare reasons. For instance, price agreements may allow for an increase in non-price competition. Or they may induce further cooperation between companies such that lower costs and increased efficiency are achieved; specifically, information costs could be reduced through collusion. Or output restriction may occur because firms speculate that product prices will be higher in the future than they are now; thus the firms cooperate to conserve resources in the present in order to offer more of these higher valued units in the future.[6] In each of these instances, it is not obvious that consumer or social welfare is unambiguously reduced, or that the prohibition of such agreements is consistent with the public interest.

The most serious problem with prohibiting price agreements is that rivalrous competition between large corporations may appear *as if* such collusive agreements always exist. Economists have been describing for years such tacit agreements and administered pricing situations in oligopolistic industries, and they have not hidden their displeasure with such arrangements. Analytically, there may be little difference between an explicit agreement to charge similar prices, and a competitive process in which Firm X increases or decreases a price and Firm Y follows. But instead of suggesting that both situations are acceptable, antitrust authorities and the courts may treat oligopolistic competition as de facto collusion.[7] And since a firm may follow a price increase, a price decrease, and may, when the price changes are over, be charging the same prices as its competitors for its products, it is possible that the entire free-market pricing process under oligopoly may become untenable. Thus the real problem with prohibiting collusion is that it is not a precise notion, and the principle may easily be extended to cripple all rivalrous corporate pricing.

Finally, as we argued in Chapter 2, even competitive outputs are always restricted, since all firms tend to equate their marginal costs with their marginal revenue, and not with market price. But how, analytically, is this restriction to be distinguished from the alleged restriction that occurs under collusion? The answer is that it cannot be distinguished. Free markets contain free-market prices, arrived at through various pricing strategies; there is no atomistic price and output that we might use as a welfare benchmark to determine some free-market supply restriction. If the market outputs were restrained by government we could speak of a monopoly restriction and a monopoly price. But in the absence of such legal restrictions on competition, interdependent pricing, in all of its manifestations, is part and parcel of the free-market process.

THE ADDYSTON PIPE CASE (1899)

We now turn to an examination of some of the landmark price-fixing cases prosecuted under the Sherman Act. The *Addyston Pipe* case is an antitrust landmark for at least three reasons.[8] In the first place, it represents one of the few early victories for the Justice Department under the Sherman Act. Second, its successful prosecution may have been a factor in significant structural changes (increasing industrial concentration) that took place in American manufacturing during the 1895–1902 period.[9] Finally the case is classic because it details vividly the difficulties of price collusion in a free and unstable market.

In 1896, the U.S. Justice Department brought suit in the Circuit Court for the Eastern District of Tennessee against six cast-iron pipe manufacturers: Addyston Pipe and Steel Company; Dennis Long and Company; Howard-Harrison Iron Company; Anniston Pipe and Foundry Company; South Pittsburgh Pipe Works, and the Chattanooga Foundry and Pipe Works. The firms were charged with rigging the bid prices for cast-iron pipe to certain municipalities. The District Court decision had argued that the combination only affected manufacturing and not interstate trade and commerce.[10] Circuit Court Judge Taft, on appeal, reversed the lower court decision on the gounds that such "associations" were always void at common law, and that there was "no question of reasonableness open to the courts with reference to such a contract."[11] Besides, Taft indicated, even if the reasonableness of the conspiracy was at issue, the facts in the case clearly demonstrated that the Addyston "group" was, indeed, charging unreasonable prices.[12]

On December 4, 1899, the Supreme Court agreed with Judge Taft's decision and reaffirmed the reversal by the Appeals Court. Justice Peckham, writing the majority opinion, simply quoted Taft's analysis of the unreasonableness of the Addyston group's prices and concluded that:

> The facts thus set forth (Taft's quoted decision) show conclusively that the effect of the combination was to enhance prices beyond a sum which was reasonable, and therefore the first objection above set forth need not be further noticed.[13]

History of the Conspiracy

The history of the Addyston Pipe conspiracy has been detailed by Almarin Phillips.[14] Phillips indicates that the object of the conspiracy was fairly straightforward. The six firms involved were the major suppliers of cast-iron pipe in the southern market area. Although there were many other cast-iron pipe producers in the rest of the country, particularly in the New Jersey area, transportation costs from the eastern plants limited competition for jobs in the "safe" areas immediately surrounding the plants of the southern manufacturers. The general idea of the conspiracy was to end competition between the six firms for the local reserved-cities jobs altogether, and to collusively prearrange a bid and a bidder for the public letting in what was termed the "pay territory." Hopefully, the internal reduction in price competition between the southern firms, and the consequently higher prices, would increase group revenues and profits.

But there were difficulties with the scheme from the beginning. The major operational difficulty concerned the allocation of "pay territory" jobs. Which firms were to get them, and how were the final bid prices determined? The prearranged bid price in the pay territory certainly had to be below the delivered price of any northern producer not a party to the conspiracy, or the southern group would get no business at all. Yet, at the same time, the price actually bid had to be high enough to realize a monopoly profit for the conspirators.

In addition, the bid price had to be at least competitive with firms within the pay territory and not a party to the conspiracy. Judge Taft admitted that there were 170,500 tons of cast-iron pipe capacity in the pay territory associated with nonconspiracy firms.[15] Some of these nonconspiracy pay territory manufacturers were in Texas, Colorado, and Oregon; more important mills were in St. Louis, Columbus, in Northern Ohio, and in Michigan.[16] Thus the prices worked out by the Addyston group would have to be tempered by potential competition from within and without the pay territory.

How were the bid prices determined? The solution to this problem was to allow secret bidding for pay territory jobs by conspiracy members. When a low-bid price was selected, the winner was then allowed to "bid a bonus" price per ton for the privilege of submitting that bid at the public letting and actually performing the production. Other things equal, the firm with the lowest marginal production costs, plus transportation, could then bid the largest bonus and get the job. Secret bidding reintroduced the element of price competition, and allowed the conspiracy to allocate the appropriate jobs to the most efficient companies. Consequently, as should be obvious, the firms that bid the largest bonus and secured the job, derived little *additional* profit from the arrangement since the bonuses were paid to the other conspirators.

Did the Conspiracy Work?

Was the attempt at price collusion successful? If the test of success is made to be a significant and sustained advance in the final price of cast-iron pipe sold by the Addyston group companies between 1893 and 1896, then clearly the collusion was not successful. For example, the first preliminary attempts to advance prices and profits in 1893 and 1894 were admitted failures.[17] During this period, prices charged by the conspiracy members were actually lower (in some cases as much as 20 percent lower) than they had been in the pre-conspiracy period. Interestingly, even prices bid in some of the reserved-city areas were significantly lower than in the period prior to the conspiracy.

Although the Addyston group did agree on a new plan in late 1895, and although some bid prices did advance briefly, most bid prices by the middle of 1896 were as low, or lower than in the previous nonconspiracy period. For example, in a statement by M. L. Holman, Water Commissioner of St. Louis, dated January 15, 1897, it is indicated that the contract price for cast-iron pipe per ton was $24.95 on April 12, 1892; $25.48 on July 26, 1892; $19.94 on August 7, 1894; $19.85 on March 26, 1895; $22.47 on September 17, 1895; $19.64 on July 28, 1896; and $19.94 on October 6, 1896.[18] These price movements were typical of the patterns in other pay territory cities.

But were the prices charged by the conspiracy "fair and reasonable"? Almarin Phillips suggests that Judge Taft likely erred when he concluded that the prices charged by the conspiracy were unreasonable.[19] The rather incomplete cost-price information available suggests, to Phillips, that conspiracy prices in the period under consideration were frequently below average costs, and possibly even below average variable costs.[20] He speculates that a price of $20 per ton would have covered full costs, including transportation, if the mills had been operating close to capacity. But since they were operating well below capacity in 1896, Phillips concludes that the "charge that the general level of prices was exorbitant seems unjustified."[21]

The United States Supreme Court *Record and Briefs* in the *Addyston Pipe* case supply additional information concerning the fairness of the prices charged by the conspiracy during the period. Although Judge Taft summarily dismissed the fifty-odd affidavits from private contractors, gas and water companies, and public officials testifying to the reasonableness of the prices charged, nothing, for our purposes, could be more relevant. Affidavit after affidavit swore to the fact that the buyer was acquainted with all the firms that manufactured cast-iron pipe, with the prices of pipe past and present, and with the price of the basic raw material, pig iron. On that basis, all testified that the prices actually charged for pipe were fair and reasonable. The last paragraph from the affidavit of A. W. Walton dated December 30, 1896 stated that:

> The prices at which said pipe, and all other pipe, which aggregated large amounts have been purchased by me and furnished by the Addiston Pipe and Foundry Company and others are the lowest that could be obtained from any of the pipe works in the United States. From my knowledge and long experience, extending over a number of years past, respecting the cost of manufacturing cast-iron pipe, the loss entailed, and the capital required, I consider the prices at which said pipe was purchased as fair, reasonable and just. From my knowledge of such things I do not believe that the prices could reasonably have been less. The prices at which cast-iron pipe has sold since December, 1894, have been uniformly moderate, even low in a number of instances, much lower at all times than pipe could be purchased prior to that time.[22]

Now surely the sworn testimony of the supposed victims of this conspiracy, the buyers of cast-iron pipe, to the effect that they believed that they were not being victimized is important and relevant information. Yet almost all accounts of the Addyston conspiracy conveniently ignore this information.[23]

The probable reason for the inability of the conspiracy to increase and sustain monopoly prices is not difficult to discover. Although many of the theoretical factors discussed earlier in this chapter would appear to favor successful price collusion here, the one crucial nonfavorable factor was the level of demand. The period of the middle 1890s was one of extremely poor and unstable economic performance, even depression. In that context, it is doubtful that the number of bids for cast-iron pipe sought by contractors and municipalities would have been sufficient to sustain then existing plant capacity without a severe reduction in market price. Further, idle capacity on the part of the nonconspiracy firms would have made them hungry for additional business at any price that covered their out-of-pocket expenses. With a decrease in demand for pipe on the part of private contractors, and the uncertainty associated with the demand for pipe on the part of the municipalities, it is not surprising that prices could not even be maintained at preconspiracy levels, let alone pushed higher. The general level of demand and the level of operating capacity of all pipe works (there were 21 firms operating in the United States) were, it appears, much more important influences on market price than conspiracy. Thus, in one of the landmark price-fixing cases of all antitrust history, monopoly prices were not realized and monopoly profits were certainly not obtained.

THE TRENTON POTTERIES CASE (1927)

A. D. Neale, in his widely respected volume, *The Antitrust Laws of the U. S. A.*, declares that the *Trenton Potteries* case is the leading Supreme Court decision on price-fixing.[24] And so it may well be. But few antitrust volumes, including Neale's own excellent survey, supply any substantial conduct performance information that would allow the reader to determine what actually transpired during this alleged conspiracy, and during the very interesting proceedings at the trial court. The most general and repeated summaries of the *Trenton Potteries* decision are legalistic. In this case, almost all accounts relate, Supreme Court Justice Stone reaffirmed the *Addyston Pipe* case precedent on price-fixing agreements and stated that:

> Agreements which create such potential power may well be held to be *in themselves unreasonable* or unlawful restraints, without the necessity of minute inquiry whether a particular price is reasonable or unreasonable . . .[25]

Thus price-fixing agreements were always illegal, and there was to be no rule of reason with regard to such conspiracies.

Such a legalistic approach leaves the most interesting economic questions unanswered, or even unasked. Did, for example, these so-called price agreements in *Trenton Potteries* actually accomplish agreement, that is, were the actual market prices for vitreous pottery bathroom and lavatory fixtures "uniform, arbitrary, and noncompetitive," as the federal grand jury indictment had charged?[26] It would be both informative and ironic, indeed, if in the "leading case on price-fixing," it could be determined that prices were not actually fixed and not uniform. Before we explore this and similar questions concerning the conduct performance of the firms involved, a brief sketch of the industry and the alleged conspiracy is required.

Background to Trenton Potteries

At the time of the alleged illegal agreements, the pottery industry in the United States was regionally concentrated in New Jersey along the Delaware

River.[27] Although there were pottery firms in Chicago, Kalamazoo, Evansville, and Wheeling, West Virginia, at least eight important firms, including Trenton Potteries and Thomas Maddock & Sons, (the two largest firms), were located in Trenton, New Jersey. Also headquartered in Trenton was the Sanitary Potters Association, the trade organization to which at least twenty-three firms representing 82 percent of the industry's output belonged.

The activities of the Sanitary Potters Association were varied, and eventually controversial. There is evidence to suggest that the Association encouraged its members to adopt a more standardized approach to the design of certain bathroom fixtures, and that it strongly encouraged the use of a uniform system of cost accounting. It also kept records of the particular wholesalers (jobbers) to whom Association members sold so-called first-line class A material, and occasionally admonished its members for selling imperfect class B fixtures in the home market. Its most controversial activity, however, involved the preparation and publication of an official industry price list.

The price lists (there were six different lists for six different geographical areas of the country) were prepared from statistics of actual sale prices submitted monthly by the association members,[28] and also from the recommendations of the Sanitary Potters "price list committee." The lists were then sent out to the member firms and supposedly served as the basis for their own price bulletins. In an individual firm price bulletin one might find the list price on a particularly styled wash bowl; in addition, the discount off the list price might also be indicated. Further, there were surcharges that might be added to the actual order invoice on particular bathroom ware. If all firms in the same regional zone followed the same list price in their bulletins, and then applied the same discount and the same surcharges to the same class A items, the final selling prices for these particular firms would have been identical.

In August 1922, a federal grand jury returned an indictment against twenty-three vitreous pottery manufacturers, claiming that they had conspired, through their trade association, to "fix and exact noncompetitive prices for the sale of said pottery," and that the firms had "refrained from engaging in competition with each other as to the prices of said pottery."[29] In addition, the indictment also charged that the defendants had illegally conspired to confine their sales of bathroom and lavatory fixtures to "legitimate jobbers."[30] The case was tried by Judge William C. Van Fleet, and on April 17, 1923, the jury returned a guilty verdict on both counts.

The convicted defendants appealed and on May 9, 1924, a Circuit Court of Appeals reversed the trial court decision on the basis of certain procedural errors in the conduct of the trial. Circuit Court Judge Hough, speaking for Judge Rogers and Mayer, maintained that "the learned court erred" when it had refused to allow defense witnesses to testify as to the existence of competition between the defendants, and that it had erred when it instructed the jury that "if they found the defendants did conspire to restrain trade, as charged in the indictment, *then it was immaterial whether such agreements were ever actually carried out . . .*"[31]

Judge Hough argued that it "was essential for the prosecution to prove the absence of competition" and, thus, "incumbent upon the defense to show, if possible, the presence of actual competition in respect of prices."[32] This was especially important, Judge Hough observed, in view of the fact that none of the defendants lived in the district where the trial had been conducted (Southern District of New York), and that the federal indictment had not charged that the conspiracy was formed in that district.

> . . . consequently there was no jurisdiction there to bring the indictment or there to try the case, unless it was shown that the jurisdiction was conferred by the commission of an overt act within the Southern District.
>
> The pleader understood this, for otherwise all the allegations concerning acts done in the Southern District in pursuance of the object of the conspiracy were mere surplusage. Why the United States was so anxious to institute and prosecute this case in the city of New York we do not know, but the frame of indictment compared with the undisputed facts show that New York was intentionally selected, and trial of these defendants in the Third Circuit, where most of them resided, was sedulously avoided. Such a choice as this carried with it the burden of proving something done in the Southern district, i.e., an overt act—justifying the finding of the indictment. The peculiarity of this transplanted litigation was overlooked below, and *it was error, and very material error*, to instruct a New York jury in so many words that it was immaterial whether any effort had ever been made to carry out the conspiracy complained of.[33]

The essential question, therefore, and the one totally ignored by the lower court, was: had the firms successfully conspired to fix arbitrary and uniform prices and, hence, "injure the public"?

Did the Conspiracy Work?

Both the trial court record and the United States Supreme Court *Records & Briefs*[34] contain abundant evidence that selling prices during the period of the alleged conspiracy were not fixed and not uniform, and that there was active competition—active price competition—between the defendants. The many buyers of vitreous pottery, to the extent that they were allowed to testify, indicated that the defendants were in active price competition with each other, and that the bulletin prices were not actual selling prices. As one buyer put it:

> I received their bulletins . . . I did not make use of the bulletins except to put
> them in the waste basket, because I went around shopping and bought just as I
> found the market ripe to buy. My prices were not affected or controlled by
> these bulletin prices that I know of . . .[35]

Although the government attorney objected again and again, and trial court
Judge Van Fleet sustained almost all objections to the introduction of defense testimony as to whether actual competition did exist in the market for
the wares of the defendants, the official record of the case still contains overwhelming evidence that vigorous price competition did exist. The following
excerpt is a summary statement from respondent's *Brief* pertaining to price
determination in the market. (The trial court record page references are in pa-
rentheses.)

> During all of the period in question sales of sanitary pottery were made at
> prices below those announced in the current bulletins (R., p. 344, fols.
> 1030–1031; p. 375, fol. 1123; p. 397, fols. 1189–1191; p. 422, fol. 1264; p. 442,
> fols. 1324–1325; p. 445, fol. 1335; p. 459, fols. 1375; p. 459, fol. 1376; p. 460,
> fol. 1378; p. 498, fol. 1453; p. 512, fol. 1535; p. 516, fol. 1547 and p. 521, fol.
> 1562). Some buyers never paid bulletin prices. (R., p. 424, fol. 1271). Others
> bought oftener below than at the bulletin prices, (R., p. 448, fol. 1342; p. 452,
> fol. 1356; p. 459, fol. 1375; p. 459, fol. 1376; p. 460, fol. 1378: p. 464, fol.
> 1391). The prices at which the various companies sold were usually different.
> (R., p. 528, fol. 1582) Sometimes the bulletin prices varied. (R., p. 450, fol.
> 1348; p. 459, fol. 1376). The prices charged by some of the companies were
> always lower than those of any of the others. (R., p. 381, fol. 1142). Some of
> the manufacturers regularly gave certain customers a stated reduction from
> their published prices (R., p. 513, fol. 1539) Salesmen of defendant companies
> found themselves in competition as to price with those of other companies (R.,
> p. 398, fols. 1193–1194), and manufacturers, if they wanted the business, met
> their competitors' prices. (R., p. 471, fol. 1412). Buyers found manufacturers
> bidding against each other for their business (R., p. 422, fols. 1265–1266; p.
> 492, fol. 1475; p. 514, fol. 1541; p. 525, fols. 1573–1575) and reducing their
> prices to get orders (R., p. 439, fol. 1317; p. 446, fol. 1336; p. 450, fol. 1349).
> Some buyers obtained prices from several manufacturers at the same time and
> found that these prices differed (R., p. 436, fol. 1306; p. 438, fol. 1314; p. 440,
> fols. 1318–1319; p. 446, fol. 1336; p. 450, fol. 1349). Some buyers obtained
> prices from several manufacturers at the same time and found that these
> prices differed (R., p. 436, fol. 1306; p. 438, fol. 1314; p. 440, fols. 1318–
> 1319; p. 446, fol. 1336; p. 465, fol. 1393; p. 528, fol. 1582). Some of the buyers
> thought so little of price bulletins that they threw them away (R., p. 439, fol.
> 1316).[36]

Further, an analysis of the actual sales invoices of twenty-one of the twenty-
three defendants between June 1, 1918, and July 31, 1922, showed that 26

percent of the tanks sold by the defendants sold at bulletin prices, while 64 percent sold below bulletin and 10 percent above bulletin. Of the bathroom bowls invoiced, only 28 percent sold at bulletin prices, while 68 percent sold below bulletin and 4 percent above bulletin.[37] And the differences from bulletin prices were not slight. Almarin Phillips has noted that some actual prices for tanks and bowls may have varied as much as 40 percent from the official bulletin prices. Clearly, then, the Trenton Potteries conspiracy was not able to fix uniform, arbitrary and noncompetitive prices for vitreous pottery in the period under consideration. And in the leading case on price-fixing, market prices were not actually fixed at all.

One can speculate as to why the conspiracy failed. Almarin Phillips suggests that the industry lacked "the leadership required to establish an effective market organization."[38] The markets were disorganized, the pottery firms had widely different objectives, and since there was no assurance that anybody was following bulletin prices, all had to "cheat" to insure their proper share of new orders. In addition, since there were no penalties associated with "shading" bulletin prices (outside of occasional admonishments), the financial benefits of competition simply exceeded the very insecure gains to be associated with any agreement. Besides, since the agreements themselves were probably being employed to obtain better market information, they encouraged more efficient rivalry and competition. Under such conditions, rigid price collusion was extremely unlikely.

The 1918–22 period was also high in other economic uncertainties. The disequilibriums of World War I were severe, especially in an industry as sensitive to construction spending and housing starts as pottery. At the same time, a major technological change had threatened to revolutionize the manufacturing process in the industry.[39] All these factors together must have placed intense competitive pressure on the existing market structure of independent pottery manufactures, and certainly made them extremely price conscious.

The Supreme Court, however, regarded such contextual information as "immaterial," and reversed the appeals court decision that such economic evidence should have been part of the deliberations of the jury. In 1927, and rather consistently since then,[40] any price agreement, or any sort of combination that "tampers with price structures,"[41] has been regarded as unlawful. Whether prices have actually been fixed, or whether they have been fixed at unreasonable levels, has been immaterial to a determination of guilt or innocence. To automatically presume that price-fixing antitrust cases must demonstrate that successful price-fixing is easy or common throughout the American business system, or would be without a protective Sherman Act, is not justifiable. In almost all instances, the information relevant to decide such an issue has been "immaterial" at federal court.

THE GREAT ELECTRICAL EQUIPMENT CONSPIRACY (1961)

The most celebrated price-fixing antitrust case of modern times is the electrical equipment manufacturers price conspiracy of the late 1950s. Involved were some of the nation's largest and most prestigious corporations, such as General Electric, Westinghouse, Allis-Chalmers, Federal Pacific, I-T-E Circuit Breaker, and Carrier. Various employees of these firms were charged with, between 1956 and 1959, combining and conspiring to "raise, fix, and maintain" the prices of insulators, transformers, power switchgear, condensors, circuit breakers, and various other electrical equipment and apparatus, involving an estimated $1.7 billion dollars worth of business annually.[42]

A series of Philadelphia grand jury indictments were returned during 1960. After much discussion between the defendants and the Department of Justice, the firms were allowed to plead guilty to some of the more serious charges, and *nolo contendere* to the rest. On February 6, 1961, Judge Ganey sentenced seven executives to jail, gave twenty-three others suspended jail sentences, and fined the firms involved nearly $2 million.[43] Subsequent triple damage suits brought against the equipment manufacturers by the TVA and private firms that had been allegedly "overcharged," increased the financial penalty manyfold. And so ended the most publicized price conspiracy in all business history.

Background To Conspiracy

The fact that there were secret price meetings among various electrical equipment producers between 1956 and 1959 was indisputable. The meetings were reportedly a "way of life" in the industry.[44] Some of the meetings were little more than hastily called "gripe" sessions where the various firm representatives complained about price discounting and foreign price competition. But others were more sophisticated and, apparently, involved the determination and application of secret bidding formulas and the formal allocation of some market business, particularly government jobs. Certainly the most incredible aspect of the conspiracy was not the price meetings, but the absolute disclaimer by top General Electric and Westinghouse executives of any knowledge of any "conspiracy." The middle-management executives actually involved in the meetings took the brunt of the social penalties.

If an agreement to fix prices constitutes illegal price-fixing, then the electrical manufacturers were certainly guilty of price-fixing. If "tampering with price structures" constitutes illegal price-fixing, then these meetings were in clear violation of the Sherman Act. But for the purposes of this discussion, the important questions are not legal or moral but economic. Did the conspiracy, in fact, "raise, fix and maintain" unreasonable prices as the twenty-odd indictments had charged? Did it "restrain, suppress and *eliminate*" price competition with respect to the selling of various kinds of electrical machinery or apparatus? Did the conspiracy, in fact, work to cheat the public of the benefits of free competition?

The Pricing Process

To correctly comprehend the issue of price collusion, one must understand the normal pricing practices that were in effect in this multiproduct, oligopolistic industry during the 1950s. General Electric, Westinghouse, and to a lesser extent the small manufacturers, sell hundreds of thousands of electrical products that have been standardized to a high degree by the industry's trade association. The products are sold out of huge catalogs where potential customers may obtain a detailed description of the product and its suggested list price. Almost all the catalog products are so-called shelf items, which the huge manufacturers produce continuously and hold in inventory. When an order is received, a computer fills the request and directs that the particular product be shipped from the closest warehouse to the customer.

Since many of the products produced by the electrical equipment manufacturers are nearly identical, and since all firms quote delivered prices, the selling prices for standardized shelf items are nearly identical to all buyers.[45] Any price change by one seller, usually announced with a mimeographed price sheet to customers, is quickly matched by other competitive sellers. On sealed-bid business, the price change is announced when the bids are opened. In any case, the pressure of the marketplace—that is, the desire on the part of each manufacturer to keep or increase his customers and his profits—makes the new price the new catalog price, which is, again, nearly identical for all firms. Although there may be recognized quality differences that eventually "sell" an order, it appears that the price of the higher quality product must approximate its lower quality competitor. The testimony of Mr. John K. Hodnette, executive vice president of Westinghouse, illustrates the pricing process with respect to such a shelf item, electric meters:[46]

> There is a standard item. It is the meter that goes on the outside of the house that measures the use of current, protects the customer, tells the utility how much electricity has been used so that they can render a bill. We have been manufacturing these meters for 75 years. The selling price is approximately $16. . . . About 60 days ago, I think it was, one of our competitors decreased the price of his watt-hour meter that corresponded to the one in question in Cleveland. When we learned of this, which we do very promptly, because they send out published catalogs, and our customers call them to our attention, so with the large number that are printed it is very easy matter to get a copy of a competitor's catalog and determine his prices, they reduced the price of the

meter 30 cents per meter, when the new pricelist came out. We had just concluded the development of a meter which we thought was superior, better than
any in the industry. We advised our field salespeople that we were not at that
time planning to reduce our prices. We felt that we could sell a superior product at a higher price. We very soon learned that customers would not pay us
the price, and many of them came to us and asked us to reduce our price to the
same as those charged by competitors, so that they could continue to buy
meters from us.[47]

Thus, Mr. Hodnette argued, the competitive process tended to produce similar prices. And the pricing process was not essentially different with reference
to sealed bid business. As he explained:

The City of Cleveland and many other people recognize no brand preference
or quality preference of one meter manufactured by one company as against
another. In order to obtain business in any location, it is necessary that he be
competitive with respect to price. This is total cost to the customer, whether he
be the city of Cleveland or TVA, delivered to him at the site he wants it. He
will not pay more. . . . In order for a manufacturer to get an order, he must
quote a competitive price. He must quote a price that is equal to that of any of
his competitors, delivered to the customer, and without any qualifications.[48]

From these remarks, it is clear that a dynamic competitive process could account for nearly identically quoted list prices in the electrical equipment
manufacturing industry during the late 1950s. To regard such quotations as
per se evidence of collusion or conspiracy, therefore, would certainly be incorrect. A final note on this important issue from Mr. Ralph Cordiner, president of General Electric during this period, will suffice.

In the course of these hearings, considerable attention has been devoted to the
frequent identity of prices charged by competitors. It has been suggested that
this identity, where it occurs, indicates a lack of competition, or even continuing conspiracy, among competing manufacturers. In all candor, may I say that
identity of prices on standard, mass-produced items normally indicates no such
thing. On the contrary, such price identity is the inevitable and necessary result
of the force of competition—a force that requires sellers of standardized items
to meet the lowest price offered in the market. The manufacturer who makes a
product on a mass-produced basis and where minimum performance or quality
standards are a part of the customer specifications will not long be in business if
he prices that product above the market. The customers will purchase elsewhere unless his product has demonstrable additional values accepted by a reasonably large number of customers. The manufacturer who prices his products
below the market will quickly discover there is no advantage to him because his

competitors drop their prices to the price level he establishes. . . . It is simply not true that uniformity of prices is evidence of collusion. Nor is it true that uniformity of prices on sealed bids amounts to an elimination of price competition. The facts are that vigorous price competition continually takes place with one effect being a uniformity of catalog prices and, therefore, a uniformity of sealed bid quotations. Suppliers come to the conclusion—some possibly reluctantly—that if they want to continue to offer a particular product for sale that they will have to offer it at market prices equal to the lowest available from any supplier of any acceptable product.[49]

Even if the product being sold is not a standardized shelf item, firms that intend to be competitive will meet the established market price. This procedure will hold even if a firm has not as yet manufactured the specialized electrical apparatus; it will quote the price of its competitor so as to announce to potential customers that it can and will be competitive should orders appear. Thus the costs in the short run, or even before the product is actually made, are not the major determinants of market price. The businessmen that testified before the Senate Subcommittee on Antitrust and Monopoly in 1961 pointed out repeatedly that market prices were determined by the firm willing to sell at the lowest price. But many of the senators on the committee, particularly Senator Kefauver, refused to accept that explanation. Like some economists, Kefauver implied that competitive prices should have been determined by costs—completely ignoring the fact that buyers of electrical apparatus have no idea what producer costs are, and care less. Note in particular, the following exchange of views with respect to costs and competition:

Senator Kefauver: How does it happen that each one of these other companies comes up with exactly the same cost figures and decides that should be their price?

Mr. Hodnette: I have no idea what their costs are. The prices are determined by competition in the market place, not by cost.[50]

Or note the discussion below between Senator Kefauver and Mr. Mark W. Cresap, Jr., president of Westinghouse, with respect to the nearly identical prices ($17,402,300) submitted by different companies on a 500,000 kilowatt turbine:

Senator Kefauver: . . . did you arrive at that price independently?

Mr. Cresap: Yes, sir.

Senator Kefauver: You figured it yourself?

Mr. Cresap:	We arrived at that particular one on the basis of the fact that General Electric Co. had lowered its costs for this type of machine, and we met it.
Senator Kefauver:	You mean you copied it from G.E.?
Mr. Cresap:	No, we met the price.
Senator Kefauver:	Have you ever made one?
Mr. Cresap:	Have we ever made . . .
Senator Kefauver:	A 500,000 kilowatt turbine?
Mr. Cresap:	We had not at that time, no sir.
Senator Kefauver:	Have you made one yet?
Mr. Cresap:	No.
Senator Kefauver:	Has G.E. ever made one?
Mr. Cresap:	Yes, they are making one.
Senator Kefauver:	They have never made one, though?
Mr. Cresap:	Well, this is the price that they established for this machine, and we met it.
Senator Kefauver:	You mean you copied it?
Mr. Cresap:	We didn't copy the machine. We met the price because it was the lowest price in the marketplace.
Senator Kefauver:	In other words, you copied the figures exactly, $17,-402,300, from General Electric?
Mr. Cresap:	Senator, we had a higher price on the machine on our former book, and when they reduced, we reduced to meet them, to meet competition.
Senator Kefauver:	If you never made one, how would you know how much to lower or how much to raise?
Mr. Cresap:	You would know by the basis of how much you needed the business, what the conditions of your backlog was, what your plant load was, what your employment was, and what you thought you had to do in order to get the business.
Senator Kefauver:	In any event, you would not know whether you were making money or losing money on this bid, because you had never made one, and Mr. Eckert told us you had no figures on which to base this price. You just followed along with G.E. Is that the policy of your company?
Mr. Cresap:	The policy of our company is to meet competitive

	prices, and this is the manner in which the book price on this particular machine was arrived at . . .
Senator Kefauver:	Even if you lost money?
Mr. Cresap:	Even if we lost money, if we needed the business to cover our overheads and to keep our people working . . .
Senator Kefauver:	On something that you had never sold, that had never been made and that you have not made yet, and they have not made one yet, their price is $17,402,300, the same as yours.
Mr. Cresap:	They would have to be, Mr. Chairman, if we are going to be competitive. We cannot have a higher price than our competition.
Senator Kefauver:	How about a lower price?
Mr. Cresap:	If we had a lower price, I am sure they would meet it, if they wanted to get the business very badly.[51]

In short, price identity may imply intense competition and a working out of the market process. Or it may imply collusion and conspiracy. The next section will attempt to determine what it did imply in this case.

The Effectiveness of Conspiracy

Did the electrical equipment manufacturers conspire successfully to raise, fix, and maintain prices? Did the meetings, which many executives admitted attending, actually fix the level of prices and price changes, or were prices set ultimately by market competition? Was the driving force behind price-identity collusion, or oligopolistic competition?

The most acceptable generalization concerning the nature of the price conspiracy meetings must be that they were a failure or, as one executive rather disgustedly put it, "a waste of time." Without exception, every witness queried before the Senate Subcommittee on Antitrust and Monopoly in 1961 stated that the meetings were not effective. (Why they attended will be discussed below.) Because this particular aspect of the conspiracy is important, and because it has been neglected, it must be substantiated with direct testimony. The following exchange concerns collusion on medium turbine sales:

Senator Kefauver:	How would it work out? Just tell us how it worked.
Mr. Jenkins:	It didn't work very good.
Senator Kefauver:	It looks as if it had the possibilities of working good.

Mr. Jenkins: The thing that is important, this is a dog-eat-dog business and everybody wanted it. There has never been enough business.[52]

And, again, with Mr. Jenkins with respect to the end of the price meetings on turbines:

Senator Kefauver: When did they break up?
Mr. Jenkins: In early 1959.
Senator Kefauver: What happened then to cause this cessation?
Mr. Jenkins: It was a waste of time and effort. There was very little business. We were at the bottom of a buying cycle. Everybody wanted every job, and it was of no value.[53]

The following exchange concerns price collusion on electrical condensors.

Senator Blakley: If I understand, then if your competitors were of the same mind as you, then it would be a general feeling that these meetings for the purpose of fixing prices would be in order; is that the way to interpret it?
Mr. Bunch: An attempt may have been made to fix these prices, but, it was entirely unsuccessful.[54]

The following exchange concerns price collusion on small turbine generators.

Mr. Flurry: What was decided at that meeting with respect to price level?
Mr. Sellers: This meeting consisted of perhaps—I say "perhaps"—there were six manufacturers in this small turbine generator business represented. This was recognition of the fact that the prior bid price discussions which had been going on among the manufacturers *was so ineffective as to be rather useless,* and to try to determine whether or not people were serious in this endeavor or whether—well, it had become so useless that there was a question as to whether you should continue, and this was a meeting to discuss that. Also, an effort to stabilize the market at some place within a few percent of a published price, rather than 10 or 15 percent, where the market had drifted. Again, the meeting *was so ineffectual as far as I am concerned, because it promptly all fell apart.* This rugged individual type of business that we are in simply

ignored—I will put it a different way. The forces that were coming about from lack of volume, and the pressure that was on a manufacturer to get volume, negated any price discussion. It just did not amount to anything.[55] (Emphasis added.)

The following exchange concerns meetings and alleged price collusion with respect to medium voltage switchgear.

Mr. Flurry: I understood you to say that this broke off some time before 1959?

Mr. Hentschel: That is right, sir.

Mr. Flurry: What was the cause of that break-off?

Mr. Hentschel: Basically the thing just wasn't working. In other words, everybody would come to the meeting, the figures would be settled, and *they were only as good as the distance to the closest telephone before they were broken.* In other words, so the thing just wasn't working.[56] (Emphasis added.)

The following exchange concerns meetings that were designed to set and maintain the prices of power transformers.

Mr. Ferrall: What do you mean, Mr. Smith, when you say you did not know whether any good would come of it or not?

Mr. Smith: Well, I meant by that, whether there was anything done at the meetings with competitors, which would in any way improve the price situation. Past meetings with competitors had been rather unfruitful in that respect.

Mr. Ferrall: You mean you did not know whether they would abide by their agreements?

Mr. Smith: I don't know whether you can say that we had real agreement at any time . . .[57]

Mr. Smith: (continuing) My experience in meeting with competitors, as I have said before, indicated to me that *it was a rather fruitless endeavor.* It might be two days, after a meeting, before jobs would be bid all over the place, and there seemed to be no real continuity that came out of those meetings in the way of stabilizing prices at any level.[58] (Emphasis added.)

And again with Mr. Smith of General Electric with respect to price agreements on power transformers:

Senator Carroll:	In other words, you reached agreement that there could be some stabilization?
Mr. Smith:	There could be, but we agreed upon no stabilization.
Senator Carroll:	I understand that. I am not asking you to commit yourself, but there was this general agreement that you could stabilize?
Mr. Smith:	General understandings that it would probably be best if it was possible.
Senator Carroll:	Did you remove the threat of price cutting?
Mr. Smith:	No, sir.
Senator Carroll:	Was there any price cutting after that?
Mr. Smith:	Surely, sir.
Senator Carroll:	Did it continue?
Mr. Smith:	Yes, sir . . .
Senator Carroll:	(Continuing) I think I have asked this question, but I will ask it again. Do the records then reflect that you got some price stabilization after that time? I mean, not the records, but the practice, your profits.
Mr. Smith:	The price curves which were maintained by the power transformer department all the way through this whole period is one of this kind of picture, up and down all the time.
Senator Carroll:	Did it improve after your last conference, the conference in 1958? Did it improve in 1958 after the two presidents got together?
Mr. Smith:	No, sir, not to amount to anything.
Senator Carroll:	Did it improve any in 1959?
Mr. Smith:	It got worse in 1959.[59]

The following exchange again concerns price meetings with respect to fixing prices on power transformers.

Senator Hruska:	By and large, Mr. Ginn, you have had considerable experience in the business of meeting with competitors. How effective were those meetings to get the job done that they purported to have as an objective?
Mr. Ginn:	Senator, this is the way I will put it. *If people did not have the desire to make it work, it never worked. And if people had the desire to make it work, it wasn't necessary to have the meetings and violate the law.*

Senator Hruska:	So that your preliminary discussions and meetings with competitors . . .
Mr. Ginn:	*Were worthless.*
Senator Hruska:	Were not necessarily controlling?
Mr. Ginn:	*Were worthless. . . . I think that the boys could resist everything but temptation.* No sir, I'll tell you frankly, Senator, I think if one thing I would pass on to posterity, that it wasn't worth it. *It didn't accomplish anything,* and all you end up with is by getting in trouble.[60] (Emphasis added.)

And a final exchange with respect to the effectiveness of fixing transformer prices:

Mr. Rosenman:	And you fixed prices, you participated in the fixing of prices?
Mr. McCollom:	That is right.
Mr. Rosenman:	Fixing of the book price . . .
Mr. McCollom:	We discussed those in meetings.
Mr. Rosenman:	But you maintain that there was no agreement as to these?
Mr. McCollom:	We discussed these generally, and I say that there was no agreement, because *it didn't result in prices being quoted at those levels that were discussed.* There was just no evidence of any agreements in the actions that were taken by the parties in the meetings. There was no formal definite agreement in writing on this thing.
Senator Kefauver:	None of it was in writing?
Mr. McCollom:	There was no verbal agreement, just a discussion.
Senator Kefauver:	Just an understanding?
Mr. McCollom:	Just a discussion of it.
Senator Kefauver:	Was there, or was there not, an understanding about what was going to be done?
Mr. McCollom:	*Well, I think the results indicate that there was no understanding.*
Senator Kefauver:	I am not talking about results. I am asking whether at the meeting there was an understanding about what was going to be done?
Mr. McCollom:	Well there was a discussion of price levels 15% off

> book. I might have gone out of the meeting thinking
> the other people understood it; they might have gone
> out thinking I did; *but there was no action that sup-*
> *ported any understanding of it,* that there was any un-
> derstanding because it did not occur. *It did not hap-*
> *pen.*[61] (Emphasis added.)

In short, throughout the entire period of the conspiracy, the firms were not able to suspend price competition. Although there had been repeated attempts to fix prices, the attempts rather monotonously failed. Price agreement might last a day or two, and "then somebody would break the line and there would be another meeting."[62] In most cases, in fact, the meetings were an attempt to restore agreements that were being openly and regularly violated in the marketplace. In other instances, the meetings were an attempt by some firms to "get the line on prices," that is, to find out what a competitor might do with his price in the near future.[63] Indeed, it can be maintained that the meetings served an important informational purpose. Such information would allow a firm to discover a competitor's costs and bid just under its competitor in order to secure the desired business. As Mr. Raymond Smith, former general manager of the transformer division at General Electric, put it: ". . . my prime objective was to find out whether the Westinghouse people had received any instructions from their people, and failing to do so, I thought the meeting was worthless."[64]

Were the Prices Fixed?

The Bureau of Labor Statistics (BLS) index of wholesale prices shows substantial increases for various kinds of electrical apparatus during the conspiracy period. Switchgear prices, for example, increased from an index number of 112.7 in 1950 to 127.4 in 1952, to 135.1 in 1954, to 154.1 in 1956, to 172.8 in 1958, and to 176.6 in 1960.[65] Since there were meetings with respect to the prices of switchgear, at least during the latter part of the 1950s, the impression conveyed by the index is that prices were rather routinely raised and maintained at unreasonable levels.

The impression conveyed by the BLS statistics, however, is an altogether incorrect impression. The statistics are based on catalog prices and not on actual invoice prices. The fact remains that throughout the conspiracy period, switchgear sold at sharp discounts from book or catalog prices. This discounting was particularly pronounced during the infamous "white sale" in 1954 and 1955, when switchgear was selling for as much as 45–50 percent off the listed book price.[66] This "sale" was repeated in late 1957 and early 1958 when some market prices were as much as 60 percent off the book price.[67] Ironically, the entire purpose of the switchgear meetings was to do something with respect to the unreasonably low switchgear prices. The price meetings ended in failure and were abandoned before the conspiracy was discovered by the Department of Justice. There was no effective price-fixing in switchgear at all.[68]

The fact that there was no effective price-fixing in switchgear, or in many other electrical products, might be supported further by an examination of profit data for some of the firms involved during the period of conspiracy. Although a positive relationship between periods of conspiracy and profit need not prove cause and effect, the complete absence of any such positive relationship might reflect a thoroughly ineffectual collusion.

The twenty separate indictments returned by the grand jury in 1960 charged that a price conspiracy had been in effect in the electrical equipment manufacturing industry between 1956 and 1959. A comparison of the rates of return, on both capital and sales for that period, with some previous nonconspiracy period, is reproduced in Tables 1–4 for four of the largest firms involved.[69]

It can be observed from these tables that in all cases, without exception, the rates of return on capital and on sales were actually lower during the period of alleged conspiracy than during the immediately preceding period.[70] If the conspiracy were profitable, the price and rate of return behavior of some of the firms involved certainly does not reflect any great success. It will be maintained, instead, that the conspiracy was ineffectual from start to finish.[71]

Table 1.   General Electric

Years	Profits on Capital	Profits on Sales
1950–1955	20.5%	5.9%
1956–1959	20.1%	5.8%

Table 2.   Westinghouse

Years	Profits on Capital	Profits on Sales
1950–1955	10.8%	5.1%
1956–1959	7.0%	3.0%

Table 3.   Allis-Chalmers

Years	Profits on Capital	Profits on Sales
1950–1955	11.3%	5.1%
1956–1959	6.6%	3.7%

Table 4.   Carrier

Years	Profits on Capital	Profits on Sales
1950–1955	12.9%	4.4%
1956–1959	7.9%	3.5%

The Failure of Conspiracy

To gain an understanding of why the conspiracy was generally ineffectual, it is necessary to examine two crucial elements of the electrical equipment manufacturers industry: the industry's cost structure, and the nature of the demand for electrical apparatus.

Although there are thousands of firms that produce and sell electrical apparatus and machinery, and although entry has remained relatively easy,[72] the important parts of the industry are dominated by a relatively few, extremely capital-intensive firms. As might be expected, these firms are rather sophisticated innovators, and all maintain substantial research and development facilities at great expense. Importantly for our purposes, the extremely high capital intensity, and the resultant scale economies,[73] generates continuous pressures for selective price reductions when demand is slow to gain volume.

The demand for electrical equipment is derived almost proportionately from industrial firms and electric utility companies. Since a high proportion of the total demand for electrical equipment is associated with new constuction, or new generating capacity on the part of utilities, it is extremely sensitive to money market conditions. In addition, since it is a demand for a postponable producer's durable good, it can be expected to display the violent instability commonly associated with the feast-or-famine capital goods industry. Both factors foretell an extremely cyclical demand for electrical apparatus.

Given the instability in the economy and in the money markets during the period 1955–1960, and given the cost structure of the equipment manufacturers, it is not at all surprising to discover that price competition was severe and that catalog prices were not being honored. Here were expensively equipped firms with huge overhead costs, and they were hungry for a volume of business that did not materialize at existing price levels; this volume simply had to be attracted. In such circumstances price reductions were inevitable.

Testimony has already been presented to support this view,[74] but the remarks of Mr. George E. Burens, former division general manager of switchgear at General Electric, can summarize the actual situation: "Everybody has their plant in shape. They have the facility. They have the organization. But they have no business. So, they are out grabbing. I think that is the thing."[75] It was, indeed, the thing.

Price-fixing was also difficult because there were always competitors that did not sell on a national basis. When demand was flat or falling, electrical firms closer to potential customers might simply figure the cost of a particular job, and quote a price to cover that cost.[76] Hence, selective market prices could be significantly different from national catalog prices, and "could be anywhere over the lot." In addition, there were so-called tin makers (e.g., firms that made inferior electrical equipment) that would make it a practice to underbid national competition, especially on sealed bid jobs.[77] Rarely did the non-national firms or the "tin makers" abide by any price agreement.

Further, there was always the problem of price competition from foreign firms. They could not be controlled directly, and they were not a part of the price conspiracy; accordingly, their pricing practices made it difficult, if not impossible, to raise, fix, and maintain prices on domestic electrical equipment. For example, prices on certain domestic turbogenerators were cut 20 percent when foreign competition entered the market, and meetings to fix that particular situation were "unsuccessful . . . quite unnecessary and very foolish."[78] The ability of such meetings to contain price competition under such circumstances was nil.

Thus price collusion was ineffective in the electrical equipment manufacturers industry because demand was unstable, economies of scale were substantial, competitors had different price-and-profit objectives, honesty and trust were non-existent, and imports were (increasingly) important. Under such circumstances, a generally successful price conspiracy would have been nearly impossible. The Justice Department, it appears, with all its legal bluster, fines, and headlines, ended a nearly impotent arrangement.

The Sultan Research—A Final Note

A thorough two-volume study of pricing and competition in the electrical equipment industry was completed by economist Ralph Sultan in 1975.[79] The Sultan study substantiates the position outlined above that corporate pricing behavior during the conspiracy period was competitive, and that the effect of the meetings and agreements on prices was insignificant. Sultan argues persuasively that market transactions prices were determined by demand, technological development, and minimum backlog, and not directly by either costs or conspiracy.[80] Importantly, he presents substantial empirical evidence that is consistent with the hypothesis of his pricing model.[81] The

Sultan research and analysis completely invalidates earlier judgments that the private treble-damage actions against the equipment manufacturers were demonstrable evidence of effective conspiracy.[82]

CONCLUSION

The general meaning of this chapter should not be misunderstood. It is not being argued that business collusion is impossible (formal merger, for instance, could allow effective and permanent collusion), or that a successful conspiracy might not reduce output and raise prices in a neoclassical sense.[83] What is being argued is that (1) all business agreements are evidence of *ex ante* benefit and are, therefore, efficient from our perspective; (2) that the natural economic factors in a free market make most price conspiracies ineffectual in terms of higher prices or monopoly profits; and (3) that a sampling of some of the most famous price-fixing antitrust cases in business history involved ineffectual price and output agreements.

NOTES

1. D. T. Armentano, "A Critique of Neoclassical and Austrian Monopoly Theory," Louis M. Spadaro, ed., *New Directions in Austrian Economics* (Kansas City: Sheed Andrews and McMeel, Inc., 1978), pp. 94–110.
2. Robert Bork, *The Antitrust Paradox: A Policy at War With Itself* (New York: Basic Books, Inc., 1978). For an exceptional dissenting view see Donald Dewey, "Information, Entry, and Welfare: The Case for Collusion," *American Economic Review*, Vol. 69, No. 4 (September 1979), pp. 588–593.
3. Roger Pilon, "Corporations and Rights: On Treating Corporate People Justly," *Georgia Law Review*, Vol. 13, No. 4 (Summer 1979), pp. 1245–1370.
4. Murray N. Rothbard, *Towards a Reconstruction of Utility and Welfare Economics* (New York: Center for Libertarian Studies, 1977).
5. Some commentators (such as Robert Bork) feel that mergers are to be preferred to price agreements since "integration" creates the possibility for additional efficiencies. But why there should be efficiencies with mergers that are induced *solely* by the prohibition on price agreement is not obvious.
6. Walter Block, "Austrian Monopoly Theory: A Critique," *Journal of Libertarian Studies*, Vol. 1, No. 4 (Fall 1977), pp. 271–279.
7. *American Tobacco Co. v. United States*, 328 U.S. 781 (1946).
8. *Addyston Pipe and Steel Company v. United States*, 175 U.S. 211.
9. Donald Dewey, *Monopoly in Economics and Law* (Chicago: Rand McNally and Company, 1959), pp. 53–55.
10. *United States v. Addyston Pipe and Steel Co.*, 78 F. 712 (1897).

11. 85 F. 293.
12. *Ibid.*, pp. 293–295.
13. 175 U.S. 238.
14. Almarin Phillips, *Market Structure, Organization and Performance* (Cambridge, Mass.: Harvard University Press, 1962).
15. The defendants' capacity was estimated at 220,000 tons. See 85 F. 291.
16. *Ibid.*, p. 292.
17. Phillips, *op. cit.*, p. 108.
18. *Addyston Pipe et al. v. United States*, 175 U.S. 211, "Transcript of Record," Supreme Court of the United States (October Term, 1899), No. 51, pp. 196–197.
19. Phillips, *op. cit.*, p. 111.
20. *Ibid.*, p. 112.
21. *Ibid.*
22. *Addyston Pipe et al. v. United States*, 175 U.S. 211, United States Supreme Court *Records and Briefs*, p. 195.
23. The mention of the affidavits is omitted from Justice Peckham's quoted decision in the *Addyston Pipe* case as excerpted in Irwin M. Stelzer, *Selected Antitrust Cases: Landmark Decisions*, 5th ed. (Homewood, Ill.: Richard D. Irwin, 1976), p. 65.
24. (London: Cambridge University Press, 1970), p. 33.
25. *United States v. Trenton Potteries Company et al.*, 273 U.S. 397 (emphasis added).
26. Phillips, *op. cit.*, p. 164.
27. *Ibid.*, pp. 162–173.
28. This practice was reportedly abandoned in 1920.
29. 300 F. 551.
30. It was the common practice of almost all manufacturers to market products exclusively through wholesalers. There was no evidence presented to indicate that any particular wholesaler had been discriminated against. See Phillips, *op. cit.*, p. 168.
31. 300 F. 552 (emphasis added).
32. *Ibid.*, p. 555.
33. *Ibid.*, p. 552 (emphasis added).
34. *United States v. Trenton Potteries Company et al.*, 273 U.S. 392, Brief for Respondents, No. 27, United States Supreme Court *Records & Briefs* (October Term, 1926).
35. Phillips, *op. cit.*, p. 167.
36. United States Supreme Court *Records and Briefs*, Brief for Respondents, No. 27, pp. 10–11.
37. *Ibid.*, p. 11.
38. Phillips, *op. cit.*, pp. 173–176.

39. *Ibid.*, pp. 175–176.
40. *Appalachian Coals, Inc. v. United States*, 288 U.S. 344 (1933), is an exception to the per se approach in price-fixing cases. See Stelzer, *op. cit.*, pp. 68–72.
41. *United States v. Socony-Vacuum Oil Company*, 310 U.S. 150 (1940), quoted in Stelzer, *op. cit.*, p. 77.
42. Clarence C. Walton and Frederick W. Cleveland, Jr., *Corporations on Trial: The Electric Cases* (Belmont, California: Wadsworth Publishing Company, Inc., 1964), p. 12. Background information concerning the conspiracy can be obtained from Richard Austin Smith, "The Incredible Electrical Conspiracy," *Fortune* (April and May, 1961); John Fuller, *The Gentlemen Conspirators* (New York: Grove Press, 1962); John Herling, *The Great Price Conspiracy* (Washington: Robert B. Luce, Inc., 1962).
43. *City of Philadelphia v. Westinghouse Electric*, 210 F. Supp. 483.
44. The best public source of information about the conspiracy meetings is the Hearings on Administered Prices by the United States Senate Committee on the Judiciary, Subcommittee on Antitrust and Monopoly, *Price-Fixing and Bid-Rigging in the Electrical Manufacturing Industry*, Parts 27 and 28, 87th Congress, 1st session (April, May, and June 1961).
45. There was testimony to the effect that the Robinson-Patman Act made quantity discounts legally difficult. See *Price-Fixing and Bid-Rigging . . .* p. 17619.
46. All the quoted testimony to follow in this chapter is taken from *Price-Fixing and Bid-Rigging in the Electrical Manufacturing Industry*, unless otherwise indicated.
47. *Ibid.*, p. 17430.
48. *Ibid.*, p. 17431.
49. *Ibid.*, pp. 17672–17673.
50. *Ibid.*, p. 17438.
51. *Ibid.*, pp. 17628–17630.
52. *Ibid.*, p. 16608. Mr. Jenkins was sales manager of medium turbine sales for Westinghouse.
53. *Ibid.*, p. 16614.
54. *Ibid.*, p. 16639. Mr. Bunch was manager of the condensor division of Ingersoll-Rand Company.
55. *Ibid.*, p. 16669. Mr. Sellers was manager of the turbine generator division of the Carrier Corporation.
56. *Ibid.*, p. 16884. Mr. Hentshel was general manager of the medium voltage switchgear department for General Electric.
57. *Ibid.*, p. 16961. Mr. Smith was the general manager of the transformer division for General Electric.
58. *Ibid.*, p. 16962.
59. *Ibid.*, pp. 17013, 17029.
60. *Ibid.*, pp. 17069–17070. Mr. Ginn was vice president and general manager of the turbine division for General Electric.

61. *Ibid.*, pp. 17378–17379. Mr. McCollom was the manager of the power transformer department for Westinghouse.

62. *Ibid.*, p. 17883.

63. *Ibid.*, p. 17523.

64. *Ibid.*, p. 17013.

65. *Ibid.*, p. 17767. It is important to note that these are price index numbers of
constant technology. Yet the technology and efficiency of the equipment increased rapidly throughout the period. See Ralph G. M. Sultan, *Pricing in the
Electrical Oligopoly*, Vol. I (Boston: Harvard Business School, Division of Research, 1974), p. 36.

66. *Ibid.*, p. 16740.

67. *Ibid.*, p. 17103.

68. The same conclusion might be made with respect to the prices of "large circuit
breakers." See George J. Stigler and James K. Kindahl, *The Behavior of Industrial Prices* (New York: National Bureau of Economic Research, 1970), p. 31.
See also Jules Backman, *The Economics of the Electrical Machinery Industry*
(New York: New York University Press, 1962), Chapters 5 and 6.

69. The tables are based on figures taken from *Moody's Industrial Manual*, and
from *Price-Fixing and Bid-Rigging in the Electrical Manufacturing Industry*,
Exhibits 54A, B, C, pp. 17960–17961.

70. The profits were reduced for a good many reasons; the 1957–58 recession in the
economy is the best possibility. The point, however, is that collusion did not
generate any extraordinary profits. Further, General Electric's profits were consistently higher than their competition because their costs were consistently
lower. For supporting evidence on comparative costs see Ralph G. M. Sultan,
Pricing in the Electrical Oligopoly, Vol. 2 (Boston: Harvard Business School,
Division of Research, 1975), pp. 147, 157.

71. This negative relationship between "collusion" and profitability seems to be the
general case. See P. Asch and R. Seneca, "Is Collusion Profitable?" Vol. 58,
Review of Economics and Statistics (1976), pp. 1–12.

72. The *Census of Manufacturers* reports that there were 7066 "establishments" in
the electrical machinery industry in 1958, compared with 3970 in 1947.

73. Walton & Cleveland, *op. cit.*, p. 13.

74. See, for example, *Price-Fixing and Bid Rigging in the Electrical Manufacturing
Industry*, p. 16614.

75. *Ibid.*, p. 16876.

76. *Ibid.*, pp. 16693–16694.

77. *Ibid.*, p. 17472.

78. *Ibid.*, pp. 16945, 17061.

79. Ralph G. M. Sultan, *Pricing in the Electrical Oligopoly*, 2 Vols. (Boston: Harvard Business School, Division of Research, 1974, 1975).

80. *Ibid.*, Vol. 1. See especially Chapter 2, "The Impact of Conspiracy on Pricing,"
pp. 37–38.

81. *Ibid.*, Vol. 2. See esp. p. 111.
82. Charles A. Bane, *The Electrical Equipment Conspiracies: The Treble Damage Actions* (New York: Federal Legal Publications, Inc., 1973), esp. pp. 386–387.
83. G. Hay and D. Kelley, "An Empirical Survey of Price Fixing Conspiracies," *Journal of Law and Economics*, Vol. 17 (April 1974), pp. 13–38. See W. B. Erickson, "Price Fixing Conspiracies: Their Long-Term Impact," *Journal of Industrial Economics*, Vol. 24 (March 1976), pp. 189–202. But see also R. M. Townsend, "The Eventual Failure of Price Fixing Schemes," *Journal of Economic Theory*, Vol. 14 (February 1977), pp. 190–199.

CHAPTER SIX

Price Discrimination and the Competitive Process

Although there is a high degree of professional unanimity over the theory and practice of the Sherman Act, Section 2 of the Clayton Act (with its Robinson-Patman Act amendments and Federal Trade Commission enforcement) enjoys no such unanimity of favorable opinion. Indeed, Section 2 of the Clayton Act has always come in for an unusual, yet entirely appropriate, amount of "roasting" from economists, consumer advocates, business spokesmen, lawyers, and jurists alike.[1] The sum and substance of the criticism is the contention that Section 2 tends to make vigorous price competition more difficult, and that it tends to protect particular competitors, rather than the competitive process. It has been argued persuasively that this section of the Clayton Act is an anticompetition law and not an antitrust law.

Some of the criticism stems understandably from the origins of the Clayton and Robinson-Patman Acts themselves. Unlike the Sherman Act, it is readily admitted that Section 2 of the Clayton Act and its important Robinson-Patman Act amendments, were passed in order to protect small, independent business firms from the buying and selling practices of larger corporations, particularly large chain stores.[2] Large store chains, for reasons to be discussed below, were able to purchase less expensively and sell at lower prices than some of their smaller rivals. The inevitable economic pressure, supposedly, was to force "independents" out of particular product lines of business and even, perhaps, out of business altogether. The independents argued that the price concessions enjoyed by the large firms could not often be justified by any real cost savings, and that it was the economic power of the large companies, and not any real cost savings or efficiencies, that allowed the chains to be more competitive. To curb this "unreasonable" economic power in the "public interest," small-business interest groups pushed through legislation that created a strong antiprice discrimination statute.

A THEORY OF PRICE DISCRIMINATION

The general theoretical objection to price discrimination is rooted deeply in the static, perfectly competitive model and in its welfare implications. In the perfectly competitive equilibrium, no seller would have any monopoly "power" and would be unable to discriminate on the basis of price. With homogeneous products and perfectly elastic demand functions in the factor and product markets, prices for "goods of like grade and quality" would be identical. In short, the absence of price discrimination coincides with the preassumed welfare ideal that exists in atomistic competition. Presumably, that is the general theoretical perspective that supports the legal prohibition.

But as we argued in Chapter 2, atomistic competition is hardly realistic or optimal in any dynamic context. And if a static, perfectly competitive equilibrium is not realistic or optimal, then it follows that a state of zero price discrimination is not always optimal either. In a non-purely competitive economic world with nonhomogeneous sellers and buyers, price differences could be expected and could be efficient. A competitive process would certainly contain price differentials, and they would not be considered anticompetitive, per se. For instance, differences in price to different buyers might typically be based on the frequency of orders and number of units purchased, the distance delivered, the incomes of the buyers and their relative demand for the product, the estimated demand elasticity, the price decisions of other sellers, the degree of product familiarity, the specific marginal cost associated with selling to a buyer, and many other factors.[3] Some discriminations, as noted, might be based on so-called real cost differences. But in a non-purely competitive disequilibrium, the typical selling situation, one would not expect that all price discriminations would be related directly to cost, or that all seller cost differences would be instantly and fully reflected in buyer price differentials. Thus, price differences, even those that do not fully reflect cost differences, ought to be considered part and parcel of a fully competitive disequilibrium process.

What is Illegal Price Discrimination?

Section 2 of the Clayton Act as amended makes price discrimination on goods of like grade and quality illegal when the effect may be to substantially lessen competition or tend to create a monopoly. Price discrimination at law has meant a difference in price.[4] Illegal price discrimination is a price difference that cannot be "justified" on the basis of either a specific cost savings, or one made in good faith to meet the lower price of a competitor.

There are many conceptual difficulties with a law that makes price discrimination illegal. The first serious problem concerns the threshold phrase, "of like grade and quality." What goods are to be classified of like grade and quality? Will minute physical differences in fundamentally similar commodities be enough to exempt them from the application of the price discrimination statute? Who will determine what a minute difference is and what is fundamentally similar? Will firms successfully avoid prosecution by making marginally physical adjustments in essentially similar products? Or will the FTC and the courts interpret such changes as artificial, and as evidence of the fact that the goods are truly of like grade and quality? Are chemically similar products that sell under different brand names and different labels to be considered "like" under the law? Certainly, the market (buyers) may treat chemically similar products differently and, hence, in the minds of the buyers the products would not be equivalent. To automatically assume that physically identical commodities are of like grade and quality would be to neglect the subjective utilities associated with popular brand names. Yet the Robinson-Patman Act was probably intended to ignore such "artificial" differentials.[5]

A second difficulty is more fundamental and has been well documented by many scholars. While the law aims at preventing price discrimination—price differences—from occurring, it may enhance what some economists define as economic price discrimination. Economic discrimination is a price differential that does not correspond to an actual cost differential. Thus, price identity when actual costs differ would be economic discrimination. To the extent that the price discrimination law aims at price uniformity, and particularly at a uniformity at some higher price, it tends to promote economic discrimination against the low-cost seller.[6]

Yet even the notion of economic discrimination has its difficulties. Here, in its clearest form, is the simple neoclassical presumption that only final prices based on costs, particularly long-run marginal costs, are truly competitive. It can be admitted that there might be a tendency under open market competition for prices (actually marginal revenue) to tend towards marginal cost, especially as additional supplies are channelled to high profit-margin markets; nonetheless, there is no reason to expect any particular price at any given moment in time to fully reflect costs. Prices are determined by demand and competition and not directly by costs. Most prices in most competitive markets are discriminatory; nondiscriminatory uniform prices, or prices that *always* reflect "costs," are reserved for the perfectly competitive equilibrium. Hence, both the law and neoclassical economic theory, to the extent that they condemn price discrimination, are dealing in competitive fantasy and illusion. They are decrying and condemning a kind of disequilibrium pricing behavior that is efficient, and is to be expected in a free market.

A third serious difficulty with the law is that the cost justification defense assumes a level of sophistication in cost accounting that has not been attained. Costs, as every economist is aware, are difficult to define and even harder to measure accurately. For example, there are troublesome joint costs and overhead costs, and these make the specific expenses associated with specific products almost impossible to determine accurately. As a practical matter, no multi-product firm could confidently justify a particular price discrimination on the basis of cost savings, especially if the cost savings must equal or be proportional to some specific price difference. Moreover, as we have argued previously, the costs that affect decision making are an inherently subjective phenomenon, and they can never be objectively measured or quantified. Thus as will be shown more clearly below, the cost justification defense is not a defense at all, but only a legal pretense at a defense.

There are certain parts of Section 2 of the Clayton Act where all pretense concerning "cost justification" is dropped, and the actual meaning of the price discrimination law is clearly revealed. For example, Section 2(c) makes price allowances for brokerage that an integrated buyer performs illegal per se, regardless of whether or not it can be cost justified.[7] And a proviso in Section 2(a) states that certain quantity discounts may be declared "unjustly discriminatory" and hence, illegal, even if full cost savings fully support these price discounts. It might be noted that here, at least, the price discrimination law is refreshingly honest concerning its intent to limit price competition and restrain the rivalrous process of an open market.

A fourth difficulty with the law is the identical one encountered in Sherman Act cases: definition of terms. What particular business conduct shall be interpreted as "substantially lessening competition" or tending to create a monopoly? Will price reductions that attract new customers be interpreted as "an attempt to monopolize"?[8] Will price reductions that prevent competitors from taking business away be considered an injury to competition? Will the loss of some undetermined amount of business, or the potential loss of some business be enough to violate the antitrust statute? Since there is no way to determine the answers to these questions beforehand, the price discrimination law is arbitrary and ambiguous in the extreme.

A fifth difficulty surrounds the so-called good faith provision; that is, that prices may legally be lowered to meet the prices of a competitor in good faith. But how is a seller to know *ex ante* whether the price it is about to meet is itself a legal discount? To meet an illegal discount has been deemed illegal.[9] Yet unless a seller is able to analyze the cost information of another seller (and that would likely be illegal collusion), it can never be sure whether the price discount it is meeting is a just price. In addition, why should sellers be required to wait for an actual price reduction before they price discriminate and lower some of their own prices? And why is it unfair to lower prices *below* the prices of competitors? Finally, how is a good faith reduction to be distinguished from a "bad" faith reduction? Such practical difficulties will surely discourage the likelihood that any prices will be cut at all, to anyone.

And finally, it appears that a strict interpretation of Robinson-Patman would rule out delivered pricing with freight absorption, and all so-called basing point pricing arrangements. Imagine a market with different sellers located at different distances from some important group of buyers. To be competitive with customers and the closest potential seller, other sellers might find it necessary to absorb freight and handling charges, and charge a price for their product that does not fully reflect costs in that market. Since the pricing practice is voluntary, one could assume that the firms find it more profitable to lower their prices than to lose the business altogether. The net result of the competitive process is that buyers are presented with additional alternatives, no customers are considered safe, and the extent of geographic rivalry is broadened considerably. Large sellers with extremely low production costs can choose to absorb freight costs and compete almost everywhere. The overall effect is to extend rivalrous pressures throughout the market economy.

Under the Robinson-Patman Act, as might be expected, the matter has been viewed quite differently. Freight absorption is a price concession that cannot be cost-justified and it is discriminatory vis-à-vis buyers located nearer the plant of the seller. While some buyers located far away have costs absorbed, buyers closer by may not. The situation is deemed inequitable since the prices that buyers pay do not reflect true costs. According to this line of reasoning, only f.o.b. (free-on-board) pricing, where sellers quote prices excluding delivery charges, would not be inherently discriminatory.

The controversy over freight absorption is an excellent example of the clash between the theory that prices should be determined by costs, and the theory that prices are determined by demand and competition. And nowhere is the trade restraining effect of Robinson-Patman more obvious, and odious. Rigidly enforced, a freight-absorption prohibition would all but end free-market competition between national firms, and would return local buyers to the mercy of geographic monopolists.[10] There, indeed, prices would reflect costs with a vengeance. The only thing more regrettable than this vision is the fact that some economists would appear to support such pricing systems.[11]

The Robinson-Patman Act is an economic and civil liberties nightmare. Imagine a seller, for instance, who knows that buyer A is a poorer bargainer than buyer B; he cannot legally charge A a higher price if competition might thereby be lessened. Imagine a seller who knows that lower prices to buyer A will produce additional orders, but that lower prices to buyer B will not; he cannot charge A lower prices unless he can demonstrate a cost savings. Imagine a seller who does meet the lower price of a competitor and discovers that "meeting competition in good faith" requires a price differential between his product and the product of his competitors; he must, therefore, raise prices back to the accustomed differential! Imagine a buyer who accepts a discount and discovers ex post that it was illegal. Imagine salesmen in the field complaining that they are losing business because they cannot bargain rates that differ from uniform book rates without either lowering all rates, or determining an exact cost saving associated with a particular order. And finally, imagine an efficiently integrated seller that cannot even employ its in-house brokerage activity as a cost justification for offering lower prices to consumers. And then ask, again, what the price discrimination statute was designed to preserve and what it was designed to prohibit.

Section 2 of the Clayton Act, with its Robinson-Patman Act amendments, is simply not intelligible unless it is recognized that it was, indeed, active price competition that it meant to end. Like the National Recovery Act "codes" during the Depression, resale price maintenance with nonsigner clauses, and many other anticompetitive statues legislated in the 1930s, Section 2 as amended was designed to restrict and punish free market competition.[12] Since discriminations are created and destroyed continuously in the open market, and since such discriminations are, indeed, an important aspect of the competitive process, it must be clear that it was competition that such antitrust statutes attempted to legislate out of existence. That they have failed to end all price competition is due more to modest enforcement levels, and to occasional court resistance, than to any error of legislative intent.

The following material is a selective examination of some classic price discrimination cases taken from the hundreds of FTC actions over the last forty years. Hopefully the author has selected some of the more representative antitrust cases in the area of price discrimination. The cases are meant to be illustrative of the real meaning of the law, the FTC enforcement procedures, the attempted defenses by the corporations involved, the various court interpretations of FTC rulings, and the ultimate absurdity of attempting to prosecute competitive behavior in the name of protecting competition.

THE CORN PRODUCTS (1945) AND THE STALEY (1945) CASES

The Corn Products Case (1945)

One of the first important price discrimination cases under Robinson-Patman involved a firm named the Corn Products Refining Company, the largest producer of corn syrup (glucose) in the country in the early 1940s.[13] At that time, the Corn Products Company did an estimated 45 percent of the business in the market, with manufacturing facilities located in Argo, Illinois and Kansas City, Missouri. In addition, seven other companies within a 400-mile radius of Chicago sold syrup in competition with the acknowledged industry leader.

Between 1940 and 1942, the Federal Trade Commission charged seven of the eight glucose manufacturers, including Corn Products, with illegal price discrimination on sales of glucose to different candy makers, and issued cease-and-desist orders to end the practice. The discriminations allegedly occurred because the glucose firms all sold on a delivered-price basis only, with Chicago as the basing point, as far as freight charges were concerned. Syrup sellers with no Chicago-area plants apparently absorbed freight costs to sell competitively to candy makers near Chicago. Syrup sellers with a plant, say, twenty miles from a customer—but a hundred miles from Chicago—apparently charged "phantom freight," since they quoted the base price for glucose plus the Chicago freight rate, yet shipped their syrup from the closer plant. Since the candy makers that bought the glucose in the different areas did not pay prices that reflected true costs, price discrimination occurred. And since these different candy makers were allegedly intensely competitive with each other, the probable effect of the discrimination, asserted the FTC, was to injure competition and violate the law.

The Lower Court Decision

Two glucose manufacturers, Corn Products and A. E. Staley Manufacturing Company, appealed the FTC cease-and-desist orders.[14] Corn Products, as already mentioned, had manufacturing plants near Chicago and in Kansas City. The Chicago-area plant had been constructed in 1911; the Kansas City facility was built in 1922. Circuit Court Judge Lindley, hearing the case on appeal, stated the conclusions of the FTC on the original cease-and-desist order.

> The Commission found that a purchaser located nearer freight-wise to Kansas City than Chicago who receives delivery from Kansas City is forced to pay a price which includes an item for delivery not actually incurred; that Chicago purchasers receiving delivery from Kansas City but at a price which does not include any freight, artificial or real, and that any purchaser located near Chicago than Kansas City who receives delivery from the latter point is charged a price which does not include all of the actual freight. Its ultimate finding was that such discrimination results in substantial injury to petitioner's competitors . . .[15]

The substantial injury allegedly stemmed from the fact that candy makers in cities other than Chicago had higher costs of production due to higher glucose prices. Consequently the court reasoned that they would either have to increase their prices for candy—and, thus, be noncompetitive with other sellers—or accept lower profits of manufacture. In either case there would be injury, and competition would probably be lessened. "We think it irrefutable from the facts that resulting substantial loss is *reasonably likely* to accrue to purchasers in the less favorably located communities. The statute *does not require proof of actual injury.*[16] As a final note, the court stated that several candy manufacturers had moved closer to Chicago in an effort to decrease their costs of delivery.[17]

The Supreme Court Decision

In 1945 the Supreme Court agreed in all essential respects with both the FTC findings and the Circuit Court decision. Supreme Court Justice Stone stated that Corn Products' pricing system "inevitably" produced "systematic price discriminations" that "created a favored price zone for the purchasers of glucose in Chicago and vicinity."[18] Such discriminations were "unrelated to any proper element of actual cost" and were, therefore, unjustified. Since glucose, a crucial element in candy making, was cheaper in Chicago, the Chicago-based candy makers were "in a better position to compete for business" than the more distant manufacturers.[19] There was a "reasonable probability" that the effect of the discriminations may be to lessen competition substantially.[20] And, again, this reasonable probability was illustrated with the FTC findings that several candy makers had moved their factories to Chicago.[21]

The Supreme Court rejected Corn Products' argument that there was no discrimination under the basing-point system, since all buyers at the same location paid the same price. Stone argued that the Robinson-Patman Act had made no specific reference to the fact that the buyers had to be at the same location. And besides "the injury to the competition of purchasers in different localities is no less harmful than if they were in the same city."[22]

The Court also rejected Corn Products' argument that the Congress had sanctioned delivered-pricing and basing points, since the Congress had not outlawed them specifically when drafting the price discrimination law. The Congressional action, stated Stone, meant only that "Congress was unwilling to require f.o.b. factory pricing, and thus to make all uniform price systems and all basing point systems illegal per se."[23] Whether any particular delivered-pricing systems was legal or illegal rested, however, on a careful examination of that system in light of Section 2(a) of the Robinson-Patman Act. Since in this case the FTC had shown that there were systematic price discriminations that may tend to lessen competition, the company was violating the statute.

The Staley Case (1945)

The companion *Staley* case, also decided in 1945, is similar to the *Corn Products* case.[24] A. E. Staley Manufacturing, a competitor of Corn Products, had a glucose processing plant at Decatur, Illinois. Like its competitors, Staley sold its glucose on a delivered price basis only with Chicago as the basing point. The Circuit Court of Appeals confirmed the FTC charge that there was evidence to indicate that the pricing system was discriminatory and did tend to "substantially lessen competition."[25] But Circuit Judge Minton argued for the majority that Staley Manufacturing had rebutted the *prima facie* case of the FTC when the former had demonstrated that their prices had been made in good faith to meet the prices of their competitors.

The basing-point system had existed before Staley had come into business in 1920. When Staley began selling glucose, it became apparent "that business could be had only by meeting competitors' prices."[26] Thus Judge Minton concluded, Staley merely followed a system established by its competition; "that this was done in good faith is not questioned in the evidence."[27]

Dissents were made by Circuit Judges Evans and Major. Evans argued that there was no evidence that Staley was attempting to jusify a lower price in good faith: It just adopted an existing system so as not to "stir up the animals" by starting a price war.[28] Major, on the other hand, argued just as vigorously that:

> there was no evidence in the record to support the finding that the discrimination shown tended substantially to lessen competition or to create a monopoly. I am not convinced that we were in error in this respect. In my view, the basing point system has the opposite effect, that is, it has a tendency to preserve competition and prevent monopoly.[29]

Judge Major was concerned that f.o.b. pricing would be forced on the defendants and geographic "competition become a thing of the past," with each manufacturer having "a monopoly of the trade in its own area."[30]

The Supreme Court Decision

On the same day that the Supreme Court affirmed the *Corn Products* decision, it reversed the *Staley* ruling of the Circuit Court. Chief Justice Stone argued that the Robinson-Patman Act's "good faith" provision applied only when a seller's lower price was "reduced to meet an equally low price of a competitor." According to Stone, the Act placed the "emphasis on individual situations, rather than upon a general system of competition."[31] Since Staley apparently had not lowered any particular price to meet a lower competitive price, but had only "slavishly" followed "their competitor's higher prices" and thereby copied a system which resulted in systematic discriminations, they could not avail themselves of the good faith defense.[32] Further, "... the fact that Staley's prices are *lower than those they might have charged, but never did charge*, does not tend to show the establishment of a lower price to meet an equally low price of a competitor."[33] Hence, the original FTC order against Staley to cease and desist its discriminations was sustained.[34]

Comment on the Corn Products and Staley Decisions

Eugene Singer has summarized two important economic difficulties associated with the *Corn Products–Staley* decisions.[35] He has noted that candy manufacturers located near Kansas City were not necessarily entitled to cost savings when Corn Products built their new glucose plant there. In the short run, Singer argues that the cost savings and resultant profits should have gone to the glucose manufacturer. Further, Singer emphasizes that it is difficult to understand how the pricing policies of the glucose manufacturers injured competition among the candy makers. If candy makers in Kansas City really compete with Chicago-based candy makers (and the Supreme Court accepted that they did), how were the Kansas City candy makers any worse off after the construction of Corn Products' Kansas City facility? Lower prices in Kansas City, or f.o.b. prices at the factory in Kansas City would, of course, have allowed Kansas City-based candy makers to extend their marketing area. But how were they injured now vis-à-vis the competitive situation that existed before the Kansas City glucose facility was constructed? They were not much better off,[36] but they were no worse off, either. If Kansas City candy makers had wanted to sell primarily in Chicago markets, then they should have located there, and not in Kansas City.

Another difficulty with both decisions is that there was no real proof that there had been any serious injury to competition as a result of the price discriminations. It is hard to believe or accept the idea of "several" candy makers moving closer to a cheap source of supply, and to a potentially larger market (Chicago) as evidence of a substantial lessening of competition or even of a probable lessening. In fact, a movement by candy firms to Chicago would have increased their ability to sell in Chicago and surrounding markets. It would have lowered their glucose costs under the basing point system, and also lowered their freight charges for candy into Chicago markets. Thus if anything, one would have expected competition among candy makers to have been intensified rather than lessened substantially.

Actually, the movement to Chicago may have been unrelated to basing-point pricing. Corwin Edwards reports that one of the greatest advantages of Chicago-based candy makers was their ability to purchase sugar at rates based on water shipment and ship candy at pool-car rates quoted from Chicago.[37]

In addition to these difficulties, the precise price discriminations calculated by the FTC and accepted unquestioningly by the courts in both cases are open to serious question. The FTC calculated "phantom freight" by subtracting the actual freight charge from Kansas City—from where the goods were actually shipped—from the freight charge from Chicago, the basing point, with respect to some delivery area. For example, the actual freight charge to Waco, Texas, from Kansas City was 63 cents. Since the freight from Chicago actually charged was 85 cents, candy manufacturers allegedly paid 22 cents of "phantom freight." And it was this price discrimination resulting from this systematic inclusion of the freight differential that was unlawful.[38]

There are two serious issues here. One issue is the magnitude of the freight absorptions vis-à-vis the phantom charges. Although the Court did not determine what percentage of business paid phantom freight and what percentage did not, it appears likely that a very great percentage of freight was absorbed rather than charged as phantom. Judge Minton stated, for example, that Staley—whose plant was located at Decatur—sold the "bulk" of its glucose in the Chicago area.[39] This would imply that the bulk of Staley's transportation expenses were in fact absorbed. Although absorbing freight is still price discrimination in the eyes of the law, it is surely much less odious from an economic perspective than charging phantom freight.

An even more serious issue, however, is the fact that the phantom freight calculated above on the shipment to Waco, Texas, can *not* be correct. The corn syrup producers enjoyed what are termed "freight in-transit" discounts from the railroads on corn and corn syrup shipped various distances. A "back haul" with glucose on the same railroad that delivered raw corn to the glucose manufacturer earned a differential freight charge. Hence, the simple FTC calculations that supported their (preconceived) conclusions, and later grounded the decisions of the Circuit Court and the Supreme Court, can hardly be accurate.[40]

Although the basing point, delivered-pricing system might create the impression that there was little price competition between glucose sellers, and although some authors have stated boldly that the firms "avoided all rivalry in their price quotations,"[41] such was just not the case. An infrequently mentioned part of the case sustained by the Circuit Court and the Supreme Court against Corn Products, was the fact that the firm often sold to favored customers at old prices long after the old prices had been increased.[42] Such booking practices, which tend to increase competitive pressures among syrup sellers, were regarded as discriminatory by the FTC and the courts, and the firms were subsequently ordered to end the activity. Thus although the firms publicly quoted identical prices in the same geographic area, the terms of the actual exchange and the exact nature of the competitive process may have been far different than supposed.

Finally, the pricing techniques adopted after the 1945 decisions against Corn Products and Staley were still "discriminatory." Although each glucose maker quoted an f.o.b. mill price, freight was still being absorbed to meet prices in distant markets.[43] Final prices still did not relate precisely to "costs," and, presumably, candy makers outside Chicago were still being injured when attempting to sell candy in competition with Chicago-based firms. It is certainly questionable whether the post-decision pricing system (with tightened booking practices) was significantly more competitive from a neoclassical perspective than the predecision pricing system.

THE MORTON SALT CASE (1948)

On September 18, 1940, the FTC issued a complaint and a cease-and-desist order involving the Morton Salt Company.[44] The complaint alleged that Morton discriminated in price between different purchasers of its Blue Label table salt, and that the effect of the discrimination "has been and may be substantially to lessen competition . . . and to injure, destroy and prevent competition between those purchasers receiving the benefit of said discriminatory prices and those to whom they are denied . . ."[45]

The discriminatory prices were a necessary consequence of Morton's volume discount system. As far back as 1922, Morton, like its closest competitors, had granted remittances or rebates to those customers that met particular quantity requirements for salt during the year. Buyers, for example, that bought in less-than-carload lots paid a delivered price of $1.60 per case; the price paid for carload lot purchases was $1.50 per case. In addition, customers that bought as many as 5000 cases or more paid $1.40 per case, while an additional five-cent discount was available to those customers that bought 50,-000 cases or more in any consecutive 12-month period.

Buyers using this volume discount system could be small single purchasers, wholesalers, or groups of small retailers or wholesalers that combined their salt purchases to take advantage of the cost savings on large volumes. "Combine selling" and "pool car arrangements" were encouraged by Morton Salt and, as a result, few buyers actually paid the highest ($1.60) delivered price for Blue Label salt.[46] As a final point, there were four large chain stores (American Stores Co., National Tea Co., Safeway Stores, Inc., A&P Co.) that obtained the lowest rate ($1.35), since they purchased 50,000 or more cases of salt from Morton.

The FTC first charged that Morton Salt's discounts discriminated against certain wholesalers since they

> must either sell at competitive prices and in so doing reduce their possible profits which they might reasonably obtain by the amount of the discriminations

against them, or attempt to sell at higher prices than the favored customers of respondent charge for the same product, with the result of inability to secure business and a reduction in the volume of their sales.[47]

In addition the discounts "injured" small retailers in competition with large chain stores since they forced "retail customers of such wholesalers to pay prices which *prohibit competition in price* between such small retailers and the large retail chain stores."[48] For these reasons, the Morton Salt Company was ordered to cease and desist "discriminating directly and indirectly in the price of such products of like grade and quality as among wholesale or retail dealers purchasing said salt when the differences in price are not justified by differences in the cost on manufacture, sale, or delivery . . ."[49] Morton *had* offered a cost defense, but it had been struck down by an FTC trial examiner because it was, supposedly, based on "estimates, hypothesis, or mere guesses," and not on facts.[50]

The Circuit Court Decision

A Circuit Court of Appeals reviewed and reversed the FTC order against Morton Salt.[51] Judge Briggle (with whom Judge Sparks concurred) first noted that Morton's discounts were open and available to all on equal terms. There were no secret, personal, or special discounts to favored customers. In this way, Briggle explained, the discounts conformed with the normal trade practices of many other producers and sellers of staple merchandise. If Morton's quantity discounts were inherently discriminatory, then such illegal discrimination was also inherent in the selling practices of many other firms.[52]

Judge Briggle then attempted to distinguish between illegal price discrimination and "harmless differentiation." Drawing "any distinction" produces discrimination, but the kind of discrimination outlawed by Section 2 must be unfair, injurious, and prejudicial.[53] Since not all price distinctions "inherently impart an adverse effect upon competition" and since "injury or threat of injury is not inferable from the price structure alone," Judge Briggle argued that the FTC would have had to prove that the price discriminations were likely to cause injury forbidden by the law.[54] But this, Briggle concluded, the FTC had not done.

The FTC had interrogated witnesses as to whether their business would be affected if they had to pay higher prices for Morton's salt than their larger competitors. Fifty-one witnesses were so questioned, and twenty-two thought that their business might be affected. But having one's business affected was not enough to infer competitive injury. To quote Judge Briggle:

Twenty-nine (some of the 32 included) observed that while the competitor enjoying the discount might have an opportunity *to make more profit, there would be no effect on competition*, if, as the record demonstrates to be the fact, the discount was not used to reduce the sale price of the product. This had not occurred in the past.

Any businessman would readily admit that to some degree the price paid by a competitor for a product sold by him affects his business. . . . This does not inferentially establish that the competitive position of either of them is being or may be injured, or that competition in the wholesale or retail business in the same line of commerce in general is being or may be injured or that the price differentials in question actually affect or may affect the competitive re-sale fluctuations in the trade.[55]

Contrary to the inferences drawn by the FTC, Judge Briggle noted that the evidence in the case demonstrated that there had been substantial *increases* in sales of salt to all nondiscount customers.[56] Hence, the actual facts in the case rebutted entirely the FTC suppositions, and rendered "wholly insufficient" the hypothesis of injury or probable injury to competition.[57]

As a final point, Judge Briggle turned to the troublesome issue of whether Morton Salt's volume discounts were related to actual cost differentials. According to the judge, the quantity carload discounts were related by "substantial and uncontroverted evidence to the cost of the sale and delivery of petitioner's product."[58] The other discounts may have been cost related, but it was not up to Morton Salt to have to prove such a relationship. Since Judge Briggle had already deduced that there was no evidence that Morton's prices were "inherently discriminatory," or that they tended to injure competition or even competitors, no cost defense was necessary. As the judge so curtly put the issue: "One does not justify an act which is harmless, inoffensive and legal."[59] The FTC complaint and order against Morton Salt was, therefore, dismissed.

Circuit Judge Minton dissented, arguing that the quantity discounts were discriminatory per se, and that they were illegal whenever the effect may be substantially to lessen competition.

It does *not have* to be shown, and therefore found by the Commission, that such discriminations actually lessened competition. It is sufficient if it is found that there is a *reasonable possibility* that the discriminatory acts "may" have such an effect.[60]

Since the "expert judgment" of the Commission had found such a reasonable possibility, Judge Minton thought that the FTC order against Morton Salt should have been sustained.

The Supreme Court Decision

A majority of the Supreme Court agreed with Judge Minton's argument and reversed the Circuit Court decision in 1948. They declared that Morton's quantity discounts did result in "price differentials between competing purchasers" and that it was "obvious" and "self-evident" that the competitive opportunities of certain merchants were injured when they had to pay more for salt than did their competitors.[61] And since Morton could not demonstrate that the "full amount of the discount was based on . . . actual savings in cost," the discounts were illegally discriminatory.

The Court also noted that while Morton Salt's discounts on volume were theoretically open and available to all, functionally they were not, since no small retailer could purchase at the 50,000 case rate. The implication here, apparently, was that a discount system which excluded all but the very large firms from the biggest discount savings was not, in fact, open and available to all.

Finally, and embarrassingly, the Court stressed the fact that the Congressional intent of the Robinson-Patman Act was "with protecting small businesses which were unable to buy in quantities, such as the merchants here who purchased in less-than-carload lots."[62] Since it was an "evil" that large buyers could secure competitive advantages based only on their purchasing ability, the Supreme Court ruled that Morton had indeed violated the law regarding price discrimination.[63]

Mr. Justice Jackson and Mr. Justice Frankfurter dissented in part with the majority's interpretation. They argued that the law had always required a "reasonable probability" of injury to competition, rather than a "reasonable possibility," as the majority had accepted. "Possibility" was simply too "slender a thread of inference" and the Justices felt that it could easily be "translated into a rule which is fatal to any discount the Commission sees fit to attack."[64]

> The law in this case, in a nutshell, is that no quantity discount is valid if the Commission chooses to say it is not. That is not the law which Congress enacted and which this Court had uniformly stated until today.[65]

It was also argued that a distinction should have been made between the discounts condemned by the majority. The 10- and 15-cent discounts to the large purchasers vis-à-vis the smaller merchants inevitably accelerated the trend "towards monopoly" (!); it was correct, therefore, that the majority had condemned these. But the 10-cent carload differentials vis-à-vis the non-carload purchasers probably did not tend to reduce competition substantially. Since these latter discounts did relate generally to handling and delivery expenses, and since only about 1/10 of 1 percent of Morton's shipments did not contain them, Justices Jackson and Frankfurter thought they should have been allowed. To clinch their argument, they maintained, rather unconvincingly, that Morton might have to raise prices to its carload customers to eliminate the illegal discrimination.[66]

Comment on the Morton Salt Decision

The *Morton Salt* decision confirms the suspicion that FTC rulings and Supreme Court reviews are made in a kind of misty wonderland, where everything is, apparently, not what it seems. Morton had used a quantity discount system for almost twenty years. If there were "substantial reductions of competition" inherent in such a pricing system, they would have surfaced well before the trials. Yet, as the lower court had importantly noted, sales of salt to the nondiscount customers had increased throughout the period. Even so, the Supreme Court simply declared that it was "self-evident" that the "possibility" of such competitive reductions in the future still existed.

Where was one to look for the possible injury to competition, or more honestly, to competitors? Was the fact that the profits or sales of particular wholesalers might be affected, enough to signify possible injury? But why should the government and the courts attempt to preserve particular profit positions for particular competitors, when the free market and the free competitive process tended to reduce them? Were any wholesalers or retailers actually driven from the market? There is no evidence in the decision that any were—but they would not even have had to have been. The mere possibility that they might have had their profits or sales influenced by Morton's discount system, was quite enough to infer a violation of the law in this case.

Throughout its written decision, the Supreme Court tried to convey the impression that the small merchant purchasing salt with no discount at $1.60 per case had to compete with firms such as A&P that were able to purchase salt at $1.35 per case. Actually, as has already been indicated, less than 1/10 of 1 percent of all salt sold at less than carload-lot prices. Thousands of retailers bought through wholesalers that bought 5000 cases or more and, therefore, enjoyed the $1.40 price per case. The National Retail-Owned Grocers, Inc., for example, with 18,917 retail store members, bought Morton Blue Label salt at the $1.40 price per case. In the preponderant number of competitive situations, therefore, the cost differential might have been no more than 5 cents per case or 1/5 of a cent per package. It is impossible to accept the inference that such a price discrimination might have had any substantial effect upon competition. The evidence in the case bears out the fact that it did not have any substantial effect. Thus, the Court's statement that it was "almost inevitable" that the discounts would accelerate the trend "towards monopoly" in this industry is both insulting and absurd.[67]

While the High Court spent little time analyzing "costs," and while Morton's "cost defense" had failed to satisfy the FTC, there was evidence introduced to indicate that there were accounting cost savings associated with serving the large discount buyers.[68] The savings were directly related to the size of the delivery order and to the fact that there was no "merchandising expense" associated with the largest purchases. Only Morton's ineptly prepared statistical report prevented these actual cost savings from justifying their price discounts.

Even, of course, if there were no cost advantages associated with the largest customers, the discounts might still have made excellent economic sense. These were extremely large orders and Morton could ill afford to lose them to the competition. Thus whether the cost savings precisely covered the discounts was entirely irrelevant; Morton Salt did what it had to do in order to secure or retain business that was a substantial percentage of its total volume. Otherwise, why grant any price concessions at all? If Morton Salt might have done the same volume of business at a nickel *more* a case, why didn't it? Certainly a court order was not necessary to get a firm to raise its price, and stop discriminating, if it would have been increasingly profitable to have done so.

The *Morton Salt* case confirms the opinion expressed in the beginning of this chapter that the Robinson-Patman Act's major purpose was to make price competition and price reductions more difficult. It also substantiates the opinion that the so-called cost defense is no defense at all, but is provided only to create the public impression that legitimate discounts can somehow be distinguished from illegitimate ones.

THE MINNEAPOLIS–HONEYWELL (1951), STANDARD OIL OF INDIANA (1951, 1958), AND SUN OIL (1963) CASES

The open hostility of the Federal Trade Commission to effective price competition, in the name of saving competition has been continued in more recent cases. In many instances the courts have set aside the more ludicrous FTC orders; in some instances they have not. In the *Minneapolis–Honeywell* case, for example, the FTC held—contrary to the trial examiner's findings— that Minneapolis–Honeywell had tended to substantially reduce competition in the selling of oil burner controls by discriminating in prices offered to certain oil burner manufacturers. The Circuit Court of Appeals rejected the commissioners' case, however, and upheld Honeywell's right to reduce prices in an attempt to gain back a declining market share.[69]

In the *Standard Oil of Indiana* case, the FTC held, contrary to the trial examiner's findings, that lowering prices in good faith to meet competition was "immaterial" if such discounts were potentially injurious to competition, that is, to *other competitors*. Standard Oil had granted discounts of 1.5 cents per gallon to four jobbers that sold some gasoline at retail in competition with other retail stations that did not receive jobber discounts. Standard had offered an elaborate cost defense,[70] which the FTC rejected, and had argued further that the jobber discounts were necessary to meet rival competition. In 1951, the Supreme Court rejected the FTC version of the "meeting competition" defense,[71] and in 1958 it rejected the FTC rebuttal that the prices Standard Oil was attempting to meet were illegal.[72]

In 1963, the Supreme Court found in favor of the FTC and rejected Sun Oil Company's argument that it had legally reduced prices to a particular dealer that was attempting to meet competition at the retail level.[73] Such price discrimination, argued the Court, was likely to injure other Sunoco dealers that did not receive the Sun Oil discount,[74] and might also injure independent petroleum suppliers that might be "the only meaningful source of price competition offered the major oil companies, of which Sun is one."[75] Thus the FTC's continuing hostility to competition, and especially to the "meeting competition in good faith" provision, was sustained in this case.[76] For a final and extensive examination of the FTC's hostility to free market competition, we turn to the classic *Borden* case.

THE BORDEN CASE (1966)

In April of 1958, the Federal Trade Commission issued a complaint against the Borden Company.[77] Borden was accused of selling goods of like grade and quality to different buyers at different prices with the effect that such selling might reduce competition substantially. The goods of "like grade and quality" were Borden's own brand of evaporated milk and some "identical" milk that it made and sold under private label. The price difference between the two milks was substantial.[78] The FTC charged that it was this difference that violated the Robinson-Patman Act.

The Hearing Examiner's Decision

The hearing examiner for the Federal Trade Commission, Abner E. Lipscomb, offered the initial decision on the complaint in December of 1961. Although Mr. Lipscomb admitted that there was a decided consumer preference for Borden's evaporated milk vis-à-vis the private brands Borden also made, he argued that this did not tend to prove that "Bordon brand and Bordon's private label brands are of a different grade or quality of evaporated milk."[79] The raw milk was the same, it was all processed in exactly the same manner, and it was put into identical cans; "no magic of the market-place thereafter" could change those facts. The different labels that were then affixed, and the different prices that Bordon charged, did not change the fact that the milk was of "like grade and quality." And since there were different prices for goods of like grade and quality there was *prima facie* price discrimination within the intent and meaning of the antitrust laws.

But had the price discriminations caused a substantial lessening of competition? The hearing examiner explained that Borden had first begun selling private-labeled milk as early as 1938. In May of 1957, Borden had been approached by three "orphaned" customers of another creamery that had gone out of business, and they had requested that Borden "pack" milk for them under their own private label. Bordon agreed, and offered them and subsequent customers open and comparable terms.

> The evidence shows that all of these new private-label purchasers came to the respondent of their own accord, and were not solicited by the respondent; that respondent dealt with them in the same manner in which it had dealt with its previous private label customers; and that respondent made no distinction between large and small accounts. Respondent's private label prices were in each instance determined by the use of its cost-plus pricing formula.[80]

Examiner Lipscomb then reported that seven small canners of evaporated milk had testified in support of the FTC complaint against the Borden Company. They argued that Borden's willingness to expand its private-label business had "placed *severe competitive pressure* on the entire unadvertised brand of private label milk structure and that has . . . largely been felt in the way of *lowered market price.*"[81] Some of the testifying canners had lost business directly to Borden; some had not. Some were selling more cases of evaporated milk in 1957 than they had been selling in 1950; some were not.[82] But competition in the market had definitely increased, and the small canners did not like that fact one bit. As one witness complained:

> The competition has forced our prices down from the level we had previous to that and some of the competition has been selling on a different basis. On an f.o.b. basis and it is made highly competitive because of these factors.[83]

The counsel supporting the price discrimination complaint against the Borden Company had argued that there were three factors that the company employed to restrain trade: (1) Borden's size; (2) the location of Borden's plants; and (3) the consequent ability ("power") of Borden to sell its private label milk f.o.b. Borden's size was an important factor in selling milk because some small canners could not handle the entire business of some of the large potential customers such as Winn-Dixie. Its convenient plant locations were also a factor, since Borden sold strictly f.o.b. The FTC examiner estimated that Borden had a clear freight advantage in approximately 86 percent of the new business that it had acquired from its Midwest competitors.[84] Thus the economic advantages that free competition tended to pass along to buyers were the primary factors, according to counsel, that "effectively foreclosed the independent packer group from selling to certain of the most desirable private-label accounts . . ."[85] Borden was being accused of possessing and employing the very economic virtues that are the hallmark of an open competitive process.

The FTC hearing examiner would not accept the argument that the inherent cost savings employed by Borden were detrimental to competition and, hence, had to be condemned. It is best to quote his full statement in this respect:

These competitive advantages which council supporting the complaint would have us condemn as unlawful are the accumulated benefits of that private initiative, industry and business acumen which our system of free enterprise is designed to foster and reward.

If a supplier is to be penalized because its size enables it to negotiate and fulfill contracts for a product in larger amounts than its competitors can produce, then the efficient conduct of a business, and its resultant growth have become legal detriments.

If a supplier be forbidden to pass on to its customers a savings in transportation costs, made possible by the fact that its plant is more advantageously located than those of its competitors, then the supplier is, in effect, required to add to its selling price a "phantom freight"—a charge equal to the difference between its cost and transportation and that of its less conveniently located competitors.

Furthermore, if a supplier is to be penalized for selling its product at a lower price f.o.b. its plant, instead of adding thereto the cost of transportation to the customer's plant and selling at a higher delivered price, the supplier's right to conduct its business in the manner it deems most practical is abrogated and its customers are thereby deprived of the legitimate saving in cost which they might otherwise obtain by electing to take delivery at the supplier's plant. Such an edict would injure both the respondent and its customers, by depriving them of what would appear to be a basic right of free business enterprise.

We conclude that the above-described contentions are beyond both the allegations of the complaint and the theory upon which it is predicated. We conclude further that all the above factors, whether considered separately or collectively, constitute lawful commercial advantages of the corporate respondent.

Furthermore, we conclude that respondent has made only lawful use of such lawful advantages, and that the resulting effect upon the sales of its Midwest competitors has been only that of the normal give-and-take of healthy competition inherent in the free-enterprise system. Such competition is not unlawful.[86]

The examiner also concluded that the price discrimination had not substantially lessened competition between wholesale customers or retail customers of Borden, nor was "there any reasonable probability of such danger to competition in the future."[87]

Examiner Lipscomb then turned to a cost analysis prepared for Borden by the accounting firm of Haskins & Sells.[88] The analysis demonstrated to Lipscomb's satisfaction that the lower costs of selling private-label milk justified the lower prices charged by Borden for that milk; in fact, the lower costs more than substantiated the price discrimination.[89] The average cost per case of private-label milk was cheaper because the labels and cartons were cheaper, the freight charges were nonexistent (Borden sold all of its private label milk f.o.b.), there were no consignment storage fees or advertising expenses and brokerage fees, and the clerical charges were significantly smaller than with Borden's own evaporated milk. In short, once the milk was packed and labeled for private-brand customers, Borden's responsibility—and expenses—ended. This was demonstrably not the case with its own nationally branded milk. One would, therefore, have expected "cost savings" on the private-brand sales, and they were demonstrated to Lipscomb's full satisfaction.

The examiner next turned to a rebuttal criticism of Borden's cost defense by a Mr. Melvin C. Steele. Mr. Steele offered a two-plant cost study which alleged to demonstrate that Borden's cost savings could not justify the price concession that they granted. It was noted that this rebuttal study was not itself a "correct" cost study, but was simply an attempt to show distortions in Borden's own case. Lipscomb, however, tersely rejected the criticism: "The two-plant study presented by counsel supporting the complaint does, as they suggest, show a distortion, but we believe that the distortion is in the two-plant study itself."[90] Lipscomb then declared that Borden's cost analysis constituted a "full justification" for the price differentials, and ordered the entire complaint against Borden dismissed.[91]

The Federal Trade Commission Decision

On November 28, 1962, the Federal Trade Commission reversed the hearing examiner's decision and ordered Borden to cease price discriminating on goods of like grade and quality sold to different buyers at different prices.[92]

Borden was given 60 days to file a report detailing the manner and form in which it would comply with the cease-and-desist order.[93]

The FTC decision written by Commissioner Dixon is analytically embarrassing due to its unbridled sentimentality and confused equivocations. To suggest that this decision does not relate the facts and logic of the Borden case is to grossly understate the issue.

The implication throughout the Dixon judgment is that Borden, because it is a multi-product, larger firm with "broad resources," could and did employ its vast "prestige and power in the market" to the economic detriment of its smaller, "precarious" rivals.[94] The evidence and analysis offered by the hearing examiner, and reviewed above, that this was not so, had not happened, and was unlikely to happen, was totally ignored. The fact that Borden's share of the market had climbed less than 1 percent during the period under consideration (9.9 percent to 10.7 percent) was also, apparently, irrelevant. The fact that most (86 percent) of Borden's new business was gained through legitimate freight advantages and the proximity of Borden's plants to its customers, was summarily rejected by Dixon as containing "isolated examples" that proved nothing.[95]

It was somehow relevant, however, that a number of smaller companies had gone out of the evaporated milk business during the 1950s. No argument was offered to indicate that Borden had helped to close them down. In fact, a few of the creameries had ceased doing business well before May 1957, when Borden had first begun to acquire additional private-label business. The closed companies were just listed by Commissioner Dixon, and the implication was that in some undefined and perhaps undefinable way, Borden must have been implicated in their demise.[96] Then after being told for the third time that Borden was a large and "powerful" concern, and that its competitors were small and "precarious," Dixon abruptly concluded:

> In this market setting, respondent's price discrimination is a clear threat to the entire competition provided by the Midwest concerns. If the price discrimination is continued, the elimination or the serious impairment of competition from small competitors in the industry is likely. This is enough to satisfy the injury requirement of the Act.[97]

As a final point, and almost as an afterthought, Borden's extensively prepared and previously accepted cost defense was declared to be "inadequate and unacceptable."[98] Without debate or comment, Dixon simply asserted that "broad averaging," and the inclusion of investment costs and brokerage in the cost defense, was completely unacceptable—period. Thus, with no careful analytical rebuttal of the hearing examiner's findings and conclusions even attempted, the Federal Trade Commission issued a cease-and-desist order against the Borden Company.

The Circuit Court Decision

On December 4, 1964, a Circuit Court of Appeals dismissed the FTC's cease-and-desist order against the Borden Company.[99] Circuit Judge Joseph C. Hutcheson, Jr., reviewing the undisputed facts in the case, argued that the first issue was "whether or not the Commission applied the correct legal test in deciding that the commodities sold at different prices were of 'like grade and quality.' "[100]

Judge Hutcheson indicated that the record clearly showed that Borden's own brand of evaporated milk did command a premium price in the market, and that the Borden product was recognized as a premium product by both consumers and dealers who sold evaporated milk. To support these conclusions, the court quoted the testimony of grocers that had stated that consumers asked for the Borden brand by name, and could not be convinced to accept some other brand. Significant price differentials had to exist, apparently, before dealers would even stock and sell other brands.[101] That dealers continued to purchase both products at the different prices indicated, to the court, that one was a "premium line" and one was not.

But was the "demonstrated consumer preference" for the Borden brand to receive legal recognition? The Circuit Court thought it should. Contrary to what the FTC had declared, there was no clear Congressional intent on the matter of "private brands" and price discrimination. In fact, if the intent of the Robinson-Patman and the rest of the antitrust statutes generally was to avoid price rigidity and price uniformity, then "commercial factors" had to be considered in pricing.

> An established brand name may have a large following among purchasers. This fact can be of great economic significance in a competitive market. We do not believe it was the intention of Congress that such clearly demonstrable consumer preference should simply be ignored in determining when products may be priced differently. As a practical matter, such preferences may be far more significant in determining the market value of a product than are its physical characteristics.[102]

There was, according to Hutcheson, no clear legal precedent on the matter. The five cases cited by the FTC to support their argument were not at all comparable to the Borden controversy.

> In none of those cases was there any showing that the purchasers paying the higher prices received brand-name products which readily commanded a premium price in the market, while the purchasers paying the lower prices did not. The brand names were not shown to have any effect on the ultimate price the products could command. Here the Borden brand label was clearly of com-

mercial significance. At all levels of distribution it imparted a premium market value to the Borden product which the private label product did not enjoy. That the Borden brand product should sell for a higher price than the lesser known private brands came as no surprise to anyone.[103]

Thus since the commercial value of the Borden brand had clearly been demonstrated, the court argued that Borden "should be allowed to take it into account in pricing its products."[104] The FTC order against Borden was set aside.

The Supreme Court Decision

The Supreme Court, with Mr. Justice White delivering the opinion, reversed the Circuit Court of Appeals decision on the issue of "like grade and quality," and remanded the *Borden* case back to the Appeals Court so that the remaining matters might be decided.[105] The argument to reverse was a virtual replay of the FTC decision; that is, that the products under discussion were chemically the same, and that the Congressional intent had been to treat national brands and private brands alike if they were chemically the same.[106]

In addition, the Supreme Court hypothesized, if a manufacturer sold its branded, higher priced milk to a retailer, but refused to sell the private-label brand to him, then the

retailer who was permitted to buy and sell only the more expensive brand would have no chance to see to those who always buy the cheaper product or to convince others, by experience or otherwise, of the fact which he and all other dealers already know—that the cheaper product is actually identical with that carrying the more expensive label.[107]

What this particular hypothesis had to do with the Borden Company, which had not been charged with such conduct (or even with the possibility of it) was never explained.

There was a sharply worded dissent in the *Borden* case written by Justice Stewart, with whom Justice Harlan joined. Justice Stewart argued, as had the Circuit Court, that products were not of like grade and quality if consumer preference demonstrated that they were not.[108] Stewart was impressed by the fact that Borden took extra precautions with its own branded milk such that a "flawed product" did not reach the consumer; no such precautions were taken with the private brand.[109] To ignore what the majority of the Supreme Court had termed "intangibles," was to ignore the obvious market determination that the products were indeed different, and were not to be considered of like grade and quality. And even if a relevant "cost determination" could be made, ". . . the cost ratio between Borden's premium and private label products is hardly the most significant factor in Borden's pricing decision and market return on those products."[110] Here, it can be observed, the inherent conflict between "costs (should) determine prices" and "prices are determined by demand" is made explicit. But this was a minority opinion endorsed by only two members of the Supreme Court.

Finally, Stewart argued, the supposed threat to competition was unclear. Since there had been no allegation that Bordon had used its position in "the premium brand market to subsidize predatory price-cutting campaigns in the private-label market," and since the consumer of the private brand had been shown to be different from the consumer of the premium brand, "conventional notions of price discrimination under the Robinson-Patman Act may not be applicable."[111] Rather disgustedly, Stewart concluded:

> In the guise of protecting producers and purchasers from discriminatory price competition, the Court ignores legitimate market preferences and endows the Federal Trade Commission with authority to disrupt price relationships between products whose identity has been measured in the laboratory but rejected in the marketplace. I do not believe that such power was conferred upon the Commission by Congress . . . [112]

Comment on the Borden Controversy

In many important and embarrassing ways, the *Borden* controversy is a fitting climax—a climax of absurdity—with respect to price discrimination under the anitrust laws. It is the theoretical dead-end to which a mechanistic, demand-ignoring, "costs (should) determine prices" theorem can be pushed. The products under discussion were clearly distinguished in the mind, and in the market behavior of the consumers; the products did not really compete directly with each other; the products had different brand names, sold in different ways and at different prices, to different buyers. Yet they were declared by an "expert" regulatory commission and by the highest court in the land to be "equal" and of like grade and quality. Declaring it, apparently, would make it so.

What was the Borden Company to do under the circumstances? Were they to adulterate the production of private-brand evaporated milk in order to make it chemically "unequal"? Or were they to raise the price of the private-label milk to the Borden brand "equivalent"? The latter proposal would surely end the alleged "discrimination," although it could bring a huge loss in sales to Borden on their private-label accounts. Of course they could lower the price of the Borden brand to the private label rates; but this action could bring the Justice Department down upon Borden for attempting to eliminate competition from the market. One would also have to assume, since Borden had not voluntarily adopted this policy, that such a reduction in price would lower, rather than increase, Borden's profits. In summation, therefore, Borden was illegally discriminating in price, and no change in its prices could have, it appears, been wholly consistent with the antitrust laws. Any change Borden might have made, other than giving up its private-label business altogether (a refusal to deal?), might have tended to "injure" someone in violation of the law.

But what of the supposed reductions in competition in this case: where exactly were they? How precisely was competition being injured? Are we to accept the idea (an idea that the FTC hearing examiner could not accept) that there is "injury to competition" within the meaning of the law whenever a firm with production and locational advantages decides to pass along some of these advantages to buyers? It should be apparent by now that with or without the alleged "price discrimination," the essence of the FTC complaint was that Borden's prices for private label milk were attractive enough to take some business away from some smaller rivals. This inherently competitive behavior is really what the FTC objected to. If Borden never sold another ounce of its own brand of evaporated milk, the effect of its low prices for private-brand milk on "competition" would still have concerned the FTC. The price discrimination charge, as Justice Stewart had hinted, was a sham from beginning to end.

And finally, what of "cost justification"? If Borden's elaborate cost defense was unacceptable, then any cost defense can be declared unacceptable. Borden demonstrated beyond a shadow of a reasonable doubt to the hearing examiner that the costs associated with its private brand business were proportional to the prices that it charged. Herbert Taggard, Chairman of the FTC's own Advisory Committee on Cost Justification, had assisted in the preparation of the Borden document, and the FTC hearing examiner had accepted the report as a "complete justification." Yet the FTC rejected it as "inadequate," and the courts remained silent on the entire question. Such is the nightmare of antitrust in the "public interest" under Section 2 of the Clayton Act.

As an optimistic postscript to the Borden Company's ordeal, the Circuit Court again considered, and again dismissed, the FTC cease-and-desist order. It found that "the record does not contain substantial injury to competition at the seller's level."[113] The legal outrage against the Borden Company was over.

CONCLUSIONS

Many learned commentators have recognized the economic nonsense that is inherent in Section 2 of the Clayton Act, as amended, and have called for repeal, or for a dramatic revision of the intent and language of the law. For example, the *Neal Report* suggested that the law should be extensively rewritten such that only substantial and persistent price discriminations be made unlawful, and only when the discrimination had particular effects on competition, not competitors.[114] It also would ease the burden of the "cost defense" and do away completely with the competitive-reducing prohibitions on "brokerage" and other services. The companion *Stigler Report* was even more critical, although less explicit concerning proposed changes.[115] A still more recent review of the antitrust laws echoes these recommendations on price discriminations.[116]

Ironically, such scholarly reports and studies are almost beside the point. There is little evidence that Congress has been moved by such criticism, and it is unlikely to revise anything significantly in either the Clayton or the Robinson-Patman Acts.[117] And the reason seems perfectly clear. The economic nightmare that is Robinson-Patman is working exactly as it was intended to work back in 1936 when the important amendments were drafted. The law, through the threat of enforcement or actual enforcement, can make serious price competition almost impossible,[118] and that may have been exactly the purpose of the statute. After decades of frustration with price discrimination cases, it would be rather naïve to assume otherwise.

NOTES

1. See, for instance, M. A. Adelman, *A&P: A Study in Price–Cost Behavior and Public Policy* (Cambridge, Mass.: Harvard University Press, 1959). See also Wesley J. Liebeler, "The Robinson-Patman Act: Let's Repeal It!" 44 *Antitrust Law Journal*, 18 (1975).

2. The Robinson-Patman Act of 1936 was actually drafted by the U. S. Wholesale Grocers' Association. See Richard Caves, *American Industry: Structure, Conduct, Performance*, 2nd ed. (Englewood Cliffs, N.J.: Prentice-Hall, 1967), p. 86. For an interesting discussion of the origins of the Clayton Act and the Federal Trade Commission see Gabriel Kolko, *The Triumph of Conservation: A Reinterpretation of American History, 1900–1916* (Chicago: Quadrangle Books, 1967), pp. 261–267. For an excellent criticism of the Federal Trade Commission, see Alan Stone, *Economic Regulation and the Public Interest: The Federal Trade Commission in Theory and Practice* (Ithaca, N.Y.: Cornell University Press, 1977).

3. For a good review of these factors, see Ralph Cassady, Jr., "Techniques and Purposes of Price Discrimination," *The Journal of Marketing*, Vol. 1 (October 1946), pp. 135–150.

4. *Federal Trade Commission v. Anheuser-Busch, Inc.*, 363 U.S. 536.

5. *Federal Trade Commission v. Borden*, 383 U.S. pp. 641–644 (1966).

6. Adelman, *op. cit.*, p. 60.

7. "... brokerage payments are per se illegal, even though no injurious or destructive effect on competition has resulted and even though the challenged concession reflected actual savings in the seller's distribution costs." *Federal Trade Commission v. Simplicity Patterns Co.*, 360 U.S. p. 55 (1959).

8. *Standard Oil of Indiana v. Federal Trade Commission*, 340 U.S. 231 (1951).

9. See the discussion in *Federal Trade Commission v. A. E. Staley Manufacturing Co. et al.*, 324 U.S. 746 (1945).

10. Murray N. Rothbard, *Power and Market* (Menlo Park, Cal.: Institute for Humane Studies, 1970), p. 47.

11. Clair Wilcox, *Public Policies Toward Business* (Homewood, Ill.: Richard D. Irwin, 1966), pp. 232–233.

12. Adelman, *op. cit.*, pp. 53, 177.

13. *Corn Products Refining Company v. Federal Trade Commission*, 324 U.S. 726 (1945).

14. *Corn Products Refining Company v. Federal Trade Commission*, 144 F. 2d 211.

15. *Ibid.*, p. 214.

16. *Ibid.*, p. 215 (emphasis added).

17. *Ibid.*

18. 324 U.S. pp. 732, 738.

19. *Ibid.*, p. 738.

21. *Ibid.*

22. *Ibid.*, p. 734.

23. *Ibid.*, p. 737.

24. *Federal Trade Commission v. A. E. Staley Manufacturing Company*, 324 U.S. p. 746.

25. *A. E. Staley Manufacturing Company v. Federal Trade Commission*, 144 F. 2d 221.

26. *Ibid.*, p. 224.

27. *Ibid.*, p. 225.

28. *Ibid.*

29. *Ibid.*, p. 230.

30. *Ibid.*, p. 231.

31. 324 U.S. p. 753 (emphasis added).

32. *Ibid.*, p. 754.

33. *Ibid.*, p. 755 (emphasis added).

34. *Ibid.*, p. 760.

35. Eugene Singer, *Antitrust Economics* (Englewood Cliffs, N.J.: Prentice-Hall, 1968), pp. 231–232. Also see his *Antitrust Economics and Legal Analysis* (Columbus, Ohio: Grid Publishing, Inc., 1981), p. 122.

36. To the extent, of course, that they received faster deliveries than they would have from Chicago, they were better off.

37. Corwin D. Edwards, *The Price Discrimination Law* (Washington, D.C.: Brookings Institution, 1959), p. 395.

38. 324 U.S. p. 733.

39. 144 F. 2d. p. 224.

40. Frederick M. Rowe, *Price Discrimination Under the Robinson-Patman Act* (Boston: Little, Brown and Company, 1962), p. 379.

41. Joel B. Dirlam and Alfred E. Kahn, *Fair Competition: The Law and Economics of Antitrust Policy* (New York: Cornell University Press, 1954), p. 126 (emphasis added).

42. 144 F. 2d p. 223

43. Edwards, *op. cit.*, pp. 391–395.

44. *Federal Trade Commission v. Morton Salt Company*, 334 U.S. p. 37.

45. *In the Matter of the Morton Salt Company*, 39 Federal Trade Commission, p. 39.

46. The Supreme Court would admit that "less than 1/10 of 1 percent of all salt sold was not sold at some discount." See 334 U.S. p. 60.

47. 39 Federal Trade Commission 43.

48. *Ibid.*, p. 44 (emphasis added).

49. *Ibid.*, p. 45.

50. For a detailed review of Morton's cost defense see Herbert F. Taggard, *Cost Justification* (Ann Arbor: University of Michigan, School of Business Administration, 1959), pp. 171–85.

51. *Morton Salt Company v. Federal Trade Commission*, 162 F. 2d 949.

52. *Ibid.*, p. 953.

53. *Ibid.*, p. 954–955.

54. *Ibid.*, p. 955.

55. *Ibid.*, p. 956 (emphasis added).

56. *Ibid.*, p. 957.

57. *Ibid.*

58. *Ibid.*

59. *Ibid.*

60. *Ibid.*, p. 959 (emphasis added).

61. 334 U.S. p. 47, 50.

62. *Ibid.*, p. 49.

63. *Ibid.*, p. 43.

64. *Ibid.*, p. 58.

65. *Ibid.*

66. *Ibid.*, pp. 59–61.

67. *Ibid.*, p. 60.
68. Taggard, *op. cit.*, pp. 171–176.
69. *Minneapolis-Honeywell Regulator Company v. Federal Trade Commission*, 191 F. 2d 766 (1951).
70. Taggard, *op. cit.*, pp. 187–236.
71. *Standard Oil of Indiana v. Federal Trade Commission*, 340 U.S. 231.
72. *Federal Trade Commission v. Standard Oil of Indiana*, 355 U.S. 396.
73. *Sun Oil Company v. Federal Trade Commission*, 371 U.S. 505.
74. *Ibid.*, p. 519.
75. *Ibid.*, p. 523.
76. In 1957, a majority of the FTC commissioners actually urged the Congress to enact a law that would set aside the right to meet a competitor's price under Robinson-Patman. See Lowell B. Mason, *The Language of Dissent* (New Canaan, Conn.: Long House, 1961), p. 117. Mason is a former FTC Commissioner.
77. *In the Matter of the Borden Company*, 62 FTC 130.
78. *Ibid.*, p. 132.
79. *Ibid.*, p. 139.
80. *Ibid.*, p. 143.
81. *Ibid.*, p. 145 (emphasis added).
82. *Ibid.*, pp. 145–149.
83. *Ibid.*, p. 145.
84. *Ibid.*, p. 150.
85. *Ibid.*, p. 151.
86. *Ibid.*, p. 152.
87. *Ibid.*, p. 155.
88. Herbert Taggard, Professor of Accounting at the University of Michigan, served as an advisor in the preparation of the cost analysis. See *Ibid.*, p. 156.
89. *Ibid.*, p. 159.
90. *Ibid.*, p. 161.
91. *Ibid.*, p. 165.
92. Two members did not participate, and one dissented; thus, only two of the five members concurred in the decision.
93. *Ibid.*, p. 193.
94. *Ibid.*, p. 174.
95. *Ibid.*
96. *Ibid.*, p. 187.
97. *Ibid.*, p. 190.
98. *Ibid.*, p. 192.
99. *The Borden Company v. Federal Trade Commission*, 339 F. 2d 133.

100. *Ibid.*, p. 135.
101. *Ibid.*, p. 136.
102. *Ibid.*, p. 137.
103. *Ibid.*
104. *Ibid.*, p. 138.
105. *Federal Trade Commission v. The Borden Company*, 383 U.S. 637 (1966).
106. *Ibid.*, pp. 640–644.
107. *Ibid.*, p. 644.
108. *Ibid.*, p. 649.
109. *Ibid.*, p. 651.
110. *Ibid.*, p. 659.
111. *Ibid.*, p. 660.
112. *Ibid.*, p. 662.
113. *The Borden Company v. Federal Trade Commission*, 381 F. 2d 175 (1967) especially p. 179.
114. *White House Task Force on Antitrust Policy*, I, (1969), Reprinted in *Antitrust and Trade Regulation Report*, Bureau of National Affairs, No. 411 (May 27, 1969), Part 11.
115. Reprinted in *Antitrust and Trade Regulation Report*, Bureau of National Affairs, No. 413 (June 10, 1969), pp. X-1 to X-8.
116. "Report to the President and the Attorney General of the National Commission for the Review of Antitrust Laws and Procedures," reprinted in *Antitrust and Trade Regulation Report*, Bureau of National Affairs, No. 897 (January 18, 1979), pp. 1–117.
117. There is some indication, however, that the Congress may attempt to restrict the power of the FTC itself in the antitrust area. See *Antitrust and Trade Regulation Report*, Bureau of National Affairs, No. 1002 (February 19, 1981), p. A-1.
118. It is difficult to exaggerate the economic nonsense in price discrimination cases. For a classic account of the Court's hostility to price competition, see *Utah Pie Company v. Continental Baking Company*, 386 U.S. 685 (1967). Also see Ward S. Bowman "Restraint of Trade by the Supreme Court: The *Utah Pie* Case," *The Yale Law Journal*, Vol. 77, pp. 70–85, for an excellent analysis of that decision.

CHAPTER SEVEN

Tying Agreements and Public Policy

A conventional *tying agreement* is said to exist when a buyer agrees to purchase or lease one commodity, conditioned on also purchasing or leasing another commodity. Such an agreement is called a *requirements contract* when a buyer agrees to purchase all requirements of several commodities from one seller. And *exclusive dealing* is an agreement wherein a buyer agrees to sell wholesale or retail only the commodities of some particular manufacturer. Although different in specifics, the agreements have a substantive common thread: In each instance, a buyer or lessee agrees to some restriction of economic activity. Under antitrust law, such contracts are illegal under Section 3 of the Clayton Act when their effect "may be to substantially lessen competition or tend to create a monopoly." They may also be prosecuted as illegal restraints of trade under Section 1 of the Sherman Act, or under Section 5 of the Federal Trade Commission Act of 1914.

A THEORY OF TYING AGREEMENTS

It is easy to understand why tying agreements merit special attention under the antitrust laws. In standard economic jargon, such contracts would inherently reduce competition and lead to a misallocation of resources.[1] A seller with some degree of "market power" in one commodity—the tying good—might require users of that commodity to purchase a second commodity or service—the tied good—at unfavorable terms. Users are then said to be injured, since they would be required to make a less than optimal purchase in the tied-good market. Moreover, potential rival sellers of the tied good might be foreclosed or excluded from the market, thereby lessening competition in that market. According to this perspective, the tie-in sale can act as a barrier to entry, limiting efficient resource employment. In short, the trade restraining effect of tying agreements can allegedly injure both buyers and rival sellers, and result in an inefficient allocation of scarce economic resources in the marketplace.

The initial presumption that tying contracts are inefficient depends upon the correctness of orthodox competition theory. It is true that in perfect competition no individual seller would have the power to require a tying agreement. In the total absence of market power, buyers would be able to acquire all of the commodities that they wanted at competitive prices from rival sellers. Tying agreements would be both impossible and unnecessary in atomistic competition.

As explained in Chapter 2, however, sellers attempt to differentiate their products and create consumer preferences ("market power") for one brand over another. To condemn such situations as resource-misallocating would be arbitrary. Once nonhomogeneous firms, products, and consumers are recognized as a fact, and once the arbitrary welfare assumptions of pure competition are set aside, it becomes difficult to conclude that voluntary market arrangements, such as tying or exclusive dealing, necessarily reduce social welfare or unfairly exclude potential sellers from the tied good market. To note that tying is a departure from atomistic competition and contains monopolistic elements, therefore, is to note only that it is like every other contract or agreement in a free-market system. If tying contracts have some particularly socially harmful feature, this feature must be demonstrated explicitly rather than assumed.

Are Buyers Injured?

The essential objections to tying contracts are that they injure buyers and foreclose rival sellers from competition. It might be appropriate to investigate the allegation that buyers are injured, in a neoclassical sense, by tying agreements. How, precisely, are they injured? Imagine, for example, a fishing rod manufacturer who offers a rod for sale on condition that a particular fishing reel, which this firm also manufactures, be purchased. If comparable fishing rods are available from other manufacturers at lower prices without tied reels, buyers are free to choose the untied, and probably less expensive, fishing rods. If buyers require reels, they are free to purchase untied reels. In this situation, buyers can compare the price and quality of the tied package with the price and quality of the separate purchases combined. The lowest priced, highest quality package, whether put together by buyers or manufacturers, will then be chosen. For example, to save on search costs, some buyers will choose (prefer) tied packages. There is certainly no reason to assume that buyers voluntarily injure themselves under such circumstances.

In situations where no fishing reel is desired, buyers can compare the fishing rod under discussion, with its unwanted accessory, against similar rods without such accessories. Since buyers would place no value on the reel whatever, the price of the combination would represent the value of the desired rod only, as if the reel did not exist. To speak of two goods being tied in this instance is ambiguous, since there is only one good actually involved—the fishing rod. This fishing rod, as in the former situation, would then have to be compared by buyers with comparable fishing rods, and a choice at the margin would then be exercised. Again, there is no reason to assume that buyers would voluntarily injure themselves, or would be injured, under such circumstances.

But what if the fishing rod manufacturer is dominant or has market power in the rod market? This means, apparently, that consumers prefer these fishing rods over comparable ones, and that they will pay more for that particular rod, other things being equal. Cannot a manufacturer in such a position extend this market power into reels, using the "leverage" in rods to enlarge the profits in reels? And will not this policy injure buyers?

A simple numerical example may be helpful in understanding the issue of leverage. Assume that the fishing rod "differentiation" is worth, at the most, $3 to customers. While other competitive rods sell for, say, $20, the one with the market power sells for $23. In other words, the manufacturer of the dominant fishing rod is already charging the highest price consistent with profit maximization; any higher price would lead to lower revenues and profits. Now assume that the manufacturer ties a reel to the rod and charges $35 for the combination. If comparable reels sell for approximately $12 in the market, there has been no leverage. If the manufacturer attempts to raise the price of the combination to, say, $40, the increase in price will be functionally equivalent to charging $28 for the rod. But we have already argued that the profit-maximizing price for the rod was $23 and that still higher prices would have lowered profits. We must conclude, therefore, that there is no practical way to "leverage" market power from one market to another, assuming that it has been fully exploited in the first market. We must also note, consistent with what was said in Chapter 2, that consumers are not injured when they prefer differentiated products, and are willing to pay higher prices for different goods.

The longer the time period under consideration, the weaker becomes the argument that buyers are harmed by tying agreements. Certainly, if a group of buyers were unhappy with certain tying contracts, sellers of alternative products would enter the market to offer more favorable terms. Some alternative sellers would offer nontying terms to formerly tied buyers, and over time, a rivalrous process would be expected to purge the relatively undesirable practice from the market. If this did not occur, it must be concluded that buyers prefer such arrangements vis-à-vis other alternatives. It would certainly be incorrect and foolish to believe that buyers are victimized by a system that is voluntarily perpetuated, in the face of open market alternatives, by the very same buyer-victims.

This is not to say that buyers approve of every aspect of every business agreement. No business agreement satisfies all desires, and all such agreements are a compromise. In the context of any given market situation, however, a buyer can be expected to choose that package of business services that generates the greatest net utility or satisfaction. When a particular agreement is completed in a free market, it must be concluded that the traders tend to find the terms preferable to other arrangements that they could have chosen. Not all aspects of the contract will ever be perfect from either's perspective. But, on balance, the agreement must, *ex ante*, intend a mutually satisfactory relationship. If the tying agreements are renewed and extended, it must be assumed that the agreements are also mutually satisfactory *ex post*.

If the tying good is leased rather than sold, it is still difficult to conclude that the lessee is somehow injured by the agreement. Some tying agreements that may appear to injure lessees and involve the employment of leverage, may only be a special kind of price discrimination. For example, a copying machine might be leased at low rentals on the condition that the paper for the machine be purchased from the machine lessor. In this case, the lessor can employ the tied good (the paper) as a meter that registers the intensity of the demand for the leased machines. By tying the paper to the machine, the lessor can, in effect, charge the more intensive machine user a higher overall rate that reflects the value of the machine to the lessee. Similar results could be accomplished by attaching a meter to the leased machines and billing the more intensive users for the additional operations. Rather than inflict any net injury on the lessee, the lessor is simply attempting to discover (and recover) the precise value of each machine to each of the different users.

Still other tying agreements arise in order to protect a manufacturer's good will, or to control "free rider" problems. For instance, a seller may employ exclusive dealing contracts with distributors in order to encourage them to promote and advertise that seller's products. In the absence of such agreements, it may be difficult for local sellers to sufficiently capture the economic benefits of the product information that they provide. Or similarly, tying agreements might encourage local sellers to make substantial investments in quality repair and service which, in the absence of such agreements, might be discouraged if low quality rival sellers of the same products could freely compete in the same territory. Finally, some equipment lessors may choose to tie-in service of the equipment in order to enhance the reputation and good will of their product. In each of these instances, the exclusive dealing arrangement helps to secure the value of a property right; it is not obvious why this is "inefficient" from a social perspective.

In conclusion, tying agreements, like all voluntary agreements, tend to exist and be extended because they provide benefits to the parties to the contract. They are frequently a less-costly way of accomplishing some particular business objective, and they relate not to any general output restriction, but often to a more effective interbrand competitive rivalry between sellers in the market. Some sellers may prefer such agreements because they enhance good will, allow effective price discrimination, limit free riding, and serve to encourage investment in promotion and service by distributors. Purchasers, on the other hand, can prefer such agreements for similar reasons; each of the advantages identified can allow a more effective competition with sellers of rival brands of products. In addition, tying and exclusive dealing can assure availability of necessary supplies, reduce search costs, and even, under certain circumstances, allow lessees to shift some of the risk and uncertainty of their own business back to the lessors of the equipment. In short, there is no reason why tying agreements can not be considered consistent with efficient resource allocation.

Foreclosure and Exclusion

We now turn briefly to an examination of alleged foreclosure and exclusion due to tying agreements. To review, the implication is that rival sellers of the tied good are unfairly excluded from market opportunities because of the existence of tying contracts. The tying good is said to be a barrier to entry that effectively forestalls competition in the tied-good market and ultimately injures consumers.

But the reasonableness of this analysis is certainly open to debate. If the percentage of the market that is tied is relatively small, and if the tied good is sold under openly competitive conditions, the effect of any alleged foreclosure must certainly be negligible. And certainly if tying exists because the tied good is offered at rates lower than alternative rates, it is not obvious that resources are misallocated or that the exclusion is "unfair." The fact remains that rivals can always attempt to compete in the tied-good market by simply lowering their prices in that maket.

But even more fundamentally, the concept of unfair foreclosure seems to beg the question. All purchases of any commodity from anyone necessarily foreclose and exclude other sellers at the moment of sale, and if the particular commodities are relatively durable, the disappointed sellers stay excluded for some time to come. Yet it would be ludicrous to describe such actions as "lessening competition" or "misallocating economic resources." Presumably, all sellers competed *before* any particular buyer made a specific selection of commodities; the conditions in the market prior to sale give the only relevant perspective for appraising competition. All buyer choice forecloses less desirable options; that is the purpose of free consumer choice in an open market. To inhibit such choices and such contracts would be to restrain efficiency and the competitive process.

It should now be apparent that the standard criticisms concerning the inefficiency of tying arrangements are misplaced. Tying often serves to lower prices, reduce market uncertainties and risk, assure regular deliveries of future supplies, limit free riding, increase investments, or allow effective price discrimination. And buyers need not be injured nor rival sellers unfairly foreclosed from tied-good markets. In addition, since tying is an agreement, it is explicit evidence of an increase, *ex ante*, in efficiency and benefit as far as the parties to the contract are concerned. With these preliminary thoughts in mind, we now turn to an examination of some of the most important tying agreement cases in antitrust history.

THE INTERNATIONAL SALT CASE (1947)

The first of the modern classic cases to be examined concerns International Salt.[2] The International Salt Company owned two patents on machines that prepared salt for certain industrial processes. The "Lixator" dissolved salt into brine; the "Saltomat" injected salt tablets into cans during the canning process. International Salt leased the machines widely, and had 840 "Lixator" and 73 "Saltomat" leases outstanding in 1947.

The government brought suit under Section 1 of the Sherman Act, and Section 3 of the Clayton Act, alleging that International Salt had illegally restrained trade by tying the purchase of its salt to the lease of its patented machines. In most of the leasing contracts for machines, the following "offensive" phrase appeared: ". . . that the said Lixate Process Dissolver shall be used for dissolving and converting into brine only those grades of rock salt purchased by the Lessee from the Lessor . . .[3] In 1944, the dollar value of salt tied to the patented machines was approximately $500,000.

The Supreme Court Decision

Justice Jackson delivered the opinion of the Supreme Court in 1947. He stated that while patents conferred a limited, and legal, monopoly on International's use of its machines, they conferred "no right to restrain use of, or trade in, unpatented salt."[4]

The District Court had issued a summary judgment on the government's charges, and had not taken evidence as to the "reasonableness" of the tying restraints. Justice Jackson thought this proper since, as with price-fixing, "it is unreasonable per se to foreclose competitors from any substantial market."[5] Since the volume of trade in the tied-good (salt) was not "insignificant or insubstantial," the tendency of the agreements to accomplish monopoly appeared obvious. And, the Court reminded, this tendency towards monopoly need only be a "creeping one," and not necessarily one in "full gallop."[6]

International Salt argued that its tying contracts were saved from being illegal per se by the insertion of the following provision:

> If at any time during the term of this lease a general reduction in prices of grades of salt suitable for use in the said Lixate Process Dissolver shall be made, said Lessee shall give said Lessor an opportunity to provide a competitive grade of salt at any such competitive price quoted, and in case said Lessor shall fail or be unable to do so, said Lessee, upon continued payment of the rental herein agreed upon, shall have the privilege of continued use of the said equipment with salt purchased in the open market, until such time as said Lessor shall furnish a suitable grade of salt at the said competitive price.[7]

Thus, lessees who could purchase salt cheaper from other salt sellers were free to do so and could still retain International's patented machines.

The Court, however, was not convinced that this particular provision relieved the tying contract from being an illegal restraint of trade. Although the provision made the restraint "less harsh," the agreement still stifled potential competition.

> The appellant [International Salt] had at all times a priority on the business at equal prices. A competitor would have to undercut appellant's price to have any hope of capturing the market, while appellant could hold that market by merely meeting competition.[8]

Finally, the Court dismissed International Salt's argument that the high quality salt standards of its leased machines necessitated tying. While quality standards might be appropriate, International's machines were surely not "allergic" to the high quality salt produced by a competitor. International was free to set reasonable quality standards but not free to tie its own salt to its leased machines.[9]

Comment on International Salt

The *International Salt* case is a classic because it appeared to condemn all exclusive or tying arrangements involving a "not insubstantial" volume of business. In short, it established a kind of per se rule with respect to tying contracts. But from an economic point of view, the case left a host of relevant questions unasked and, therefore, unanswered.[10]

For example, International Salt did have two important machine patents, and patents are a monopoly of sorts.[11] But before one can infer unfair leverage in the tied-good market (in this case, salt), one must discover whether (1) the machines were sub-optionally priced, and (2) whether there were similar machines leased by competitors at relatively comparable rates. On the latter issue, the Supreme Court indicated that there were such machines and such competitors.[12] Clearly, the more vigorous the competition in the tying good market, the less significant becomes the issue of alleged leverage. Yet since the Supreme Court treated the tying agreement like price-fixing, it did not hear, and would not instruct the district court to hear arguments relating to the economic reasonableness of such agreements. Thus, the extent and degree of competition in the tying good remained an unexamined—and as far as the Supreme Court was concerned, irrelevant—issue.

The Court never asked, nor was it revealed, whether competition in the market for salt was significantly affected by the tying arrangement between International and its machine customers. But how can it be determined whether $500,000 is "not insubstantial," if no determination of the entire market for salt is made? How many firms sell salt, and how many purchase it? Had International Salt's market share been increasing or decreasing over time? What percent of all salt sold was involved in the tying agreements under discussion? Since tying was treated as a per se offense, these questions, relevant to this inquiry, were never raised. Thus, the Court's conclusion that a "not insubstantial" amount of business was involved must relate to absolute dollar figures only, a rather useless guidepost in determining competitive restraint, even from a strict neoclassical perspective.

Finally, it is likely that International Salt was employing the tied-good (salt) as a vehicle for price discrimination in the lease of its machines. This presumption is strengthened by International's strong objection to a paragraph in the District Court's summary judgment which directed the sale or lease of the salt machines on "non-discriminatory terms and conditions."[13] Yet this issue, which could have been of great explanatory value, was not explored in that context at court.

THE STANDARD STATIONS CASE (1949)

Standard Stations, Inc. was a wholly owned subsidiary of Standard Oil of California. Prior to 1949, Standard Stations had marketed petroleum products and auto supplies through its own retail gasoline stations, and through 5197 independently owned stations that were under exclusive supply contracts to Standard Stations. The government charged that these contracts violated Section 1 of the Sherman Act and Section 3 of the Clayton Act, and a trial began on January 2, 1947.[14]

Judge Yankwich wrote the decision of the District Court in 1948. He admitted that: (a) the independent dealers voluntarily chose to tie themselves to Standard Stations; (b) the typical contract was for only six months, and did not include additional auto accessories; (c) Standard assisted the dealers financially, expended huge funds for advertising, helped repair and improve independent stations, and generally educated dealers in the handling of its products; (d) Standard's percentage of the gasoline market was only 6.7 per cent (1.8 per cent in replacement battery sales) and had been declining over the years; and that (e) Standard's major competitors employed such a system, had since 1938, and "split pump" retailing (retailing more than one brand in the same station) represented only 1.6 per cent of all gasoline sales.[15] Yet relying heavily on Justice Douglas's opinion in the *Socony–Vacuum* case,[16] Judge Yankwich was required to conclude that these facts, and the resultant economic benefits that might flow from the contracts, were irrelevant when it came to the legality of the exclusive dealing arrangements. "The fact that it may be beneficial is not material, if, in effect, it is an unreasonable restraint . . . *economic benefits cannot be taken into consideration if, in fact, there be substantial restriction of commerce.*"[17] This did not mean, supposedly, that exclusive supply contracts were illegal per se,[18] or that the determination of illegal restraint would rest solely on the fact that certain outlets were closed to competitors for the length of the contracts.[19] It would rest, instead, on whether an appreciable segment of trade had been restrained.[20]

But what was an "appreciable segment of trade"? The court's own statistical data, drawn from the trial court record, demonstrated that Standard Stations was a comparatively minor factor in the petroleum retailing market. In percentage terms, Standard was certainly not monopolizing, or even tending to monopolize anything. But the court was not interested in percentages. In one of the most amazing statements in all antitrust history, Judge Yankwich wrote:

> But while the comparative figures bear on the questions, they are not determinate. Substantiality of restraint or tendency to create monopoly is established by (a) the market foreclosed—here represented by the controlled units—and (b) the volume of controlled business, totalling here in value $68,000,000.
>
> Fractionally speaking, the business done by the competitors with their own outlets or with those under contract is much greater than the business of Standard—both in volume and in money value. Nevertheless, the business of Standard is considerable. In effect, it amounts to a substantial lessening of competition and a monopoly of a sizeable segment of a line of commerce in a definite area—the seven Western states. What has the *tendency* to achieve such result becomes, *in actual effect*, an unreasonable restraint.[21]

There was a "substantial restraint" in this case, because the court said that there was; there is no other way to read the above quotation. The restraint was established by the absolute number of dealers "controlled," and the volume of business accomplished. The volume of business was then declared to be considerable and a sizeable segment of the market, even though Standard's share of the market was less than 7 percent. The exclusive supply contracts constituted an unreasonable restraint of trade—period. So as to leave no room for doubt, the court summarized its position as follows:

> *Grant* that on a comparative basis and in relation to the entire trade in these products in the area, the restraint is not integral. Admit also that control of distribution results in lessening of costs and that its abandonment might increase costs. . . . *Concede further*, that the arrangement was entered into in good faith, with the honest belief that control of distribution and consequent concentration of representation were economically beneficial to the industry and to the public, that they have continued for over fifteen years openly, notoriously, and unmolested by the government, and have been practiced by other major oil companies competing with Standard, that the number of Standard outlets so controlled may have decreased, and the quality of products supplied to them may have declined, on a comparative basis.
>
> . . . despite all this, there confronts us the inescapable fact that such 'balanced distribution'—as counsel for the defendants characterized it—calls for concentration of representation, which, in turn, results in an unreasonable restriction of trade, and a substantial lessening of competition, so far as the 5297 outlets, their independent operators and those who seek to supply them are concerned. As the restriction corners a market of the value of $68,000,000, it is illegal, even considered on a comparative basis.[22]

This is, of course, a revealing admission. While the court grants that the exclusive supply contracts lower costs and benefits the industry and the public, it finds that they restrain trade. But how do they restrain trade? They simply exist. But why do they exist? Because, apparently, they lower costs and benefit the industry and the public. In short, economic benefits are not just irrelevant and immaterial in this case. Here they are positively damaging to the defendant since by the court's own logic, the contracts would not have existed but for their benefits. Firms restrain trade, therefore, when they economize on scarce resources, the exact opposite of the truth. Such is the twisted economic logic in the *Standard Stations* case.

The Supreme Court Decision

The Supreme Court reviewed the *Standard Stations* decision in 1949.[23] Justice Frankfurter suggested that the real issue was whether "the requirement of showing that the effect of the agreements 'may be to substantially lessen competition' may be met simply by proof that a substantial portion of commerce is affected, or whether it must also be demonstrated that competitive activity has actually diminished or probably will diminish."[24] Prior to 1947, Frankfurter explained, the precedent had been that "domination of the market" was "sufficient in itself to support the inference that competition had been or probably would be lessened."[25] But the share of the market held by Standard Stations was "hardly large enough to conclude as a matter of law that it occupies a dominant position, nor did the trial court so find."[26]

The *International Salt* case, however, had changed the rules in tying contract cases. That decision "rejected the necessity of demonstrating economic consequences once it has been established that 'the volume of business affected' is not 'insignificant or insubstantial' . . ."[27] Since tying arrangements "hardly serve any purpose beyond the suppression of competition,"[28] and since the Court steadfastly refused to review the economic effects of the contracts,[29] the exclusive supply contracts were illegal because a substantial share of a line of commerce was affected.[30] In a final parting comment, the Court stated:

> Standard's use of the contracts creates just such a potential clog on competition as it was the purpose of Section 3 to remove wherever, were it to become actual, it would impede a substantial amount of competitive activity.[31]

Thus, the lower court decision against Standard Stations was affirmed.

Justice Douglas's celebrated dissent in the *Standard Stations* case is, in the main, an emotional polemic on the alleged growth and power of big business in America.[32] Yet its relevance was the argument that the majority's decision would force independent gasoline dealers out of business, and encourage large oil companies to "build service station empires of their own." Thus, in Douglas's view, the Court's legal medicine in this case, the ending of tying agreements, was even worse than the disease.

> The requirements contract which is displaced is relatively innocuous as compared with the virulent growth of monopoly power which the Court encourages. The Court does not act unwittingly. It consciously pushes the oil industry in that direction. The Court approves what the Anti-Trust Laws were designed to prevent. It helps remake America in the image of the cartels.[33]

Chief Justice Vinson and Justices Jackson and Burton also dissented in a separately written opinion. They argued that the government had not proven that the actual or even probable effects of Standard's exclusive supply contracts were to substantially lessen competition or tend to create a monopoly, and that the mere quantity of business affected, in itself, was not sufficient proof of illegal activity.

> Proof of their quantity does not prove that they had this forbidden quality; and the assumption that they did without proof, seems to me unwarranted.

Moreover, the trial court not only made the assumption *but did not allow the defendant affirmatively to show that such effects do not flow from this arrangement.* Such evidence on the subject as was admitted was not considered in reaching the decision that these contracts are illegal.[34]

No comment that we might add could be more devastating than the comments of the Court's own dissenters. In this case, there simply was no proof of illegal restraint nor was the defendant allowed to show that its contracts did not do what the government said they must do. The evidence that was admitted concerning "beneficial economies" was either immaterial or, as has been previously argued, positively damaging to the defendant's case. Thus the idea of a defense in this case was a charade from start to finish: *No defense was possible.*

THE AMERICAN CAN CASE (1949)

The American Can Company was the nation's largest maker of "packers cans" and had been since the firm had been formed in 1902. American sold its cans to food processors through requirements contracts that bound the customers to purchase their complete requirement of cans from American. Although there were many different types of contracts, the typical agreement at the time of the trial was a full requirements contract for a period of five years. In addition, machines that completed the can (e.g. put the top on) were available on a leasing basis from American Can.

American Can had been in the courts previously with respect to its can and can-closing machine business. In 1916, American had narrowly escaped divestiture under the Sherman Act; in 1924 the FTC had prohibited American from formally tying can-closing machine leases to its can sales. The Justice Department, however, was not satisfied that competition had been restored to the can industry. In 1948, they brought suit under the Sherman and Clayton Acts, charging that American's requirement contracts for cans and its can-closing machine leases illegally restrained trade.[35] As a remedy they petitioned the court to end the requirements contracts altogether, and to divest American of its can-closing machine business.[36]

The District Court Decision

Judge Harris delivered the District Court decision in the *American Can* case on November 10, 1949. Harris first established that although there were 125 competitive can makers in the United States, American Can was the market leader with over 40 per cent of the business.[37] Further, even though American's percentage of business had slipped continuously from an estimated 90 percent in 1902, and even though the firm was "not in a position of complet-monopoly" at the time of the trial, it was still dominant in its industry.[38] Finally, following the guidelines set forth in *Standard Stations*, Harris concluded that there was no question that a not "insubstantial" volume of business was affected.[39]

But what specific business practices had restrained trade? According to the government, the five-year total-requirements contract was able, in itself, to unreasonably exclude or limit competition from rival can makers. But how had American repeatedly "coerced" its customers into such unreasonable restraints? *By offering generous and attractive terms!* The court reported that American offered an attractive discount on quantity can purchases, paid money (occasionally) to obtain certain business, furnished equipment in addition to closing-machines at nominal rates, paid large claims to can users when it appeared good business, and purchased can making equipment from customers at "inflated values" in order to secure their business.[40] In addition, the customers were guaranteed delivery of their requirement of cans regardless of the particular supply conditions in the industry. In short, American treated its customers to economies and efficiencies apparently not obtainable from other can makers, and the customers were generally satisfied with the requirements agreements. Yet the court detected the evil inherent in these economic benefits:

> The incidents, when examined realistically and not as mere abstractions, are deeper than the typical run-of-the-mill, day-to-day business transactions. They represent a studied, methodical and effective method of restraining and acquiring by refined, gentlemanly and sauve means, plus an occasional 'commercial massage,' the dominant position which American has had and maintained for at least a generation on and over the canning industry. A detailed analysis of this phase of the Government's case convinces that there is little room left in a competitive sense, for the independent small business man. As a competitive influence, he has slowly and sadly been relegated into the limbo of American enterprise.[41]

But were the requirements contracts illegal per se, or was the court to weigh the costs and benefits of such arrangements? Judge Harris approvingly quoted the *Standard Stations* decision, where it was indicated that any such economic analysis was "immaterial" and "not determinate" with respect to the legal questions involved.[42] Also not determinate were the desires of the consumer of cans.

> In analyzing a contract in terms of its effect on competition, the condition of the consumer should not be completely ignored, although, as it appears, *the wishes or desires of the consumer are not determinative in reaching a finding as to whether a monopoly or a tendency to create a monopoly exists.*[43]

What was to be "determinative," therefore, was the fact that competition (read "competitors") was being limited by the length and favorable terms of the requirements contract. The five-year length of American's requirement contract was then declared to be "unreasonable," and a one-year requirements contract was approved by the court.[44]

The same sort of judicial reasoning was employed to condemn American's can-closing machine business. The government had made much of the fact that American leased 54 per cent of all the machines in the industry,[45] leased machines only to customers that bought its cans,[46] and allowed the lease on can machinery and its can requirements contracts to run concurrently. Yet the court admitted that the success of American's machine leasing policy rested on the quality of the machines manufactured by American, and on the low rentals charged for such machines. To quote Judge Harris:

> An important factor which induces canners to lease their machines has been the low rentals charged for such machines. The defendant admits that low rentals provide an effective 'sales tool.'

> American, over the years, has imposed rentals ranging from purely nominal to a rate sufficient to pay for the cost of the equipment furnished. Recently defendant standardized its charges so that today they represent an amount equivalent to 8.2 per cent of the depreciated value of the machines. Such a charge approaches a fair standard, but even present rentals are insufficient to cover the complete cost of furnishing and servicing the machines.[47]

But how can economies restrain trade? They "restrict" the market for closing machine manufacturers (there were two independent firms in existence with 12 percent of the business) and thereby limit the number of concerns in that business!

> The record disclosed that others would engage in the manufacture of closing machines if there were a free market in which sellers might compete on an equal basis with the canmakers who now lease their machines.[48]

Reflect on this statement. The desire (read "wish") of the potential competitors is now, apparently, to be determinative. We are to pity the poor machinery firms that cannot enter the market or expand their market share because they cannot match the low rentals and terms offered by American and other can companies. If there were only a "free market," laments the court. *Free* market? That is exactly the sort of market that did exist, and as a consequence, it limited the entry of high-cost, high-price, would be "producers." The pleading for competition on an "equal basis" is the familiar refrain of the less efficient business organization. Yet instead of exposing this embarrassing economic nonsense for what it was, the District Court enshrined it in legitimate tones that would have the force of law.

The final decree by the District Court (a) prohibited American from offering any annual cumulative volume discounts; (b) lowered the time period of requirements contracts to one year; (c) ordered American to sell its closing machines at extremely low prices for a period of ten years, train buyers in technology and service, and license closing machine patents without royalty; and (d) required that American lease any machine to anyone at rentals that were fully compensatory, including a fair profit. As was the case with United Shoe Machinery, stiff legal measures were required to relegate American Can to the same status as the rest of its rivals, such that they might all compete on an "equal" basis.[49]

The McKie Article

James W. McKie has written the classic defense of the *American Can* decision.[50] In it, McKie pointed out some of the advantages of the decision. He noted that: (1) "the independent manufacturers of machines will be able to market closing machines directly to the canning industry"; (2) "small firms are now better able to detach fragments of business which used to be held firmly by the large can suppliers"; (3) "the market position of smaller manufacturers has been greatly strengthened"; and (4) "that large buyers can no longer be pacified with volume discounts."[51] Dissolution of the leading can companies would have, in McKie's view, produced more "spectacular" results, but the 1950 decision had restored a "workable competition" to the metal container industry.

But certainly there had always been a kind of "workable competition" in the metal container industry, even prior to the decision. Witness the relative decline of American Can's market share and the number of eager can companies in the industry. How is it to be determined objectively whether the post-decision situation was preferable to the pre-decision situation? The fact that the smaller can companies and independent machinery companies were "stronger" or could do more business proves nothing. For example, as part of the District Court decree, American (and Continental) were ordered to *raise* their leasing rates on closing machines and end their volume discount sales on cans. Are we to infer that such actions are automatically in the public interest? Does this action tend to promote a more optimal resource allocation? McKie's concern for the smaller firms is touching but economically unconvincing. To raise leasing rates by law and then cheer at the sight of more "competition" is a situation difficult to comprehend. To prevent large firms from passing along economies, by law, and then cheer that smaller rivals are suddenly more "competitive" is ambiguous economic analysis, to put it mildly. Why, if this be sound economic policy, the possibilities for increasing "competition" throughout the economy by raising the costs and prices of the leading firms, would be staggering. The flaws in such an analysis are, hopefully, truly too obvious for further comment.

The same sort of questions can be raised regarding McKie's approval of the court-ordered can-closing machine sales. He claims, much to American and Continental's surprise, that over 75 per cent of the machines that were being leased in 1949 had been sold under the court-established procedures by 1954. Serious competition in can machinery could now begin, and the "commercial leverage" exercised by the large can makers in the can market could now be ended.

But given the costs imposed on the major can makers, is the outcome so surprising, or necessarily an occasion for rejoicing? Purchases of can-closing machinery became popular because the court purposely set bargain prices for machines, and because additional court ordered gifts (e.g., technical services and patents) made the purchase of machinery irrational to forego. In short, machinery buyers were made the beneficiaries of a court sanctioned expropriation of property. In our view, this certainly does not promote either efficiency or competition.

What acceptable formula would allow a conclusion that competition in 1954 was "more optimal" than competition in 1949? McKie's only suggested method, apparently, is structural. But serious objections have been raised to this approach to competition (see Chapter 2). Since McKie had previously admitted that American Can and Continental Can had held their market shares with superior research, customer service, volume discounts, and progressive can-closing machinery,[52] what besides structural considerations would allow a conclusion that the *American Can* decision advanced the ever elusive public interest? McKie's assurances that it did?

THE TIMES–PICAYUNE CASE (1953)

The Supreme Court, in 1953, reversed a District Court decision that had found the Times–Picayune Publishing Company of New Orleans guilty of illegal tying arrangements.[53] That company's policy had been to sell certain kinds of advertising in its morning newspaper—the *Times-Picayune*—and in its evening newspaper—the *States*—as a unit; it was impossible to purchase ad space in one or the other paper separately. The government claimed that such "unit contracts" illegally restrained trade and tended to monopolize in violation of the Sherman Act. After a lengthy trial, the District Court agreed with the government and enjoined the practice. The Supreme Court, however, reversed the order in a 5–4 decision.

Justice Clark delivered the majority opinion of the Supreme Court. Although he admitted that tying contracts "flout the Sherman Act's policy that competition rule the marts of trade,"[54] certain conditions had to be met before such arrangements could be condemned as illegal restraints of trade under the Sherman Act. Precedent indicated to Clark that the seller must enjoy a monopolistic position in the market for the tying product, and that a substantial volume of commerce in the tied product must be restrained.[55] But in the majority's opinion, *Times-Picayune* was not in a monopolistic, or even in a "dominant" position, in the newspaper advertising market in New Orleans.

There were three newspapers being published in New Orleans at the time of the trial: the *Times-Picayune*, the *States*, and the independently owned *Item*. According to the Court, the sales of both general and classified advertising linage for the *Times-Picayune* (the tying good) was about 40 percent of the total in the market. This ruled out "monopoly" according to Clark.

> If each of the New Orleans publications shared equally in the total volume of linage, the *Times-Picayune* would have sold 33%; in the absence of patent or copyright control, the small existing increment in the circumstances where disclosed cannot confer that market 'dominance' which, in conjunction with a 'not insubstantial' volume of trade in the tied product, would result in a Sherman Act offense . . .[56]

In addition, the unit contracts for advertising could hardly be compared with standard tying agreements. Under illegal tying agreements, dominant sellers use their power and leverage in the tying-good market to suppress competition and inflict economic harm in the tied-good market. The *Times-Picayune* situation, however, was quite different.

> Here . . . two newspapers under single ownership at the same place, time and terms, sell indistinguishable products to advertisers; no dominant 'tying' product exists (in fact, since space in neither the *Times-Picayune* nor the *States* can be bought alone, one may be viewed as 'tying' as the other); no leverage in one market excludes sellers in the second, because for present purposes the products are identical and the market the same.[57]

Hence, it was doubtful whether there was tying here at all; two services were simply being sold as a unit.

Finally, the Court noted, approvingly, that the *Times-Picayune* advertising rates were significantly lower than the corresponding *Item*'s rates,[58] that many of the nation's publishers, including the *Item*, had switched to the unit system,[59] and that the unit system "was viewed as a competitive weapon in the rivalry for national advertising accounts."[60] The Supreme Court could find no Sherman Act violations in any of this.

THE NORTHERN PACIFIC RAILWAY COMPANY CASE (1958)

In the nineteenth century, the Northern Pacific Railroad—like most of its important transcontinental competitors—had been gifted with extensive land grants by the federal government. In the case of the Northern Pacific, the grants had totaled almost 40 million acres. By 1949, most of this resource-rich land had been sold or leased to outside parties on condition that all commodities produced or manufactured on the land be shipped over the Northern Pacific's line, provided that its rates, and in some instances its services, be equal to those of competing carriers. The government charged that these "preferential routing" agreements were unreasonable restraints of trade in violation of Section 1 of the Sherman Act.[61]

Justice Black wrote the majority decision for the Supreme Court in this case.[62] He stated that there were "certain agreements or practices which because of their pernicious effect on competition and lack of redeeming virtue are conclusively presumed to be unreasonable and therefore illegal without elaborate inquiry . . ."[63] He listed price-fixing, division of markets, group boycotts, and tying contracts among those illegal practices. And with respect to tying agreements, Black stated:

> They are unreasonable in and of themselves whenever a party has *sufficient economic power* with respect to the tying product to appreciably restrain free competition in the market for the tied product and a 'not insubstantial' amount of interstate commerce is affected.[64]

But did Northern Pacific have "sufficient economic power" in the tying product market? Black suggested that such power could simply be inferred by virtue of Northern Pacific's "extensive land holdings." The fact that there were such holdings and that the tying agreements existed was proof enough that Northern Pacific possessed economic power.

> The very existence of this host of tying arrangements *is itself* compelling evidence of the defendant's great power, at least where, as here, no other explanation has been offered for the existence of these restraints.[65]

Finally, the Supreme Court rejected the defendant's argument that the preferential routing clauses did not unreasonably restrain trade, since they contained the escape provision providing for the matching of a competitor's lower rates. Arguing as in the *International Salt* decision, they held that the agreements were still "binding obligation[s] held over the heads of vendees which deny defendant's competitors access to the fenced-off market on the same terms as the defendant."[66] The clauses were, therefore, unreasonable, and the district court decision to end the restrictive practices was affirmed.

Justice Harlan, with whom Justices Frankfurter and Whittaker joined, wrote a dissenting opinion in the *Northern Pacific* case. He argued that neither the District Court nor the majority of the Supreme Court had determined whether Northern Pacific was actually dominant in the market where the alleged violations had occurred. The tying market was land, and there had been no determination of Northern Pacific's relevant market share in that market. The District Court had simply assumed dominance, or worse, had simply assumed that Northern Pacific dominated "the lands now owned by them and had dominance in the lands formerly owned at the time of sale of such lands."[67] But dominance over one's own property was hardly the test of illegality under the Sherman Act!

> The District Court should have taken evidence of the relative strength of appellants' landholdings vis-à-vis that of others in the appropriate market for land of the types now or formerly possessed by appellants . . . Short of such an inquiry I do not see how it can be determined whether the appellants occupied such a dominant position in the relevant market as to make these tying clauses' illegal per se under the Sherman Act.[68]

Thus, in Harlan's view, Northern Pacific was convicted without a determination that they were dominant in the tying-good market, and without a determination that they could exercise leverage in the tied-good market.

THE TAMPA ELECTRIC (1961) AND LOEW'S (1962) CASES

In the *Tampa Electric* case,[69] the Supreme Court appeared to modify the extreme position it had taken in *Northern Pacific*. In this instance, the Court let stand a long-term requirements contract for coal between the Tampa Electric Company and the Nashville Coal Company. Nashville, at Tampa's request, had agreed to supply one million tons of coal annually for twenty years for Tampa's newly constructed electric power plant. Although the exclusive supply contract involved upwards of $128 million, the Supreme Court ruled that in the relevant market for coal (an eight-state area), the foreclosure of potential suppliers amounted to less than 1 percent. And less than a 1 percent foreclosure rate was not enough to make the agreement illegal under Section 3 of the Clayton Act.

In the Loew's case,[70] the Supreme Court reaffirmed a District Court decision—with some modifications—ending the block booking of films by distributors to television stations. Block booking was a practice whereby distributors allegedly sold or leased commercially "desirable" films on condition that less than desirable films also be bought or leased. Similar practices had been ended by the Court in the film industry,[71] but television block booking or tying of films was a new experience.

The distributors argued that: (1) dominance could not be demonstrated; (2) the uniqueness attributed to copyrighted film shown in moviehouses could not be assumed to automatically exist with respect to television viewing; (3) feature films represented only 8 percent of all television programming; and (4) that there was "reasonable interchangeability" of films with other programming shown on television. The Supreme Court, in rejecting these notions, agreed with the district court, which had thus summarized the essential issue in this case:

> There can be no dispute that the evidence showed that *no defendant had market dominance over the feature film market as such.* Each defendant owned its own feature films. There are numerous feature films on the market and there was intense competition among the defendants to market their own films. *However, each film was in itself a unique product.* Each film was copyrighted. Each film was unique in its subject matter and presentation. *Each defendant had market dominance as to its own feature films.*[72]

The copyright created "uniqueness," and the uniqueness generated "sufficient economic power" to impose an "appreciable restraint on free competition in the tied product . . . as demanded by the *Northern Pacific* decision."[73] The "appreciable restraint" may have only tied up as little as $60,800, but that was enough to bring it within the law's prohibition.[74] Hence, to dominate one's own property—but not the market for similar property—and use the "monopolistic advantage" inherent in that dominance to tie one commodity to another violated the antitrust statutes.

Some Conclusions on Tying

It seems safe to conclude from these cases that tying arrangements on the part of any firm can be judged illegal, and that information on economic benefits is immaterial with respect to the issue of illegal restraint. Further, illegal restraint can be inferred if the tying agreements exist, since the existence of the contracts themselves evidence "sufficient economic power" on the part of seller. Finally, the volume of trade "restrained" in the tied-good market can certainly be very small, since "not insubstantial" can mean anything the court chooses to have it mean. Therefore, any firm with a patented good, a copyrighted good, or any "unique" product of any sort, that employs that "uniqueness" to tie buyers to another product or service can violate the antitrust statutes with respect to tying agreements. No damage to the public interest need even be demonstrated; it is simply assumed to exist. As a final illustration of this thesis, observe the analysis of the Supreme Court in the *Fortner I* case below.

THE FORTNER ENTERPRISES I CASE (1969)

Fortner Enterprises, Inc. had filed an antitrust suit against the U. S. Steel Corporation and its wholly owned subsidiary, U. S. Steel Homes Credit Corporation, claiming that it (Fortner) had been victimized under an illegal tying agreement.[75] The tying agreement consisted of the fact that Fortner, in order to obtain $2 million from the Credit Corporation to purchase and develop lands in Kentucky, had agreed to erect prefabricated homes manufactured by U. S. Steel on the lots purchased with the funds. Subsequently, Fortner experienced financial difficulties—allegedly due to the fact that the prefabricated homes proved to be "defective and unusable"—and sued U. S. Steel for treble damages under the Sherman Act. The suit that first reached the Supreme Court in 1968 was over the District Court's decision (affirmed by the Court of Appeals) to enter a summary judgment for U. S. Steel, and to dismiss the antitrust charge.

The Supreme Court Decision

Justice Black delivered the majority decision for the Supreme Court on April 7, 1969. He agreed with the District Court that a traditional tying agreement was involved, but he disagreed with the manner in which the district court had analyzed the legal issues involved. The District Court had held that U. S. Steel did not have sufficient economic power over credit, and that the amount of land foreclosed to competing sellers of prefabricated homes was "insubstantial."[76] Thus, according to the precedents set in the *Northern Pacific* case, the agreements under discussion were not illegal.

Black noted, however, that while the tying agreements might not be illegal per se, this did not mean that they were legal. The failure to meet the per se prerequisites of the *Northern Pacific* opinion did not necessarily doom the petitioner's case against U. S. Steel. As Justice Black explained:

A plantiff can still prevail on the merits whenever he can prove, on the basis of a more thorough examination of the purposes and practices involved, that the general standards of the Sherman Act have been violated. Accordingly . . . the summary judgement against petitioner still could not be entered without further examination of petitioner's general allegations that respondents conspired together for the purpose of restraining competition and acquiring a monopoly in the market for prefabricated homes.[77]

Thus, if necessary, a detailed examination of the economic issues involved could and should proceed at court, and a summary dismissal prior to such an examination was inappropriate.

Justice Black found further fault with the District Court's analysis. The District Court had determined that the percentage of land foreclosed to competing sellers of prefabricated homes because of the tying agreements involving U. S. Steel was only .00032 percent, and had, accordingly, determined that the trade restrained in the tied-good market was "insubstantial."[78] Black noted, however, that a "not insubstantial" volume of trade was not meant to apply to market share in percentage terms, but to dollar volume of business in absolute terms. And $190,000 (the amount of annual purchases of homes from U. S. Steel by Fortner) was clearly not "paltry" or insubstantial.[79] In addition, it was the total volume of sales tied by such a policy with anyone that was the determining amount. Since U. S. Steel did more than $2 million worth of business under such agreements in 1962, the amount "could scarcely be regarded as insubstantial" by the Supreme Court.[80]

The District Court also erred with respect to its examination of sufficient economic power, according to Justice Black. No monopoly or even dominant position was necessary in the tying good. Quoting the Loew's decision approvingly, Black argued that economic power could simply be inferred "from the tying product's desirability to consumers, or from uniqueness in its attributes."[81] All that was necessary was that the seller be able to "exert some power over some of the buyers in the market, even if the power is not complete over them and over all other buyers in the market."[82]

The "product" offered by U. S. Steel was apparently unique. A. B. Fortner, president of Fortner Enterprises, Inc., testified that he had accepted the tying agreement only because the 100 percent financing "was unusually and uniquely advantageous to him."[83] No alternative financing on such liberal terms was available to his corporation during the 1959–62 period. No other financial institution in the Louisville, Kentucky area was able to match U. S. Steel's terms and rates. Whether the reason for this "competitive advantage" was "economies resulting from the nationwide character of its [U. S. Steel] operations," or whether state and federal statutes might have prevented such terms from being offered by banks, was not clear to the Court. But the presence of "market power" was certainly apparent enough to justify a trial on the tying agreements, as far as Justice Black was concerned.

Finally, the Supreme Court dismissed the argument that the agreements between U. S. Steel and Fortner were not tying contracts at all, and that only one product, the prefabricated homes, was actually involved. The Court admitted that offering credit for the purchase of a product was harmless enough. But credit financing was:

> a far cry from the arrangement involved here, where the credit is provided by one corporation on condition that a product be purchased from a separate corporation, and where the borrower contracts to obtain a large sum of money over and above that needed to pay the seller for the physical products purchased.[84]

In Black's view, credit could be as much of a tying good as any other product, and its potential harm was just as great. As an example, he noted that important barriers to entry had been raised by the tying agreements. Sellers of prefabricated homes in competition with U. S. Steel must also be able to offer credit on comparable terms, but this was probably impossible.[85] Hence, equally efficient or more efficient competitors who produced prefabricated homes would be excluded from the market solely because of the economic power of U. S. Steel in the credit market. This, however, was exactly the sort of "evil" that the antitrust laws had been designed to prevent. Therefore, the Supreme Court reversed the order of the Appeals Court, and directed that the case proceed to a full trial.

There were two written dissents in the *Fortner I* case. Justice White reviewed the meaning of tying agreements and the historic rationale for making them illegal, and emphasized that it was the existence of "some market power in the tying product" that was the crucial determination in such cases. Without a determination of market power, the economic "distortions" suggested by the theory could not occur. But what proof of market power in the tying product—credit—was there in this case?[86] Was the fact that credit was available at favorable rates and terms from U. S. Steel evidence of monopoly power? Did low prices infer market power? Justice White thought not: "A low price in the tying product . . . is especially poor proof of market power when untied credit is available elsewhere."[87] But what of the supposed barriers to entry imposed by the tying agreements? They were easily overcome, according to White. The low price of the credit was "functionally equivalent" to a price reduction on prefabricated homes. Since buyers could easily secure untied credit elsewhere, competitors of U. S. Steel could always compete by simply cutting the prices of their homes. There was no good reason why U. S. Steel "should always be required to make the price cut in one form rather than another."[88]

White also argued that if equally available credit terms were not available to Fortner, then the charge that U. S. Steel foreclosed the market to competition had to be incorrect. *To whom could they be foreclosing the market?* If U. S. Steel assumed risks that no one else would assume, then they certainly were not foreclosing any competitor from any market.[89] The Sherman Act could hardly be used against a kind of behavior that, in White's view, it was meant to encourage.

Nor would White infer "market power" simply because the agreements existed. Buyers were not "burdened" when they could buy tied and untied products elsewhere on "normal" terms. And competing sellers were not foreclosed since they could always lower their prices on the tied product and compete. Far from evidencing market power, lower credit rates were

> more likely to reflect a competitive attempt to offset the market power of others in the tied product than it is to reflect existing power in the credit market. *Those with real power do not offer uniquely advantageous deals to their customers; they raise prices.*[90]

Justice Fortas wrote a separate dissent in the *Fortner I* case. He argued, quite simply, that the contract between Fortner and U. S. Steel was not a tying agreement. U. S. Steel, in the opinion of Justice Fortas, was not "selling credit in any general sense"; they were selling prefabricated homes with an "incidental provision of financing."[91] Almost all the loaned $2 million was related to the purchase and installation of homes. It was simply "not a sale of one product on condition that the buyer will not deal with competitors for another product or will buy the other product exclusively from the seller."[92] It was, rather, a quite common agreement in the business world whereby a seller extends financing to a purchaser. That such an agreement could violate the Sherman Act was almost inconceivable as far as Fortas was concerned.

> It is hardly conceivable except for today's opinion of the Court, that extension of such credit as a part of a general sale transaction or distribution method could be regarded as 'tying' of the seller's goods to the credit, so that where the business man receiving the credit agrees to handle the seller-lender's product, the arrangement is *per se* unlawful merely because the amount or terms of the credit were more favorable than could be obtained from banking institutions in the area.[93]

To condemn such credit arrangements out of hand was, in Fortas's words, to use the antitrust laws "as an instrument in restraint of competition."[94]

Comment on the Fortner I Case

In an ironic way, *Fortner I* is a fitting climax to any discussion of tying theory and cases. It represents the dead end to which the per se approach can be pushed in antitrust. It also reveals the utter nonsense of an antitrust enforcement that is based on traditional notions of monopoly power.

Was the contract between Fortner and U. S. Steel a tying contract of the kind prohibited by the law? Since all business contracts bind the participants to certain specific terms and limit their freedom of action, tying contracts must somehow be distinguished from all other business relationships. But what can distinguish them? Tying arrangements can provide that one independently identifiable good or service be sold or leased on condition that some *other* independently identifiable good or service also be purchased or leased. But if this is tying, then the *Fortner I* case did not involve tying contracts. U. S. Steel was not selling homes and credit but instead selling homes through the mechanism of a credit transaction with a subsidiary. The credit was a conduit through which the singular product, the prefabricated homes, was sold. Many products are sold through advertising (them), but advertising a product is not a tying agreement in restraint of trade—at least not yet. The credit in this case would, presumably, have not existed or been extended but for the fact that the prefabricated homes could not have been sold without the credit. Clearly the agreement expanded rather than restrained trade and competition in the sale of prefabricated homes.

Another curious issue in this case concerns the relevance of economic evidence. We have already seen in many cases that the economic benefits associated with tying contracts are not determining, and that they are immaterial with respect to the legal questions involved. Yet, in this case, the Supreme Court makes it perfectly clear that a petitioner—on failure to demonstrate a per se violation of the antitrust statutes—can employ any such economic evidence as is necessary to demonstrate a possible violation of the Sherman or Clayton Acts. So while the petitioner can use evidence of economic effects in an attempt to demonstrate illegal restraint of trade, an attempt by the defense to employ similar evidence to rebut such accusations is likely to be termed "irrelevant and immaterial."

The determination that the uniqueness of U. S. Steel's credit terms conferred economic power on the defendant is the most interesting, though not unprecedented issue in the *Fortner I* case. The groundwork for such a ruling, as we have shown, had been laid before. Here, the Supreme Court reasoned that U. S. Steel evidenced economic power because it, and only it, could offer superior terms on the financing of its prefabricated homes. How U. S. Steel had obtained that particular market position was irrelevant. The fact remained that it offered a uniquely advantageous financing arrangement, and such arrangements "can reflect a creditor's unique economic advantage over his competitors." Thus it again appears that the ability to generate unique circumstances for buyers is legally suspect, and that the acceptance of such circumstances by buyers is then evidence of economic power. Even more, the Court appears to sanction the theory that a buyer may then turn around and sue a seller, claiming coercion into an agreement that has already been admittedly described as "uniquely advantageous." That this reasoning was ultimately rejected in *Fortner II* some eight years later is hardly adequate justice in this case[95]

THE SCHWINN (1967), CHICKEN DELIGHT (1972), AND GTE–SYLVANIA (1977) CASES

The hostility of the courts to tying agreements and other so-called customer restrictions was further extended in *United States v. Arnold, Schwinn & Co.*[96] In this case, the District Court had enjoyed Schwinn from territorially restricting any wholesaler or jobber that resold Schwinn products (bicycles). The Supreme Court, on appeal by the federal govenment, further enjoined Schwinn from restricting the distributor's "freedom ... to dispose of the Schwinn products, which they have bought from Schwinn, where and to whomever they choose." Schwinn had argued in vain that its challenged distribution system would strengthen its dealer outlets and allow more effective competition with mass merchandisers such as Sears. Allowing franchised dealers to sell to any retailer would "subvert the whole distribution scheme" (by allowing, presumably, unfranchised sellers to "free ride" off of franchised sellers). Yet while the Court appeared sympathetic to the competitive situation that had given risc to the distribution program, the reselling restrictions were, nonetheless, condemned as illegal per se.

In *Siegel v. Chicken Delight, Inc.*,[97] the Court struck down agreements that had required licensed franchises to purchase specific cookers, fryers, packaged mixes, and spices from their franchiser, Chicken Delight. Chicken Delight had maintained that its trademark ought not to be considered distinct from its mixes and equipment; that the existence of many other fast-food franchisers prevented any finding of "sufficient economic power"; and that the tying agreements were a "reasonable device" for measuring and collecting revenue (it charged no franchise fee or royalty). The Court, however, could not agree with any of this argument. The attempt to extend or leverage a legitimate trademark to "common articles" was not legitimate, especially where the alternative of specification (to protect goodwill) was to be presumed simply from the fact that the registered trademark (like a copyright) created a legal barrier to entry. And finally, Chicken Delight was free to collect its revenues through alternative methods of compensation (such as royalty) that had been employed by its competition—but not through tie-in sales which always have "undesirable anticompetitive consequences." What these undesirable anticompetitive consequences were in this case was never documented.

Continental T.V., Inc., v. GTE–Sylvania Incorporated[98] may well represent an important benchmark in judicial thinking concerning the legality of exclusive dealing arrangements. In this decision the Supreme Court affirmed an Appeals Court ruling which had maintained—contrary to the District Court—that a "locational restriction agreement" ought not be judged per se illegal but, instead, ought to be examined in light of a "rule of reason." The Court overturned the per se rule in *Schwinn*, since it was convinced that some vertical non-price restraints could provide substantial "social utility" with relatively little "pernicious effect" upon competition.

The case arose out of a dispute over Sylvania's decision to impose a territorial restriction on its franchisee, Continental. Continental operated retail stores in San Francisco and desired to open a new store in Sacramento. Sylvania, believing the Sacramento market to be adequately serviced by the existing Sylvania retailers, denied Continental's request to market Sylvania sets in the new location. Continental eventually brought a claim against Sylvania, alleging that the franchise agreement that restricted sales to other than specified locations violated Section 1 of the Sherman Act.

Most of the *Sylvania* decision is given over to a review of *Schwinn*. Justice Powell, writing for the majority, argued that there were important similarities between the restrictive agreements in both cases. For instance, both Schwinn and GTE–Sylvania had sought to reduce competition among their respective dealers with locational restrictions, and in both instances these agreements "limited the freedom of the retailer to dispose of the purchased products as he desired."[99] But, Powell argued, to treat the reduction of intraband competition as per se illegality "has been the subject of continuing controversy and confusion, both in the scholarly journals and in the federal courts. The great weight of scholarly opinion has been critical of the decision . . ."[100] Thus *Schwinn* had to be reconsidered in light of these objections and because of the commercial importance of these agreements.

The problem with *Schwinn* is that there had been no explicit recognition that territorial agreements that might decrease in*tra*brand competition, might also lead to an overall increase in in*ter*brand competition. Economists, according to Justice Powell, had "identified a number of ways in which manufacturers can use such restrictions to compete more effectively against other manufacturers."[101] For instance, such agreements may solve the "free rider" problem and thereby induce distributors to more heavily invest in promotional activity and in after-sale service. And since there was "substantial scholarly and judicial authority supporting the economic utility of such agreements," and "relatively little authority to the contrary," the per se rule in *Schwinn* was overruled.[102]

Mr. Justice White concurred in the decision but wrote a separate opinion. He agreed that a "location clause" ought to be judged under a rule of reason, but did not agree that this required the overruling of the rule in *Schwinn*. While there were similarities with *Schwinn*, as Justice Powell had noted, the differences, particularly with respect to interbrand competition, was substantial. What made the agreements "reasonable" was the fact that Sylvania, unlike Schwinn, had an insignificant market share and, thus, had no "economic power in the generic product market."[103] Since Sylvania was a "faltering, if not failing" producer of television sets with negligible economic power, Justice White felt that the competitive impact of the restraint was negligible, and enough to justify a "rule of reason standard."

CONCLUSIONS

Except, perhaps, for *Sylvania*, the classic decisions reviewed in this chapter confirm our initial judgment that the courts have consistently misconstrued the plan coordinating and competitive benefits associated with tying arrangements. The agreements attacked in these cases were hardly exploitative of or injurious to consumers; indeed, the agreements existed in the first place (as in *Fortner*) because they provided unique benefits that could not be obtained elsewhere in the marketplace. And yet in all the pre-*Sylvania* cases, economic benefits were treated as implicitly harmful, since they were transformed by the court into evidence of "sufficient economic power" on the part of the defendant.

A "rule of reason" approach to tying agreements is certainly to be preferred to absolute illegality,[104] but it must be admitted that such an approach is subject to the same criticisms noted earlier in this book. Simply put, there is no objective way to compare the costs and benefits associated with restrictive agreements and no way, therefore, to make unambiguous judgments as to their social cost or utility from a neoclassical perspective. An alternative approach would be to hold that all such agreements are legitimate because they necessarily tend *ex ante* to coordinate the plans of the respective parties involved. From this perspective, tying agreements are *always* efficient—unambiguously efficient—since they represent demonstrable evidence of increased social coordination.

NOTES

1. The literature on tying agreements is vast. For some excellent neoclassical discussions see, Eugene Singer, "Market Power and Tying Arrangements," *Antitrust Bulletin*, Vol. 8 (July–August 1963), pp. 653–657; W. S. Bowman, Jr., "Tying Arrangements and the Leverage Problem," *Yale Law Journal*, Vol. 67 (November 1957), pp. 19–36; Donald Turner, "The Validity of Tying Arrangements Under the Antitrust Laws," *Harvard Law Review*, Vol. 82 (No-

vember 1958) pp. 50–75; and Richard A. Posner, *Antitrust Law: An Economic Perspective* (Chicago: University of Chicago Press, 1976), pp. 171–211.

2. *International Salt Co. v. United States*, 332 U.S. 392.

3. *Ibid.*, p. 394.

4. *Ibid.*, pp. 395–396.

5. *Ibid.*, p. 396.

6. *Ibid.*

7. *Ibid.*, pp. 394–395.

8. *Ibid.*, p. 397.

9. *Ibid.*, p. 398.

10. Joel B. Dirlam and Alfred E. Kahn, *Fair Competition: The Law and Economics of Antitrust Policy* (Ithaca, N. Y.: Cornell University Press, 1954), p. 97.

11. Patents are a monopoly over one's own property. They do not usually prevent others from using their own property to compete. For an excellent review of the antitrust controversy over patents, see Ward S. Bowman, *Patents and Antitrust Law* (Chicago: University of Chicago Press, 1973); see also my review of the Bowman book in *The Wall Street Review of Books*, Vol. 1, No. 3 (Fall 1973), pp. 334–337, for a "natural rights" approach to patents.

12. 332 U.S. 399.

13. *Ibid.*, p. 398.

14. *United States v. Standard Oil of California and Standard Stations, Inc.*, 78 F. Supp. 850.

15. *Ibid.*, pp. 855, 856, 868, 869.

16. 310 U.S. 150.

17. 78 F. Supp. 858 (emphasis added).

18. *Ibid.*, p. 863.

19. *Ibid.*, p. 864.

20. *Ibid.*, pp. 865–866.

21. *Ibid.*, p. 872 (emphasis in original).

22. *Ibid.*, pp. 874–875.

23. *Standard Oil of California and Standard Stations v. United States*, 337 U.S. 293 (1949).

24. *Ibid.*, p. 299.

25. *Ibid.*, p. 301.

26. *Ibid.*, p. 302.

27. *Ibid.*, p. 304.

28. *Ibid.*, p. 305.

29. *Ibid.*, p. 313.

30. *Ibid.*, p. 314.

31. *Ibid.*

32. *Ibid.*, pp. 315–319.
33. *Ibid.*, p. 321.
34. *Ibid.*, p. 322 (emphasis added).
35. *United States v. American Can Company,* 87 F. Supp. 18 (1949).
36. Continental Can (the second largest can maker in the country), under similar indictment, agreed to accept the decision in the *American Can* case.
37. 87 F. Supp. 21–22.
38. *Ibid.*, p. 23.
39. *Ibid.*, p. 30.
40. *Ibid.*, pp. 27–28.
41. *Ibid.*, p. 28.
42. *Ibid.*, p. 30.
43. *Ibid.*, p. 31 (emphasis added).
44. *Ibid.*, p. 32.
45. *Ibid.*, p. 23.
46. *Ibid.*, p. 26.
47. *Ibid.*, p. 23.
48. *Ibid.*, p. 24.
49. 110 F. Supp. 295. The major similarity with *United Shoe Machinery* is that the tying agreements here probably were intended to shift the risk (of a poor crop; hence, low utilization of expensive can-closing machines) from small packers to stronger and more diversified can producers. For supporting argument, see David Flath, "The *American Can* Case," *The Antitrust Bulletin,* Vol. 25 (Spring 1980), pp. 169–193. See also Wesley J. Liebeler, *California Law Review,* Vol. 66 (Dec. 1979), p. 1321.
50. "The Decline of Monopoly in the Metal Container Industry," *American Economic Review, Papers and Proceedings,* Vol. 45 (May 1955), pp. 499–508.
51. *Ibid.*, pp. 506–507.
52. *Ibid.*, p. 504.
53. *Times-Picayune Publishing Company et al. v. United States,* 345 U.S. 594 (1953).
54. *Ibid.*, p. 605.
55. *Ibid.*, p. 608.
56. *Ibid.*, p. 613.
57. *Ibid.*, p. 614.
58. *Ibid.*, p. 622.
59. *Ibid.*, p. 623.
60. *Ibid.*, p. 624.
61. Suit was brought under the Sherman Act since "land" was not explicitly included in the Clayton Act, Section 3 prohibition.

62. *Northern Pacific Railway Company v. United States*, 356 U.S. 1 (1958).
63. *Ibid., p. 5.*
64. *Ibid.,* p. 6 (emphasis added).
65. *Ibid.,* p. 8 (emphasis added).
66. *Ibid.,* p. 12.
67. *Ibid.,* p. 15.
68. *Ibid.,* p. 16.
69. *Tampa Electric Co. v. Nashville Coal Co.,* 365 U.S. 320.
70. *United States v. Loew's Incorporated et al.,* 371 U.S. 38 (1962).
71. *United States v. Paramount Pictures, 334 U.S. 131 (1948).*
72. *United States v. Loew's Incorporated et al.* 180 F. Supp. 381 (emphasis added).
73. 371 U.S. 48.
74. *Ibid.,* p. 49.
75. *Fortner Enterprises, Inc. v. United States Steel Corporation and United States Steel Homes Credit Corporation,* 394 U.S. 495 (1969).
76. *Ibid.,* p. 499.
77. *Ibid.,* p. 500.
78. *Ibid.,* p. 501.
79. *Ibid.,* pp. 501–502.
80. *Ibid.,* p. 502.
81. *Ibid.,* p. 503 (emphasis added).
82. *Ibid.,* p. 503.
83. *Ibid.,* p. 504.
84. *Ibid.,* p. 507.
85. *Ibid.,* p. 509.
86. *Ibid.,* p. 511.
87. *Ibid.,* p. 515.
88. *Ibid.*
89. *Ibid.,* pp. 516–517.
90. *Ibid.,* p. 519 (emphasis added).
91. *Ibid.,* pp. 521–522.
92. *Ibid.,* p. 522.
93. *Ibid.,* p. 524.
94. *Ibid.,* p. 525.
95. The District Court—on remand—and the Appeals Court both agreed that the "uniqueness" of the agreement made the tying arrangement illegal; the Supreme Court in *Fortner II*, however, held that United States Steel did not possess any appreciable monopoly power in the credit market, and set aside the decision. See 429 U.S. 610 (1977), esp. 622.

96. 388 U.S. 365 (1967).

97. 405 U.S. 955 (1972). The District Court decision is 448 F. 2d 43 (9th Cir. 1971).

98. 433 U.S. 36 (1977).

99. *Ibid.*, p. 46.

100. *Ibid.*, pp. 47–48.

101. *Ibid.*, pp. 54–55.

102. *Ibid.*, pp. 57–58.

103. *Ibid.*, p. 63.

104. See the argument in W. David Slawson, "A Stronger, Simpler Tie-In Doctrine," *The Antitrust Bulletin*, Vol. 25, No. 4 (Winter 1980), pp. 671–99, esp. 699.

CHAPTER EIGHT

Mergers, Competition, and Antitrust Policy

One of the most important areas of antitrust law throughout the last two decades has been Section 7 of the Clayton Act, as amended, dealing with corporate mergers and acquisitions. This section prohibits any corporation from acquiring the stock or assets of any other corporation when the effect of the acquisition may be "substantially (to) lessen competition, or tend to create a monopoly." The alleged intent of the amended statute was to prohibit "monopolistic tendencies in their incipiency," before they matured into Sherman Act transgressions.

CORPORATE MERGERS AND THE LAW

The significance of Section 7 has been highlighted by the pace of recent merger activity in the economy. For instance, beginning in the late 1960s we witnessed the start of one of the most spectacular corporate merger movements in all business history. These mergers have been spectacular in at least three different respects. In the first place, the number of absolute corporate marriages per year has been far higher than it has ever been; the average number of mergers for the 1965–69 period, for example, was 1,630 per year, as against 670 per year for the 1955–59 period.[1] Secondly, the mergers have been larger in dollar value than they had ever been; in 1969 alone, the total value of "large acquired assets"[2] equaled $12.6 billion.[3] Third, the mergers increasingly involved firms that bore no obvious economic relationship to each other; for instance, 82 percent of all recorded mergers between 1966–68 were classified as "conglomerates."[4] And although merger activity slackened considerably in the early 1970s, it has resumed its frenzied pace in the late 1970s and early 1980s, continuing at well above average levels.

This continuing wave of mergers is not, of course, without some precedent in business history. The first great wave of corporate marriages in the

1898–1902 period had produced upwards of 2500 consolidations with an estimated total value of $6 billion.[5] Some of America's largest and most prominent industrial giants (e.g., U. S. Steel, Standard Oil of New Jersey) were constructed during that active period. Another wave of intense merger activity occurred between 1925 and 1931 when there were a reported 5846 corporate consolidations.[6] As in the first wave, a considerable percentage of the merger activity was involved with the formation of giant corporations. The recent merger movement, however, has broken all records in its duration, and for the absolute number of consolidations and dollar value of acquired assets.

Although Section 7 of the Clayton Act had been in effect since 1914, the Justice Department and the Federal Trade Commission had not, prior to the post–World War II period, taken an aggressive antimerger position with respect to corporate consolidations. As a general rule, and with few exceptions, the giant corporations that had been put together through merger between 1898 and 1950 were left intact. This is not surprising, since Section 7 had originally been intended to prevent the formation of holding companies; furthermore, the unamended statute specifically did not apply to asset acquisitions. The law did not (and apparently was not meant to) dampen the enthusiasm of corporate combinations, generally. The Celler–Kefauver Antimerger Act of 1950, however, "clarified" the intent of Section 7 and removed the asset loophole in the law; the way was now open to a much tougher enforcement policy.[7]

Since neoclassical competition theory, with its emphasis on market structure, has been the theoretical foundation of antitrust policy, it would not have been difficult to predict that the Justice Department and Federal Trade Commission would be concerned with the anticompetitive effects of mergers. To review briefly, the strict structural approach to competition holds the perfectly competitive equilibrium as a welfare ideal, and assumes that movements away from that atomistic market structure imply less competition and a misallocation of scarce economic resources. Since corporate mergers affect structure directly, they are an immediate and obvious threat to efficiency and to competition from this perspective.

No one has stated the hypothesis concerning mergers, market structure, and "competition" more exactly than Donald F. Turner, former chief of the Antitrust Division of the U. S. Department of Justice. In 1966, in an article first published in *Fortune*, Turner argued that the fundamental purpose of the antimerger law was to prevent an increase in "market power," and that this could be accomplished by preserving competitively structured markets.[8] According to Turner, economic theory instructed that concentration increased market power and led to poor economic performance; the chances for resource misallocation would be minimized with competitively *structured* markets. It should not be surprising, therefore, that an antitrust policy firmly rooted in traditional structural considerations would be generally hostile to business merger.

A THEORY OF MERGER POLICY

Horizontal Merger

When there is a merger between two corporations that sell the same product or service in the same market, the consolidation is termed a *horizontal merger*. A horizontal merger always decreases the number of independent competitors by one, increases the market share of the acquiring firm, and may increase the industry concentration ratio. In simple structural terms, therefore, horizontal mergers would tend to decrease the effectiveness of "competition," increase the possibility of an output restriction and, consequently, tend to lower economic welfare.

As we observed in Chapter 2, however, a simple decrease in the number of competitors or an increase in the concentration ratio does not indicate anything significant with respect to the level of rivalrous competition. Competition in the sense of a rivalrous process may well be more vigorous after any merger. Since competition is a process that cannot be cardinally measured, there is no way to proceed from the number of sellers, the change in market shares, or an increase in concentration ratios, to specific conclusions concerning the degree of competition. All previous attempts to quantify competition (or monopoly) in this fashion have failed. To attempt to judge the wisdom of mergers on simple structural factors alone would, therefore, be quite irrational.[9]

It is easy to suggest a situation where a business merger would increase competitive pressures even though some structural factors might be sacrificed. Assume, for example, that two beer producers compete in the same market area. A corporate merger between them could economize on expenses associated with management, purchasing, advertising, research, production, and marketing, and could allow their respective beers to be marketed in different areas, increasing competitive pressures on existing sellers in those areas. This merger would be particularly competitive if broadening the product line allowed a more effective rivalry with, perhaps, some larger, more established company. Although there is one less independent beer producer, and although market share and concentration ratios might even increase, consumers would likely be more efficiently served by the new market arrangement.

A more difficult example, perhaps, is the so-called large consolidation where, say, several substantial oil or steel corporations decide to merge their respective properties. In this and similar instances, assert the critics, the threat of control over market price through output restriction is increased substantially, and any mergers that can create such market power ought not to be permitted.

But as we have argued previously, all business organizations in the real world have some market power; the existence of market power is not unique with large mergers. Moreover, all relevant market definitions and all such determinations of "high" market concentration or "large" mergers are strictly arbitrary and not scientifically defensible. What may appear to be "high" concentration to one analyst is certain to appear "reasonable" to another. Is a consolidation that generates a 38 percent market share (issues of relevant market aside) dangerously "high " or is it "reasonable"? How about 41 percent? Can anyone really take this approach seriously? The fact remains that the knowledge concerning a socially efficient market structure in an industry (in the future) is knowledge beyond the grasp of any economist or committee of experts. Lacking any rational basis to restrict voluntary mergers, therefore, we hold that all mergers can be socially efficient in a plan-coordinating sense and ought to be allowed as a matter of right.

Mergers Encourage Mergers. A "domino" theory of mergers suggests that a successful horizontal merger in an industry could spawn other mergers and that the effect, ultimately, would be to weaken market competition. Through such a process, an atomistic market structure might deteriorate into oligopoly; the wisest public policy would be to stop the merger process in its incipiency. To continue this line of reasoning, it would be more rational to prevent "competition" from declining in the first place, than to attempt to restore competition (through divestiture) after the process is well along.

But this theory suffers from a number of fatal difficulties. The primary difficulty is the pretense of knowledge as to the socially efficient structure of an industry. What is the socially efficient number of independent business units in a market place at any given point in time? If the market structure enthusiasts could supply that information, we would then know how many mergers to allow and how many to prohibit. Lacking that information, there is no sound basis for concluding that many mergers are somehow less optimal than fewer mergers or no mergers at all. The alternative is to allow an open competitive process to determine the ultimate structure of any market.

A secondary problem with this view can be illustrated by asking: Why do some mergers encourage other mergers? Are the subsequent mergers consummated in order to be better able to compete with previous corporate combinations? Did the first consolidation realize economies and profit opportunities that other firms desire to imitate, and indeed must imitate in order to remain competitive? But low-cost operations throughout an industry should be imitated, and the sooner the better. If more efficient methods of production, distribution, and organization are discovered, it is imperative that rival firms and the consumers they serve be able to enjoy these same economies, whatever the alleged structural sacrifices. To impede such a discovery process with arbitrary merger "guidelines" is unjustified.[10]

Vertical Merger

When a manufacturing firm merges with a supplier or with a distributor, the merger is termed vertical integration or a *vertical merger*. The manufacturing firm is combining one or more of the stages of production in the product line from raw material to the final delivered product in the hands of some buyer. Since such mergers are not between direct competitors, the antitrust issues are more subtle than with strictly horizontal combinations. Nevertheless, such mergers are reputed to be a threat to competition.

Efficiency and Foreclosure.   The essence of the concern over vertical integration centers around the concept of foreclosure, a rather familiar issue at this point. According to this concept, to purchase a supplier would be to preempt and foreclose rivals from sources of supply; to purchase a retailer would be to preempt or foreclose some competitors from channels of distribution. In either case, it is alleged that nonintegrated rivals would find it more difficult to compete since their access to certain markets would be impeded. The tendency would be to substantially reduce competition or to tend to create a monopoly.

But how exactly are competitors foreclosed from markets? Assume, for example, that a firm that makes steel ingot purchases a coal producing firm. Certainly the steel firm can, and probably will, increase its own purchases of coal from its own firm (assuming that its own firm is at least price competitive), but this action will hardly foreclose rivals from coal purchasing opportunities. Why should there be fewer aggregate opportunities after the merger than before the merger? Economic activity is emphatically not a zero-sum game. Increased purchases by one firm do not necessarily imply that other firms must purchase less. If the steel company is interested in operating the coal subsidiary profitably, that firm will be interested in selling additional units of output. And nothing would prevent other coal firms, especially those that have lost orders for coal, from doing additional business. Why should anyone be foreclosed from anything?

The same analysis applies to a vertical merger involving a distributor. The natural tendency is to conclude that the manufacturer will increase its requirements of its own product with that distributor, thereby excluding some of the products of its competitors. This is, of course, a possibility, but consider the situation just prior to the merger. The distributor is attempting to sell that combination of products that render the greatest total profit. Assuming that the merger has just been completed, where does that distributor now get the leverage to force more of one supplier's product on the public than before, and thereby foreclose rival manufacturers from final markets? If it had been profitable to sell more of brand X, and preempt competitors, prior to the consolidation, why hadn't the distributor already done so? Precisely how does the merger alter demand conditions in the final market to make foreclosure profitable?

It has also been asserted that nonintegrated competitors may be put at a disadvantage if vertical merger realizes certain economies for the firms involved. It may, for example, be easier, more convenient and ultimately cheaper for some business organizations to retail goods through their own subsidiaries rather than through independent distributors. If this allows lower costs, lower prices, or greater profits, then nonintegrated firms would be at a competitive disadvantage in the selling market. But, of course, such "disadvantages" are absolutely desirable and are the essence of a free-market competitive process. They are the particular business practices that insure that scarce economic resources will tend to be channeled toward their most productive employment. The disadvantage arises precisely because, and only because, final consumers prefer lower prices and tend to reward those sellers that curb their expenses. If they did not, then the merger could not and would not create any disadvantages for any rivals. To condemn the creation of such situations, therefore, is to strike at the heart of the process of efficient resource allocation, and directly at consumer tastes and preferences. To do so in the name of "protecting" consumers from monopoly is the ultimate irony of antimerger policy.

Efficiency as a Barrier to Entry. The foreclosure of competitors by companies that realize economies of production and selling has also been termed a barrier to entry. As already explained, the fact that some manufacturers are vertically integrated can make competition with them more difficult. If consumers reward efficient, integrated sellers, for example, a kind of barrier is created, vis-à-vis firms that do not offer consumers similar advantages. But, again, it would be illogical to blame consumers for the welfare reductions allegedly associated with such barriers, when such barriers are sustained by consumer preference itself! All such barriers are in reality economies that some firms have achieved and others have not achieved; and such economies may act as a barrier to entry. They exclude firms that cannot organize their inputs and outputs in a manner that is as pleasing to consumers. Those who argue that such a condition is unfair, or unfairly limits competition, do not really understand the nature and purpose of a rivalrous competitive process.

Subsidization and Squeezing. An interesting element in vertical merger theory is the concept of subsidization and its corollary, *squeezing*. Subsidization implies that vertically integrated firms have competitive advantages over nonintegrated firms, since certain stages of production can be used to subsidize or finance other stages. A steel firm, for example, might purchase coal from its own subsidiary at cost, or below cost, and use this advantage to depress the final price of steel ingot. Nonintegrated ingot rivals that are purchasing relatively more expensive coal, could then be "squeezed" between higher coal costs and lower ingot prices. The tendency would be to reduce competition and to create a monopoly in ingot production.[11]

There are many objections to this line of reasoning, however. In the first place, it would appear that successful squeezing of rivals depends upon a near monopoly in the supply of the input resource. Nonintegrated manufacturers that can turn to alternative suppliers at lower prices cannot be squeezed. Squeezing would seem to depend upon monopolization in some unique input and extreme barriers to entry in resource markets, which is an extremely unlikely occurrence in an open, free market.

Furthermore, if there were no monopoly over the resource, and squeezing did occur, it would not necessarily be condemnable from any consumer perspective. The essence of the process of squeezing is to lower the costs of each of the stages of production so that final goods prices can be as low as possible. Properly understood, what is being squeezed is cost or profit margins. Nothing would or should prevent other firms from making similar mergers to enjoy the same advantages of vertical integration. Thus, mergers and competition between firms that squeeze costs and profit margins is never to be regretted.

Firms that "subsidize" (invest in) one stage of production can choose to temporarily forego a return in some alternative investment. But, of course, nonintegrated firms can make the same "investments." And since an integrated firm has already made a substantially larger investment than its nonintegrated rivals, it must eventually secure a greater overall profit on its larger investment. If it voluntarily foregoes a return in one stage of production, it must plan to recoup it in another.

But how will it be able to recoup that return? If final product markets are openly competitive, how will the integrated seller be able to earn a higher than normal rate of return there? Will the lower ingot prices bring a volume and a profit sufficient to cover subsidization through the stages of production? Perhaps, but this can in no way be guaranteed or assured. If it does occur, it would be a delightful development as far as the consumer of ingot is concerned. Such low-priced high-volume operations are the very essence of openly competitive markets.

If final markets for ingot are not openly competitive, higher prices would allow classic profit recoupment in the spirit of a true monopoly. But why is subsidization necessary before final goods prices can be increased? If prices can be increased profitably, they can be increased with or without any subsidization. The cost advantages associated with vertical integration have nothing, apparently, to do with raising prices to final consumers.

To summarize, the competitive problems associated with vertical integration are illusionary. There is no reason to accept the proposition that such mergers—employing foreclosure, subsidization, and squeezing—can work any serious injury to consumers. Indeed, mergers such as this are a serious threat to relatively inefficient nonintegrated rivals, and not to consumers. They may upset status quo market structures, but their danger to the competitive process in an open market is not apparent.

Conglomerate Merger

There is no generally accepted definition of the term *conglomerate*, nor of the mergers that should be classified as conglomerate.[12] In the following discussion mergers that are not clearly horizontal or vertical will be classified as conglomerate. The term will refer to corporate marriages between firms that are not direct competitors, suppliers, or distributors. Some conglomerate mergers may involve firms in related but not identical product lines; some may involve firms whose product lines are complimentary rather than strictly competitive or unrelated. Some conglomerate mergers may involve firms with high degrees of concentricity and a mutuality of interest. Although these latter terms defy precise definition, the general impression is that the acquired firm acts as a kind of catalyst to the potential market performance of the acquiring firm. The term *synergy* has also been used to describe the effects of such mergers on the acquired or acquiring firm.[13] Finally, the term conglomerate may apply to any so-called free-form merger, even where no concentricity or synergy is obvious.

Since conglomerate mergers do not directly involve competitors, suppliers or distributors, the structural approach to competition would not appear immediately applicable. At first blush it would seem that conglomerate mergers could not endanger the competitive process in any measurable way. Yet the belief that "large conglomerate enterprises possess kinds of power that may involve jeopardy to competition" has certainly been widespread in key governmental as well as in some academic circles.[14] The following section will explore how conglomerate power purportedly endangers the competitive system.

Foreclosure and Potential Competition.   It has been argued by critics that conglomerate mergers decrease competition because they foreclose the acquiring firm from the market as an independent competitor. This theory assumes that the acquiring firm would have entered the market of the acquired firm by, say, constructing a plant there. If it had, the number of competitors would have increased and the market shares and concentration ratios in that market would now be lower. In short, when a firm buys its way into a market that it might have entered on its own, it forecloses some competition and, accordingly, lowers economic performance.

Moreover, it has also been argued that a firm on the brink of market entry serves as a competitive restraint vis-à-vis existing firms in the industry. Existing firms in the market are conscious of the potential competitor and behave themselves accordingly. When that firm purchases an existing competitor, potential competition is thereby lessened, and if the purchasing firm was a substantial potential competitor, competition is said to be "substantially" lessened.

There are many problems, however, with this theory of potential competition and self-foreclosure. In the first place, it is difficult to believe that a firm can be rationally condemned for something it did not do. It was a potential competitor, it did not construct a plant to compete, ergo it decreases competition (substantially?) because it might have (but did not) entered the market as an independent competitor. The real issue—whether or not the merger *itself* reduces competition in some intelligently explainable manner—is conveniently skirted. But why is independently entering a market more competitive than purchasing an existing firm? Because the former procedure produces one more competitor than the latter? It appears that the self-foreclosure argument can be reduced to the numbers game inherent in the market structure approach to competition.

Second, why might a business organization purchase an existing firm rather than build an independent facility? The major reason for such a decision would be that the former investment promises a greater rate of return than the latter. The increased profit would be associated with specific economies; the merger would be cheaper than the next-best economic alternative. Scarce economic resources would flow into those areas where they render the maximum service to consumers. To condemn such allocations of resources and to condemn "cheapness" is to condemn efficiency and consumer welfare. That economies foreclose less desirable and more costly options is always true. But such efficient foreclosure is to be applauded and not condemned.

The potential competition theory always attempts to prove too much. All business organizations are potential competitors with each other; even firms yet unborn are potentially competitive with existing firms. Are companies never to be allowed to merge because they might someday enter some new market and produce some product? Such a view could be used to prohibit every corporate merger. But such a conclusion, and the theory that produces it, cannot be taken seriously.

Reciprocity. One theoretical factor concerning conglomerates that may appear new, but that actually is not new, is the concept of reciprocity. Reciprocity is the practice of buying products or services from those sellers that also purchase products and services from you. To put the concept in antitrust jargon, certain firms are able to exert "market power" on suppliers such that they become customers. The alleged effect of the practice is to foreclose rival competitors from sales, and to reduce competition.

Reciprocal dealings between firms predate conglomerate mergers, and purchasing agents have always been keenly aware of the potential value of reciprocal arrangements. An article in *Fortune* once reported that over 60 percent of the top 500 corporations used trade relations men that promoted reciprocal dealings.[15] The antitrust issue, however, is not the existence of reciprocal agreements per se, but the idea that suppliers are coerced into purchases, or that rival competitors are unfairly shut out of markets.

Imagine a situation with no reciprocal agreement, where a buyer is purchasing materials from some independent seller. The buyer, presumably, is making the best deal possible, and obtaining the best product at the lowest possible price. We can assume that all of the buyer's market power has been employed to obtain the most optimal and beneficial package. Under such circumstances, where would the buyer obtain the additional power to dictate an unfair reciprocal agreement?

If the seller were a subsidiary of the buyer (conglomerate), noncompetitive reciprocity could be mandated. But how does such an arrangement do anyone any good? To obtain goods far below cost would be to sacrifice the return on that investment; to obtain goods above cost would be inefficient and, ultimately, unprofitable. Unless all competitors can be permanently crushed by such action (what theory would suggest this?), enforced reciprocity between subsidiaries is foolish and foolhardy.[16]

It is possible, of course, that a buyer may make a reciprocal sale so attractive to a supplier that some reciprocal agreement is established. Buyers, for example, may agree to pay slightly higher prices for their supplies in exchange for slightly better terms on some reciprocal sale. It is not obvious, however, that such agreements endanger the competitive process or injure consumers. Finally, since many conglomerates operate under the profit-center concept, noncompetitive reciprocity within the conglomerate itself would be minimized. In short, noncompetitive reciprocal dealings are an illusionary hobgoblin in an openly competitive market.

Conglomerate Power. It has also been argued that conglomerates can reduce competition in an industry into which they have merged, by unfavorably affecting the price-making calculus of the smaller independent competitors.[17] This argument holds that independent companies facing conglomerates in competition would be more reluctant to reduce prices, for fear of retaliation by the multiproduct giant. Thus rigid pricing, the allegedly familiar pricing behavior of oligopolies, would come to prevail in an industry that was formerly competitive and the net effect would be to reduce economic welfare.

There are many familiar difficulties here. In the first place, interdependence among rival sellers is a factor in *all* open markets; its appearance is *not* unique with conglomeration. Even "small" firms in "competitive" industries must integrate the likely reactions of rivals into their own pricing decisions. Since competition is never atomistic, all firms *have* a pricing policy and all pricing decisions *are* affected by competitors. Conglomerates, therefore, do not spoil some perfectly competitive economic wonderland.

Moreover, the implications concerning corporate retaliation and predatory practices are becoming a bit tedious at this point. Where is the documented empirical evidence—even the smallest shred of it—that leading firms in actual rivalrous situations *ever* systematically employ such practices?[18] And even if they ever *did* employ such practices, where is the convincing argument that consumers would be injured and resources "misallocated" by such behavior?[19]

Lacking a rational and consistent theory to explain the anticompetitive effects of mergers, the arguments against business mergers have often deteriorated into irrelevant antitrust concerns. For instance, it has been stated that an important reason for mergers is the tax advantages and promoters' profits associated with such consolidations. Perhaps. But what has this to do with competition or, more specifically, with a threat to competition? Whether it would be wise to legislate on tax advantages and stock promotions is a separate issue from the one that is under examination in this chapter. Do mergers restrain trade, lessen competition, and tend to subvert consumer sovereignty and social welfare? If they do, how do they? Tax advantages and stock promotions are relevant issues if it can first be demonstrated that mergers are destructive of competition. Lacking such a demonstration, discussions of tax advantages and stock promotions are beside the point.

The same argument applies to the human dislocations that are alleged to accompany mergers, particularly where regional firms are acquired by growth-oriented conglomerates. Although such issues might be relevant in sociology and management, they are bogus antitrust issues. They do, however, serve to demonstrate the almost total bankruptcy of antitrust theory with respect to corporate mergers.

The first part of this chapter has reviewed and analyzed critically some popular merger theories. The second part will be devoted to an examination of some classic merger cases in recent antitrust history. If mergers actually restrain trade, tend toward monopoly, foreclose substantial amounts of competition, encourage noncompetitive reciprocity, and generally reduce social welfare, an examination of some leading merger cases ought to reveal such activity.

THE BROWN SHOE CASE (1962)

The *Brown Shoe* case involved the legality of a 1956 merger between the Brown Shoe Company and the G. R. Kinney Company.[20] Prior to the merger, Brown was the nation's fourth-largest shoe manufacturer, with 4 percent of total domestic manufactured shoe output; in addition, Brown owned 845 retail shoe outlets, all of which had been acquired between 1950 and 1955. Kinney, a very small shoe manufacturer (½% of industry output) was the nation's largest family-style shoe store chain, with over 400 stores in 270 cities. Although there were a reported 1048 shoe manufacturing plants in the United States in 1956, and over 70,000 retail outlets that sold shoes (not including shoes sold in department stores), the government charged that the pending merger between one of the nation's largest shoe manufacturers and the nation's largest family-owned chain of shoe stores violated the amended Section 7 of the Clayton Act. After failing, in 1955, in an attempt to obtain a permanent injunction to stop the merger, the Justice Department sued for divestiture in 1956.

The District Court Decision

The District Court, with Judge Weber presiding, found against the Brown-Kinney merger on November 20, 1959.[21] In summary it stated that the merger would (1) increase manufacturing and retailing concentration in the shoe industry; (2) eliminate competition between Kinney and Brown at the retail level; and (3) "establish a manufacturer–retailer relationship that would foreclose other firms from a fair opportunity to compete for Kinney's business."[22]

There can be little doubt that concentration, and trends in concentration, were the decisive issues in the District Court decision. Judge Weber emphasized that it had been the Congressional intent in passing the Antimerger Act of 1950 to "encompass minute acquisitions which tend toward monopoly and to do so in their incipiency."[23] Even though the share of the shoe market held by Brown, or even by Brown-Kinney, might be small in percentage terms, that was not to be the determining issue: "We are not so much concerned with percentages as such, but with what these percentages mean in examination under the light of the fact of the case and the economic realities involved."[24] The "economic realities" demonstrated, according to Weber, that there was a "definite trend" toward concentration in the shoe industry. The most important aspect of the concentration movement took the form of leading shoe manufacturers obtaining additional retail outlets. The record showed that the large shoe manufacturers had acquired over 1000 independent retail shoe stores between 1950 and 1956; in fact, the thirteen largest shoe manufacturers operated 21 percent of all shoe outlets by 1956.[25] And this trend, coupled with the declining number of shoe manufacturers, was the very sort of thing that the Congress had meant to "arrest in its incipiency" when it had amended Section 7.

The concentration trend was not just important for its own sake. When shoe manufacturers acquired shoe retailers, they "definitely increased the sale of their own manufactured product to these retail outlets," thus "drying up the available outlets for independent manufacturers."[26] Judge Weber held that the smaller manufacturers were "losing that market" through foreclosure, and that this "substantially lessens competition between manufacturers."[27] Therefore, the tendency in the shoe industry was toward the elimination of small manufacturers and small independent retailers.[28]

The Brown-Kinney merger could also have lessened competition at the retail level, since there might have been substantial cost savings associated with vertical integration in the shoe industry. Weber admitted that company-owned retail outlets had cost advantages in advertising, insurance, inventory control, and price control. These advantages would likely be reflected "in lower prices or in higher quality at the same prices." But of course, the independents would have a much harder time competing with company-owned stores if such conditions prevailed.

Finally, after much discussion, the court admitted that competition was likely to be lessened in the men's, women's, and children's shoe markets. It was determined that there were at least 141 cities of over 10,000 people where Brown and Kinney retail outlets competed directly.[29] The merger would eliminate Kinney as an independent competitor, and simply make the company an "adoptive child" of a larger shoe family.[30] For all of these reasons, therefore, Judge Weber ordered Brown to divest itself of Kinney.

The Supreme Court Decision

The Supreme Court decision, written by Chief Justice Warren, affirmed the lower court decision against Brown.[31] Warren first reviewed the lower court's findings and the legislative history of Section 7 of the Clayton Act. He agreed that the "relevant market" in this case was the market for "men's, women's and children's" shoes. These were lines of commerce easily recognized by the public, typically manufactured in separate plants, not directly competitive, and clearly directed at different classes of consumers.[32] An analysis of whether the vertical aspects of the Brown-Kinney merger reduced competition substantially in those lines of commerce was now required.

The Supreme Court first convinced itself that the issue of foreclosure in this case was somewhat akin to foreclosure in tying contract clauses.[33] They then went on to argue that the foreclosure in *Brown* was not just *"de minimis,"* since "no merger between a manufacturer and an independent retailer could involve a larger potential market foreclosure."[34] And since there was a definite trend toward vertical integration in this industry, and since the District Court had found a "tendency of the acquiring manufacturers to become increasingly important sources of supply for their acquired outlets," the tendency must be to "foreclose . . . independent manufacturers from markets otherwise open to them."[35] But this tendency went against the clear Congressional intent in passing the Celler-Kefauver Act:

> Congress was desirous of preventing the formation of further oligopolies with their attendant adverse effects upon local control of industry and upon small business. When an industry was composed of numerous independent units, Congress appeared anxious to preserve this structure.[36]

Hence, the Court concluded that the vertical aspects of the merger might foreclose competition from a substantial share of the relevant market, and that there were no "countervailing competitive, economic, or social advantages" associated with the merger. Strangely, there had been no discussion whatever of such countervailing advantages until the point in the decision when they were suddenly declared not to exist![37]

Chief Justice Warren then proceeded to discuss the horizontal aspects of the merger. He accepted the District Court's finding, over Brown's strong objection, that the relevant markets under consideration were men's, women's, and children's shoes in cities of over 10,000 people. He also agreed that the District Court had taken enough of a sample to estimate the competitive consequences of the merger in those markets.[38] In 118 cities, for example, the Court estimated that the combined Brown-Kinney share of the relevant market exceeded 5 percent. But was market share to be directly related to a lessening of competition, and was 5 percent a "substantial" volume of trade? Justice Warren answered affirmatively on both counts:

> In an industry as fragmented as shoe retailing, the control of substantial shares of the trade in a city may have important effects on competition. If a merger achieving 5% control were now approved, we might be required to approve fur-

ther merger effort by Brown's competitors seeking similar market shares. The oligopoly Congress sought to avoid would then be furthered and it would be difficult to dissolve the combinations previously approved. Furthermore, in this fragmented industry, even if the combination controls but a small share of a particular market, the fact that this share is held by a large national chain can adversely affect competition.[39]

But how would competition (read "competitors") be adversely affected? Why through certain economies and efficiencies realizable from the merger! Integrated national chains could alter styles in footwear quickly, eliminate wholesalers, and "market their own brands at prices below those of competing independent retailers."[40] And this sort of process was to be condemned if it endangered the economy of "numerous independent units" envisioned by Congress. In one of the most amazing and revealing statements of all antitrust, Warren declared:

> Of course, some of the results of large integrated or chain operations are beneficial to consumers. Their expansion is not rendered unlawful by the mere fact that small independent stores may be adversely affected. It is competition, not competitors, which the Act protects. But we cannot fail to recognize Congress' desire to promote competition through protection of viable, small, locally owned businesses. Congress appreciated that occasional higher costs and prices might result from the maintenance of fragmented industries and markets. It resolved these competing considerations in favor of decentralization. We must give effect to that decision.[41]

This is classic antitrust double-talk, and exposes the antitrust hoax completely. The Act protects competition, not competitors, by protecting competitors. Economies that adversely affect small, independent businesses are not to be condemned unless they adversely affect small, independent businesses. No amount of economic or legal rationalization can possibly put this antitrust house back together again.

Justice Harlan wrote a separate decision in which he dissented in part, and concurred in part, with the majority decision. Harlan dissented in part because he would have dismissed the case for lack of jurisdiction.[42] More importantly, he dissented because he felt that the District Court's conclusions on the vertical aspects of the merger were sufficient to condemn the merger, without regard to any examination of the horizontal issues.[43] Since "Brown's merger with Kinney potentially withdraws a share of the market previously available to the independent shoe manufacturers," and since these manufacturers would have to "enter some other market or go out of business," the Brown-Kinney consolidation was condemnable on vertical foreclosure grounds alone.[44] Harlan concluded his opinion by admitting that the cost economies of integration would tend to work a competitive disadvantage on nonintegrated retailers.[45]

Comment on the Brown Shoe Case

Much of the argument in the *Brown Shoe* case was premised on the assumption of increasing concentration in the shoe industry. The District Court had stated, and the Supreme Court had agreed, that there was a "definite trend" toward concentration in shoe manufacturing and shoe retailing, and that it was the Congressional intent to halt such movements in their incipiency. We will not restate previously made arguments that changes in concentration prove nothing *a priori* about competition. But we will observe that the Court-observed trends in concentration are open to the most serious question. It is true that there had been an absolute decline in the number of domestic shoe manufacturers between 1947 and 1956,[46] but concentration ratios for the largest group of firms actually declined during that period. Justice Harlan had noted (in a footnote) that while the fourth, eighth, and fifteenth largest shoe firms had accounted for 25.9 percent, 31.4 percent and 36.2 percent of industry output respectively in 1947, they accounted for 22 percent, 27 percent and 32.5 percent of industry output respectively in 1955.[47] Was this the legendary "tendency toward oligopoly" that the Congress had supposedly legislated against?[48]

Even stronger doubts linger over the inference that there was increasing concentration in retail outlets, or in the percentage of retail outlets owned by manufacturers or chains. Although the absolute number of such outlets purchased by the larger shoe manufacturers undoubtedly increased throughout the period, Brown introduced data that indicated that retail sales by chains with eleven or more stores stood at a constant 19.5 percent of national dollar volume in both 1948 and 1954.[49] In addition, there were unquestionably more shoe retailers in 1955 than there had been in 1948. Any talk of concentration in an industry with nearly 100,000 units, and with such ease of entry, must not be taken seriously unless it can be supported with incontrovertible fact. Yet there was no such fact in this case. Nonetheless, a good part of the case against the Brown-Kinney merger rested upon such "evidence."

Even more importantly, the entire argument concerning "substantial foreclosure" and the supposed "drying up of available outlets for independent manufacturers" depends upon and is logically derived from the concentration myth just exposed. Outlets could not be drying up if the retail shoe markets were not becoming increasingly concentrated, if the number of retail outlets was growing, and if the volume of business done by these shoe stores was increasing. Even if Brown switched some of its shoe business to its own stores, the old outlets from which Brown had switched the shoes were now opened to independent shoe manufacturers. While particular independent manufacturers may have been foreclosed from particular outlets, therefore, they should not have been foreclosed from the general retail shoe market.

But even admitting this is admitting too much. Both the District Court and the Supreme Court noted the fact that Kinney's purchases of shoes from Brown had gone from zero prior to the merger, to 7.8 percent after the merger.[50] Information supplied from other Brown acquisitions indicated that Brown had a habit of increasing its own shoe requirements at outlets which it owned or franchised. The clear impression conveyed by both court decisions is that the independent shoe manufacturers must have sold fewer shoes to Brown retail outlets, and particularly to Kinney, after the merger, and that the independents were "losing that market" as the purchases of Brown shoes by Kinney increased.[51] But this impression is wholly inaccurate since independent sales to Kinney did not decrease. The trial court record indicates that independents sold as many shoes to Kinney after the merger as they had before the merger.[52] In fact, even the Supreme Court admitted that "the dollar value of Kinney's outside shoe purchases in 1955 was between 16 and 17 million dollars, and this amount has increased to 19.4 million by 1957."[53] Thus the Court mistakenly inferred consequences concerning foreclosure that had *not* happened from concentration assumptions that were *not* accurate.

Finally and briefly, the Supreme Court's open hostility to the economies of vertical integration must be the most embarrassing part of the decision against the merger. Again we are told by the highest tribunal in the land that economies and efficiencies restrain trade and tend to reduce competition— the very opposite of the truth. When it is demonstrated that competitors with admittedly "higher costs and prices" have to be "preserved," and vertically integrated firms that would pass economies on to consumers have to be dissolved, antitrust stands naked, stripped of all of its pro-consumer pretense. That antitrust law can still find substantial intellectual support after decisions such as this is the most incomprehensible aspect of this public policy.

THE CONTINENTAL CAN AND ALCOA CASES (1964)

The hostility to mergers became even more pronounced in the *Continental Can*[54] and *Alcoa*[55] cases, both decided by the Supreme Court in 1964. In *Continental*, the Court struck down a merger between the nation's second largest can maker (Continental) and the third largest producer of glass containers (Hazel-Atlas). Although the Court admitted that the products of the two companies were different and certainly not perfectly interchangeable, the justices ruled that there was sufficient inter-industry competition to permit rational discussion of a "glass and metal container market" as a separate line of commerce. Since in that market the share of the combination was high (25 percent), and since a dominant, multi-product firm would hold advantages over single-product smaller rivals, and perhaps, also tend to trigger additional mergers, the Continental-Hazel merger could not be permitted. In addition, Continental and Hazel were potential competitors in the future, and to allow this merger would reduce potential competition. Justice Harlan's strong dissent argued that the Court's "bizarre" calculations of a "non-existent" market had enabled them to dispense with any elaborate proof that competition had been substantially reduced, but it was to no avail.[56]

In the *Alcoa* case, a majority of the Supreme Court overturned a lower-court decision that had allowed the merger between the Aluminum Company of America and the Rome Cable Company. Justice Douglas held that aluminum and copper conductor cable were different enough to form their own sub-markets, and that in the aluminum conductor market, Alcoa held 27.8 percent of industry sales, Rome 1.3 percent, and the nine largest firms over 95 percent. Since the market was already highly concentrated, and since Rome was a substantial and aggressive competitor, the merger violated Section 7.[57]

Justices Stewart, Harlan, and Goldberg joined in an emphatic dissent in *Alcoa*. The essence of the dissent was that the Supreme Court majority had "clearly failed to prove its line of commerce claims." The District Court's long (3,500-page) trial record and careful analysis demonstrated to these Justices that insulted aluminum conductors and insulated copper conductors were part of the same relevant market; the Supreme Court majority was simply mistaken on that crucial point.[58] And the District Court's opinion that the merger was a " 'combination of an aluminum and an essentially copper manufacturing company' undertaken by Alcoa in the face of its declining market for the purpose of obtaining insulating know-how and diversification, needed 'to overcome a market disadvantage rather than to obtain a captive market. . . . or to eliminate a competitor' " was more nearly representative of the facts than the Supreme Court majority opinion.[59] But the findings and conclusions of the District Court were not to be determining in this case.

THE CONSOLIDATED FOODS CASE (1965)

In 1965 the Supreme Court reversed the Court of Appeals and found that Consolidated Foods should divest itself of Gentry as the FTC had ordered in 1961.[60] Consolidated Foods, a large, diversified food processor and wholesaler had purchased Gentry, Inc., a manufacturer of dehydrated onion and garlic, in 1951. The FTC alleged that the acquisition violated Section 7 of the Clayton Act, since the threat of reciprocal purchasing might create "for Gentry a protected market which others cannot penetrate despite superiority of price, quality or service."[61] Supposedly, Consolidated could and did pressure some of its suppliers to deal with Gentry, thus foreclosing some competition. Since "the share of the market that might be insulated from the effective interplay of fair competition" was substantial (25 percent of all Consolidated's suppliers required onion and garlic), a "substantial" lessening of competition was probable and the FTC ordered divestiture.

The Circuit Court of Appeals Decision

The Circuit Court of Appeals reversed the FTC decision in 1964.[62] Although Judge Castle (speaking for Judges Knoch and Mercer) admitted that Consolidated Foods had "overtly *attempted* to use its purchasing power as a device to obtain business for its Gentry division," the trial record indicated that (1) it was not apparently a consistent company policy and (2) it was completely ineffective in a number of instances.[63] Most importantly for the Circuit Court

> ten years of post-acquisition experience—during which Consolidated attempted overt enforcement of reciprocal buying practice where it deemed it might be successful—serves to demonstrate that neither the acquisition of Gentry, in and of itself, nor the overt attempts to use buying power to influence sellers to Consolidated to purchase from Gentry resulted in substantial anticompetitive effect. No substantial impact on the relevant market occurred, and . . . we are of the view that the experience reflected by this post-acquisition period must weigh heavily in appraising future probabilities.[64]

Between 1951 and 1958, Gentry's share of the market in dehydrated onion sales rose from 28 percent to 35 percent, while its dehydrated garlic sales declined from 51 percent to 39 percent. Since the industry as a whole was growing rapidly, Gentry's "slight gain" in onion and "significant loss" in garlic demonstrated that reciprocity, implied or overt, was completely ineffectual and of no concern as far as competition was concerned.[65]

The Supreme Court Decision

The Supreme Court reversed the Appeals Court decision on April 28, 1965.[66] Justice Douglas was sympathetic to the FTC argument that in an industry that was already extremely concentrated (the industry leader, Basic, and second-ranking Gentry combined produced 85 percent of all sales), anticompetitive obstacles like potential reciprocity should be removed. The fact that reciprocity had been tried repeatedly was sufficient cause to infer that a substantial lessening of competition was probable.[67] And the post-acquisition evidence, Douglas argued, tended to confirm the FTC allegations with respect to the potential anticompetitive effects of the merger.[68]

Justices Harlan and Stewart concurred in the majority opinion, although both expressed some disagreement with Douglas' opinion. Justice Stewart argued that neither the "mere effort at reciprocity" nor the peculiar structure of the industry would be sufficient for a finding of a substantial lessening of competition.[69] In fact, he hypothesized, it was perfectly possible that the merger intensified competition between Basic and Gentry; certainly the outputs and qualities of product were more impressive in 1958 than in 1951.[70] Moreover, there was no evidence to indicate—contrary to the FTC implications—that barriers to entry were particularly severe in this industry.[71]

Stewart would have placed much more weight on the post-acquisition evidence than did the Supreme Court. For it was here, he said, that Consolidated's probable effect on competition was evidenced. Stewart maintained that while Consolidated was unable to wield reciprocal pressure against large, brand-name food processors like Armour and Swift, it could and did "strong-arm" smaller, private-label food processors.[72] Since these independents were substantial purchasers in the dehydrated onion and garlic market, the Commission was right to order divestiture on the probable effects of reciprocity.

Brief Comment on the Consolidated Foods Case

Stewart's criticism of the Supreme Court majority decision is certainly well taken. We can easily agree with the argument that simple market structure and concentration statistics combined with a few (mostly unsuccessful) efforts at reciprocity are not enough to infer a substantial competitive restraint. But neither, of course, is Stewart's suggestion that certain small independents were "pressured" to deal with Gentry—evidence of a substantial competitive restraint. What is crucial and completely unexamined in this case is the nature of the wholesale market for food. If this market is openly competitive (and there is no reason to believe that it is not) then it becomes difficult to accept the idea that any sellers are "injured" by Consolidated's actions.[73] A competitive wholesale market would make effective anticompetitive reciprocity extremely unlikely with anyone, and completely undermine Justice Stewart's conjecture. But since the Supreme Court's decision was based on the fact that the structural organization of the market gave rise to potential reciprocity, and that actual reciprocity had been attempted, such an examination and analysis was beside the point.

THE VON'S GROCERY CASE (1966)

The mistaken inference that certain structural factors lead inevitably to substantial competitive restraint reached a climax of absurdity in the *Von's Grocery* case, decided by the Supreme Court in 1966.[74] In that decision, Justice Black concluded—contrary to the District Court—that the merger between the Von's Grocery Company and Shopping Bag Food Stores would tend to restrain competition substantially in the retail grocery market in the Los Angeles area.

Black's conclusion was based completely on structural factors and suppositions: the merger combined the third- and sixth-largest retail grocery sellers; their combined sales represented 7.5 percent of total grocery sales in the Los Angeles market in 1960; the number of owner-operated single grocery stores had decreased from 5365 in 1950 to 3590 in 1963; and the grocery business was falling into fewer and fewer hands.[75] Since Congress was anxious "to prevent economic concentration in the American economy by keeping a large number of small competitors in business," and since mergers and acquisitions had continued at a rapid pace after the Von's merger, it was logical to conclude that competition might have been substantially reduced by the Von's–Shopping Bag consolidation.[76] Thus in the most completely mechanistic approach to antitrust yet applied in merger cases, the Supreme Court ordered divestiture.

As some sort of consolation, there was a long, careful and devastating dissent by Justice Potter Stewart in the *Von's Grocery* case. The following excerpt will set the tone and the context of his criticism:

> The Court makes no effort to appraise the competitive effects of this acquisition in terms of the contemporary economy of the retail food industry in the Los Angeles area. Instead, through a simple exercise in sums, it finds that the number of individual competitors in the market has decreased over the years, and, apparently on the theory the degree of competition is invariably proportional to the number of competitors, it holds that this historic reduction in the number of competing units is enough under Section 7 to invalidate a merger within the market, with no need to examine the economic concentration of the market, the level of competition in the market, or the potential adverse effect of the merger on that competition. This startling *per se* rule is contrary not only to our previous decisions, but contrary to the language of Section 7, contrary to the legislative history of the 1950 amendment, and contrary to economic reality.[77]

Stewart offered rebuttal on every phase of the Supreme Court decision. He first argued that there was no incipient trend toward a lessening of competition in the grocery business in Los Angeles. The simple "counting-of-heads game" played by the Court majority could not be rationally equated with a lessening of competition. In fact, the grocery markets in Los Angeles were competitive to a fault, with intense rivalry among chain stores and between chains and single grocery stores.[78] An exploding population and the buying and selling of cooperatives made entry into the industry easy, and made competition between all sizes of stores possible.[79] The numerical decline in single-store units was only the result of a "transcending social and technological change" in consumer tastes and retailing techniques; there could be no reasonable inference that competition had suffered because of the "attrition" of some smaller stores. Yet, Stewart added bitterly, the Supreme Court's decision was "hardly more than a requiem for the so-called 'Mom and Pop' grocery stores," and an indirect attempt "to roll back the super market revolution."[80]

Even more crucial to the opinion in this case, Stewart maintained that the Court erred when it implied that concentration in the Los Angeles grocery business was increasing. Between 1948 and 1958, the leading grocery chain's percentage of total market sales declined from 14 percent to 8 percent; and the top chains' percentage declined from 21 percent to 14 percent.[81] Although the combined share of the top 20 stores had increased from 44 percent to 57 percent, the substantial turnover in the membership of the top 20 made that concentration ratio an unreliable measure of concentration and, most assuredly, of competition in the marketplace.[82] Further, the empirical evidence that the Court had relied upon to prove that the bigger firms were buying out the smaller firms and, therefore, that concentration was increasing in the retail market, did not appear to substantiate its allegations.[83]

Stewart also noted that a "great majority" of the post-Von's–Shopping Bag mergers in the grocery market were market-extension mergers that neither eliminated direct competitors nor increased concentration. In fact, the District Court had determined that the Von's–Shopping Bag consolidation itself involved firms that competed in different areas of Los Angeles.[84] Stewart suggested that that particular merger was three parts product extension, and only one part horizontal; with this interpretation, less than 1 percent of total grocery sales could have been foreclosed by the Von's–Shopping Bag merger.[85] Yet the Supreme Court majority had not even mentioned this important aspect of the merger controversy.

Finally, Stewart noted that the supposed victims in this case—the small independent firms—were aggressive, able, and efficient competitors; the District Court had "found not a shred of evidence that competition had been in any way impaired by the merger."[86] The defendants, therefore, were being punished for "the sin of aggressive competition," and not for any lessening or probable lessening of competition.[87] Clearly, any additional comment concerning the economic irrationality of this Supreme Court decision would be superfluous.

THE PROCTER & GAMBLE–CLOROX CASE (1967)[88]

Because the history of the Procter & Gamble–Clorox affair is extremely complicated, a short summary of the major legal issues might be helpful. Procter & Gamble (referred to as Procter hereafter) purchased Clorox in August 1957; the FTC issued a complaint against the merger in September 1957; after 14 months of hearings, an FTC hearing examiner found that the merger violated Section 7 and ordered divestiture on June 17, 1960; the FTC, on appeal by Procter, set aside the hearing examiner's original opinion because it was based on "treacherous conjecture"; a second hearing examiner's report of February 28, 1962 found against Procter and ordered divestiture of Clorox; the FTC supported the second examiner's report and issued a formal divestiture order on November 26, 1963; a Federal Appeals Court dismissed the FTC complaint against Procter in 1966 because the FTC decision was "not supported by substantial evidence"; and finally, on April 13, 1967, almost ten years after the case had begun, the U. S. Supreme Court reversed the Appeals Court and ordered Procter to divest itself of Clorox.

The Second Opinion of the FTC (1963)

Commissioner Elman wrote the FTC decision—and summarized some of the undisputed facts in the case.[89] Procter was one of the nation's fifty largest manufacturers with net sales of over $1 billion in 1957. Moreover, Procter was the nation's largest advertiser, and had spent $80 million on advertising, mostly television, in 1957. Prior to its purchase of Clorox, Procter had sold soaps, packaged detergents, and household cleaning agents, and many other low-priced, high-turnover consumer products, but had not sold liquid bleach. A stock swap valued at over $30 million with the Clorox Chemical Company in the summer of 1957, changed all that, however.

The Clorox Chemical Company, prior to 1957, was a relatively small firm ($12 million assets; $40 million sales), but one which had come to dominate the nation's production and sale of liquid bleach. Although liquid bleach was a standardized commodity (5¼ percent sodium hypochlorite, 94¾ percent water), unprotected by patent and made by upwards of 200 different firms, Clorox brand bleach represented almost 50 percent of industry sales by 1957. More importantly, Clorox was the only bleach selling on a national basis; with the exception of the Purex Company (Purex had about 15 percent of total bleach sales), almost all Clorox's competitors were smaller, regional, so-called down-cellar producers. Thus the Procter–Clorox merger united the nation's largest advertiser and the nation's largest liquid bleach firm.

The structure of the liquid bleach market prior to the merger first interested FTC Commissioner Elman. That market was "highly concentrated and oligopolistic" and one firm, Clorox, had almost half the industry sales. Clorox had created, probably through advertising, a "definite consumer preference" for its brand of bleach which allowed it to be sold at prices equal to or greater than competitive products.[90] It would be extremely difficult for a new firm to compete with Clorox, since "a new entrant into the bleach industry would have to advertise and operate from the outset on at least a broad regional scale, and consequently incur a very heavy initial investment for advertising."[91] But even if a competitor were able to accomplish the initial entry thrust, Clorox could not afford to "remain passive in the face of a significant encroachment upon its market position." In the resulting "competitive struggle," Clorox, by reason of substantial accumulated consumer preference, would undoubtedly have a "great advantage." Therefore Clorox, even prior to the merger with Procter, was a "significant impediment to new entry" and "an effective barrier to the growth or expansion . . . of existing rivals in the bleach industry, and thus an inhibitor of vigorous competitive activity."[92] Even without the Procter merger, the bleach industry was already concentrated "to a degree inconsistent with effectively competitive conditions."[93]

Elman then argued that the merger of Procter and Clorox would undoubtedly worsen competitive conditions in the bleach industry. This was likely, since there were "substantial cost savings and other advantages in advertising and sales promotion, especially in television advertising" available to Procter–Clorox.[94] Supposedly, the maximum-volume discounts in advertising amounted to 25–30 percent for network television; magazine, newspaper, and radio volume discounts were equally substantial. Even worse for competition (again, read "competitors"), the Clorox advertising could be placed in better time slots, and selectively shown in areas of the country where Clorox faced particularly intense competition.[95] In addition, the economies obtainable from joint promotions and the more efficient use of Procter's large sales force "would in all likelihood substantially increase Clorox's already great market power."[96] This market power could presumably be applied against retailers to obtain more valuable shelf space, and might even support tie-in and full-line forcing agreements with other Procter products. In short, the overall effect of Procter in the bleach market would be to enhance the already considerable power of Clorox.

Procter's size advantages were also allegedly crucial in another area—pricing. Elman stated that only a firm with "ample reserves" could offer merchants the "price concessions" needed to gain increased shelf space.[97] And

since Procter was a multi-product firm, it might be able to offer such concessions and engage in systematic underpricing to the detriment of its single
product rivals. Even worse, if local price cutting flared, the smaller, single-
product rivals, short on reserves, would be in a precarious position: "In a price
fight to the finish, Procter, whose aggregate scale of operations and fiscal resources dwarf the entire liquid bleach industry, can hardly be bested."[98] Since
the "appropriate standpoint for appraising the merger is, then, that of
Clorox's rivals and of the firms that might contemplate entering the liquid
bleach industry," the FTC was forced to conclude that the Procter–Clorox
merger had "increased the power of Clorox, by dominating its competitors
. . . discouraging new entry . . . and foreclosing effective competition in the
industry."[99]

Elman granted that the merger restrained competition in the bleach industry; but was a substantial lessening of competition probable? He noted that
the Procter–Clorox merger was not a horizontal or vertical combination, and
that the "ready crutch of percentages" common to all such cases was not to
be available in this one. Therefore, other methods that were "non-percentile
and non-quantitative—of roughly, but fairly, estimating the substantiality of
a merger's probable adverse effect on competition in the relevant market"
had to be discovered.[100] He then went on to suggest five criteria that would
substitute for "percentage ratios" in this product-extension or conglomerate
merger case:

> (1) the relative disparity in size and strength as between Procter and the largest
> firms in the bleach industry; (2) the excessive concentration in the industry at
> the time of the merger, and Clorox's dominant position in the industry; (3) the
> elimination, brought about by merger, of Procter as a potential competitor of
> Clorox; (4) the position of Procter in other markets; and (5) the nature of the
> "economies" enabled by the merger.[101]

Most of Commissioner Elman's discussion of the size disparity issue is a virtual replay of his previous comments on the effects of the Procter–Clorox
merger on competition; the only difference is the inclusion of the word "substantial" in his remarks. For example, we are told that Procter's size would
realize "substantial cost savings which impart a substantial competitive advantage to the acquired firm."[102] The most important effect of the size disparity, however, would be on the merger activity of the smaller firms:

> The remaining firms may now be motivated to seek affiliation by merger with
> giant companies. The practical tendency of the instant merger, then, is to
> transform the liquid bleach industry into an arena of big business competition
> only, with the few small firms that have not disappeared through merger even-
> tually falling by the wayside, unable to compete with their giant rivals.[103]

But this "transformation" was the essence of the Congressional concern in amending the Clayton Act in 1950. Nothing, therefore, could be more relevant than the likely effect of this merger on concentration in the bleach industry generally. Although bigness was not to be condemned per se, and although disparity of size was not to be relevant in every merger case, it was certainly condemnable and relevant in this one.[104] It would "eliminate virtually all possibility of an eventual movement toward deconcentration in the liquid bleach industry," and that was sufficient to find against this particular merger.[105]

Another crucial element in the argument against Procter was that the merger eliminated Procter as a potential competitor of Clorox in the bleach industry. Prior to the merger, Elman declared, "Procter was not only a likely prospect for new entry into the bleach market, it was virtually the only such prospect"; the merger, therefore, removed a substantial competitive threat.[106] It destroyed one of the "last factors tending to preserve a modicum of competitive pricing . . . in the liquid bleach industry." Since Procter's potential effect on Clorox's pricing policies no longer existed, the merger tended to reduce competition substantially.

Procter's "market power" in related markets and industries was also a legitimate factor in appraising the competitive effects of the merger according to Commissioner Elman. Procter was unquestionably able to subsidize Clorox's activities with profits from other products if it chose to do so.[107] But even if it chose not to do so, the "psychological response" of Clorox's competitors to Procter's "prowess as a competitor gains an added, *even sinister dimension*" in terms of the impact of the merger on competition.[108] Procter could, presumably, frighten off competition by its very presence; certainly no smaller bleach firms would dare do battle with such a powerful, multi-product combination.

Finally, a merger "so productive of efficiencies" would undoubtedly heighten the barriers to new entry into the bleach industry.[109] Since the explicit concern of the Congress was with the competitive effects of merger, and not necessarily with efficiency, economies and efficiencies were certainly not to be determining in any merger case. In fact, to the extent that economies and efficiencies made it difficult for other firms to compete, they would actually reduce competition and not, therefore, be in the consumers' interest. Elman stated the matter as follows:

A merger that results in increased efficiency of production, distribution or marketing may, in certain cases, increase the vigor of competition in the relevant market. But the cost savings made possible by the instant merger serve, we have seen, not to promote competition, but only to increase the barriers to new entry into the relevant market, and thereby impair competition . . . while we do not doubt that marketing economies, including those of advertising and sales promotion, are as socially desirable as economies in production and physical distribution, there does come a point 'at which product differentiation ceases to promote welfare and becomes wasteful, or mass advertising loses its informative aspect and merely entrenches market leaders.' We think that point has been reached in the household liquid bleach industry. In short, *the kind of 'efficiency' and 'economy' produced by this merger is precisely the kind that*—in the short as well as the long run—*hurts, not helps, a competitive economy and burdens, not benefits the consuming public.*[110]

Although the post-acquisition evidence was "entitled to little weight," it did tend to confirm, in Elman's view, the FTC analysis of the merger. Clorox's share of the liquid bleach market had increased from 48.8 percent in 1957 to 51.5 percent in 1961.[111] To remove the anticompetitive effects of the merger on the bleach industry, a divestiture of Clorox from Procter was necessary; it was so ordered.[112]

Comment on the FTC Statement

Since the Appeals Court and Supreme Court decisions to follow are based almost completely on this Federal Trade Commission decision, it might be appropriate to examine and critically analyze some of the arguments made above. Commissioner Elman's first significant point in this case was to argue that advertising created "barriers to entry" in the bleach industry and that this would effectively deter new entrants. He emphasized that the Clorox company was the only truly national producer, and that it would be difficult for any firm, particularly any new firm, to compete with Clorox on a national scale, since advertising expenditures were so crucial to success in this industry. Since Clorox, even prior to the merger, spent more on advertising than anyone else, and since a Procter–Clorox combination was the largest potential bleach advertising combination in the economy, it was clear to Elman that "the industry was barricaded to new entry."[113]

But logic and the facts in the case bely the FTC arguments completely. Household bleach was a fairly standardized item, easily produced, and unprotected by patent. Since it was a relatively heavy product and had a relatively low price-per-unit of weight, effective competition was always limited to about a 300-mile radius from the point of actual production. One did not have to be some sort of "national" seller to be able to compete with Clorox or anyone else in this industry. Competition always takes place in particular markets for particular customers, and individual bleach markets were actively competitive, with over 200 firms vying for the consumer dollar. In addition, a high percentage of liquid bleach was sold in supermarkets under a store's own label. Unless Clorox was required to have the same competitor in different markets, whether one was a "national producer" had nothing at all to do with rivalrous competition in the marketplace.

Elman also made the usual market-structure error with respect to competition in the bleach industry: He moved directly from the fact that concentration ratios were high in the bleach industry, to some negative and rather dismal conclusions concerning competition in that industry. But where in this case is the slightest bit of empirical information that would allow a conclusion that competition in the bleach industry was, say, less vigorous in 1957 than it had been in 1951? Or in 1941? Had there not been substantial market turnover? Had outputs of bleach been restrained and prices increased as a consequence? Had Clorox engaged in successful predatory price cutting in the bleach market? Was Clorox, in fact, suppressing competitors, consumers, or the competitive process, in an intelligible way? What information, beside raw structural concentration ratios, would allow the conclusion that competition in the liquid bleach industry had all but been extinguished as the FTC inferred, and that the Procter merger would be the last nail in the competitive coffin? Since absolutely no proof that competition had been extinguished was offered by the FTC, is it reasonable to assume that no such proof existed? Apparently the "inevitable inferences" of the market structure approach to competition worked their mysterious hocus-pocus in still another antitrust case.

The Federal Trade Commission could never really make up its mind on the pricing dangers inherent in the merger of Procter and Clorox. On the one hand, the commissioners argued that the substitution of Procter for Clorox would lend further rigidities to an already oligopolistic industry, and would tend to eliminate what little price competition remained in the industry.[114] On the other hand, they argued that the substitution of Procter for Clorox would tend to create a situation of "extreme pricing flexibility available only to a firm with ample reserves."[115] With its typical disregard for consistency, the FTC argued that both pricing practices were likely, and would tend to reduce competition substantially.

The latter pricing policy, as might be expected, was the greater competitive danger. It would allow "cross-subsidization" from Procter's other product markets and allow Procter to subsidize Clorox's activities in the bleach industry. As explained earlier in the chapter, however, such inferences depend on some crucial assumptions. Where, for example, did Procter possess the "monopolistic advantage" to fund such subsidization? The FTC assumed, again mistakenly, that its casual reference to the fact that Procter was a "large" firm, and possessed high "market shares" in other product lines would be enough to demonstrate that the company earned monopoly profits that might fund subsidization.[116] It should be apparent, however, that if simple market-structure assumptions do not allow accurate inferences about

competition in the bleach industry (where at least some additional information was provided), they can hardly allow accurate inferences with respect to
competition in Procter's other markets (where no information whatever was
provided). Again, all the FTC's inferences were based on simple structural
assumptions in this case.

One of the most novel and telling aspects of the FTC decision was the
"potential competition" thesis: Procter lessened competition in the bleach industry, since by its merger with Clorox, it removed itself as an independent
competitive threat. Since we have already commented upon this issue, it will
suffice to indicate here that it was not established that Procter was a likely
entrant into the bleach business, nor—as the FTC boldly stated—"virtually
the only such prospect" for entry. There was no evidence whatever in the
FTC account that would lead inevitably to the conclusion that Procter was a
likely entrant. The only mention of Procter's plans in the FTC decision was a
statement to the effect that Procter, after a two-year study, had decided *not* to
enter the bleach industry.[117] Are we to infer that they were a potential competitor because they had decided not to enter the bleach industry?

Why the FTC believed Procter to be virtually the only prospect for entry
was never explained. Why weren't Colgate-Palmolive, Lever Brothers, B.T.
Babbit, or any number of established firms that made household products to
be considered potential competitors? Were not these firms as likely to enter
the bleach industry as Procter? In fact, why weren't any of America's industrial giants to be considered potential competitors? Weren't they "potential"
enough? When introducing one "potential" competitor—Procter—the FTC
should have been prepared to admit that there could have been dozens of
other potential competitors. That the number of potential competitors was
reduced by one (and that one became an active competitor in the bleach industry), therefore, certainly cannot lead to the FTC conclusion that competition in the bleach industry was substantially lessened because Procter bought
Clorox.

The most embarrassing part of the FTC decision concerns Commissioner
Elman's discussion of the trade-restraining possibilities of "economies and efficiencies." We are repeatedly told that cost savings achievable from the consolidation will only increase the bleach industry's barriers, and will thus impair competition. Relying heavily on Professor Joel Dirlam's notion that
product differentiation and advertising beyond a certain point is "wasteful"
and merely entrenches market leaders,[118] and on the FTC's belief that it had
discovered that certain point, Commissioner Elman boldly asserted that any
further economy and efficiency would burden, not benefit the consuming
public.[119]

But how had the FTC come to its decision on this crucial issue? What was
that certain point, and how did the FTC know that it had been reached or

exceeded in this case? Were they to be the judge of what product differentiation was wasteful? In a free market, the concept of what is "wasteful" is relevant to voluntary consumer preference. Since consumer demand determines the priorities for the use of scarce economic resources, consumers determine what product differentiation they consider wasteful and not wasteful. If they have free choice, they will tend to support just that degree of product differentiation that they desire. To assert that product differentiation is wasteful in spite of apparent consumer preference is to substitute one's own preferences for those of the consumer's in the marketplace. Professor Dirlam and the Federal Trade Commission should at least be honest enough to admit that they are speaking for themselves and not for the consumers of bleach.

Economies and efficiencies in production, distribution, or marketing are never to be regretted, and successful product differentiation is never wasteful. The thrust of economic activity in a free market is to produce whatever consumers value most highly, and at the lowest cost, thereby economizing on scarce factors of production. To cripple this competitive process because certain competitors might find it difficult, or because certain economic experts are confident that economies or differentiations past some arbitrary point are wasteful, is to strike at the heart of efficiency in the name of defending and protecting it.

The entire FTC decision is the logical culmination of a long series of cases where economies and efficiencies have been suspect. Here, of course, they are more than just suspect; they are blatantly condemned, since they would create regrettable burdens that the public would have to bear should the merger be allowed. No hypothetical decision that this author might invent could better illustrate the argument of this volume that antitrust theory and policy is fundamentally misguided.

Finally, the most ironic part of the entire issue with respect to cost savings, particularly advertising economies, is that they may not have been achievable after all. The essence of the FTC arguments concerning barriers to entry was that the smaller bleach firms (even Purex) would be at a severe disadvantage in purchasing network advertising time as compared with Procter–Clorox. Yet David Blank has argued that in reality no such disadvantages actually existed.[120] He has charged that the FTC, like some scholars in similar studies, unquestionably accepted the "book prices" for advertising time, rather than the actual transactions prices for such advertising time. From Blank's analysis, it is clear that there was little if any price advantage for the large buyers; if anything, the larger buyers may have had to pay higher rates per unit of time than smaller buyers. Thus still another FTC case had been built around some fundamental assumptions that turn out, upon analysis, to be incorrect. Is there any salvageable theory or fact left in this case?

The Court of Appeals Decision

Much of the criticism related above concerning the FTC decision in the *Procter* case is certainly not original. A good share of it can be found in a reading of the Appeals Court decision of 1966 which reversed the FTC divestiture order.[121]

Chief Judge Weick of the Appeals Court first reviewed the circumstances of the FTC proceedings. He emphasized the fact that the first FTC ruling on the Procter merger had set aside an initial hearing examiner's decision, because "the evidence was insufficient to support a finding of illegality"; the remand and rehearing was for the sole purpose of taking post-acquisition evidence in the matter.[122] Yet, surprisingly, the second FTC decision (Commissioner Elman's decision), while it admitted that there had been no dramatic change in market structure or behavior in the post-merger market, dismissed the relevance of such information and found against Procter's purchase of Clorox. The second FTC decision, therefore, was based solely on a record that the first FTC decision "had ruled insufficient to support a finding of illegality."

But was there any substantial evidence to support the FTC's second decision? Judge Weick thought not. In the first place, Weick argued, there was just no evidence that Procter planned to engage in the manufacture or distribution of liquid bleach prior to the Clorox merger, as the FTC had mistakenly assumed.[123] The "potential competitor" hypothesis was based on "mere possibility and conjecture," and not on any supportable facts.

> Household liquid bleach is an old product; Procter is an old company. If Procter were on the brink it is surprising that it never lost its balance and fell in during the many years in which such bleach was on the market. It had never threatened to enter the market.[124]

Second, the Appeals Court rejected the FTC notion that Procter was virtually the only potential competitor, and that the barriers to entry surrounding the liquid bleach industry made new entry impossible. Certainly a moderately sized firm like Clorox would not deter

> large companies like Lever Brothers and Colgate-Palmolive Peet Co. (Procter's largest competitors) from entering the field on a national basis if they concluded that the profits were sufficiently attractive to justify the expenditure required.[125]

In addition, there were several other large firms (Monsanto Chemical, Diamond Alkali Company) that might have either entered the industry independently or combined in a conglomerate merger to produce bleach. And finally, the fact that there were upwards of two hundred smaller producers of bleach "would not seem to indicate anything unhealthy about the market conditions."[126]

Judge Weick next turned to the issue of possible economies that were likely to accrue from the merger. There certainly were possible cost savings in marketing and advertising, but the court was not overly impressed with their size, nor with their probable effect on competition in the bleach industry. That some economies might be effected from a merger otherwise lawful was insufficient reason to condemn such a consolidation.

The court was also not impressed with the "sinister" aspects of Clorox's market power, nor with the market power of the Procter–Clorox combination. Clorox-brand bleach was an excellent product with a high degree of quality control; its ability to get "shelf space" was clearly a function of the corresponding "great consumer demand" for the product. Procter, on the other hand, had never engaged in predatory practices, and the singular example of a "price war" offered by the FTC only proved that the Procter–Clorox combination would retaliate to meet the competitive price thrusts of other firms.[127] Nothing in either the history of Clorox or Procter, therefore, could substantiate the "sinister" market power assumptions of the FTC.

Finally, all the FTC conjecture of what might happen to competitors and consumers was belied by the post-acquisition evidence on what did happen. There had been no important change in market shares, and Clorox's rivals were selling "substantially more bleach for more money than prior" to the merger.[128] Certainly such evidence, virtually ignored by the Commission, "does not prove the anticompetitive effects of the merger." The Appeals Court set aside the FTC divestiture order and remanded the case to the District Court with instructions to dismiss the entire matter. The FTC, however, appealed the decision to the Supreme Court.

The Supreme Court Decision

Mr. Justice Douglas delivered the unanimous opinion of the Supreme Court in the *Procter–Clorox* case on April 11, 1967.[129] After sympathetically reviewing the FTC's major hypothesis, Douglas concluded that the Court of Appeals had "misapprehended the standards for its review."[130] That court, it will be remembered, had noted (but only as a final point) that the post-acquisition evidence did not prove that the Procter–Clorox merger had any anticompetitive effects. But Justice Douglas argued that no such proof of anticompetitive effects was required in Section 7 cases. Since the Act dealt with "probabilities" and not with "certainties," no "manifestation" of anticompetitive power was necessary for conviction.[131]

But was it even probable that competition would be substantially lessened because of the merger? The Supreme Court thought that it was, for apparently the same reasons as the FTC had suggested and the Appeals Court had rejected. Justice Douglas merely repeated the unsubstantiated FTC arguments that Procter's advertising economies would raise entry barriers, and that Procter's size would "dissuade the smaller firms from aggressively competing."[132] He also drearily repeated the "potential competition" hypothesis that Procter was the most likely entrant, that the FTC evidence clearly supported such a conclusion (!), and that the merger, therefore, eliminated the potential competition of the acquiring firm.[133] Accordingly, the Court of Appeals decision was reversed, and the original FTC decision to divest was sustained.

Justice Harlan's concurring opinion in the *Procter* case was a serious attempt to formulate some standards for judging the legality of product-extension and conglomerate mergers. Unfortunately, most of Harlan's suggested standards are founded on traditional market-structure assumptions. Harlan did, however, maintain a healthy degree of skepticism about "the state of our economic knowledge," and two of his standards certainly substantiate this skepticism. His four suggested standards are reproduced below:

> First, the decision can rest on an analysis of *market structure* without resort to evidence of post merger anticompetitive behavior. Second, the operation of the premerger market must be understood as the foundation of successful analysis. The responsible agency may presume that the market operates in accord with *generally accepted principles of economic theory* but the presumption must be open to the challenge of alternative operation formulations. Third, if it is reasonably probable that there will be a *change in structure* which will allow the exercise of substantially greater market power, then a *prima facie* case has been made out under Section 7. Fourth, where the case against the merger rests on the probability of increased market power, the companies may attempt to prove that there are countervailing economies reasonably probable which should be weighted against the adverse effects.[134]

Harlan's standards for conglomerate mergers still rest heavily upon "generally accepted principles of economic theory"; that is, on the market-structure approach to competition. Market structure changes create market power and a *prima facie* case against any merger. If the increase in market power is probable, however, evidence of economies and efficiencies may be introduced to countervail the "adverse" effects of the merger. Thus, Harlan closed the *Procter* case with a call for a much watered down rule-of-reason approach in conglomerate merger cases.

THE INTERNATIONAL TELEPHONE AND TELEGRAPH CASE (1970)

A reasonably significant test of the government's full arsenal of conglomerate theories is *United States v. International Telephone and Telegraph.*[135] The

Department of Justice had at first sought a preliminary injunction to prevent the merger of ITT (ninth largest industrial corporation in 1969) with Grinnell Corporation (286th largest industrial corporation in 1969) and, failing this, sued in District Court (Connecticut) to divest the companies. Judge Timbers, however, ruled against the government on every important economic and legal issue of substance, and dismissed the entire complaint.

Judge Timbers first noted that it was "well settled" law that the acquisition of a "dominant competitor"in an oligopolistic market by a much larger company violated Section 7 of the Clayton Act, since it provided "marketing and promotional competitive advantages" that were likely to further entrench market position.[136] The court, however, was not persuaded that Grinnell was a dominant competitor in its market "within the recognized meaning of that term in the antitrust field."[137]

Grinnell, to be sure, was an important national supplier of automatic sprinkler devices and systems, power piping (piping used in utility power plants) and pipe hangers. But its market positions were hardly overwhelming. In sprinkler systems, for instance, Grinnell was the "leading" installer in the country, but its share of the national market was only 20 percent.[138] Even more to the point, Timbers argued, its market share had declined dramatically in the five years prior to the acquisition, indicating (to him) a healthy state of competition—not "dominance"—and the absence of significant barriers to entry into the market.[139]

Timbers also rejected arguments by the government that Grinnell would gain unreasonable competitive advantages because of its association with ITT and another ITT subsidiary, The Hartford Fire Insurance Company. For instance, the government claimed that ITT–Grinnell could offer additional products in its automatic sprinkler line and even begin to engage in so-called package or system selling.[140] Further, it was alleged that an association with Hartford Fire might give Grinnell a competitive advantage, since Hartford agents could provide "leads" for sprinkler business to Grinnell, and even recommend Grinnell sprinklers to their customers.[141]

Timbers reasoned, however, that neither of these consequences could be reasonably expected to occur. Package or system selling of sprinklers, plumbing, heating, and air conditioning was not the accepted procedure in the industry, since it offered no real economic advantages.[142] Further, there was no evidence whatever that Grinnell intended to engage in such system selling. And finally, even if such system selling were to occur, the court was unable to determine how Grinnell would gain a substantial competitive advantage over its competition.[143]

The Hartford Fire affiliation was equally benign, according to Timbers. Sprinkler systems were awarded overwhelmingly on the basis of competitive bidding and not on "recommendations" of insurance companies or agents.[144] More importantly, Grinnell could not afford to "abuse" its association with

Hartford since Hartford's share of the "sprinkled risk" market was but 2.4 percent. Any alliance between Hartford and Grinnell "would cause other insurance companies to be less friendly with Grinnell and less inclined to furnish leads to, or to make recommendations of, Grinnell."[145] Thus, the court reasoned that economic self-interest and competition neutralized the Grinnell–Hartford Fire connection.

On a related issue, the government had argued that Grinnell's market position would be further enhanced through "reciprocal" deals caused by ITT's large purchasing power.[146] ITT, allegedly, would be able to pressure suppliers to deal with Grinnell to the detriment of Grinnell's less formidable competitors. Timbers ruled, however, that the government's fears concerning reciprocity were totally without foundation.

In the first place, a good share of the sprinkler installations were accomplished for nonindustrial customers that could not, presumably, be pressured by ITT.[147] Secondly, the bulk of the sprinkler contracts were awarded on the basis of competitive bid which "minimized reciprocity."[148] Finally, and perhaps most importantly, ITT was organized into distinct "profit centers" which operated independently of each other.[149] The success of each unit depended upon how profitably its operations were managed, and this profit-center approach ruled against noncompetitive reciprocity. Timbers noted, too, that the government had "adduced no evidence that any ITT unit has ever obtained business as a result of reciprocity or reciprocity effect."[150]

Finally, Timbers sharply rejected the government's novel claim that increasing concentration in the economy somehow established that anticompetitive consequences would appear in "undesignated individual lines of commerce." On the contrary, Section 7 mandated that the courts were to deal with the anticompetitive effects of mergers within the context of specific product and geographic markets. To broaden the explicit meaning of Section 7 was to engage in "judicial legislation"; but this the court "emphatically" refused to do.[151]

CONCLUSIONS

It is not obvious from our review of these cases, that antitrust law makes any more sense in the merger area than elsewhere. The business organizations involved in these mergers were not shown to be restraining output or increasing prices, and they were not shown to be engaging in practices destructive of any competitive process. Indeed, the most likely inference from these cases is that the challenged mergers were themselves part of an intensely competitive process. Yet the courts' implicit acceptance of atomistic competition and the market-structure approach to competition led them, inevitably, to condemn most of these mergers and acquisitions. And although the radical position adopted in *Von's* and *Procter–Clorox* may have been moderated somewhat in recent cases, the breadth and depth of this moderation (given the irrationalities in this area) is hardly sufficient reason for any general optimism.[152]

NOTES

1. Calculated from statistics given in Federal Trade Commission, *Current Trends in Merger Activity, 1969* (March 1970), p. 9.
2. Mergers involving acquired firms with assets of $10 million or more. See Federal Trade Commission, *Current Trends in Merger Activity: 1968* (March 1969), pp. 1–7.
3. *Ibid.*
4. Federal Trade Commission, *Economic Report on Corporate Mergers*, Hearings on Economic Concentration, Subcommittee on Antitrust and Monopoly, U.S. Senate, 91st Cong., 1st Sess. (Washington 1969), p. 63.
5. Ralph L. Nelson, *Merger Movements in American Industry* (Princeton, N.J.: Princeton University Press, 1959), p. 60.
6. Samuel R. Reid, *Mergers, Managers, and the Economy* (New York: McGraw-Hill, 1968), p. 56.
7. For an excellent review of the legislative history of Section 7, see *Brown Shoe Company v. United States*, 370 U.S. 294 (1962) at pp. 311–323.
8. Turner's article, "The Antitrust Chief Replies," is reprinted in Edwin Mansfield, ed., *Monopoly Power and Economic Performance*, 4th ed. (New York: W. W. Norton & Co., 1974), p. 190.
9. Irrational or not, the judicial approach to antitrust, and particularly to mergers, has been thoroughly structural. See Richard E. Low, *Modern Economic Organization* (Homewood, Ill.: Richard D. Irwin, 1970), p. 48. Also see Peter Asch, *Economic Theory and the Antitrust Delimma* (New York: John Wiley & Sons, 1970), pp. 317–321.
10. The courts have been explicitly hostile to "economies" associated with merger. See *Brown Shoe Co. v. United States*, 370 U.S. 294; and *Federal Trade Commission v. Procter & Gamble Co.*, 386 U.S. 586.
11. For an excellent discussion of this issue, see Eugene Singer, *Antitrust Economics* (Englewood Cliffs, N.J.: Prentice-Hall, 1968), pp. 262–266.
12. For three different views on this issue of definitions, see Betty Bock, *Antitrust Issues in Conglomerate Acquisitions* (The National Industrial Conference Board, Studies in Business Economies, No. 110, 1969), p. 8; Donald F. Turner, "Conglomerate Mergers and Section 7 of the Clayton Act," *Harvard Law Review*, Vol. 78, No. 7 (May 1965), p. 1315; and John C. Narver, *Conglomerate Mergers and Market Competition* (Berkeley: University of California Press, 1967).

13. Editors of Fortune, *The Conglomerate Commotion* (New York: The Viking Press, 1970), p. 81.

14. Corwin Edwards, "The)Large Conglomerate Firm: A Critical Appraisal," Edwin Mansfield's *op. cit.*, p. 110. The Federal Trade Commission has held this position since at least 1949. See Narver, *op. cit.*, p. 39. For an excellent dissenting view, see L. G. Goldberg, "The Effect of Conglomerate Mergers on Competition," *Journal of Law and Economics*, Vol. 16 (April 1973), pp. 137–58.

15. Edward McCreary, Jr., and Walter Guzzardi, Jr., "Reciprocity: A Customer Is a Company's Best Friend," *Fortune*, Vol. 71, No. 6 (June 1965), pp. 180–182, 192, 194.

16. Robert H. Bork, "Antitrust in Dubious Battle," *Fortune*, Vol. 80 (September 1969), p. 160. See also J. Lorie and P. Halpern, "Conglomerates: The Rhetoric and the Evidence," *Journal of Law and Economics*, Vol. 13 (April 1970), p. 149, esp. pp. 150–153.

17. See John M. Blair, "Conglomerate Mergers—Theory and Congressional Intent," in J. Fred Weston and Sam Peltzman, *Public Policy Toward Mergers* (Pacific Palisades, Calif.: Goodyear Publishing Company, Inc., 1969), pp. 186–188.

18. Even Donald F. Turner has admitted that there is no empirical evidence to verify the thesis that large firms, particularly conglomerates, engage in predatory pricing practices. See Turner, "Conglomerate Mergers and Section 7 of the Clayton Act." *Harvard Law Review*, p. 1340. See also Ronald H. Koller II, "The Myth of Predatory Pricing: An Empirical Study," *Antitrust Law and Economics Review*, Vol. 4, No. 4 (Summer 1971), pp. 105–123.

19. Some economists have tried—unsuccessfully in my view—to determine under what conditions "predatory" practices should be permitted or made illegal. See Phillip Areeda and Donald Turner, "Predatory Pricing and Related Practices Under Section 2 of the Sherman Act," *Harvard Law Review*, Vol. 88 (1975), pp. 697–733. For a criticism of their position, see Oliver E. Williamson, "Predatory Pricing: A Strategic and Welfare Analysis," *Yale Law Journal*, Vol. 87 (1977), pp. 284–340.

20. *Brown Shoe Company v. United States*, 370 U.S. 294 (1962). For an excellent economic analysis of this case, see John L. Peterman, "The Brown Shoe Case," *Journal of Law and Economics*, Vol. 18 (April 1975), pp. 81–146.

21. *United States v. Brown Shoe Company*, 179 F. Supp. 721.

22. *Ibid.*, p. 741.

23. *Ibid.*, p. 737.

24. *Ibid.*

25. *Ibid.*, pp. 737–738.

26. *Ibid.*, p. 738.

27. *Ibid.*, p. 739.

28. *Ibid.*, p. 740.

29. *Ibid.*, p. 735.
30. *Ibid.*, p. 741.
31. 370 U.S. 294.
32. *Ibid.*, p. 326.
33. *Ibid.*, pp. 330–331.
34. *Ibid.*, p. 332.
35. *Ibid.* (emphasis added).
36. *Ibid.*, p. 333.
37. *Ibid.*, p. 334.
38. *Ibid.*, pp. 334–343.
39. *Ibid.*, pp. 343–344.
40. *Ibid.*, p. 344.
41. *Ibid.*
42. *Ibid.*, p. 357.
43. *Ibid.*, p. 366.
44. *Ibid.*, p. 372.
45. *Ibid.*, p. 372–373.
46. There were, however, almost 500 more shoe manufacturers in 1947 than there had been in 1937; the Court failed to mention this! See *United States v. United Shoe Machinery Corp.* 110 F. Supp. 295, at p. 301.
47. 370 U.S. 374.
48. It should also be remembered that no account was taken of foreign manufacturers.
49. 370 U.S. 374.
50. 179 F. Supp. 738 and 370 U.S. 304.
51. 179 F. Supp. 739.
52. See "Proceedings of Section 7, Subcommittee A.B.A.," *The Antitrust Bulletin*, Vol. VIII, No. 2 (March–April 1963), p. 249.
53. 370 U.S. 371.
54. *United States v. Continental Can Company et al.*, 378 U.S. 441.
55. *United States v. Aluminum Company of America*, 377 U.S. 271.
56. 378 U.S., pp. 470–477.
57. 377 U.S., p. 281.
58. *Ibid.*, pp. 285–286.
59. *Ibid.*, p. 287.
60. *Federal Trade Commission v. Consolidated Foods Corporation* 380 U.S. 592.
61. 62 FTC 960.
62. *Consolidated Foods Corporation v. F.T.C.*, 329 F. 2d 623.
63. *Ibid.*, pp. 625–626.

64. *Ibid.*, p. 626.
65. *Ibid.*, pp. 626–627.
66. 380 U.S. 592.
67. *Ibid.*, pp. 596–597.
68. *Ibid.*, p. 598.
69. *Ibid.*, p. 604.
70. *Ibid.*
71. *Ibid.*, p. 605. (A firm by the name of Gilroy Foods, Inc., had entered the industry in 1959.)
72. *Ibid.*, p. 608.
73. See discussion in Singer, *op. cit.*, p. 233.
74. *United States v. Von's Grocery Company*, 384 U.S. 270.
75. *Ibid.*, pp. 272–273.
76. *Ibid.*, pp. 274–275.
77. *Ibid.*, 282–283.
78. *Ibid.*, p. 287.
79. *Ibid.*, p. 288.
80. *Ibid.*
81. *Ibid.*, p. 290.
82. *Ibid.*, p. 290.
83. *Ibid.*, pp. 292–294.
84. *Ibid.*, p. 295.
85. *Ibid.*, p. 296.
86. *Ibid.*, pp. 298–300.
87. *Ibid.*, p. 297.
88. *Federal Trade Commission v. Procter & Gamble Company*, 386 U.S. 568.
89. *In The Matter of the Procter & Gamble Company*, 63 FTC 1465.
90. *Ibid.*, p. 1562.
91. *Ibid.*
92. *Ibid.*, p. 1563.
93. *Ibid.*
94. *Ibid.*
95. *Ibid.*, p. 1564.
96. *Ibid.*, p. 1566.
97. *Ibid.*, pp. 1566–1567.
98. *Ibid.*, 1567.
99. *Ibid.*, p. 1569 (emphasis added).
100. *Ibid.*, pp. 1570–1571.
101. *Ibid.*, p. 1571.
102. *Ibid.*, p. 1572.

103. *Ibid.*, p. 1573.
104. *Ibid.*, p. 1574.
105. *Ibid.*, p. 1575.
106. *Ibid.*, p. 1578.
107. *Ibid.*, p. 1578.
108. *Ibid.*, p. 1579.
109. *Ibid.*, p. 1580.
110. *Ibid.*, pp. 1580–1581.
111. *Ibid.*, p. 1583.
112. *Ibid.*, p. 1585.
113. *Ibid.*, p. 1563.
114. *Ibid.*, p. 1575.
115. *Ibid.*, p. 1567 (emphasis added).
116. *Ibid.*, p. 1579.
117. *Ibid.*, p. 1541.
118. *Ibid.*, p. 1580.
119. *Ibid.*, p. 1581.
120. David M. Blank, "Television Advertising: The Great Discount Illusion, or Tonypandy Revisited," *Journal of Business,* Vol. 41 (January 1968), pp. 10–38. See also John L. Peterman, "The Clorox Case and the Television Rate Structures," *Journal of Law and Economics,* Vol. 11 (October 1968), pp. 321–432.
121. *Procter & Gamble v. Federal Trade Commission,* 358 F. 2d 74 (1966).
122. *Ibid.*, p. 78.
123. *Ibid.*, p. 80.
124. *Ibid.*, p. 83.
125. *Ibid.*, p. 80.
126. *Ibid.*
127. *Ibid.*, p. 82.
128. *Ibid.*
129. 386 U.S. 568 (1967).
130. *Ibid.*, p. 576.
131. *Ibid.*, p. 577.
132. *Ibid.*, pp. 578–579.
133. *Ibid.*, pp. 580–581.
134. *Ibid.*, pp. 589–599.
135. 324 F. Supp. 19 (1970).
136. *Ibid.*, p. 24.
137. *Ibid.*, p. 30.

138. *Ibid.*, p. 27.
139. *Ibid.*, p. 28.
140. *Ibid.*, p. 30.
141. *Ibid.*, p. 33.
142. *Ibid.*, pp. 31, 32.
143. *Ibid.*, p. 32.
144. *Ibid.*, p. 34.
145. *Ibid.*, p. 36.
146. *Ibid.*, p. 42.
147. *Ibid.*, p. 43.
148. *Ibid.*, p. 44.
149. *Ibid.*, p. 45.
150. *Ibid.*, p. 46.
151. *Ibid.*, p. 52.
152. *United States v. General Dynamics Corp.*, 415 U.S. 486 (1974).

CHAPTER NINE

The Antitrust Laws
and a Free Society

We are now in a position to review the major findings of this study. The most important conclusion is that the entire antitrust system—allegedly created to protect competition and increase consumer welfare—has worked, instead, to lessen business competition and lessen the efficiency and productivity associated with the free-market process. Like many other governmental interventions, antitrust has produced results that are far different from those that were allegedly intended.

The second general conclusion of this study is that these perverse economic consequences could have been predicted, since antitrust law has continued to rely primarily upon the static models of perfect competition and monopoly. These models (as we have demonstrated) are highly misleading in the antitrust area, and attempts to base antitrust judgments upon them have produced economically absurd cases with harmful social consequences. That these unfortunate consequences are now admitted by some practitioners is gratifying,[1] but this recent enlightenment in certain academic and legal circles is not yet general, and it is still far too little and far too late. Until academic economists and enforcement officials adopt a thoroughly process-oriented theory of competition—and recognize government intervention, and not the free market, as the source of monopoly power—antitrust policy will not have been sufficiently reformed.

If these two general conclusions are correct, then they tend to cast additional doubt upon the conventional explanation for the existence of antitrust in the United States. As we noted in Chapter 1, important scholars have maintained that the "sole purpose" of antitrust was and is to prevent an artificial output restriction and the subsequent enhancement of prices to consumers.[2] We have argued previously that there has always been some reason to doubt this "sole" purpose, particularly with respect to the Clayton Act, the Federal Trade Commission Act of 1914, the Antimerger Act of 1950, and especially—and most obviously—the Robinson-Patman Act of 1936. But it is even more apparent at the conclusion of this study to observe that no such "sole purpose" was in evidence in *any* of the classic antitrust cases reviewed. In each and every case the indicated corporations were engaging in an intensely competitive process; yet in each and every case, such behavior was condemned, by the FTC or by the Justice Department, as a "restraint of trade" and as an alleged violation of the antitrust laws. Serious doubts, therefore, must remain concerning the social purpose of antitrust and antitrust enforcement.

These suspicions as to the exact meaning of antitrust become even more disturbing when one turns to an examination of the *private* antitrust cases. In the vast majority of these private cases, it is perfectly clear that the legal concern is not monopoly or resource misallocation at all, but an obvious and blatant attempt by the plaintiff to restrain and restrict the competitive rivalry emanating from the more efficient defendant company. It is almost standard procedure—a literal cost of doing business—that successful corporations will be sued under the antitrust laws by their less-than-successful competitors. The relevant issue in such cases is never injury to consumers, but always "injury" to some competitor, so-called cut-throat competition, predatory practices, the advantages associated with some superior technology adopted by the defendant, and like-sounding complaints concerning the rigors of the competition process in a free marketplace.[3] Here, at last, we must applaud the honesty of the antitrust laws; in these private cases, there is no pretense at least that the interest that is being served here is the public interest. But, of course, say the supporters of antitrust policy, this is not what we intend (or what the Congress intends) for the antitrust laws generally.

Our suspicions concerning the alleged intent of antitrust policy are increased even further when it is realized that monopoly has always been associated with governmental entry restrictions such as licenses, quotas, tariffs, and prorationing laws. Such devices limit competition by law, injure consumers, shut out suppliers, and tend to reduce economic efficiency in the economy. But the bulk of this monopoly—the real monopoly in the system—is immune from antitrust prosecution and always has been. In short, we are asked to accept the idea that the government and the courts, concerned about the public interest effects of monopoly, have *unknowingly* (1) employed the antitrust laws against competitive firms taking competitive actions in open markets, and (2) protected and sheltered the actual monopolists in the industrial system with governmental privileges and total antitrust immunity. If this hypothesis concerning the meaning of the antitrust laws can be swallowed as reasonable truth, then a good part of this study has clearly been in vain.

It makes far more sense and requires a far smaller degree of faith to consider the revisionist notion that antitrust policy in America is a misleading myth that has served to draw public attention away from the actual process of monopolization that has been occurring throughout the economy. The general public has been deluded into believing that monopoly is a free-market problem, and that the government, through antitrust enforcement, is on the side of the "angels." The facts are entirely the opposite. Antitrust, therefore, whatever its intent, has served as a convenient cover for an insidious process of monopolization in the marketplace. Such is the deeper and more subtle meaning of antitrust policy.

This process of governmental monopolization has been well documented. There is now solid historical evidence that a number of American industries welcomed governmental intervention in an attempt to restrict and restrain competition, and in order to preserve positions of wealth and power within the industrial order. We have detailed that process within the petroleum industry (see Chapter 3), but a very similar historical process of business and government interventionism has also been in evidence in the railroad industry,[4] the airlines industry,[5] electrical power production and distribution,[6] medicine,[7] and in other industries. Leading executives, trade associations, and other influential business spokesmen have argued that "special" circumstances required that their particular industrial situation be spared the "perennial gale" of open competition. According to their perspective, open competition would have been "destructive", "unfair" and even "wasteful"; what was required was governmental regulation and entry restriction to create a more orderly market. Thus while the antitrust laws were blasting away at competitive firms in open markets, other business interests were quietly employing the power of government to achieve state-approved and state-sanctioned restrictions on competition. In short, antitrust has always been irrelevant to the actual monopoly problem in America.

THE ANTITRUST CRITICS

There is now a fairly important group of scholars within the antitrust and industrial organization area that appreciate most of the arguments reviewed in this volume, and the fact that antitrust enforcement has been something less than desirable from an economic perspective. Robert Bork and Ward Bowman from the Yale Law School have always been in the forefront of effective antitrust criticism, and both have authored book-length criticisms of antitrust theory and policy.[8] Likewise Donald Dewey has never been much of an antitrust enthusiast, while Simon Whitney has eloquently warned of the economic consequences of present antitrust policies.[9] Betty Bock of the National Industrial Conference Board has always been an active critic of specific antitrust policies.[10] And finally some of the most trenchant criticism of antitrust theory and policy has come from Yale Brozen, John McGee, Wesley J. Liebeler, Richard Posner, and Harold Demsetz. Demsetz has even admitted that if certain antitrust policies were continued, he would favor the outright repeal of the Sherman Act.[11]

There is evidence that these criticisms may have been partially responsible for some recent court decisions that have shown an awareness of the limitations of the market-structure approach to competition. Decisions such as *United States v. General Dynamics Corp.*[12] and especially *Continental T.V. v. GTE–Sylvania, Inc.*[13] would have been inconceivable thirty years ago (or even fifteen years ago), and the progress made—especially with respect to the importance of economic analysis and reasoning—is encouraging and, perhaps, reason for some optimism. Yet, as we will argue below, the antitrust battle is nowhere near being won, and it might be useful to speculate on some of the difficulties with the current criticism of antitrust policy.

One of the most important difficulties is that the critics—excepting the libertarian critics[14]—are not really objecting to antitrust in principle but only to antitrust in practice. The critics are not generally opposed to the very idea of antitrust regulation in a free society, but only to the specific irrationalities of many current enforcement policies. Some critics, for instance, believe that the current antimerger regulations seriously impede efficiency-producing consolidations, and thus reduce productivity and welfare. Yet, on the other hand, some of these very same critics of antitrust have strongly endorsed antitrust enforcement in the price-fixing and market division area. Indeed, they have called for the expenditure of more governmental resources in this area. Thus, some of the critics seem to believe that although antitrust is misguided in *some* areas, it could be made useful in still *other* areas and certainly should not be abandoned altogether.

There are several critical observations that can be made of such a position. The first is the strategic contention that any opposition to a public policy that is not, in fact, an opposition in principle is bound to be relatively ineffective. The entire antitrust establishment is committed in principle to antitrust, and to a sharp increase in both the depth and breadth of the antitrust enforcement effort. Anything less than an opposition in principle must end up by granting and conceding some of the premises and assumptions of the antitrust enthusiasts. Yet, as this study has argued, *none* of these premises or assumptions need be granted. Antitrust theory and antitrust policy (whatever that policy) is not intellectually respectable; moreover, from a civil liberties perspective, the laws and their enforcement are a gross travesty of justice. Therefore, we need not worry about being too extreme on this issue. Nothing less than an extreme opposition in principle to all antitrust law appears justified by the facts.

Even more importantly, however, the view held by some of the critics that certain antitrust policies can be rationally defended on efficiency grounds is dangerously naive. The efficiency standard that the critics would adopt is the very same efficiency standard embraced by the more knowledgeable antitrust enthusiasts, that is, the notion of efficiency associated with the static equilibrium models of competition and monopoly. But as we have argued previously, such notions of static efficiency are faulty and are based on theories of measurement and aggregation that are simply not legitimate. The vision of a rational antitrust policy depends almost entirely on the myths of "efficiency" and we should never want to put ourselves in the position (as critics of antitrust) of employing the faulty methodology of the opposition.

Social efficiency, if the expression has any meaning whatever, is to be associated with a society that allows full scope for free and voluntary exchange agreements. Social arrangements are efficient if they provide the widest opportunity for private plan fulfillment and private plan coordination.[15] A free society is both the necessary and the sufficient condition for efficient action and efficient resource allocation.

To attempt to prohibit certain merger agreements or price-fixing agreements in the name of enhancing social efficiency is a contradiction in terms. Such agreements *are* efficient since they represent explicit evidence of social coordination. To condemn or restrict such agreements in the name of efficiency is to employ that term in the restricted neoclassical manner, and in a way that must invite accusations of market failure and calls for regulation and state intervention. To accept the conventional notion of efficiency is to legitimize an antitrust enforcement based on additive notions of utility and cost and interpersonal utility comparisons that are totally inappropriate from our perspective. In short, the critics, though an important intellectual force in essentially the right direction, grant far too much in this crucial debate and, thus, weaken opposition to the antitrust juggernaut.

Another weakness in the critics' argument against antitrust is the general lack of appreciation of a revisionist historical perspective. Some of the critics assume that while current policies are misguided, antitrust in the older cases and back in the good old days was fruitful and even necessary. Antitrust had historical relevance it is assumed, but it is the increasingly complex nature of the business world today that makes current policies uncertain and even dangerous. Times change, some of the critics argue; policies that might have been rational and relevant in the past may not be rational and relevant today. Consequently, given this approach we could never be sure what new governmental antitrust policy might be "necessary" next month or next year to cope with some new manifestation of alleged market power.

In accepting the past rationality and relevance of antitrust, the critics knowingly or unknowingly ignore the information brought to light in this volume and in other revisionist works. Simply put, there was no "golden age" when monopolistic abuse was running rampant in a free market and when, accordingly, antitrust policy was magnificently relevant. Antitrust law has always been ambiguous, the theoretical foundations of antitrust theory have always been faulty, and the empirical "evidence" has always been nonexistent. Although the belief in some golden age of antitrust might be emotionally satisfying, and although it is consistent with the critics' position that antitrust is acceptable in principle, it is the ultimate in naiveté and deserves no support whatever.

Finally, most of the criticism of antitrust has not yet been directed at the fundamental assumptions of antitrust theory, that is, the atomistic theory of competition, and the market-structure/industrial organization paradigm. Almost all the critics, for instance, admit that present antimerger policies are misguided, and that potentially competitive situations that would realize economies for consumers are prevented by inappropriate antitrust rules and court decisions. But how far would the critics go with antitrust in the merger area, how would they rationally tell how far to go, and what would they be going toward?[16] Is a 46 percent market share competitive or monopolistic? How are we to know that there is market power with a merger that results in a 53 per cent market share? Can anyone take these arbitrary numbers seriously? What tests to measure competition would the critics devise? What is their particular vision of an ideally competitive market, or of an optimal allocation of resources? Would they really give up the idea of perfect competition as some sort of a welfare ideal, or would they simply attempt to make atomistic competition more "realistic," and market structure tests more "practical"? To refine and modify existing theories, however, is to work within the system of antitrust and to accept its most basic neoclassical premises. But it is the fundamental welfare premises of neoclassical theory that are the problem, and it is these premises that require challenging.

Most of the current criticisms of antitrust policy are important, therefore, but they are not fundamental. They accept the legitimacy of governmental intervention in a free-market system; they criticize the particular form of the intervention. They accept the antitrust laws (primarily the Sherman Act) as a legal bulwark against actual or potential monopolistic abuse; they criticize present merger guidelines or court interpretations of monopoly power, particularly in the area of corporate mergers. They tend to accept the idea that antitrust was relevant historically; yet they ignore the fact that there is little or no documentation to support that thesis. And finally, and most importantly, most of the critics refuse to challenge seriously the *sine qua non* of antitrust theory: the equilibrium models of neoclassical price theory. Apparently they realize that to challenge such models in any radical manner would be to undermine the entire rationale for governmental intervention in a market economy. And this the critics will not do or cannot do.

THE ANTITRUST ENTHUSIASTS

It would be incorrect to create the impression that the antitrust establishment is reeling from a frontal assault by its academic critics. Antitrust is still a very firmly entrenched public policy with wide support, both in the political and in the academic community. Most of the ideas of the critics have yet to even reach the primary textbooks in economics and industrial organization, much less reach and convince the general public or the Congress. The supporters of the antitrust philosophy—and those that would push for an extension and an expansion of antitrust enforcement—still command the high ground in this important public policy debate.[17]

Indeed, the antitrust movement has recently taken on a new intellectual enthusiasm since it has been adopted by those reformers who would radically restructure the industrial system and, indeed, the entire societal order. Ralph Nader's proposals for federal chartering and for "constitutionalizing" the large corporations have all contained generous amounts of antitrust medicine.[18] Nader and others are convinced that competition within oligopolistic industries is negligible, and that large corporations in concentrated industries hold and employ an arbitrary power to the detriment of consumers and the political process. To dissolve such aggregations of private power, employing existing law or new legislation, is the explicit goal of the new antitrust activists. Spectacular divestiture suits against major American corporations in concentrated industries would begin to fulfill these critics' vision of an appropriate antitrust policy in a democratic society.

But this approach to efficiency, concentration, and power is flawed, and is based on assumptions which are not rationally defensible. The critics of American business are right to be concerned about the manifestations of political power in society, but they are wrong to argue that monopoly power is to be associated with product differentiation or with concentration and market share. Nader, Green, and others, despite some promising early work,[19] have continued to blur the essential difference between private persuasion and government coercion, between efficiency as a barrier to entry and pernicious legal barriers, between power and production, and between economic and political accountability. Large corporations in open markets—regardless of their size—must earn their market positions each day through voluntary exchange. They are continuously accountable to consumers and owner-investors, and their fortunes depend upon their competitive performance.

There are, of course, business organizations that do benefit from the power to restrict entry and competition. This power, however, is not a function of product differentiation, or of advertising, or of the "technostructure," or of market concentration, but is a function of explicit favors and privileges obtained from government. The sole source of the monopoly power, and of the problem, is the state. Yet it is the very state that most of the critics of business (and supporters of antitrust) would expand and enlarge to suit their particular vision of the good society. Knowingly or unknowingly, the critics of big business would enhance the very institution, and the very relationships that are at the root of the social problem they claim to abhor. Either they are naively unaware of this paradox, or they hold a vision of society that is far different from the one they claim to support.[20]

The only principled and practical way to end monopoly power is to end it at its source. Government regulation, entry control, subsidization, *and antitrust*, are all manifestations of a governmental interventionist power that has been employed by private firms to private advantage and to the detriment of society. These manifestations cannot be justified from either a natural rights, utilitarian, or subjectivist perspective. In short, we must seek to end governmental interventionist power, including antitrust, and move to create a free and open society where individuals can fulfill their own vision of the good society.

NOTES

1. See *Business Week* (January 12, 1981), pp. 90–91.

2. Alan Stone, *Economic Regulation and the Public Interest: The Federal Trade Commission in Theory and Practice* (Ithaca, N.Y.: Cornell University Press, 1978), p. 24.

3. See, for instance, *Berkey Photo, Inc., v. Eastman Kodak Co.,* 603 R. 2d 263 (1979), or almost any of the private suits involving the International Business Machines Corporation.

4. Gabriel Kolko, *Railroads and Regulation: 1877–1916* (Princeton: Princeton University Press, 1965).

5. Charles J. Kelley, Jr., *The Sky's the Limit: The History of the Airlines* (New York: Coward McCann, 1963), p. 102.

6. Greg Jarrell, "The Demand for State Regulation by the Electric Utility Industry," *Journal of Law and Economics,* Vol. 21, No. 2 (October 1978), pp. 269–296.

7. Ronald Hamowy, "The Early Development of Medical Licensing Laws in the United States, 1875–1900," *Journal of Libertarian Studies,* Vol. 3, No. 1 (1979), pp. 73–119.

8. Robert Bork, *The Antitrust Paradox: A Policy at War with Itself* (New York: Basic Books, 1978); Ward Bowman, *Patents and Antitrust Law* (Chicago: University of Chicago Press, 1973). Their earlier coauthored assault upon antitrust was, "The Crisis in Antitrust," *Columbia Law Review,* Vol. 65 (1965), p. 363.

9. Donald Dewey, "The Economics of Antitrust: Science or Religion" in Richard

Low's, *The Economics of Antitrust* (Englewood Cliffs, N.J.: Prentice-Hall, 1968), pp. 61–73; Simon Whitney, "Antitrust Threats to the Market Economy," *The Intercollegiate Review* (January–February 1968), pp. 70–77.

10. See, for example, her *Antitrust Issues in Conglomerate Acquisitions: Studies in Business Economics*, No. 110 (New York: National Industrial Conference Board, 1969).

11. Excellent criticism by Brozen, McGee, Demsetz, and other economists can be found in Yale Brozen, ed., *The Competitive Economy: Selected Readings* (General Learning Press, 1975). See also H. Goldschmid, H. M. Mann, and J. F. Weston, eds., *Industrial Concentration: The New Learning* (Boston: Little, Brown and Company, 1974). (For Demsetz's explicit rejection of antitrust law, see esp. p. 235.) Finally Richard A. Posner's, *Antitrust Law: An Economic Perspective* (Chicago: University of Chicago Press, 1976), contains some excellent criticism of antitrust theory and cases.

12. 415 U.S. 486 (1974).

13. 433 U.S. 36 (1977).

14. Murray N. Rothbard, *Man, Economy and State*, Vol. 2 (Princeton, N.J.: D. Van Nostrand Company, Inc., 1962), p. 790.

15. Israel Kirzner, *Market Theory and the Price System* (Princeton, N.J.: D. Van Nostrand, Inc., 1963), pp. 34–45.

16. This problem is most obvious in the generally excellent *Antitrust Paradox*, and especially in Bork's treatment of large mergers. It is also evident in Posner, *op. cit.*, pp. 96–134.

17. For a well respected mainstream position on antitrust, see F.M. Scherer, *Industrial Market Structure and Economic Performance*, 2nd ed. (Chicago: Rand McNally College Publishing Company, 1980).

18. Ralph Nader, Mark Green and Joel Seligman, eds., *Corporate Power in America* (New York: Grossman, 1973) and *Taming the Giant Corporation* (New York: W. W. Norton and Company, 1976.)

Much of the current enthusiasm for deconcentration stems from the recommendations of the *Task Force to Study Antitrust Policy* (1968), reviewed in *Antitrust Law and Economics Review* (Winter 1968–69). The intellectual origins for such policies go back at least to C. Kaysen and D. Turner, *Antitrust Policy* (Cambridge, Mass.: Harvard University Press, 1959.)

19. Mark Green, ed., *The Monopoly Makers* (New York: Grossman, 1973) details for the most part, how industry uses governmental power to restrict and restrain competition.

20. See Robert Hessen, *In Defense of the Corporation* (Stanford, Cal.: Hoover Institution Press, 1979), pp. 101–115.

APPENDIX

The Antitrust Laws: Relevant Sections

SHERMAN ACT

§1. Every contract, combination in the form of trust or otherwise, or conspiracy, in restraint of trade or commerce among the several States, or with foreign nations, is hereby declared to be illegal . . .

§2. Every person who shall monopolize, or attempt to monopolize, or combine or conspire with any other person or persons, to monopolize any part of the trade or commerce among the several States, or with foreign nations, shall be deemed guilty. . . .

CLAYTON ACT

§2. (a) That it shall be unlawful for any person engaged in commerce, in the course of such commerce, either directly or indirectly, to discriminate in price between different purchasers of commodities of like grade and quality, where either or any of the purchases involved in such discrimination are in commerce, where such commodities are sold for use, consumption, or resale within the United States or any Territory thereof or the District of Columbia or any insular possession or other place under the jurisdiction of the United States, and where the effect of such discrimination may be substantially to lessen competition or tend to create a monopoly in any line of commerce, or to injure, destroy, or prevent competition with any person who either grants or knowingly receives the benefit of such discrimination, or with customers of either of them: *Provided,* That nothing herein contained shall prevent differentials which make only due allowance for differences in the cost of manufacture, sale, or delivery resulting from the differing methods or quantities in which such commodities are to such purchasers sold or delivered: *Provided, however,* That the Federal Trade Commission may, after due investigation and hearing to all interested parties, fix and establish quantity limits, and revise the same as it finds necessary, as to particular commodities or classes of commodities, where it finds that available purchasers in greater quantities are so few as to render differentials on account thereof unjustly discriminatory or promotive of monopoly in any line of commerce; and the foregoing shall then not be construed to permit differentials based on differences in quantities greater than those so fixed and established: *And provided further,* That nothing herein contained shall prevent persons engaged in selling goods, wares, or merchandise in commerce from selecting their own customers in bona fide transactions and not in restraint of trade: *And provided futher,* That nothing herein contained shall prevent price changes from time to time where in response to changing conditions affecting the market for or the marketability of the goods concerned, such as but not limited to actual or imminent deterioration of perishable goods, obsolescence of seasonal goods, distress sales under court process, or sales in good faith in discontinuance of business in the goods concerned.

(b) Upon proof being made, at any hearing on a complaint under this section, that there has been discrimination in price or services or facilities furnished, the burden of rebutting the prima-facie case thus made by showing justification shall be upon the person charged with a violation of this section, and unless justification shall be affirmatively shown, the Commission is authorized to issue an order terminating the discrimination: *Provided, however,* That nothing herein contained shall prevent a seller rebutting the prima facie case thus made by showing that his lower price or the furnishing of services or facilities to any purchaser or purchasers was made in good faith to meet an equally low price of a competitor, or the services or facilities furnished by a competitor.

(c) That it shall be unlawful for any person engaged in commerce, in the course of such commerce, to pay or grant, or to receive or accept, anything of value as a commission, brokerage, or other compensation, or any allowance or discount in lieu thereof, except for services rendered in connection with the sale or purchase of goods, wares, or merchandise, either to the other party to such transaction or to an agent, representative, or other intermediary therein where such intermediary is acting in fact for or in behalf, or is subject to the direct or indirect control, of any party to such transaction other than the person by whom such compensation is so granted or paid.

(d) That it shall be unlawful for any person engaged in commerce to pay or contract for the payment of anything of value to or for the benefit of a customer of such person in the course of such commerce as compensation or in consideration of any services or facilities furnished by or through such customer in connection with the processing, handling, sale, or offering for sale of any products or commodities manufactured, sold, or offered by sale by such person, unless such payment or consideration is available on proportionally equal terms to all other customers competing in the distribution of such products or commodities.

(e) That it shall be unlawful for any person to discriminate in favor of one purchaser against another purchaser or purchasers of a commodity bought for resale, with or without processing, by contracting to furnish or furnishing, or by contributing to the furnishing of, any services or facilities connected with the processing, handling, sale, or offering for sale of such commodity so purchased upon terms not offered to all purchasers on proportionally equal terms.

(f) That it shall be unlawful for any person engaged in commerce, in the course of such commerce, knowingly to induce or receive a discrimination in price which is prohibited by this section. . . .

§3. That it shall be unlawful for any person engaged in commerce, in the course of such commerce, to lease or make a sale or contract for sale of goods, wares, merchandise, machinery, supplies, or other commodities, whether patented or unpatented, for use, consumption, or resale within the United States or any Territory thereof or the District of Columbia or any insular possession or other place under the jurisdiction of the United States, or fix a price charged therefor, or discount from, or rebate upon, such price, on the condition, agreement, or understanding that the lessee or purchaser thereof shall not use or deal in the goods, wares, merchandise, machinery, supplies, or other commodities of a competitor or competitors of the lessor or seller, where the effect of such lease, sale, or contract for sale or such condition, agreement, or understanding may be to substantially lessen competition or tend to create a monopoly in any line of commerce. . . .

§7. That no corporation engaged in commerce shall acquire, directly or indirectly, the whole or any part of the stock or other share capital and no corporation subject to the jurisdiction of the Federal Trade Commission shall acquire the whole or any part of the assets of another corporation engaged also in commerce, where in any line of commerce in any section of the country, the effect of such acquisition may be substantially to lessen competition, or to tend to create a monopoly.

No corporation shall acquire, directly or indirectly, the whole or any part of the stock or other share capital and no corporation subject to the jurisdiction of the Federal Trade Commission shall acquire the whole or any part of the assets of one or more corporations engaged in commerce, where in any line of commerce in any section of the country, the effect of such acquisition, of such stocks or assets, or of the use of such stock by the voting or granting of proxies or otherwise, may be substantially to lessen competition, or to tend to create a monopoly. . . .

FEDERAL TRADE COMMISSION ACT

§5. (a) (1) Unfair methods of competition in commerce, and unfair or deceptive acts or practices in commerce, are hereby declared unlawful.

Index